PN 84

Surve

trop

Surveying the American Tropics
A Literary Geography from New York to Rio

American Tropics: Towards a Literary Geography

American Tropics: Towards a Literary Geography

The term 'American Tropics' refers to a kind of extended Caribbean, an area which includes the southern USA, the Atlantic littoral of Central America, the Caribbean islands, and northern South America. European colonial powers fought intensively here against indigenous populations and against each other for control of land and resources. This area shares a history in which the dominant fact is the arrival of millions of white Europeans and black Africans; shares an environment which is tropical or sub-tropical; and shares a socio-economic model (the plantation) whose effects lasted well into the twentieth century. The approach taken by the series is geographical in the sense that the focus of each volume is on a *region*. Each region is a zone of encounter, bringing together sets of writing in different languages and styles, from different literary and cultural backgrounds, all of which have in common the attention paid to the same place.

The imaginative space of the American Tropics series therefore offers a differently centred literary history from those conventionally produced as US, Caribbean, or Latin American literature. The development of the discipline of cultural geography has encouraged more sophisticated analyses of notions of place and region, which this series brings to bear on its materials. The individual volumes therefore stand at an angle to national literary histories, offering a different perspective, with each volume contributing one piece of the jigsaw towards a completely new map of the literary history of the area.

Series Editors

Maria Cristina Fumagalli (Professor in the Department of Literature, Film, and Theatre Studies at the University of Essex)

Peter Hulme (Professor in the Department of Literature, Film, and Theatre Studies at the University of Essex)

Owen Robinson (Senior Lecturer in the Department of Literature, Film, and Theatre Studies at the University of Essex)

Lesley Wylie (Lecturer in the School of Modern Languages at the University of Leicester)

Surveying the American Tropics

A Literary Geography from New York to Rio

EDITED BY
MARIA CRISTINA FUMAGALLI,
PETER HULME, OWEN ROBINSON,
AND LESLEY WYLIE

LIVERPOOL UNIVERSITY PRESS

First published 2013 by
Liverpool University Press
4 Cambridge Street
Liverpool
L69 7ZU

British Library Cataloguing-in-Publication data
A British Library CIP record is available

ISBN 978-1-84631-890-0

Typeset by Carnegie Book Production, Lancaster
Printed and bound in the United States of America

In memory of Neil L. Whitehead
(1956–2012)

Contents

List of illustrations

Introduction

Maria Cristina Fumagalli, Peter Hulme,
Owen Robinson, Lesley Wylie

M ost literary histories are written in lockstep with national stories. It is perfectly clear what such co-ordination brings to nationalism: it makes that national story deeper and longer, more rooted in its territory. It is less clear that literary history benefits. For a start many of the books herded into such national literary histories were written long before these nations ever existed: to read, say, the writings of Christopher Columbus as part of US literature is to misplace the historical and geographical co-ordinates necessary to understand Columbus. But even within the modern era, dominated by nation-states, literature itself has rarely been disciplined by national borders. Other ways of organising can tell different stories, which can perhaps persuade us to look in different ways at the multiplicity of texts available for the writing of literary history.

In this regard the American continent offers some fine complexities, from indigenous cultures which pre-date the European invasion, through the ever-shifting pattern of colonial settlements and struggles for independence, to the present mosaic of nation-states and notional supra-national designations such as 'Latin America', 'Anglo-America', and 'the Caribbean', not to mention the constant patterns of migration which have created categories like Cuban-American and Nuyorican, with writers who might belong to two or three national territories—or perhaps to none at all.

In recent years new formulations have suggested some different configurations: the idea of the Black Atlantic has emphasised connections across that ocean, particularly between Africa and America; various new versions of 'southern' literature have rediscovered connections between the southern US states and the islands of the Caribbean; and the Caribbean itself has expanded to include the coastal regions of Colombia and

1

Venezuela.[1] One major difference between these new formulations and the older national literary histories is that whereas previously writers might be struggled over—is T. S. Eliot a US or an English poet? is Paule Marshall a West Indian or a US novelist?—the new configurations are not mutually exclusive: each optic can in theory reveal a different set of relationships and trajectories. Taken together they help produce a richer literary history.

Introducing the American Tropics

This book belongs to a series called *American Tropics: Towards a Literary Geography*. Not a tightly defined geographical designation, American Tropics refers to a kind of extended Caribbean, including the south-eastern USA, the Atlantic littoral of Central America, the Caribbean islands, and north-eastern South America, with outposts even further afield. The Martinican writer Édouard Glissant called the area 'the estuary of the Americas', a term employed to reflect the fact that here the continent's three great rivers—the Mississippi, the Orinoco, and the Amazon—all meet the Atlantic.[2] This area shares a history in which the dominant fact is the arrival of millions of white Europeans and black Africans (with devastating impact for indigenous populations). It shares an environment which is tropical or sub-tropical. And it shares a socio-economic model (the plantation), whose effects lasted at least well into the twentieth century and give a further possible name: Plantation America.[3] So an anthropological geography provides a sense of area rather

---

[1] Paul Gilroy, *The Black Atlantic: Modernity and Double Consciousness*, London: Verso, 1993; Suzanne W. Jones and Sharon Monteith, eds., *South to a New Place: Region, Literature, Culture*, Baton Rouge: Louisiana State University Press, 2002; Jon Smith and Deborah Cohn, eds., *Look Away! The U.S. South in New World Studies*, Durham: Duke University Press, 2004; Sean X. Goudie, *Creole America: The West Indies and the Formation of Literature and Culture in the New Republic*, Philadelphia, University of Pennsylvania Press, 2006; Jessica Adams, Michael P. Bibler, and Cècile Accilien, eds., *Just Below South: Intercultural Performance in the Caribbean and the U.S. South*, Charlottesville: University of Virginia Press, 2007; Vera Kutzinski, 'Borders, Bodies, and Regions: The United States and the Caribbean', in Charles Crow, ed., *A Companion to the Regional Literatures of America*, Oxford: Blackwell, 2003, pp. 171–191; and John Lowe, '"Calypso Magnolia": The Caribbean Side of the South', *South Central Review*, 22, no. 1 (spring 2005), pp. 54–80.

[2] On the 'extended Caribbean', see Immanuel Wallerstein, *The Modern World-System II: Mercantilism and the Consolidation of the European World-Economy, 1600–1750*, New York: Academic Press, 1980, p. 103; for 'the estuary of the Americas', see Édouard Glissant, *Le discours antillais* [1971], Paris: Gallimard, 1997, p. 427.

[3] On Plantation America, see Charles Wagley, 'Plantation America: A Culture Sphere', in *Caribbean Studies: A Symposium*, ed. Vera Rubin, Seattle: University

different from anything currently operative within comparative literature, and perhaps particularly significant because it crosses several national and linguistic frontiers. Instead, the area has cultural and historical logics, which are based on—and inseparable from—a geographical or environmental logic.

The American Tropics is undoubtedly a special area, most of all perhaps because of those three great rivers. But it is also where Columbus thought that paradise was situated and it is home to El Dorado and the Fountain of Eternal Youth; so much American mythology belongs in this region. And it is where history has been made. Whereas until relatively recently we seemed to live in a world whose politics had been shaped by the Second World War, we increasingly seem to live in a world shaped by a US imperialism which began at the turn of the twentieth century with the occupation of Guantánamo Bay and the building of the Panama Canal, two of the key places within the area.

*

The development of the discipline of cultural geography has encouraged more sophisticated analyses of notions of space and place, which the series aims to bring to bear on its materials.[4] Other books in the series will focus on a number of key *places* which have been nodal points for the production of writing, taking these as case studies: Oriente (Cuba), New Orleans, the Haiti-Dominican Republic border, the Putumayo, and Western Trinidad.[5] Each place is seen as a zone of encounter, bringing together sets of

---

of Washington Press, 1960, pp. 3–13; cf. Philip D. Curtin, *The Rise and Fall of the Plantation Complex*, 2nd edition, Cambridge: Cambridge University Press, 1998; Jack Greene, 'Reassessing the Colonial South', *Journal of Southern History*, LXXIII, no. 3 (August 2007), pp. 525–538; Alexandra Isfahani-Hammond, *Masters and the Slaves: Plantation Relations and Mestizaje in American Imaginaries*, New York: Palgrave Macmillan, 2005.

[4] For the philosophical development of the idea of 'place', see the important work of Edward Casey: *Getting Back into Place: Toward a Renewed Understanding of the Place-World*, Bloomington: Indiana University Press, 1993; *The Fate of Place: A Philosophical History*, Berkeley: University of California Press, 1997; and *Representing Place: Landscape Painting and Maps*, Minneapolis: University of Minnesota Press, 2002. For an introduction to cultural geography, see James Duncan et al., eds., *A Companion to Cultural Geography*, Oxford: Blackwell, 2004. Cultural geography provides an approach to the Caribbean in the essays in Elizabeth M. DeLoughrey, Renee K. Gosson, and George B. Handley, eds., *Caribbean Literature and the Environment: Between Nature and Culture*, Charlottesville: University of Virginia Press, 2006.

[5] The first of these has appeared: Peter Hulme, *Cuba's Wild East: A Literary Geography of Oriente*, Liverpool: Liverpool University Press, 2011.

writing in different languages and styles, from different literary and cultural backgrounds, all of which have in common that attention to the same place. The *American Tropics* conference held at Essex in July 2009 brought together nearly 100 scholars from all over the world. From the papers presented we selected twelve for development into essays which engage with the idea of literary geography central to this series and which represent—inasmuch as twelve essays can—the rich diversity of the writing produced within its geographical area. This volume therefore stands at an angle to the others in the series, offering a *survey* across the area, sampling twelve distinct places within it, from the outpost of New York in the north to Brazil in the south.

*

Migration out of the American Tropics has been a major feature of the cultural life of Atlantic countries over the last century. Cities such as Toronto, Montreal, Amsterdam, London, and Paris have been immeasurably enriched by writers whose formative experiences or familial memories were formed in Port Antonio or Matanzas or Castries or Basseterre. New York has been a particular beneficiary because of successive waves of immigration from a wide variety of places—Jamaica and Barbados, but also Puerto Rico and the Dominican Republic and Haiti, not to mention Guatemala and El Salvador … and so many more.

The first two essays in this collection bear witness to the northern extension of the American Tropics. Paule Marshall, Edwidge Danticat, and Junot Díaz all feature for their explorations of the complex geographies interlinking New York and New Jersey with Barbados, Haiti, and the Dominican Republic. So the volume starts with this outpost of the American Tropics before working its way in a generally southern direction.

A number of writers originally from the American Tropics have lived and set their stories in Brooklyn neighbourhoods, particularly Bedford-Stuyvesant and East Flatbush. As Jamaica Kincaid puts it, recalling her first visit to Brooklyn, quoted at the beginning of Martha Jane Nadell's essay, 'A Tree Grows in Bajan Brooklyn: Writing Caribbean New York': 'I felt as if I had taken a wrong turn, slipped through a crack between worlds, and emerged in the main street of a tropical city'. At the centre of Nadell's analysis is Paule Marshall's 1959 novel, *Brown Girl, Brownstones*. The novel has often been read as a coming-of-age or an immigrant narrative, but Nadell focuses on the insistent descriptions of the urban topography—more than just a *setting*—to argue that Marshall is primarily concerned with mapping the construction of Barbadian places within Brooklyn, none more important nor more intricate than the brownstone of the title.

Marshall's novel is in one sense a history of house and family and community from the 1930s through to after the Second World War, with the house the particular site of the creation of what Nadell calls a 'vernacular landscape' containing spatial and visual indications of Barbadian identity, which inevitably echo yet clash with the images of an ideal island home—perhaps someday to be recovered, perhaps lost forever. This detailed analysis of Marshall's novel is set alongside briefer comparative considerations of a significant recent writer, Edwidge Danticat, and an earlier figure, Betty Smith, against whose iconic text, *A Tree Grows in Brooklyn*, Marshall's novel was critique and counterpoint.

María del Pilar Blanco's essay, 'Reading the Novum World: The Literary Geography of Science Fiction in *The Brief Wondrous Life of Oscar Wao*', focuses on Junot Díaz's 2007 novel about the eponymous Dominican-American science fiction aficionado living in Paterson, New Jersey. By way of a family saga, the novel narrates recent Dominican—and wider American—history. It meditates, in particular, on the over thirty-year rule of Rafael Trujillo (a period known as the Trujillato) and its consequences for the Dominican Republic, principally widespread diaspora, of which Oscar's family's life in the USA is a product.

As Blanco shows, *Oscar Wao* is a deeply reflexive work, both historically and formally. Díaz has claimed that the novel is a 'textual Caribbean', and throughout the novel he makes reference, both directly and indirectly, to Caribbean theoreticians and writers such as Édouard Glissant, Derek Walcott, and Alejo Carpentier. Central to the essay is a discussion of science fiction in Díaz's novel. Whilst, as Blanco notes, *Oscar Wao* is not a science-fiction text per se, the novel abounds in sci-fi references—from Frank Kirby's *The Fantastic Four* to J. R. R. Tolkien's *The Lord of the Rings* and the long-running BBC series *Dr Who*. Sometimes these references simply invoke events and people from the Trujillato, as when a comparison is made between the Dominican dictator and the malevolent antagonist Sauron in Tolkien's trilogy. At other times, however, science fiction produces what Blanco calls 'a particular form of planetary estrangement', providing Díaz with a fitting 'aesthetic tool' to unpick and assimilate the history—both textual and otherwise—of the Dominican Republic and the wider Antillean region. Departing from mythologies of 'unity and continuity', to quote Díaz, science fiction reveals the instabilities and fissures in Caribbean identity, in line with Stuart Hall's view of the 'critical points of deep and significant *difference*' across the region.

This 'planetary estrangement' in *Oscar Wao*, epitomised by the novel's tragi-comic protagonist, who experiences alienation both in the USA ('You really want to know what being an X-Man feels like? Just be a smart bookish boy of color in a contemporary US ghetto ... Like having bat wings or a pair of tentacles growing out of your chest') and in the macho culture of the Dominican Republic, is, Blanco demonstrates, an example of what critic Darko Suvin has, after Ernst Bloch, termed the '*novum*'—science fiction's ability to generate 'a strange newness' or a 'reality displacement'. Yet the essay also shows that such defamiliarising strategies are a feature not only of science-fiction texts but of Antillean discourse more widely. The final section of the essay, a discussion of the strikingly similar rhetorical questions posed by Carpentier in 1948 and in this 2007 novel ('After all, what is the entire history of all America if not a chronicle of the marvellous real?' and Díaz's 'who more sci-fi than us?'), reveals a long history of cognitive estrangement in the literary geography of the American Tropics, although these invocations of new worlds are, as Blanco's essay shows, not always to the same ends.

Although, strictly speaking, the tropical line of Cancer runs south of all mainland US territories, the south of the USA has always had close connections with the islands and territories across that tropic line. The plantation system flourished in states such as Louisiana and Mississippi, with climate and soil so similar to those of Cuba and Jamaica. Plantation owners often held properties on both sides of that tropic line and on occasions in the nineteenth century even dreamed of uniting them in a Southern Empire.[6] US military expeditions have consistently gone south too—into Mexico, Central America, Cuba, Puerto Rico, Haiti, the Dominican Republic, Grenada ... However, allied with this US fascination with the lands to its south is a fear of contamination by them, particularly through the illegal immigration that needs to be countered by ever longer and higher walls along the border with Mexico. No literary text has better captured or anatomised this fear of contamination than Leslie Marmon Silko's 1991 novel, *Almanac of the Dead*, the subject of Hsinya Huang's essay, 'Inventing Tropicality: Writing Fever, Writing Trauma in Leslie Marmon Silko's *Almanac of the Dead* and *Gardens in the Dunes*'.

Huang begins by sketching the role of disease in the terrible reduction of Native American population numbers after 1492, taken—within the racialist doctrines of the colonial period—as evidence of the inferiority of those populations, widely seen as passively occupying the 'virgin lands' awaiting European cultivation. On one level, *Almanac of the Dead* does what its title suggests and chronicles a chilling series of fatal diseases from 1590 onwards, though it is noticeable that the land itself seems as diseased as the bodies that inhabit it: drought and earthquake accompany pox and fever. These are

---

[6] Robert E. May, *The Southern Dream of a Caribbean Empire, 1854–1861*, Baton Rouge: Louisiana State University Press, 1973.

southern—sub-tropical—lands and scarcity of water leads to parched crops, animal fatality, and Native trauma. Tucson provides the geographical focus for the novel, a border city where, as Huang puts it, 'historical killings have been buried but where the ghosts of the departed remain'.

But the novel's almanac also offers a counterweight to all this destruction, housing as it does the ancient wisdom of the Maya, who prophesied a revolution that would begin in Chiapas and move from south to north to reclaim Native American lands—a revolution that did indeed begin there three years after the novel's publication with the appearance of the Zapatista National Liberation Army, even if it has yet to initiate its northwards sweep.

Meanwhile, contemporary pillaging continues, focused in the novel on the destruction of a fragile environment by greedy corporations who drill and pump without understanding what they thereby destroy, a theme further developed in Silko's 1999 novel, *Gardens in the Dunes*. Though its temporal focus is on the late nineteenth century, *Gardens in the Dunes* also introduces mystic elements from Mayan, Aztec, and Pueblo cultures, enriching her prose even as the Native lands become further desiccated. The gardens of the title, lovingly described, offer a potent image of what has been lost through destruction. Against all odds, however, the mythic perspective does finally offer hope of resistance, of expulsion of disease from the house of the shades of the dead. The ghost dancers gather to help, offering the possibility of salvation.

Gesa Mackenthun's essay, 'Imperial Archaeology: The American Isthmus as Contested Scientific Contact Zone', begins in 1847 at one of the turning points in the history of the American Tropics. The USA was again looking south: war with Mexico would quickly lead to a huge expansion of the US national territory, the California gold rush would lead to a massive increase in migration to the American west coast, and Central America—which offered the quickest passage between the Atlantic and Pacific oceans—would become a centre of attention, a railway line across Panama foreshadowing the complex feat of building an interoceanic canal.

The territories of Central America had been traversed by Spain since the early sixteenth century but the often forbidding terrain and climate had ensured that Spanish settlements were relatively sparse. The work of exploration needed to survey possible rail and canal routes inevitably led to greater knowledge of the area and soon started to turn up a series of spectacular sites—cities abandoned by earlier American civilisations such as the Maya, whose startling architectural achievements drew archaeological interest from the USA and from Europe.

John Lloyd Stephens's travel accounts from the early 1840s, *Incidents of Travel in Central America, Chiapas, and Yucatan* and *Incidents of Travel in Yucatan*, had given the first accounts of Maya cities, parts of which he transported back to the USA, impelled by that rigid sense of US entitlement that was especially apparent in the years after 1847. The descendants of the city-builders were now degraded and abject, Stephens thought: it was the right of the newest American civilisation to assume possession of and responsibility for such remnants. However, as a transitional figure, Stephens—who appears in the opening paragraphs of Mackenthun's essay paying homage to Alexander von Humboldt in Berlin—was also alert to the often fantastic stories of adventure and romance that cling to these regions, including that of a 'hidden' but still inhabited Maya city never reached by white men.

As always, nomenclature proves important. Central America is the most neutral of terms, merely indicating the middle of the long continent, the part where it narrows, also referred to by archaeologists as Mesoamerica or Middle America—though with varied and disputed boundaries. Meanwhile, the imperial powers were doing their best to name and shape the territory: Mosquitia was the British effort, one stoutly resisted by the USA as it carved out its own set of interests, largely through the private endeavours of individuals like William Walker and Cornelius Vanderbilt—who were quite as likely to fight each other as they were to fight the natives.

In Mackenthun's account Stephens is followed by an even more colourful figure in Ephraim George Squier, who was intimately involved in the struggle over the Mosquito coast, which stretches across the republics of Nicaragua and Honduras. An adventurer and writer, working—somewhat notionally at times—for the US government, Squier held to an imperial vision sometimes even too sweeping for his employers, however much they might actually have shared his strong anti-British views.

Squier left valuable, if tainted, accounts of the groups active in the region at this time, among them the Miskito, whom he despised as mixed and therefore degenerate (and who were in any case allied to the British), and the Caribs, exiled to this coast from the Caribbean island of St Vincent at the end of the eighteenth century. Squier's genuinely ethnological fascination with migration patterns in Central America led him towards grandiose theories which tended inevitably towards the master narrative that underlay (and perhaps still underlie) much US activity within the American Tropics. Like Stephens, Squier was attracted by rumours of lost cities and hidden remnants, a trope which Squier also fictionalised in his 1855 novel, *Waikna*, rich in imperial wish-fulfilment, and addressed in his introduction and annotations to a translation by his wife of Arthur Morelet's 1857 *Voyage dans l'Amérique Centrale*. Central America in the mid-nineteenth century is a complex translational space, a comment which could be made about most places within the American Tropics at some historical juncture, but whose significance can only fully be realised through the kind of thorough disentanglement of sources and discourses that Mackenthun offers here.

*

In March 2008 the first European Space Agency Automated Transfer Vehicle was launched on an Ariane 5 rocket from Kourou, in Guyane; as Mimi Sheller notes in her essay, 'Space Age Tropics', it was named after Jules Verne, the science fiction writer who first recognised aluminium's potential to get human beings to the moon. Sheller's essay reminds readers that underlying the cultural geographies of the American Tropics there is a physical geography of mining and resource extraction which has aluminium at its very core. She depicts the relation between North America and the American Tropics as two inextricably linked faces to aluminium: the North Atlantic's dreams of mobility, speed and communication systems represent the gleaming side of modernity, while the harsher tropical reality of mining, labour exploitation, and environmental devastation represent the dark side of modernisation.

The essay begins by offering a brief but thorough overview of the history of the aluminium industry in the Caribbean from 1917, when Alcoa first mined bauxite in Suriname, to the present. Since the 1960s, hydroelectric dams and artificial lakes have been built throughout Suriname and in Saamaka Maroon territory, exploitation that still continues, always to the detriment of Saamaka people and the ecology of the region. In Jamaica bauxite was discovered in the 1940s, in the context of bargaining between multinational corporations with financial and military backing from the US government and a weak post-war British colonial state. Here Alcoa and other transnational aluminium corporations contributed to the creation of the tourist industry in Jamaica through the luxury magazine advertisements promoting the Caribbean cruises of the Alcoa Steamship Co. from 1948 to 1958. Rather than a literary history, Sheller here offers a visual analysis of graphic illustrations that drew on literary tropes of the tropics, from botanical collection to ethnological depictions of racial types, music, and dance. While the North American tourists who are portrayed relaxing on board the cruise ships are represented as mobile, travelling beings, the islands and Caribbean coastal countries are depicted as immobile and collectable: they are catalogued as docile sites of natural beauty while their interior forests were being cleared, flooded, and strip-mined for bauxite. This alleged 'immobility' of the islands contrasts with the fact that the Caribbean working class was, as Sheller explains, one of the most mobile and politicised in the world. Indeed, at precisely this time, the power of colonial governments and transnational corporations was actively trying to break the labour movements in the region: for example, the racial polarisation between Afro-Guyanese and Indo-Guyanese has its origin in October 1953 when the British government, with US support, suspended the constitution of Guyana and deposed the labour-left government of Cheddi Jagan, which had threatened to take back mineral resources and move the colony of British Guiana towards independence.

Yet through her analysis of the transnational cultural geographies of the American tropics represented in these advertising images, Sheller also shows how the images testified to a cultural vitality and to a potentially threatening 'mobility'. As primary exemplification, she refers to the Caribbean Art Competition sponsored at this time by Alcoa, which encouraged self-representation (albeit in foreign corporate sponsorship) just when the movements for independent self-government and resource sovereignty were strengthening. By the 1960s Jamaica had become the world's largest producer of bauxite. It achieved independence in 1962, and in the early 1970s the New World Group of economists at the University of the West Indies began to call for the nationalisation of the Jamaican bauxite industry. However, Sheller explains, the corporate powers that controlled the global aluminium industry refused to allow such developments and, in 1975, they doubled their bauxite imports from Guinea whilst reducing their Jamaican imports by 30 per cent. Despite the damage done to people and environment by bauxite mining, Caribbean countries remain active in planning for the expansion of aluminium production, attesting to the ongoing power of world economic processes to shape the region.

*

The European discovery of America in 1492 had posed difficult questions for views of the world which had foundations in classical and Biblical traditions. One powerful argument, famously proposed by the French naturalist Buffon in the middle of the eighteenth century, stressed American difference: what had been called the American lion, or puma, is not a lion at all—it's actually weaker and more cowardly than the 'real lion'. European philosophers—notably Hegel—developed this view of the continent, contested by contemporaries who had actually set foot in America such as Alexander von Humboldt. Humboldt's enthusiastic descriptions of American flora and fauna, especially in the tropics, were embraced by the newly independent American republics throughout the continent. But it was the arrival of the first black revolution, resulting in an independent Haiti, which ultimately made those negative comparisons logically impossible to sustain—though logic doesn't always enter such equations.

What happened in Haiti was not a revolution that Europe wanted to be associated with—it was on the whole welcome to its uniqueness. However, no other event in the American Tropics has had such resonance, the aftershocks of which continue into the twenty-first century. Of all the works of historiography that have grappled with the significance of the Haitian revolution, C. L. R. James's 1938 *The Black Jacobins* is perhaps the most distinguished and certainly the one that has itself most resonated with academic and popular discussion. Taking the motif of comparison within and outwith *The Black Jacobins*—not least in its very title—Susan Gillman offers a textually subtle analysis of this classic text and its implicit geographies, looking in particular at how James uses blackness as a conceptual and revisionist resource for constructing world history.

Gillman's essay—'Black Jacobins and New World Mediterraneans: Spectres of Comparison?'—locates the comparative thinking of *The Black Jacobins* in its grammatical and paratextual margins, demanding some close and scholarly work on various versions of the text, the kind of exegesis that such classic texts deserve, but don't always receive. For example, although the title itself, *The Black Jacobins*, requires careful elaboration of its terms, James is also, in the 1963 edition, adept at comparing what he calls 'French San Domingo' in the late eighteenth century with Cuba in 1958—a comparison itself inflected by the implicit comparison between 1938 and 1963. James's Haiti ends up, as Gillman demonstrates, inescapably but also multiply comparative as it anchors a circuit which goes back to Africa before returning to the Caribbean.

Gillman also pursues the spatio-temporal implications of James's comparative thinking by responding to the deceptively simple question: 'Where and when was the Haitian Revolution?' Certainly, to make only the simplest points, *The Black Jacobins* itself is located at the confluence of three languages (English, French, Spanish) and four empires at different stages of development (France, Britain, Spain, the USA), making it paradigmatic for the region it so adeptly anatomises.

'New' is an important term here too—scattered like confetti across the American continent as an almost anxious assertion of how it might be different from the old world, yet carrying with it, like an elderly relative whom it can't quite manage to dump overboard, the nominative reminders of the places left behind: York, Orléans, Hampshire—not to mention those simply reproduced: the Scarboroughs and the Brightons and the Portsmouths. Yet, as Gillman points out, with respect to one of the frequent comparisons, the Caribbean is not just *the* Mediterranean transported west, but *a* mediterranean sea in its own right, forming one of the twin lodestars of modernity, both in need of proper and full comparison with the other.

*

A concern with literary geography involves the constant lengthening and shortening of focus. The American Tropics covers a huge area. There are many regions within it, their designations often changing over time, often disputed. Shortening the focus further directs attention towards examples of particular topoi—natural features such as rivers or mountains or cultural ones such as plantations or city squares or, as here, hotels and houses. The hotel in question is perhaps the most famous one in the Caribbean, the Oloffson in Port-au-Prince, Haiti, the subject of Alasdair Pettinger's essay, a hotel which has housed many writers over the years and has itself featured directly or in fictional form in much of the writing about Haiti by outsiders over the last half century. Houses—already seen as significant in the Brooklyn of Paule Marshall's work (in Martha Nadell's essay)—re-emerge as potential signifiers of class and racial belonging in Jak Peake's analysis of mostly neglected novels from 1930s Trinidad, read as symptoms of a society—and indeed a whole region—on the cusp of major social and political change.

Colonial houses have always made statements about power and have always distinguished themselves in their architecture from slave quarters or the urban dwellings of the poor—barracks or yards. In fiction, as in the real world, the amount and kind of space inhabited by an individual tells you much about their position in society. Peake therefore begins his essay, 'Dark Thresholds in Trinidad: Regarding the Colonial House', with a discussion of the key terminology here—domain, threshold, property—before moving to the contrasting work of Yseult Bridges and Alfred Mendes.

Yseult Bridges was the daughter of old French plantation families, long resident in Trinidad, and Peake reads her novels—*Questing Heart* and *Creole Enchantment*—as symptoms of white anxiety as the old colonial divisions begin to break down and Afro-Trinidadian and Indo-Trinidadian intellectuals begin to permeate the boundaries of the 'cultured' classes in Port of Spain. This is the period and place in which C. L. R. James and Eric Williams were coming of age.

Questing Heart's heroine is a poor white orphan, a woman of sound background brought low through no fault of her own and forced to work as a servant to a mixed-race family that despises her. Through the myth of imperial vulnerability, Bridges envisions the degrading of white innocence by vulgarity and libertinism, a purgatory which inevitably culminates in a sexual assault. The story of Christine's salvation is then marked by the houses in which she subsequently lives. Rescued by a wealthy white businessman, she is first installed in his ex-nanny's cottage in Belmonte, just east of Port of Spain. Though respectable, this cottage is still in a noisy black neighbourhood, not fitting for a white gentlewoman, so Carter has to find her a house of her own, a newly-built bungalow in Maraval, where Christine can assume her proper role as mistress of her home, from which tropical life can be viewed in proper picturesque perspective and to which access can be controlled, as Peake goes on to discuss. The 'natural' order is restored—in fiction.

If Bridges offers a spirited defiance of historical forces, Alfred Mendes's contemporaneous *Pitch Lake* deals with social ambition and upward mobility in a more traditional sense as its protagonist, Joe da Costa, attempts to escape from the restrictions of his family residence, a small and struggling rum shop in San Fernando—a provincial backwater compared with the capital city, Port of Spain. Joe's brother, Henry, marries into wealth and elitism, leaving Joe torn between, as Peake puts it, 'conflicting geographies, contrasting homes, and ambivalent desires', leading him to a psychological impasse which can only have a tragic outcome.

As his title suggests, Alasdair Pettinger's paper focuses on the Hotel Oloffson, currently a slightly run-down gingerbread mansion which once served as the model for the Hotel Trianon in Graham Greene's 1966 novel *The Comedians*. The Oloffson is an atypical Caribbean hotel because its guests are not tourists in search of pristine beaches but journalists, aid workers, military personnel, documentary film-makers, art collectors, and up-market literary travellers who want to stay in the many rooms named after famous visitors like Greene himself.

Drawing on several writers' accounts of the Oloffson (amongst others, Kathie Klarreich, Julia Llewellyn Smith, Ian Thomson, Madison Smartt Bell, Bob Shacochis, Herbert Gold, and David Yeadon), Pettinger investigates how such writers imaginatively inhabit the private and public spaces of the hotel and its surroundings and highlights the continuities and discontinuities between the Oloffson and the all-inclusive resorts and cruise-ships that proliferate in the Caribbean. Pettinger illustrates how the Oloffson, like the all-inclusive hotels, is depicted by the writers in question as a sort of enclave, a typical *tropical* hotel, in which they can find refuge from heat, insects, and the chaotic streets of Port-au-Prince where criminal activities are rife. Pettinger insists that, unlike the modern, postmodern and postcolonial hotels referred to or imagined by Siegfried Kracauer, Fredric Jameson, or James Clifford, the Oloffson generally figures in the works of his writers/guests as a secure fortress rather than a busy crossroads.

In the section entitled 'I must get back to my hotel', Pettinger examines the turning-point of narratives which record dangerous situations in which the writers have placed themselves, the hotel being a secure vantage point from which thrilling events can be crafted in retrospective tranquillity and rendered as aesthetic experience. He highlights how this aesthetic impulse reinforces and supports the controversial political decisions of foreign governments to classify Haiti as a highly dangerous place, much to the disadvantage of local tourist operators, and of the United Nations Stabilization Mission in Haiti (MINUSTAH) to map the city into 'red' (read: dangerous and to be avoided without armed escort) and 'green' (that is, safer) zones—the Oloffson having in fact lost business from being included in the 'red zone'.

Taking his cue from Mary Louise Pratt, who claims that scenes where narrators look out from their hotel balconies onto Third-World cities below are a modern version of the 'Monarch-of-all-I-survey' trope, Pettinger notes that the sensory experience of the Oloffson's guests is of a different nature because the hotel is set back from the streets and surrounded by tall trees. The Oloffson's veranda—'the supreme hangout in Haiti', as one writer calls it—is in fact a place from which one hears rather than sees, reminding us of how much the ear contributes to the way in which we imagine and inhabit space. The shouts, cries, cracks, and explosions heard from the veranda, Pettinger insists, appear to be a great source of anxiety for his travel writers as they prove very difficult to domesticate.

In his conclusion Pettinger invokes Michel Foucault's notion of heterotopia to argue that the 'Oloffson' that emerges from the contradictory accounts of the travel writers he has just analysed is a fractured, confused, indeterminate place simultaneously coded as safe *and* dangerous. However, he alerts us to the existence of a more poignant heterotopia, the one that can emerge only if one considers the ways in which the local people who work in the hotel (waiters/waitresses, housekeepers, cooks, or drivers) both experience and imagine it. Their perspective on the hotel might significantly challenge those guest-writers who try to maintain a clear-cut demarcation between dirty, tropical, unhealthy, lawless, and dangerous Haiti and the more temperate climates where they originate, which are invariably characterised by much higher standards of public health, cleanliness and civic governance. Any such binary opposition might be forcefully challenged, Pettinger notes, by a housekeeper who must clean up after the tourists.

Kettly Mars's 'The Last of the Tourists', where the Oloffson is mentioned together with the streets of Port-au-Prince (the city where Mars resides) and Ground Zero in New York, is finally offered as an example of what might be called 'travellee writing' in which the host writes about the guest; its insistence on reciprocity, however, points towards a heterotopic geography where the Oloffson can be transformed into a radically different place.

*

The American Tropics certainly has its share of small nations, particularly the islands dotted down the chain that runs from Puerto Rico to Trinidad. But these are Brazils compared with the 'Micronations of the Caribbean' discussed in Russell McDougall's paper. Two of his key examples are actually small islands that now form part of larger nation-states, while the third was merely a raft. Size, however, is only relative; in the case of micronations, Gross Discursive Product matters much more than the usual economic kind.

Tortuga's contemporary discursivity has a solid historical footing since it was a pirate haven in the seventeenth century, evolving its own distinctly unofficial 'national' characteristics—egalitarianism, ethnic diversity, homosexuality—anathema to the European nation-states of the day who were busily consolidating their empires in America, but subsequently an endless source of fascination which has consolidated 'Tortuga' as a key trope in the transnational discourse of piracy, from the Disney film series to the kidnapping and ransoming of individuals and ships off the Somali coast.

The literary appearances of Tortuga and its pirates are plentiful, often based on the core histories of Exquemelin and Johnson to which writers like John Steinbeck and Peter Benchley have turned for inspiration. But the richness of the trope is perhaps best captured in its imbrication with the contemporary discourses of terrorism and financial piracy—the latter in particular seemingly drawn to small islands like a honey bee to a wild flower.

While Tortuga—now Île de la Tortue and part of Haiti—is a well-populated island of substantial size, bigger for example than either St Kitts or Nevis, which together make up a nation-state, Redonda has taken on its semi-mythical status as a micronation despite—or because of—being little more than a rocky outcrop about a mile long off the coast of Antigua, unable to support a population of any kind. Redonda owes its literary renown to the understudied West Indian writer M. P. Shiel, who reported in 1929 that he had, aged 15, been crowned king of the island after his Monserratian father claimed sovereignty. Subsequent descent of title is much disputed but the acclaimed Spanish writer Javier Marías (King Javier I) is widely regarded as the current incumbent, at least in part because he seems to take the matter more seriously than anybody else.

New Atlantis, McDougall's third example, is perhaps the purest inasmuch as what physically underlay its state apparatus—constitution, flag, postal system, currency—was a 30-foot raft anchored off the coast of Jamaica, which failed to survive the first heavy sea it encountered. Literary resonances are again present, if indirect, since New Atlantis's progenitor was Leicester Hemingway, brother of Ernest.

McDougall's essay is not just historical in orientation, however. The 'micronation' is now a fully theorised concept and the author draws extensively on the language of temporary autonomous zones, repeating islands, social sargassos, refractive spaces, and fatal nests. All this, he suggests, tells us something important about the intrinsic specificity of the region, as if in the smallest unit could be found in miniature form the very essence of the Caribbean islands in particular and of the American Tropics in general.

*

Europeans first entered the American continent through the Caribbean sea and their first settlements were on its islands. But the landmass to the southwest soon became a magnet, the huge estuaries of the Orinoco and the Amazon suggesting its vastness and offering routes into its interior. The term 'El Dorado' today still sums up the dreams and nightmares of that era—vast wealth, brutal death, lingering madness—all of which feature in Neil Whitehead's exploration of the contemporary legacy of that very real but also intensely imagined space: 'Golden Kings, Cocaine Lords, and the Madness of El Dorado: Guayana as Native and Colonial Imaginary'.

'Guayana' is another of those indigenous terms—both geographical and cosmological—which have survived, against all colonial odds, to do duty as valuable designations of cultural areas long since divided politically. The word morphed into Guianas, British, French and Dutch, the British part achieving independence as Guyana, but the region of Guayana also includes parts of northern Brazil and Venezuela.

Whitehead's chapter is notable for its equal attention to actual indigenous practices, not least of gold-working, in Guayana, and to the myths and legends associated with the place. A proper understanding of native ritual and trade is essential to understanding the actions of Walter Ralegh and others, who certainly had plausible reasons for seeking gold in the region and whose long-ridiculed accounts of sophisticated conurbations along the Orinoco have largely been validated by recent archaeology.

Trade patterns are key to understanding the area's anthropology, and gold—along with jade—was at the heart of native exchange, as Whitehead elucidates. The Guayana uplands were the nub of a trade network which extended from the Caribbean islands to the southwestern edge of the tropics in the foothills of the Andes. An understanding of this network helps us to make sense of some of the lasting myths associated with the region— none more resonant than those of the Amazons and the Cannibals—and to understand some of the figures who still act as cultural reference points, such as Anacaona.

The golden dust which coated El Dorado has been replaced, Whitehead says—in a startling juxtaposition of sixteenth- and twenty-first-century icons—with the white powder of cocaine, the imagination of Guayana again becoming what he calls 'a zone of crazed violence and dissolution of self, illicit wealth, and relentless vengeance', for which the name is *kanaimà*, a shamanic complex fundamental to the understanding of many aspects of this region of the American Tropics—its mythology and its literature, but also its contemporary political reality.

Neil Whitehead died just as this Introduction was being finalised. The editors respectfully dedicate this book to the memory of a fine Americanist scholar.

*

In 'Suriname Literary Geography: The Changing Same', Richard and Sally Price offer an intriguing analysis of the neglected corpus of Surinamese literature. They begin by arguing that it is not scarcity of literature, but rather mainstream scholars' non-mastery of the relevant languages that has left Surinamese literature overlooked. Until the eighteenth century, writers engaging with the area often plagiarised one another but, later on, the literature on the three Guianas tended to restrict itself by political and linguistic boundaries: English for British Guiana/Guyana, French for Guyane (French Guiana), and Dutch for Suriname. Drawing from various archives (visual and literary, eighteenth-century and contemporary, ethnographic and journalistic, and, most importantly, European and Saamakan, written and oral) Richard and Sally Price provide an abridged literary history of Suriname which begins by identifying tropes established in the early modern period which still have currency today and constitute the 'changing same' of their title: the menacing jungle vs. the bountiful rainforest, the space of death, torture and heroic resistance vs. the idyllic plantation, the multi-ethnic paradise vs. the contemporary narcocracy.

Focusing in particular on eighteenth-century representations, the authors offer engaging and, at times, provocative readings of texts as diverse as Maria Sibylla Merian's *Metamorphosis Insectorum Surinamensium ofte Verandering der Surinaamsche Insecten* (1705), an entomological treatise which foregrounds—well before it became fashionable to do so—the ecological contextualisation of the discoveries it contains, Dirk Valkenburg's painting *Slave Dance* (1707) which, as the Prices explain, does not portray caricatures but human beings in an ethnographically contextualised setting, and the book that towers over the literature on Suriname of the time, John Gabriel Stedman's *Narrative of a Five Years Expedition Against the Revolted Negroes of Surinam* (1790). During his four-year stay in Suriname, Stedman had dealings with members of all social classes and produced a thorough description of the panorama of life in the colony which was accompanied in its published version by William Blake's well-known engravings.

Richard and Sally Price's analysis of their chosen texts is particularly poignant because of the attention they pay to non-European presences, voices, and sensibilities and their refusal to obliterate historical and ethnographic specificities in the interests of a theoretical argument. For example, their analysis of Valkenburg's *Slave Dance* demonstrates that many of the individuals depicted were among those who rebelled five years after the painting was made and are among the ancestors of the large Dombi clan of Saamaka Maroons, one of the two largest Maroon peoples of Suriname. When dealing with Stedman's depiction of slaves' stoicism under torture, their focus on the actors' mindset and not exclusively on the observers' brings them to suggest that such depictions of black pain display the victims' ultimate act of resistance rather than being a mere disempowering trope concocted by the European writer.

One section of their essay is devoted to the organised struggle orchestrated by the Saamaka maroons to protect their lands which began in 1996, when Chinese loggers, who had received official concessions from the Suriname government, occupied much of Saamaka territory. In 2000, with the help of human rights lawyers, the Saamaka filed a petition with the Inter-American Commission on Human Rights, and in November 2007 they were granted collective rights to the lands on which their ancestors had lived since the early eighteenth century. Instrumental to this petition was a richly detailed map of the 9,500 square kilometres of forest the Saamaka consider their territory, a map which was created ad hoc and combined their reticence to reveal culturally private information—it does not show sites of ritual importance and the sites that played a role in their ancestors' century-long war against the colonists—with their pride in their environmental knowledge, including as it does both natural features such as sandbanks, rapids, and waterfalls and social features such as villages and cemeteries, while signposting places where certain fish can be caught or where wild mangos grow.

The essay ends with an analysis of Saamaka oral tradition. The Prices point out that, from the perspective of today's Saamakas, their ancestors literally discovered America, forging anew everything from horticultural techniques to religious practices: Saamaka folktales recount precisely this process of discovery and creation. The stock characters of these folktales have diverse historical proveniences. Some, like the 'scrawny little kid' (usually the youngest sibling who saves his sister from disaster), appear, albeit in a different guise, throughout Afro-America. This 'scrawny little kid' (*makisá miíi*) is the Saamaka version of the Chiggerfoot (or Jiggerfoot) Boy of Anglophone West Indian tales, but amongst the Saamaka, he is a member of a normal Saamaka family living in a rainforest village and not the younger brother of a white princess in the family of a king, as is the case with Chiggerfoot. Moreover, in Saamaka, the *makisá miíi* always rescues a *black* sister (not, as in the West Indian cases, a white one) and solves *community-wide* problems rather than domestic ones like his West Indian counterpart. Overall, Saamaka folktales contrast with those of other Afro-Americans in portraying the white world (with its kings, slavemasters, and wage-labour bosses) as completely 'other', fully beyond the boundaries of Saamaka society. The very final passage offers a translation of the Saamaka tale of the great hunter Bási Kodjó and the Bush Cows, a tale where two worlds are pitted in mortal battle: the world of Maroons and the world of 'whitefolks' and the plantation.

The book's final essay crosses the equator into the southern tropics, to the furthest reach south of the plantation complex. In 'The Art of Observation: Race and Landscape in *A Journey in Brazil*', Nina Gerassi-Navarro examines the opposition between scientific observation and the lived experience of the tropics in two accounts of an expedition to Brazil undertaken in 1865 by the Swiss-born naturalist, Louis Rodolphe Agassiz, his wife, Cary Elizabeth Agassiz, and a team of Harvard academics and students, including the future psychologist and philosopher, William James. The expedition, which can be positioned in a tradition of botanical and geological journeys to tropical South America in the eighteenth and nineteenth centuries, most notably those by Agassiz's mentor and benefactor, Alexander von Humboldt, reveals a view of the American Tropics as a stage for scientific discovery. As Gerassi-Navarro notes, Agassiz set out on the voyage with high hopes that his theory of glaciation—which could account for the appearance of strange rock formations throughout the world as well as patterns of extinction in flora and fauna—would be proven in Brazil. Despite Agassiz's zeal for first-hand observation, such an approach amounted, as Gerassi-Navarro argues, to a process of 'making science fit'—what Tzvetan Todorov has called in relation to Columbus's early observations of the 'New World' 'a "finalist" strategy of interpretation', where 'the ultimate meaning is given from the start'.[7]

---

[7] Tzvetan Todorov, *The Conquest of America: The Question of the Other*, trans. Richard Howard, New York: Harper & Row, 1984, p. 17.

As this essay shows, the voyage and subsequent travel narrative, *A Journey in Brazil*, co-authored by Louis and Cary Agassiz, alongside William James's little-known travel account of the expedition and his letters, reveal a number of tensions, both within the scientific community of the time and between a scientific and 'picturesque' view of the tropics. The Agassizs set out for Brazil just six years after the publication of Charles Darwin's groundbreaking *On the Origin of Species* [1859] and much of Agassiz's motivation for the trip was to disprove evolutionary theory by way of glacial theory, hence restoring belief in divine creation. Cary Agassiz and James were, on the other hand, much more absorbed by the natural superabundance of the tropics and the people they encountered there. Cary Agassiz's commentary on the journey—a lively, subjective account filled with local colour—was praised by US poet and friend of Agassiz, Oliver Wendell Holmes, for its 'delicate observations from the picturesque side' which 'relieve the grave scientific observations'. Whilst James initially declared himself nonplussed by the landscape—a disappointment which, as Nancy Stepan has noted, is 'common in many tropical journeys'—he later corrected this view with an enraptured description of tropical nature as 'wonderful', 'very beautiful', and 'very different from the colorless state of things at home'.

The juxtaposition between Agassiz's 'scientific' writings and the 'picturesque' touches of Cary Agassiz and James culminated, as the final section of Gerassi-Navarro's essay demonstrates, in their respective views of racial mixing in the tropics. The concern with tropical 'degeneration', which many nineteenth-century commentators believed was caused not only by the climate but by widespread racial mixing, was of concern across the American Tropics in this period. During his expedition Agassiz's anxiety about the supposed dangers of miscegenation led him to undertake a project of racial documentation and classification in the Amazonian city of Manaus, principally through the new technology of photography. Yet, as Gerassi-Navarro shows, this was a project that the writings of James and, more subtly, Cary Agassiz, often undercut. The variance between Agassiz's will to 'scientific' documentation of his subjects and his wife's more tentative, and often approbatory statements about Brazilians (including her observation that the existence of Amazonian women was 'perfectly free and a thousand times pleasanter than the ladies' life') highlight a distinction between different types of observation of the people and places of the region: on the one hand, a rigorous form of surveillance often divorced from contact with the local population and, on the other, the 'interactive' approach favoured by Cary Agassiz and James who mixed daily with Brazilians, engaged with the natural environment aesthetically and emotionally, and were—at times— subjected to a kind of inverse ethnography when locals perceived them as incomprehensible or exotic. These competing strands of observation—the picturesque and the scientific—can be seen throughout the history of Western travel to the American Tropics.

We'd like to thank everyone who participated in the *American Tropics* conference at Essex in July 2009, especially Bill Marshall, who reviewed and commented on the essays collected here, and Susan Forsyth who, as well as helping organise the conference, made the index to this book.

A Tree Grows in Bajan Brooklyn: Writing Caribbean New York

Martha Jane Nadell

I had already made several research trips to Haiti, but the brief drive to Mama Lola's house was my introduction to the Brooklyn outpost of the Caribbean ... Animated conversations could be heard in Haitian, French Creole, Spanish, and more than one lyrical dialect of English. The street was a crazy quilt of shops: Chicka-Licka, the Ashanti Bazaar, a storefront Christian church with an improbably long and specific name, a Haitian restaurant, and Botanica Shango ... I was no more than a few miles from my home in lower Manhattan, but I felt as I had taken a wrong turn, slipped through a crack between worlds, and emerged on the main street of a tropical city.[1]

Brooklyn 1974. 'Sassy Antiguan' Jamaica Kincaid visits the West Indian Day Parade, and finds herself, like anthropologist Karen McCarthy Brown, in a 'tropical city' in Brooklyn. After racing across the Manhattan Bridge in a taxi, she wanders the parade route on Eastern Parkway, one of Brooklyn's two grand boulevards, designed by Central Park architects Frederick Law Olmstead and Calvert Vaux in 1866. Framed by stately apartment buildings and a tree-lined median that separates the main roadway from a narrow outlet, Eastern Parkway stretches from Evergreen Cemetery in Queens, past Ralph Avenue, the boundary between Brooklyn and Queens. It continues by the imposing Beaux-Arts Brooklyn Museum and meets Grand Army Plaza, a large oval plaza that is home to Brooklyn's own *Arc de Triomphe*, the Soldiers' and Sailors' Arch, a monument built in

---

[1] Karen McCarthy Brown, *Mama Lola: A Vodou Priestess in Brooklyn*, Berkeley: University of California Press, 2001, p. 1.

the late nineteenth century in honor of the Union soldiers that died during the Civil War.

Once per year, on Labor Day in early September, roughly on the anniversary of Trinidadian independence, Eastern Parkway is the site of New York City's version of Carnival, the West Indian Day Parade. Thousands line the streets to take in the brightly coloured, extravagant costumes of the bands that dance past them. Vendors hawk the food and flags of the many islands whose populations are represented at the event. And politicians and community leaders campaign and network among their constituents.

As she wandered through the crowds in 1974, Jamaica Kincaid took notes about the goings-on at the parade. And her notes, which were passed to Wallace Shawn at the *New Yorker*, were published without change in the magazine's Talk of the Town section. Kincaid introduces readers to the Mighty Shadow, the 'very slick' calypso singer, La Belle Christine, 'America's No. 1 limb-dance artist', and the Mighty Sparrow, 'who sang a song called "Come See Miss Mary," which was – well, *suggestive*'. Kincaid recounts for her readers the history of Carnival, told to her by Errol Payne, 'the vice-president of art and culture of the West-Indian Day Carnival Association', who locates the origins of Carnival in Trinidad during the era of slavery. She describes the 'old days', when the West Indian Day Parade was in Harlem, and eyes the dignitaries who watch the Carnival Queen as she wiggles her hips and snaps her fingers. She peers at the audience and notes the many white people who seem so out of place that they look like they are 'doing fieldwork for an extension course in Inter-Cultural Interaction: The Folk Experience'. She herself enjoys the 'jumping up', something her mother refused to let her do when she was a girl. And she concludes her series of observations delighted with the fresh Tower Isle patty she purchases along the parade route from a woman, who tells her that she can find more patties in the frozen food section of the local supermarket. This is how she knows that West Indians have arrived: 'you know an ethnic group has made it in this country when you find its food in the local grocer. As Lord Kitchener said to [her], "accessibility is the key to success"'.[2]

Kincaid's essay imagines the West Indian Day Parade and all that accompanies it as constructing a West Indian place, for at least a time, on one of Brooklyn's grandest thoroughfares. The masqueraders who parade down the Eastern Parkway and dance on its floats, those who watch them from the sidewalks and apartment windows, and those who use the event as a commercial opportunity all claim the street on that occasion as

---

[2] Jamaica Kincaid, 'West Indian Weekend', in Jamaica Kincaid, *Talk Stories*, New York: Farrar, Straus, and Giroux, 2001, pp. 15–24.

pan-Caribbean, and as Trinidadian, Jamaican, Barbadian, and of any other island of their choosing. Eastern Parkway becomes, at that moment, as much part of the Caribbean as of the USA.

It is tempting to read the West Indian Parade as deploying what Herbert Gans calls 'symbolic ethnicity'.[3] For Gans, the West Indian Parade could be an expression primarily of 'feeling' West Indian in the USA, an expression that emerges in visual and aural symbols. Indeed, newspaper and television accounts routinely report that the costumes, music, food, and flags are 'celebrations' of West Indian 'culture'. But there is more than celebration that emerges from the beef patties, feathered headdresses, and steel drums that occupy participants and observers alike. Rather, Kincaid's fragmented, non-linear notes suggest that Eastern Parkway, as the parade route on that day in early September, becomes the scene of complex and multivocal place-making.[4] Kincaid casts Carnival in Brooklyn as a multivalent site and moment. It is an occasion for the articulation of attachments to and conceptions of 'home', a site of memory for herself and for others, a location for the expression of what Rachel Buff calls 'denizenship'—a way of inhabiting and thereby making claims on space—and an opportunity to negotiate the racial hierarchy and political scene of Brooklyn's urban life.[5] On the day of the West Indian Parade, then, Brooklyn, in Kincaid's essay, sees a creation of a place simultaneously tropical and urban, of the Caribbean and of the USA, evocative of memories and experiences of the West Indies, and fraught with the complexities of US race relations.

Kincaid's notes raise a concern that preoccupies a set of authors, who may be considered part of both Caribbean and US literary histories. A number of twentieth-century writers, ranging from Eric Walrond to Edwidge Danticat, speculate about the possibility that the Caribbean may emerge in Brooklyn, or at least in a certain number of neighbourhoods. They deploy locales in New York's largest borough—Bed-Stuy and East Flatbush primarily—as both literal spaces in which their novels and short stories occur and figurative places of contestation, conflict, and complexity. They ask if these neighbourhoods are Caribbean islands themselves, bound not

---

[3] Herbert Gans, 'Symbolic Ethnicity', in Werner Sollors, ed. *Theories of Ethnicity, A Classical Reader*, New York: New York University Press, 1996, pp. 425–459, at 434. Gans describes symbolic ethnicity as an 'expressive rather than instrumental function in people's lives', 'less of an ascriptive than a voluntary role that people assume alongside other roles'. In a 1995 epilogue (pp. 452–457), Gans addresses symbolic ethnicity in the context of post 1965 immigrants.

[4] Rachel Buff, *Immigration and the Political Economy of Home*, Berkeley: University of California Press, 2001, p. 40.

[5] Buff, *Immigration*, p. 4.

by water but by the streets of other neighbourhoods whose demographic makeup is different. In the 1920s, Eric Walrond in 'Miss Kenny's Marriage' and Claude McKay in *Home to Harlem* cast Brooklyn as a slightly less urban alternative to Harlem in their accounts of New York's black population. Paule Marshall, from the 1950s on, uses Brooklyn as a central setting in a number of her novels and short stories. In her extensive meditations on Caribbean identity, family, community, and narrative, she casts the streets, houses, and stores of Brooklyn as encounter zones in which immigrants and their descendants wrestle with memory and history, and conceptions of home along with the racial politics of New York. Marshall's works in particular play with language, deploying vernacular to comment on and challenge other Brooklyn texts, thereby engaging with the construction of national and literary citizenship. Edwidge Danticat's fiction, in the 1990s and 2000s, moves back and forth between Brooklyn and Haiti, insisting on a transnational, literary geography. Loida Maritza Perez and Esmeralda Santiago draw attention to the particular experiences of immigrants from the Spanish-speaking Caribbean, attending to the complexities of situating a language other than English in what Perez calls the 'geographies of home'. Brooklyn, in the work of these writers, then, emerges as an important spatial node of meaning in an expansive American literary geography, thereby configuring a textual cartography of the tropics that refuses to be contained by and instead joins the literary histories of the Caribbean and of Brooklyn.

In this essay, I concentrate primarily on Paule Marshall's *Brown Girl, Brownstones*, for it, more than any other text, turns Brooklyn's spaces into places imbued with often conflicting meanings. Indeed, given Walrond's and McKay's depictions of Brooklyn, Marshall's work stands as a sort of foundational text in a literary history that is simultaneously of the Caribbean and of Brooklyn. Through its depictions of urban topography—its architecture, commercial and residential spaces, public and private areas, streets and sidewalks—*Brown Girl, Brownstones* constructs Caribbean places within Brooklyn, often in contrast and opposition to the socially produced functions of that urban landscape. Marshall constructs, out of the raw materials of Brooklyn's streets and houses, factories and parks, a cultural and linguistic geography that inscribes various versions of 'Barbadianess' or 'Bajaness' on New York City.

Published in 1959 and set from 1939 through the years past World War II, Marshall's text traces the coming-of-age of Selina Boyce, a young Barbadian-American girl whose family resides in the Bedford-Stuyvesant section of Brooklyn, an area whose racial and ethnic composition has shifted from predominantly white to predominantly black in the period directly before the beginning of the narrative. As participants in the first wave of immigration from the Caribbean to the USA, Selina's parents, Silla and Deighton, stand in and for the central conflicts of the text. They wage a battle over the house in which they reside and the meaning they attribute to it.

Critics have tended to understand the text in a number of ways. In the 1970s, scholars saw it as thematising the conflict between the individual and the community. Selina, in readings by Marcia Keizs and others, rejects the pressures of the Bajan community to conform in pursuit of a life as an artist. Heather Hathaway, in her astute 1999 *Caribbean Waves*, reads the novel as a migration narrative, which figures Selina as a second-generation immigrant, 'a cultural hybrid' who inhabits a 'dual location'.[6]

It is indeed tempting to read the story primarily as a coming-of-age tale or as an immigration narrative, one that thematises the dynamic between consent and descent and plays with the transformations of generations.[7] But the concerted attention to space throughout the text, that is the repeated references to houses, parks, streets, and other elements of Brooklyn's cityscape, suggests the novel's urban topography is more than simply a passive setting, a location in which the themes of immigration and racial and ethnic identity play out, or a narrative device that unifies the plot.[8] Marshall's novel unpacks the relationship between 'official', socially produced space, stemming from the governmental policies and social practices that map racial, ethnic, and economic relations in the city, and the 'unofficial', the personal and communal meanings inhabitants ascribe to the spaces in which they conduct their lives. These meanings may counter, pose alternatives to, or embrace the 'official'. They may be shared among members of the community, or they may be idiosyncratic. In *Brown Girl, Brownstones*, the characters and the narrative extract meaning out of space, thereby constructing a number of Bajan places, which may be in conflict with each other and comment on US and Barbadian economic and racial practices.

The central space in the text is the brownstone in which the Boyce family and their tenants reside. Like Eastern Parkway during the West Indian Day Parade in Kincaid's essay, the brownstone in Marshall's novel is a multivalent site, capacious enough to encompass often-competing conceptions of its significance. As both a private and public space, the building itself is an

---

6 See Marcia Keizs, 'Themes and Style in the Works of Paule Marshall', *Negro American Literature Forum*, 9, no. 3 (1975), pp. 67–76; Martin Japtok, 'Paule Marshall's *Brown Girl, Brownstones*: Reconciling Ethnicity and Individualism', *African American Review*, 32, no. 2 (1998), pp. 305–315; Heather Hathaway, *Caribbean Waves*, Bloomington: Indiana University Press, 1999, pp. 10, 86–118.

7 See Werner Sollors, *Beyond Ethnicity*, New York: Harper Collins, 1986, pp. 5–6.

8 See Kimberly W. Benston, 'Architectural Imagery and Unity in Paule Marshall's *Brown Girl, Brownstones*', *Negro American Literature Forum*, 9, no. 3 (1975), pp. 67–70.

encounter zone. Each resident—Selina's mother Silla, her father Deighton, and their tenants Suggie, a domestic worker, and Miss Mary, the maid of the former white owners, and her daughter—occupies and claims a different territory in the house. The kitchen is Silla's domain, while Deighton takes the sun porch. Suggie resides in rooms next to those of Miss Mary and her daughter. The residents are at war with each other, battling not over square footage or heat but over meaning. In particular, Silla demands authority over the entire building and, through that, over notions of Barbadian identity, community, and home.

Buying house: vernacular landscape and language

Written at the burgeoning of the civil rights movement, Marshall's text looks back to a moment of demographic shifts in Brooklyn and New York City's history, a moment that Silla and her Bajan peers take as an opportunity. In 1910, Brooklyn's population was 1,634,582. Of that number, 22,708 were black. 39% of Brooklyn's black population was native born, 49% were migrants, and 11% were foreign born. By 1930, the decade in which the novel begins, Brooklyn was home to 2,560,401, with 68,921 black residents. Of that number, according to the census, only 30% were born in New York State; 49% were migrants, and 16% were foreign born.[9]

Marshall describes this demographic change through an account of the provenance of the house:

> First there had been the Dutch-English and Scotch-Irish who had built the houses. There had been tea in the afternoon then and skirts rustling across parquet floors and mild voices. For a long time it had been only the whites, each generation unraveling in a quiet skein of years behind green shades.
>
> But now in 1939 the last of them were discreetly behind those shades or selling the houses and moving away. And as they left, the West Indians slowly edged their way in. Like a dark sea nudging its way onto a white beach and staining the sand, they came.[10]

Marshall traces shifting ownership of the brownstones in ethnic and racial terms, and, with her metaphor of the 'white beach' and the 'dark sea',

---

[9] Craig Wilder, *A Covenant with Color*, New York: Columbia University Press, 2000, p. 178, 125.

[10] Paule Marshall, *Brown Girl, Brownstones* [1959], New York: The Feminist Press, 1982, p. 4. Further references are included parenthetically in the text.

imagines a physical cartography of social inclusion and exclusion. However, in this moment, she does not refer to the politics behind this demographic shift. As part of Franklin Delano Roosevelt's New Deal programs, the Home Owners' Loan Corporation (HOLC), an agency charged with shoring up the housing market by preventing foreclosures and supporting banks, used race and ethnicity as criteria in its designation of Brooklyn's neighbourhoods as 'desirable' or 'undesirable'. Undesirable neighbourhoods, most of which were in northern Brooklyn, received little if any investment; denied financial assistance, white residents fled those areas, while African Americans and Caribbean immigrants settled there. In 1937, the *Brooklyn Eagle* called Bed-Stuy a 'copless, city stepchild', referring to the shift in municipal services away from Northern Brooklyn to Southern Brooklyn, which saw a rapid increase in white settlement.[11] The effort to determine the desirability of neighbourhoods (and hence the financial and municipal investment in those neighbourhoods) was known as redlining, for the red lines on the maps that identified the borough's areas. These redlined maps signified political and economic efforts to organise Brooklyn along lines of race, an organisation to which cities have been particularly vulnerable. As Gary Bridge and Sophie Watson write, cities 'are ... constituted spatially, socially, and economically sometimes leading to polarization, inequality, zones of exclusion and fragmentation, and at other times constituting sites of power and resistance, and the celebration of identity. Difference is constituted in all spatial relations but the particularity of the city is that it concentrates differences through its density of people and lived spaces'.[12] Marshall's novel exhibits the spatial logic of dense urban areas. It maps difference on the streets and in the houses and calls attention to the complex negotiations of national and racial identifications.

Despite its problematic racial politics, redlining, as Marshall's novel attests, did create opportunities for home ownership for recent immigrants from the West Indies, opportunities that challenged the notion of 'undesirability' and that could reconfigure the spatial organisation of political power. Indeed, the Association, a communal organisation of Barbadian property owners and businessmen modeled on 'black New York's most prominent benevolent society and credit union', the Paragon Progressive Community Association, focused on the purchase of property as a means of political

[11] Wilder, *Covenant*, p. 196.

[12] Gary Bridge and Sophie Watson, 'City Differences', in Gary Bridge and Sophie Watson, eds., *A Companion to the City*, Oxford: Blackwell, 2003, pp. 251–260, at 251–252.

advancement in New York City.[13] And throughout Marshall's novel, various members of that community, especially Silla, pursue home ownership with an almost religious fervor, a 'fierce idolatry' (4).

But it is more than just property and its economic benefits in the form of rooms to let that the women of Marshall's novel in particular desire. While the conflict over the Boyce brownstone certainly propels the novel's forward trajectory, as it creates the irresolvable conflict between Silla's seeming materialism and Deighton's longing for an imagined, ideal home in Barbados, it also affords Barbadians an opportunity to create a vernacular landscape. The brownstones come to operate, in the novel, as spatial and visual indicators of Barbadian identity, which reveal, as Jerome Krase writes, 'the history of bounded space, ... used as a way of defining political and economic power'. Vernacular landscape, in Marshall's Brooklyn, 'is the political and temporal complement of the cognitive map; it is an account of both inclusion and exclusion'.[14] The exterior of the brownstones of the West Indian residents of Bed-Stuy and later Crown Heights both herald a demographic shift—'the ones owned or leased by the West Indians looking almost new with their neat yards, new shades and fresh painted black iron fences, while the others where the whites still lived looked more faded in the hard sunlight' (53)—and transform the space into a West Indian place. The 'new cream-colored shades with fringes at every window' or 'arched windows and elaborate stonework' broadcast their proprietors and claim the neighbourhood for West Indians (54, 192).

Silla, her friends, and the members of the Association construct this vernacular urban landscape in part in response to and despite the economic and racial discrimination they experience. They combat the link between undesirability and race through their efforts not only to foster ownership but also to transform the visual landscape and the demographic make-up of the area. They are, in effect, undermining the 'official maps', as James Agee calls them, of the neighbourhood.[15] Property ownership, then, becomes the means by which the Bajans create, within Brooklyn, a Caribbean landscape and home, and this modified cityscape is simultaneously a declaration of difference and a claim of authority. The brownstones, in Marshall's Brooklyn, become an expression of the tropics in New York.

---

[13] The Paragon Progressive Community Association was founded in 1939 by Barbados-born Rufus Murray.

[14] Jerome Krase, 'Polish and Italian Vernacular Landscapes in Brooklyn', *Polish American Studies*, 54, no. 1 (1997), pp. 9–31, at 14.

[15] James Agee, *Brooklyn Is*, New York: Fordham University Press, 2005, p. 9.

Marshall's vernacular landscape is of a piece with the vernacular that shoots through her novel. In her essay, 'Poets in the Kitchen', Marshall describes her most important influences: the 'unknown bards' who scrubbed floors by day to further their 'consuming ambition to "buy house"' and who played with language and ideas by night, while sitting around her kitchen table.

> [T]hey talked—endlessly, passionately, poetically, and with impressive range. No subject was beyond them. True, they would indulge in the usual gossip: whose husband was running with whom, whose daughter looked slightly 'in the way' (pregnant) under her bridal gown as she walked down the aisle. That sort of thing. They were always, for example, discussing the state of the economy. It was the mid and late '30s then, and the aftershock of the Depression, with its soup lines and suicides on Wall Street, was still being felt ...[16]

The women were linguistic daredevils, taking 'standard English taught them in the primary school of Barbados and [transforming] it into an idiom, an instrument that more adequately described them—changing around the syntax and imposing their own rhythm and accent so that the sentences were more pleasing to their eyes'. The recipe includes: 'a few African sounds and words', 'a raft of metaphors, parables, biblical quotations, sayings, and the like'. A loose woman became a 'thoroughfare' or 'free-bee'. A pregnant woman was 'in the way' or 'tumbling big', and anything beautiful was 'beautiful-ugly'.[17]

The kitchen table, in Marshall's essay, is the locus for the imbrication of vernacular language and the daily concerns of these Bajan women. In the center of Marshall's mother's home, they navigated the often-perplexing experiences of the foreign city in which they were making their way and the language they found necessary to articulate a Caribbean homeland within the city. Marshall writes, 'Confronted therefore by a world they could not encompass, which even limited their rights as parents, and at the same time finding themselves permanently separated from the world they had known, they took refuge in language. "Language is the only homeland", Czelaw Milosz, the émigré Polish writer and Nobel laureate, has said'.[18] The women

---

[16] Paule Marshall, 'Poets in the Kitchen', *Reena and Other Stories*, New York: The Feminist Press, 1983, p. 5.

[17] Marshall, 'Poets', p. 8.

[18] Marshall, 'Poets', p. 7.

make, within Brooklyn, a Bajan home through their deployment of both vernacular language and vernacular landscape.

Kitchen scenes, indeed, are central to *Brown Girl, Brownstones*, for they link the creation of a vernacular landscape with the expression of vernacular language in the forging of a Bajan place in Brooklyn. It is in the kitchen that Silla, 'the mother' as Selina imagines her, crafts her strategy to 'buy house'. She and her friends discuss World War II, the relationship to 'England and the crown', their children, and their men.[19] Silla cooks Bajan delicacies, which she will later sell. In these moments between Silla and her friends, the text claims narrative possibilities in vernacular language, akin to social, economic, and communal possibilities of vernacular landscapes. Just as they use the creation of a vernacular landscape to negotiate the racialised urban spaces in which they reside and work, they use vernacular language—the expressions, sounds, and phrases of Barbados—to foster community and express their power outside of the contours of standard English. In both landscape and language, then, *Brown Girl, Brownstones* presents a West Indian place in Brooklyn, an island geographically far from but, pregnant with meaning, close to or even part of Barbados itself.

Cuckoo and codfish: the place of memory

Marshall's novel does not create a Caribbean place only by imagining a vernacular landscape and vernacular language. Indeed, Silla is not the only resident of the brownstone that preoccupies her and the narrative. She is at war with her two tenants, Suggie, a Barbadian domestic worker who lives with the Long Island white family for whom she works during the week and returns to Brooklyn on the weekends, and Miss Mary, the elderly white maid who lived in the home as a domestic servant of the previous white owners.

That Suggie and Miss Mary are both associated with domestic service point to the manner in which work bears the weight of race and gender in Brooklyn during the depression and earlier. According to a federal study at the beginning of the twentieth century, white women worked in thirty different 'job categories', while black women worked in four: as dressmakers, laundresses, servants/waitress, and other. The majority worked as servants. As Craig Wilder writes, 'the concentration of native and foreign-born black women in unregulated, unprotected, and unorganized domestic service jobs made them "the most oppressed section of the working class"'. Indeed, in

---

[19] Marshall, *Brown Girl, Brownstones*, p.65.

recognition of this dire situation, in 1937 the National Negro Congress briefly formed the Domestic Workers' Association.[20]

Marshall's novel attends to the problem of domestic work in spatial terms:

> It was always the mother and the others, for they were alike—those watchful, wrathful women whose eyes seared and searched and laid bare, whose tongues lashed the world in unremitting distrust. Each morning they took the train to Flatbush and Sheepshead Bay to scrub floors. The lucky ones had their steady madams while the others wandered those neat blocks or waited on corners—each with her apron and working shoes in a bag under her arm until someone offered her a day's work. Sometimes the white children on the way to school laughed at their blackness and shouted 'nigger', but the Barbadian women sucked their teeth, dismissing them. Their only thought was of the 'few raw-mout' pennies' at the end of the day which would eventually 'buy house'. (11)

The domestic workers, especially those in the worst of situations are, in effect, bereft of both space and place. They wander the streets looking for work, unable to create meaning in neighbourhoods in which they have neither economic nor social standing. However, despite the demeaning, insecure work they perform and the verbal assaults to which they are subject, many of the women, like Silla, find some comfort in the thought of ownership, the possibility of claiming a literal space and hence a legitimised place in neighbourhoods other than those of the madams. The houses and the possibilities of economic security and political power they represent offset the racialised sphere of domestic work they inhabit.

Suggie, however, does not make that move. During the week, she sleeps in a 'lonely room under the high roof' at the home of the white family that employs her. When she returns each weekend to Bed-Stuy, she uses an alternative strategy to 'nullify the long week of general house work and the lonely room in a stranger's house'. Instead of attempting to climb the ladder of social mobility, she creates, in effect, a Caribbean place carved out of the room she rents. 'Not long off the boat', she cooks and eats Barbadian food in her small Brooklyn flat, food that evokes the sensory memory of the island (18, 35, 23):

> She ate sitting on the edge of the bed, and from the way she held the bowl in her palm and solemnly scooped the food she might have been

---

[20] Wilder, *Covenant*, pp. 138–139.

home in Barbados, eating in the doorway of the small house perched
like a forlorn bird on the hillside. She could see the yam patch from
there and the mango tree with its long leaves weighted down by the
dusk, and beyond, all down the sloping hills, a susurrant sea of sugar
cane. (18)

Notice the transition from 'might have been at home' to 'could see.' Marshall's
language suggests that Suggie has been transported, while in Brooklyn, back
to the island from which she migrated and, at the same, inhabits a Caribbean
place even in her small room. Even Suggie's body language and her bodily
experiences with her lovers evoke what is simultaneously a sensory return
and a sensory creation: 'Her eyes wistfully sought the bottle of rum on the
low table between them, seeing in it a cane field at night with the cane rising
and plunging in the wild, hearing the ecstatic moan of the lover inside her'.
Suggie is, for a moment, in the cane fields of Barbados (24–25). However,
when she no longer has access to that which returns her to the island, food
or sex, she finds herself immersed in the harsh aspects of US urban life,
manifest in the grim surroundings in which she lives. Although she cannot
sustain the feeling of Barbados, her idiosyncratic creation of a Bajan place,
she does not long for a literal return:

> 'Go back? Where? Home, you mean?' The sagging bed thumped the
> floor as she sprang up, her incredulous eyes boring into Selina. 'Me
> go back there? You think I looking to dead before my time? Do you
> know how bad those malicious brutes would lick their mouth on me if
> I went back the same way I left? Tell muh, whey you think your father
> is at the bottom of the sea tonight?' (208)

Suggie's effort to negotiate the racialised economic and social system of
domestic work with her body's experience of place does not translate into
nostalgia for a lost time or locale. Rather she creates an embodied experience
of Caribbean-ness, albeit a temporary one, in her actions in space, akin to
the dancing and jumping up at Jamaica Kincaid's Carnival. Suggie's body
becomes a site of return via memory, an embrace of an embodied cultural
past that is an alternative to the assaults of domestic work.

Though she is not West Indian, Miss Mary, who lived in the house well
before Silla leased it, employs a similar strategy to that of Suggie. Rather
than construct an alternative place within the one she inhabits, she erects,
through memory, an alternative time. In the room, full of furniture, dust,
and clutter, 'relics' of the past, Miss Mary dreams of her lover, her young

master and mistress, and the days before Caribbean immigrants moved into the neighbourhood:

> In the midst of this dust and clutter Miss Mary's bed reared like a grim rock. She lay there, surrounded by her legacies, and holding firm to the thin rotted thread of her life ... Today, out of the heaped memories, she selected the days of dying: the master lying in state in the parlor ... the letter announcing her lover's death in the 1904 war even as his child swelled her stomach ... the joyless years afterward and the mistress slowly wasting. (20)

For Miss Mary, the brownstone rooms she occupies return her to a lost time, suggesting that the transformation of space into place is highly contingent on those who create it and that it may elude collective meaning.

Suggie's and Miss Mary's construction of their own places within the brownstone, however, offend Silla. The odors and sounds emerging from Suggie's room represent a Bajan past, memory that Silla wishes to deny. The clutter in Miss Mary's room too is an affront to Silla, for it signals the past of white ownership and exclusion that she wants to erase. In occupying and trying to buy the house with Suggie and Miss Mary still living in it, Silla attempts to contain and control memory that threatens her vision of Barbados in Brooklyn. In marking the brownstone as her territory, Silla rejects the possibility of multivocal, multivalent Barbados in Brooklyn and of the possibility of sharing place-making with anyone but those who abide by her beliefs.

Deportation and denizenship

Deighton represents the strongest challenge to Silla's efforts to construct a singular Barbadian place in Brooklyn through the acquisition of property. He condemns both the obsessive house buying of the Bajans and Suggie's efforts to experience the tropics in her body. Deighton rejects Suggie's strategy, in particular, for he fears that it will mark him as foreign to the USA: 'Outside in the hall, the smell of Suggie's codfish hung in a dead weight, and he hurried downstairs, afraid that the smell would insinuate itself into his clothes and he would carry it with him all night as the undisputed sign that he was Barbadian and a foreigner' (22). He does not want the odor of the island to linger on his body, to suggest that his body is a Caribbean one, rather than a cosmopolitan one, as though the two are not compatible. Suggie's approach would mark him, he believes, as having no social standing on the streets he walks; instead he wants to be part of, indeed construct, the lively, urban area:

> Unlike Chauncey Street, Fulton Street this summer Saturday night was a whirling spectrum of neon signs, movie marquees, bright-lit store windows and sweeping yellow streamers of light from the cars. It was canorous voices, hooted laughter and curses ripping the night's warm cloak; a welter of dark faces and gold-etched teeth; children crying high among the fire escapes of the tenements; the subway rumbling below; the unrelenting wail of a blues spilling from a bar; greasy counters and fish sandwiches and barbecue and hot sauce; trays of chitterlings and hog maws and fat back in the meat stores; the trolleys' insistent clangor; a man and a woman in a hallway bedroom, sleeping like children now that the wildness had passed; a drunken woman pitching along the street; the sustained shriek of a police car and its red light stabbing nervously at faces and windows. Fulton Street on Saturday night was all beauty and desperation and sadness.
> Deighton walked slowly, loving it. (37)

Like de Certeau's walker, who 'transforms the spatial signifier into something else', Deighton and the other residents and visitors make Fulton Street a vital place where life spills out, sometimes messily, from doors and windows in contradistinction to the blight implied by HOLC's label of 'undesirability'.[21] Children use the fire escape for something other than escape; music escapes the walls and doors of bars. Interdictions do not work on this street, as Bed-Stuy's residents resist even architectural and social constraints. This is a vernacular landscape, which resists containment, but it is not, here, a Bajan vernacular landscape.

---

[21] Michel de Certeau writes: 'If it is true that a spatial order organizes an ensemble of possibilities (e.g., by a place in which one can move) and interdictions (e.g. by a wall that prevents one from going further), then the walker actualizes some of these possibilities. In that way, he makes them exist as well as emerge. But he also moves them about and he invents others, since the crossing, drifting away, or improvisation of walking privilege, transform, or abandon spatial elements ... The walker transforms each spatial signifier into something else. And if on the one hand he actualizes only a few of the possibilities fixed by constructed order (he goes only here and not there), on the other he increases the number of possibilities (for example, by creating shortcuts and detours) and prohibitions (for example he forbids himself to take paths generally considered accessible or even obligatory). He thus makes a selection' (*The Practice of Everyday Life*, trans. Steven Rendall, Berkeley: University of California Press, 1988, p. 98).

In walking, Deighton attempts to claim 'denizenship'; he wants to inhabit the city in which he resides on his own terms, to claim it as he wishes. While he resists the imposition of Barbados on Brooklyn's spaces, he wants to inhabit Brooklyn, without the limits imposed on him by US race relations or by the Barbadian community by travelling where he pleases, both literally and figuratively. He wants access, without the constraints of a racialised system, to Fifth Avenue, and, as that is not available, he does not recognise the possibility of a Caribbean place in Brooklyn and wants to return home.

Deighton, however, is neither a citizen nor legal resident of the USA. Having 'jump[ed] ship into this country', he has neither political nor social standing (33). Despite his admittedly limited efforts, he can neither function effectively within the exclusionary system of labor nor make meaning out of the brownstone he shares with Silla. With a knowledge of the manner in which his national origin places him in a racialised status, and with a strong conflict with his wife and the community in which they reside, Deighton retreats to the sun parlor, where 'the house was given over to the sun', where 'sunlight came spilling through the glass wall, swayed like a dancer in the air and lay in a yellow rug on the floor' (8). This warm, sunny room is the space from which Deighton half-heartedly attempts and fails to navigate New York's landscape of labor and longs, instead, for a lost, idyllic home.

When Deighton inherits 'land', a strong contrast to buying 'house', he imagines a return, an escape from Brooklyn and from the Barbadian community there. Given the racial system within the US, 'buying house' does not, for him, make a Caribbean place in Brooklyn. Rather, it anchors him in a space in which he cannot function. Land in Barbados itself, on the other hand, would be an answer to the predicament of race he identifies: 'A lot in a place that's only 166 square miles—and a lot for a colored man to own in a place where the white man owns everything' (25). And his return, he imagines, will be accompanied by the class mobility he fails to achieve in Brooklyn:

> Then these Bajan with their few raw-mouth houses will see what real money is! But I wun get like them ... I going home and breathe good Bimshire air 'cause a man got a right to take his ease in this life and not always be scuffling ... Did I tell yuh I gon plant ladies-of-the-night round the house? (85)

Deighton is, to use Philip Kasnitz's phrase, a 'bird of passage', who considers himself a 'temporary sojourner in North American society'.[22] In his fantasy of 'tall white columns', glasses and flowers, a home built on land in Barbados means the possibility of a rise in class status and the possibility of stepping outside the US racial system altogether. He imagines another return, this time to the USA, where he would claim a class status inaccessible to him. He tells Selina 'I gon put you 'pon a plane to New York to do your shopping. And when these Bajan here see you, they gon say, "Wha'lah, wah'lah look Deighton Selina! I hear that man living like a lord home"' (87).

Silla, however, denies that possibility, undermining his imagination of Barbados by condemning Bimshire for the difficulties she experienced there. She reminds Deighton about 'People having to work for next skin to nothing' and about the treatment by whites (70). She tries to impose her notion of Barbados and her sense of the possibilities in Brooklyn for a Caribbean place on all of her family, thereby legitimising her unscrupulous actions and denying the possibility of meanings other than hers. She says to him, 'I know you. As soon as you got home you'd be ready to come back. You cun live on no small island after living in New York. But we can still buy land home if you want. Later' (115). When Deighton refuses Silla, she sells the land out from under him, thereby destroying their relationship and Deighton's dreams of 'home'.

Defeated, Deighton is not able to make place out of any space. When he discovers Father Peace, a stand in for Father Divine, he worships at a brownstone unlike any Selina has ever seen, with a 'large flickering neon sign where the cornice should have been … inside there were no walls but only one long high room, garishly lighted' (164). The brownstone is stripped of all distinguishing features and of history. Like the brownstone, Deighton's room in the 'kingdom in Brooklyn' is stripped of all place-making objects. It is bare, save for a portrait of Father Peace. A far cry from the light-filled sensuality of the sun-parlor, this room denies Deighton's denizenship in Brooklyn. And Silla, frustrated with Deighton's refusal to engage with the family and with her desire to create her version of a Bajan-Brooklyn place, reports him for his illegal status. She takes advantage of the second wave of deportation in US history, 'when an anticrime and often rather nativist and xenophobic flow met a centralizing, anticorruption, "good government" administrative ethos'.[23] Deighton's deportation represents both the imposition of an official conception of citizenship, one that recognises neither his entry (jumping off the boat) nor his status in the USA, a failure

---

[22] Philip Kasnitz, *Caribbean New York*, Ithaca: Cornell University Press, 1992, p. 35.
[23] Daniel Kanstroom, *Deportation Nation*, Cambridge: Harvard University Press, 2007, p. 163.

of his denizenship to make claim on the space in which he resides, and his ex-communication from the Bajan community. Indeed, Deighton's death, which occurs in a space betwixt and between the USA and Barbados, is the culmination of his placeless-ness.

Walking in the city

When, as a 'New York child', Selina, Deighton's and Silla's daughter, contemplates Barbados as 'home', she does not make, in some form, Barbados in Brooklyn. For Selina, space is not an opportunity to craft a Caribbean place; instead it becomes a metaphor for identity, something that stands for constraint or freedom, and the possibility of cosmopolitanism. Indeed, Selina is associated with and makes multiple meanings out of multiple spaces in the text: the brownstone, parks and streets, Clive's basement apartment, the Association's building and even Times Square.

Early in the novel, Selina exhibits an uneasy relationship to the brownstone. Not only does she imagine the house's history, but she also conceives of it as a living, vibrant entity, almost with a consciousness of its own. Marshall writes, 'Her house was alive to Selina. She sat this summer afternoon on the upper landing on the top floor, listening to its shallow breathing' (4). Selina insists on her presence in the house, and, like Silla, attempts to control its meaning, albeit in a different way: 'Slowly she raised her arm, thin and dark in the sun-haze, circled by two heavy silver bangles which had come from 'home' and which every Barbadian-American girl wore from birth. Glaring down, she shook her fist, and the bangles sounded her defiance with a thin clangor' (5). In shaking her bangles, Selina makes a claim on the house, and the house responds; 'the house, stunned by the noise, ceased breathing and a pure silence fell' (5). Selina asserts that it and Barbados are both and simultaneously 'home', and the house seems to accept that. And Selina then links her self to the island of her parents' origins and the brownstone's past residents:

> She rose, her arms lifted in welcome, and quickly the white family who had lived there before, whom the old woman upstairs always spoke of glided with pale footfalls up the stairs. Their white hands trailed the bannister, their mild voices implored her to give them a little life. And as they crowded around, fusing with her, she was no longer a dark girl alone and dreaming at the top of an old house, but one of them, invested with their beauty and gentility... It was the museum of all the lives that had ever lived here. The floor-to-ceiling mirror retained their faces as the silence did their voices. (5)

The house's former family lingers throughout the text. In the furniture, the mirror, and even the sounds of the house, they are present to Selina. Yet she, unlike Silla, does not wish to erase them. She does not have an unequivocally hostile relationship with the former inhabitants, and, in fact, identifies with them, often thinking of them and 'imagin[ing] that she was one of those children' (51). Because of her embrace of the house's history and of its present state, she is able to move freely within it, and despite her mother's objections, interacts with Miss Mary and Suggie in their rooms. Indeed, in doing so, she recognises the varieties of place-making in which all of the brownstone's inhabitants engage and defies the boundaries Silla erects between them.

As the novel progresses, Selina begins to move freely throughout Brooklyn and beyond. And it is these movements that are an integral part of the novel's *bildungsroman* form. Indeed, Selina's coming-of-age is predicated on transformations in her relationships to space. As the novel continues, she moves out farther and farther from the brownstone and from the West Indian community.

Early on, Selina thinks about space near the brownstone, expanding her world far beyond that of her mother's. 'After the house, Selina loved the park,' Marshall writes. 'The thick streets, the grass – shrill-green in the sun – the statue of Robert Fulton and the pavilion where the lovers met and murmured at night formed, for her, the perfect boundary for her world; the park was the fitting buffer between Chauncey Street's gentility and Fulton's raucousness' (13). The novel, at this point, begins to map Brooklyn in terms of Selina's identity. Selina's territory expands from the brownstone to include Fulton Park, complete with the nineteenth century monument to Robert Fulton, the well-known engineer and inventor, a monument commissioned in the late nineteenth century well before the demographic shifts in Bed-Stuy. Bridge and Watson are helpful here, for they help articulate why Selina, unlike her parents and Suggie, finds that Brooklyn's spaces belong to her on her own terms, rather than on the terms of her mother and community: 'The complex textures of a city are a rich source of memory for urban dwellers which may represent an absence for new migrants disembedding them, at least initially, from a sense of place and belonging'.[24] Unlike her parents and Suggie, 'new migrants', Selina has no memories of Barbados and creates her own in Brooklyn, claiming the monument and pavilion as her own 'cultural markers', ultimately indicative of her passage from childhood into adulthood.

As Selina ages, she finds that she requires even more expansive space. When she finds that 'she had finally passed the narrow boundary of herself

[24] Bridge and Watson, 'Introduction', *A Companion to the City*, p. 13.

and her world [and that] she could no longer be measured by Chauncey Street or the park or the nearby school', Selina begins to travel through Brooklyn's streets, interacting with them in ways vastly different from that of her mother and father (56). Consider an early moment in her travels on the trolley in Brooklyn:

> They [Selina and her friend Beryl] took separate window seats on the trolley so that they could watch the panorama of Sunday in Brooklyn strung out under the sun. To Selina the colors, the people seemed to run together. Dark, lovely little girls in straw bonnets flowed into little boys with their rough hair parted neatly on the side; into women in sheer dresses which whipped around their brown legs, into a bevy of church sisters swathed in black as though mourning their own imminent deaths... Life suddenly was nothing by this change and return. (56)

And then a later moment:

> She had never seen streets like these. The trolley might have taken her to another city, some barren waste land gripped by a cold more intense that winter's and raw with wind, a place where even the falling snow was a soiled brown. Factories stretched unending down the streets, towered blackly into the sky, their countless lighted windows offering no promise of warmth inside. Obscene drawings and words decorated the walls; the war had added its swastika and slogans, lovers their hearts pierced with arrows. Each factory was bedecked with 'Help Wanted' signs, making it look like one of the shabby men who walk the city's streets with advertisements strapped to their shoulders. (96–97)

Selina is a young flaneur. She walks and rides through Brooklyn, like James Agee in *Brooklyn Is* or Alfred Kazin in *A Walker in the City*, observing and experiencing the streets. She notes the writings of urban life, the graffiti on walls and the placards on men's backs, all indicative of place-making outside of the Bajan community. Selina reads the city in her travels, but not in terms of 'Caribbean-ness'. Instead, she recognised in what had been, initially, unfamiliar, the possibility of more than her mother and community desire.

Even on the level of plot, she resists the conception of Brooklyn as a Caribbean place. She escapes from her mother and the familial conflict by travelling first to Prospect Park and the local library and later to the basement studio of a brownstone rooming house with her lover Clive. Like Greenwich Village, Clive's basement, albeit confined, stands for freedom of thought and her body. As she grows into an adult, she adopts an understanding of space that has much in common with other Brooklyn texts, say *A Walker in the City* and *A Tree Grows in Brooklyn*, which cast Brooklyn as ethnic and provincial and Manhattan as cosmopolitan. Selina falls in love with Times Square, where she finds a space that echoes her interior life. Marshall writes,

> Times Square, that bejeweled navel in the city's long sinuous form. To Selina it was a new constellation, the myriad lights hot stars bursting from chaos into their own vivid life, shooting, streaking wheeling in the night void, then expiring but only to burst again—and the concatenation of traffic and voices like the road from the depth of a maelstrom—an irresistible call to destruction. She loved it for its chaos echoed her inner chaos; each bedizened window, each gaudy empty display evoked something in her that loved and understood the gaudy, the emptiness defined her own emptiness and that in the face flitting past her. (213)

In Times Square's 'culture of congestion: congestion not only in people, in buildings, in cars, in signs, but, most alluring of all, congestion in meaning', Selina identifies a place that stands for her.[25] The 'density of meaning' of Times Square, meaning that overwhelms and refuses to be confined, its sensory overload and sense of cosmopolitan and modern possibility, allows Selina to discard her parents' competing notions of what it means to be Bajan. Indeed, Selina insists, 'Fulton Street is nothing compared to Times Square. Nothing!' (214). Like her father, Selina does not accept the place-making of Silla and other Bajans. She neither embraces nor desires their moves to create a tropic place in New York City, in part because of the limits it would impose on her and in part because of her recognition of the manner in which black-white race relations trump her efforts to distinguish herself from her family and community.

Selina's final walk through the landscape of Bed-Stuy concludes the text. She notes 'the ravaged brownstones' and the new sounds emerging from them, 'the staccato beat of Spanish voices', the 'frenzied sensuous music joined [by] the warm canorous Negro sounds'. She arrives, ultimately, at a place of 'vast waste—an area where blocks of brownstones had been blasted to make way for a city project':

> On the far perimeter of the plain, the new city houses were already up and occupied. As Selina stared at those monolithic shapes they

---

[25] Marshall Berman, *On the Town*, New York: Random House, 2006, pp.xxi–xxii. Berman writes that Times Square is a 'primal urban experiences—being in the midst of a physical and semiotic overflow feeling the flow all over you'.

seemed to draw near, the lighted windows dangling the sky like a new constellation. She imagined she heard footsteps ringing hollow in the concrete halls, the garbled symphony of radios and television, children crying in close rooms: like moving in an oppressive round with those uniformly painted walls. The projects receded and she was again the sole survivor amid the wreckage. (309–310)

Selina witnesses further demographic change; the Barbadian immigrants, in their pursuit of class mobility, are moving to Crown Heights and a new group, a Spanish-speaking one, is taking their place. This shift could have suggested the possibility of a vital transformation and change, but Selina encounters ruins, a 'solitary wall stood perversely amid the rubble, a stoop still imposed its massive grandeur, a carved oak staircase led only to the night sky' (309). She faces the anti-democratic and anti-urban project of New York City's urban renewal, the destruction of the streets and houses in favour of large-scale public housing that erases the city streets. Again, Marshall only obliquely refers to the politics that undergirded this transformation, the unfortunate meeting of Le Corbusier's modern aesthetics and Robert Moses's political power that worked together to transform, indeed destroy, the urban landscape. Brownstones, associated now with non-white ethnic and racial identities, are reduced to rubble as the 'new city houses', housing projects, take over.[26]

Selina, as the 'sole survivor amid the wreckage', responds in a very different way than either of her parents would in the face of this extreme change. She throws only one of her bangles towards the projects, leaving something of herself in Brooklyn, as she plans leaving. At this moment she is of Brooklyn and Barbados but also fully herself by insisting on being apart from them. Selina's final act suggests a burgeoning transnationalism, as she plans to 'go away' to the 'islands' to leave the 'faces that hung like portraits in her mind' and the spaces and places they occupied (307–308).

Place-making in the post-1965 generation

This incipient transnationalism in Marshall's 1959 text comes fully to the fore in a generation of post-1965 writers. Edwidge Danticat, in particular, as well as Marshall in her later work, play with place-making in the nexus of Brooklyn and the Caribbean. Danticat explores the complexities of migration

---

[26] See Marshall Berman, *All That is Solid Melts into Air: The Experience of Modernity*, London: Verso, 1983, and Wilder, *A Covenant with Color*.

and movement in *Breathe, Eyes, Memory* and writes a translocal text in her collection of short stories *The Dew Breaker*.

Like *Brown Girl, Brownstones*, Danticat's *Breath, Eyes, Memory* depicts a vernacular landscape, albeit a commercial one, that creates a Caribbean place out of and in Brooklyn. Flatbush Avenue is the location of 'Haiti Express', where local residents send remittances, money orders and letters to Haiti. Sophie and her mother visit the 'Haitian beauty salon'. But the creation of a Haitian place within this small area of Brooklyn isn't suggested only by Danticat's use of national or what have become ethnic tags: 'All along the avenue were people who seemed displaced among the speeding cars and very tall buildings and argued in Creole and even played dominoes on their stoops ... On the walls were earthen jars, tin can lamps, and small statues of the beautiful *mulâtresse*, the goddess and loa Erzulie'.[27] Like de Certeau, who distinguishes between the observer, who peers down from his high vantage and imagines that he sees a city whose streets and buildings are legible, and the individuals on the street who maintain its illegibility by making it their own in fulfilling its possibilities or denying its interdictions, Danticat contrasts speeding cars and tall buildings, which have no regard for the individuals who inhabit the buildings and walk the streets, with the language, play, and consumption that enable residents to claim the area as theirs, as Haitian. The Haitian immigrants and their families create 'home', out of a new locale, on their terms.

The Dew Breaker enacts the transnationalism of later generations of Caribbean migrants on a formal level. The text contains stories/chapters set in both Haiti and Brooklyn, as well as other areas in the USA, and does not privilege a single locale. Rather, the book's setting is precisely in the relay between its various locations. Consider this exchange:

> 'Where are you and your daddy from, Ms. Bienaimé?' Office Bo asks doing the best he can with my last name ...
>
> I was born and raised in East Flatbush, Brooklyn, and have never even been to my parent birthplace. Still, I answer 'Haiti' because it is one more thing I've always longed to have in common with my parent.[28]

Like *Brown Girl, Brownstones*, *The Dew Breaker* explores the multiplicity of ideas of home and the idiosyncratic ways in which individuals make claims on space. However, Danticat's work turns its attention to violence, political crimes, and justice. In the attention to the wanted posters for Haitian war

---

[27]   Edwidge Danticat, *Breath, Eyes, Memory*, New York: Vintage, 1994, pp. 50–51.
[28]   Edwidge Danticat, *The Dew Breaker*, New York: Vintage, 2004, pp. 3–4.

criminals in Brooklyn, Danticat's work points to the contiguousness of Brooklyn and Haiti. While national boundaries are policed 'officially', they are easily crossed in communal and individual ways through Danticat's work.

Danticat's memoir, *Brother I'm Dying* negotiates the relationship between the official and the unofficial, between rigid boundaries between nation and permeable ones on the level of families and individuals. While Brooklyn becomes the space in which Danticat's mother and father choose to raise their family, for Danticat herself it becomes a place that is equally home, along with Haiti. She travels back and forth between the USA and Haiti twenty-five times after she first leaves Haiti to join her parents. But, of course, Danticat is in a privileged position as a naturalised US citizen. She is able to function as a denizen, someone who makes meaning and claims authority over space, and as citizen simultaneously.[29] Her uncle, on the other hand, is detained on what would become his final trip into the USA. Despite the violence from which he was fleeing, he is placed into the custody of INS in Krome, a detention center in Miami, where he dies. This memoir calls attention to the problems in the possibilities and tension between the USA and the Caribbean, given current and official immigration policies and practices and the unofficial practices of residents. Danticat's uncle is not able to make place in Brooklyn or anywhere in the USA, while her father could. However, in death, the two are united in a shared cemetery plot. But even then, Danticat speculates about the tensions between exile and home:

> My uncle was buried in a cemetery in Queens, New York. His grave sits by an open road, overlooking the streets of Cyprus Hills and the subway tracks above them. During his life, my uncle had clung to his home, determined not to be driven out. He had remained in Bel Air, in part because it was what he knew. But he had also hoped to do some good there. Now he would be exiled finally in death. He would become part of the soil of a country that had not wanted him. This haunted my father more than anything else.[30]

In the concern with the burial of the dead, a trope that is repeated, *Brother, I'm Dying* explores the relationship between diaspora and citizenship, between dignity and dehumanisation. Danticat asks if the uncle's burial

---

[29] When asked at a discussion of her work at Brooklyn College, which (Brooklyn or Haiti) she considers 'home', she responded 'both'. Edwidge Danticat, Lecture at Brooklyn College 2011 First-Year Common Reading Room Event (20 September 2011).
[30] Edwidge Danticat, *Brother, I'm Dying*, New York: Knopf, 2007, p. 251.

is a loss of citizenship, freedom, and sovereignty or the reconciliation of family. The memoir wonders, given the dynamics of Haitian migration, as described in this text, if familial reconciliation and the formation of a new home come at the expense of national identity and history. Danticat's work points to an uneasy form of place-making, one that is unable to counter the problematic immigration policies of the USA, even while some are able to claim a Caribbean place within the USA.

Place-making and making a place in literary history

Marshall's mid-century work and Danticat's later texts are clearly of a piece in that they employ Caribbean place-making in Brooklyn. Can we then claim Marshall, Danticat, and others as part of a Brooklyn and US literary history, as part of Caribbean literary history, as both; or should we reconfigure those literary histories into something else altogether?

To explore these questions, we may turn back to *Brown Girl, Brownstones*. The novel is a direct comment on and critique of the iconic Brooklyn novel by Betty Smith, *A Tree Grows in Brooklyn*, which claims a singular Brooklyn— and American—'authenticity' predicated on white ethnic identity. Smith set her own work against that of Thomas Wolfe, whose 1935 comic short story 'Only the Dead Know Brooklyn' investigates inclusion and exclusion in urban life, an investigation rendered in a strong Brooklynese. Despite its attention to and skill in rendering a Brooklyn vernacular, Wolfe's story, Smith imagined, did not do justice to the Brooklyn she knew, one populated by the white, the ethnic, the poor, and the immigrant. Her novel, a sentimental, quasi-didactic coming-of-age tale, was an attempt to depict the borough in a more 'authentic' or accurate way.

Published in 1943, *A Tree Grows in Brooklyn*, probably more than any other novel, has come to represent Brooklyn for generations of readers. Extraordinarily popular among the armed forces during World War II, celebrated by countless readers, and remaining in print since its publication, *A Tree Grows in Brooklyn*, like *Brown Girl, Brownstones*, revolves around a specific neighbourhood, in this case Williamsburg, and disseminates a particular vision of Brooklyn—one that downplays its complexity and diversity in favour of a white, ethnic, working class and poor community. This community stands for the nation, and *A Tree Grows in Brooklyn* operates as a national narrative.

Centred on Francie, a young girl of Irish and German descent, and her mother and father, who are in conflict over work, alcohol, and family life, the novel remains preoccupied with the resilience of the poor and the language necessary to portray poverty and the people who live in it. Through its elaborate descriptions of poverty, it offers a narrative of ethnic assimilation and success with a degree of realism and an occasionally sentimental and didactic streak. In its embrace of upward mobility and in its refusal to represent vernacular language, *A Tree Grows in Brooklyn* trades the ethnic and linguistic complexity of the borough for a more accessible Brooklyn that can stand for a broad range of Americans, though not all. It deploys a white ethnic identity that comes to stand for a national identity, just as the text itself comes to stand as a national narrative. As Judith E. Smith describes a soldier's comment on the book: 'I guess that's one of the freedoms we're fighting for in this bitter war, the freedom that will assure the Francies of the world the same opportunities and privileges (or BETTER!) that millions of us have capitalized in our great country'.[31]

Despite *A Tree Grows in Brooklyn*'s embrace of narratives of the white ethnic, urban poor, it erases the linguistic difference of its characters and ignores almost completely that of any non-white, non-Christian characters. Although we know that Francie, the protagonist, has a Brooklyn accent, something she hopes to lose at the University of Michigan, none of her speech is rendered in vernacular. Indeed none of the major characters speak with any sort of accent, whatever their native language. Compare this to Henry Roth's *Call It Sleep*, published in 1935, or to Wolfe's 'Only the Dead Know Brooklyn,' to which Marshall refers in *Brown Girl, Brownstones*. Both render the Brooklyn accent so strongly that it is near impossible to read them silently. The almost exclusive use of Standard English—except for the most marginal characters—allows Brooklyn to stand for the USA.

And here is where the comparisons to *Brown Girl, Brownstones* are most striking. While the plots of the two novels are remarkably similar, it is Marshall's use of the Barbadian vernacular that distinguishes *Brown Girl, Brownstones*. The novel does not merely offer up examples of the vernacular language as a sort of local color. It also insists that Brooklyn and its literary history must include Caribbean words, phrases, and lilts, and it does so in terms of space. Note the beginning:

> In the somnolent July afternoon the unbroken line of brownstone houses down the long Brooklyn street resembled an army massed at attention. They were all one uniform red-brown stone. All with high massive stone stoops and black iron-grille fences staving off the sun. All draped in ivy as though mourning. Their somber facades, indifferent to the summer's heat and passion, faced a park while their backs reared

---

[31] Judith Smith, *Visions of Belonging*, New York: Columbia University Press, 2004, p. 56.

dark against the sky. They were only three or four stories tall—squat—yet they gave the impression of formidable height.

Glancing down the interminable Brooklyn street you thought of those joined brownstones as one house reflected through a train of mirrors, with no walls between the houses but only vast rooms yawning endlessly one into each other. Yet, looking close, you saw that under the thick ivy each house had something distinctively its own. Some touch that was Gothic, Romanesque, baroque or Greek triumphed amid the Victorian clutter. Here, Ionic columns framed the windows while next door gargoyles scowled up at the sun. There cornices were hung with carved foliage while Gorgon heads decorated others. Many homes had bay window or Gothic stonework; a few boasted turrets raised high above the other roofs. Yet they all shared the same brown monotony. All seemed doomed by the confusion of their design. (3)

It is tempting to read this opening as an invitation to the reader to speculate on the exchange between the individual and the community. Indeed, in an earlier draft of the novel, Marshall uses, but later discards from the published version, a similar image for precisely that effect.[32] However, this opening passage may be read as speculation as to the narrative possibilities of a text written by and about non-white immigrants.

In its account of the streets and the houses that line it, this beginning is suggestive of the complexity of writing about difference. Rather than cast the uniformity of the houses only as a figure for ethnic solidarity and assimilation, *Brown Girl, Brownstones* asks us to attend to narrative and formal differentiation. Subtle variations of architecture among 'Victorian clutter' are differences in language, in experience, departures from the formulae of *A Tree Grows in Brooklyn*. And there is tension in these differences, for Selina feels that her 'odd speech clashed in the hushed rooms', as though she were 'something vulgar in a holy place' (6). This text thus wrestles with the construction of the American body politic and with the narrative, linguistic, and spatial forms available to that construction. Through its paralleling of space with alternative formal and linguistic strategies, *Brown Girl, Brownstones* questions the assumptions about a racially homogenous and authentic Brooklyn and its story, cast as an 'official' American story.

---

[32] In an earlier, unpublished version of the novel, located at the Brooklyn College library, Marshall introduces Selina's interest in the Association with the blending and dissolution of Fulton Street's sounds and sights into each other to figure the tension between the individual and the community.

Marshall's work, then, sets the stage in the 1950s for the coalescing of Brooklyn, standing in for US and Caribbean literary histories. In making Caribbean places out of Brooklyn's streets, store fronts, buildings, and parks, Marshall and later writers construct a textual cartography that moves beyond national borders. These texts then—*Brown Girl, Brownstones, Breathe Eyes, Memory,* Marshall's *The Fisher King,* Veronica Chambers's *Mama's Girl,* Perez's *Geographies of Home* and others—present an American literary tropics that moves from the Caribbean to the Northeast of the USA.[33] While Brooklyn may not appear on any literal map of the Caribbean, these works, taken together, form a textual cartography in which Brooklyn abuts Bimshire and Bel Air.

Brooklyn 2011. Let us return to the West Indian Day Parade. Jamaica Kincaid was right. Not only are beef patties in every grocery store, but the sounds and smells of the parade emerge from the commercial establishments of certain Brooklyn neighbourhoods, and not only on the days of the parade. Walk down Nostrand Avenue. Pause for a moment in front of Charlie Records and listen to the sounds of calypso and soka. Stop for a second as the odors of doubles and bakes emerge from the Trini Roti Shop. Notice the voices exchanging greetings in a Jamaican patois along the street and these stores. Despite the chill in the air, there is a tropical feel to this area, one that emerges from the sensory experience of walking through it and from the fact of its demographic make-up. Several neighbourhoods in central Brooklyn—Crown Heights, Bed-Stuy, East Flatbush—remain literal and figurative home to Caribbean immigrants and their descendants. Caribbean enclaves. It seems as though, on the days of the West Indian Day parade and throughout the rest of the year, Brooklyn has become a central node in a transnational Caribbean, while remaining part of New York.

---

[33] Marshall's 2000 novel *The Fisher King* returns to many of the issues in *Brown Girl, Brownstones.* Set in Brooklyn and Paris, it explores place-making, domestic work, and property. However, more than Marshall's early novel, it investigates relations between African Americans and West Indians and their descendants, couched in terms of their relationship to space and place.

Reading the Novum World: The Literary Geography of Science Fiction in Junot Díaz's *The Brief Wondrous Life of Oscar Wao*

María del Pilar Blanco

*T*he *Brief Wondrous Life of Oscar Wao* (2007) by Dominican-American author Junot Díaz is an encyclopaedic novel that presents itself as having much to say about history, literature, popular culture, and the experience of exile. As one might expect from such a wide-ranging yet oblique novel, it invites numerous types of readings. Among them, the most literalist approach is one that takes Díaz's plot on its own tragicomic terms, seeing it as the pathetic story of a Dominican-American science fiction-obsessed 'nerd' named Oscar De León and the two previous generations of his family. The novel offers a fragmented account of how these three generations directly or indirectly suffered the events of Rafael Trujillo's rule—that is the period between 1930 and 1961, commonly known as the Trujillato. Told through the perspectives of the narrator (Yunior) and Oscar's sister Lola (Yunior's onetime girlfriend), one thread recounts the downfall of Oscar's grandfather, Abelard Luis Cabral, who in the 1940s tried to keep the lustful dictator Trujillo away from one of his adolescent daughters. *Oscar Wao* also narrates the dramatic history of Abelard's youngest daughter, Hypatía Belicia Cabral, who flees the Dominican Republic after being nearly killed for having an affair with a man who was married to Trujillo's sister. The bulk of the novel recounts the life of the hardened Belicia and her two children, Lola and Oscar, after she migrates to the USA during the high point of Dominican diaspora, a trend that was spurred by the lifting of restrictions on travel

49

during Joaquín Balaguer's rule in the 1960s.[1] The family's 'eternal return' (296) to disaster culminates in Oscar's murder in 1995. Like his mother, he had fallen in love with the wrong person, in his case a prostitute named Ybón, whose boyfriend was a corrupt captain in the Santo Domingo police force. Yunior, the narrator whose identity is revealed well into the narrative, gives himself the difficult task of piecing together the family's history. An alter-ego of Díaz, Yunior attempts to narrate the silenced recent history of the Dominican Republic through the perspectives of the De León family members' unwitting encounters with Trujillo and with the traumatic aftermath of his reign of terror.

A different way to approach *Oscar Wao* could be to exercise greater alertness to its form. Díaz's novel can be seen as a self-reflexive work that catalogues and meditates upon its variety of narrative modes, and tries thereby to cover a great number of hermeneutic angles. It uses Spanglish to tell a story about an unlikely hero—the overweight, impossibly awkward Oscar—and his tormented family. It is important to note from the outset that Díaz's narration appeals to a number of readerships that range from the popular to the high theoretical. It does this in a number of ways. The first is Díaz's deployment of modes of narrative self-reflexivity and intertextuality. For one, the text contains a good number of footnotes that, besides offering personal commentary about the De León family, contain hearsay and gossip about the famous personages and victims of the Trujillato (for example, the Mirabal sisters [83n7], and the intellectual Jesús de Galíndez, who was murdered by Trujillo's men for writing a dissertation that indicted the government for corruption [97n11]). Other footnotes inform the reader about Dominican and Caribbean history (there are several, for example, that refer to the Trujillo-ordered massacre of Haitians in 1937). The text also reveals its reflexivity through the repeated instances in which Yunior addresses the reader directly, or includes parenthetical remarks that nudge the reader into a kind of complicity. At times, in the style of a Laurence Sterne or a Machado de Assis, Yunior even points the reader towards the gaps in the story that, despite his efforts, he has been unable to fill. We could say that the novel's self-containment is also displayed in the knowing manner with which it anticipates its own audience. Díaz recognises full well the novel's likely readership, together with the different critical persuasions that it will attract. Some of these readers will undoubtedly be academics, and

---

[1] Speaking of Balaguer, Díaz's narrator asserts: 'It was he who oversaw/initiated the thing we call Diaspora'. Junot Díaz, *The Brief Wondrous Life of Oscar Wao*, New York: Riverhead Books, 2007, p. 90. All further references are to this edition and are given after quotations in the text.

Yunior/Díaz knowingly pre-empts their interpretations of the text. One such moment of complicity between the narrator and the academic reader occurs in the episode in which Oscar is beaten by the police captain's cronies. Yunior describes the scene as being 'like one of those nightmare eight-a.m. MLA panels: *endless*' (299). The reference to the Modern Language Association annual conventions may not translate to all readers of the novel, but assures a knowing nod from a specialised arts and humanities contingent. This formulation of complicity with an academic reader is further enhanced by Yunior's hints at how the novel can be intellectualised. To this end, Díaz introduces into his lively narration the names of important figures from Antillean intellectual history (for example, Fernando Ortiz, author of *Cuban Counterpoint*), lending the novel a further interpretive layer. More than name-dropping, Díaz's references point to the diverse hermeneutic levels that have been employed to understand this region, which range from the biographical to the theoretical.

One of these allusions can be found in a footnote that follows Yunior's address to the reader as 'your humble Watcher': '... it's hard as a Third Worlder not to feel a certain amount of affinity for Uatu the Watcher; he resides in the hidden Blue Area of the Moon and we DarkZoners reside (to quote Glissant) on '*la face cachée de la Terre*' (Earth's hidden face)' (92n10). This quotation contains references from different literary environments. Readers stand a chance of understanding all, some, or none of them. The Martinican theorist may not be recognised by a number of the novel's readers. But the quotation from Édouard Glissant's *Le Discours antillais* (1981) allows Díaz to align his novel with what has been the ongoing effort to rationalise the Antillean experience from an autochthonous perspective.[2] Among his many contributions to contemporary Antillean thought, Glissant has critiqued the historicisation of the Antilles by European discourses, and ultimately suggests a revision of the methods that had been previously employed to write this history. While Glissant uses the expression 'Earth's hidden face' to refer to the ahistorical place to which the Antilles have been relegated, Díaz (through his narrator) is himself resisting this ahistoricity by offering his own, annotated, version of the Dominican condition that is representative of a wider Antillean reality in the twentieth century.

In the passage from *Le Discours antillais* in which Glissant gestures to the

---

[2] The term 'Antillean' refers to the archipelago within the Caribbean basin. In the novel as in interviews, Díaz uses both Antillean and Caribbean interchangeably. Stuart Hall, who is cited throughout this essay, does as well. I will employ the term 'Antillean' in the essay to refer specifically to the geography and cultural output of these islands.

'hidden face' of the planet that must reveal itself, he makes a comparison of this eclipsed region to the 'moon's hidden face' [*face cachée de la lune*] that had been a mystery to mankind in the past.[3] In the footnote from *Oscar Wao*, the reference to Glissant follows another allusion, this time to Frank Kirby's *The Fantastic Four* science-fiction comic book series. In *The Fantastic Four*, Uatu the Watcher, an extraterrestrial who possesses immense intellectual powers, has the task of studying the Earth from the dark side of the moon. In what looks like one fell swoop, Antillean cultural theory meets science fiction. Is this conflation jarring, or is Díaz bringing together two dissimilar forms of discourse that have a lot to learn from one another? How can science fiction and Antillean history complement each other? Díaz takes Glissant's observation, which has a home in a critical/theoretical context, and includes it within another form of specialised canon (the multimedia universe of the science-fiction genre). Likewise, Kirby facilitates a reading of high theory because his character, Uatu, personifies, in Díaz's view, the 'Third Worlder's' exile outside of what Glissant calls the Western construction of 'History' (a concept that Glissant marks with a capital 'H').[4] Díaz's approximation of Glissant and Kirby highlights how two types of discourse with such dissimilar aims have in common the necessity to spell out a particular form of planetary estrangement. The incorporation of science fiction into Antillean intellectual discourse not only permits Díaz to appeal to different readerships, but also to advance a revitalised reading of Antillean geography through what Carl H. Freedman has called the 'shared perspectives' of critical theory and science fiction.[5] On a different level, the correspondence between this genre and Glissantian discourse also raises the interesting question of which aesthetic forms are best suited to describe the contemporary Antilles and the circumstances of its many diasporas. Glissant questions the Western version of world history, thus foregrounding the need for the differentiated narratives that can come out of 'Earth's hidden face'. Science fiction allows Díaz to draw from a different literary imaginary, and a differentiated canon, that invites his reader to assimilate the experience of Antillean diaspora.

In what follows, I will examine Díaz's conjugation of geography and

---

[3] Édouard Glissant, *Le Discours antillais*, Paris: Seuil, 1981, p. 191.

[4] See Glissant, *Le Discours antillais*, p. 141.

[5] As explained later in this essay, Freedman argues that 'the dialectic standpoint of the science-fictional tendency, with its insistence upon historical mutability, material reducibility, and, at least implicitly, utopian possibility' align it with critical theory, especially theory of the historical-materialist persuasion. Carl Howard Freedman, *Critical Theory and Science Fiction*, Hanover, MA: Wesleyan University Press, 2000, p. 32.

the science-fiction genre in order to address the extent to which science fiction promotes a new reading of the Antillean region. It is important to note from the outset that, while *Oscar Wao* is not a science-fiction novel, it nevertheless *draws on* science fiction as a multivalent hermeneutic model to understand this region. Díaz's uses of the science-fiction canon, as detailed below, can range from allusions to characters and events in specific texts, to more generalised reflections on tropes within the genre, such as the figure of the alien or outsider (as in his commentary on Kirby's Uatu). There are even some instances in which the author appears to be emulating the rhetorical stylisations of science-fiction narrators. These varied homages to the genre work together to suggest the role of science fiction as a compelling aesthetic tool with which to understand the different narratives that make up Antillean history. Díaz employs this genre to facilitate a portrayal of the Antilles as a region and the Dominican Republic as an island nation that have had the propensity to be read from inside and outside, but whose recent and contemporary histories have yet to be written. Describing how Díaz 'science fictionalises' the Antilles, I ask how this genre, as he interprets it, offers a distinctive engagement with the particularity of this region, at the same time as keeping open the question of how the theorisations of the genre can help elucidate the meaning behind Díaz's conception of what he calls the 'sci-fi' space of the Antilles (6). Science fiction's ultimate interest in unknowing the known—what Darko Suvin has called '*cognitive estrangement*'—leads us to a more profound understanding of why Díaz's description of the Antilles as a 'sci-fi' region is a persuasive assessment.[6] Alongside paratextual episodes in which Díaz/Yunior nudge the reader into this new visualisation of the Antilles, the author also invites us to see the Caribbean region through the eyes of Oscar, who is an ardent reader of science fiction. His gradual accrual of knowledge about the genre allows the main character to make sense of the many layers of estrangement he experiences as a Dominican-American subject. More generally, it enables Díaz to use Oscar as a cipher for an alternative reading of Antillean history. The final part of this essay considers the manner in which Díaz employs science fiction to comment on this region's position as the epicentre of the New World. Using Suvin's persuasive argument that science fiction introduces what he calls a 'novum', a never-before-experienced newness, I argue that Díaz engages with previous Antillean critiques of the term 'New World' to promote a more accurate portrait of a 'Novum' World—a decentred Antillean geography that has been indelibly affected by mass diaspora. In order to demonstrate how

---

[6] Darko Suvin, 'On the Poetics of the Science Fiction Genre', *College English*, 34, no. 3 (1972), pp. 372–382, at 372.

Díaz should be read as part of a longer tradition that has reflected on what is at stake in thinking of this American region as a new world, this essay concludes with a comparison with Cuban author Alejo Carpentier, who in 1948 declared that America was an exceptional hemisphere because of the pervasive occurrence within it of 'the marvellous real'. While it would be inaccurate to call the marvellous real a genre in the way that science fiction is, Carpentier's view is an earlier manifestation of a call for a renewed sense of cognition in order to better understand the so-called 'New' World.[7] What interests me in this comparison is the idea that, as with Díaz's proclamation of the Antilles as a sci-fi space, inherent in Carpentier's formulation is a need to feel estranged from the place one calls home, in order to be able to assess it again with a fresh perspective.

Science-fiction references pervade Díaz's novel. At various points throughout *Oscar Wao*, Yunior and Oscar address the Antilles, and the Dominican Republic specifically, as a preferred location of the science-fiction genre. 'Who more sci-fi than us?' (21n6), asks Yunior in a footnote that is an echo of an earlier reference to Oscar's worldview: 'He was a hardcore sci-fi and fantasy man, believed that that was the kind of story we were all living in. He'd ask: What more sci-fi than the Santo Domingo? What more fantasy than the Antilles?' (6). This approximation of existing geography and a diverse artistic genre that so often appeals to an imagination of places estranged from our here and now prompts a number of questions. Is the author launching these islands into the stratospheres of a fantastic aesthetic form that loses touch with reality, or is this a defamiliarising strategy asking for a wholly different interpretation of what science fiction can accomplish? In the context of a novel that elucidates the urgency to revisit twentieth-century Dominican history, and to dispel from it the mythologies created by the devastating Trujillo dictatorship, what are the benefits of this repeated synchronisation of genre and lived space? As an author born in the Dominican Republic, but who has lived most of his life in the USA, why is Díaz incorporating the Antilles into the folds of a literary universe whose main practitioners and followers have overwhelmingly been associated with the global north?

---

[7] Critics commonly conflate Carpentier's 'marvellous realism' with the literary genre of 'magical realism'. One recent example is Monica Hanna who, in her essay on Junot Díaz, speaks of 'Alejo Carpentier's and Gabriel García Márquez's vision of the genre of magical realism' as one and the same project. See Monica Hanna, '"Reassembling the Fragments": Battling Historiographies, Caribbean Discourse, and Nerd Genres in Junot Díaz's *The Brief Wondrous Life of Oscar Wao*', *Callaloo*, 33, no. 2 (2010), pp. 498–520, at 510.

The integration of geography and literature is an organising principle behind Díaz's novel. 'In my mind', he said in a 2008 interview, '[*Oscar Wao*] was supposed to take the shape of an archipelago; it was supposed to be a textual Caribbean'.[8] Díaz promotes *Oscar Wao* as one text within a given literary tradition that problematises the history of this particular region. The 'archipelago' that Díaz envisioned, however, was meant to dispel any 'myth' of these islands forming a monolithic whole. To this effect, he says in the interview: 'Take a brief look at Caribbean or Dominican history and you'll see that the structure of the book is more in keeping with the reality of this history than with its most popular myth: that of unity and continuity'. Díaz's critique of a mythology of wholeness responds to the many discourses that address the Caribbean region as one, and it also counters the more localised myth of a singular nation under Trujillo's 30-year rule. Díaz's vision of his 'fragmented world' (a phrase he employs in the same interview) is reflected as much in his representation of the divided Dominican society during the Trujillato, as in the details of the repercussions that this dictatorship had on the De León family's migration. Here, Díaz's 'archipelago' in many ways echoes Stuart Hall's description of the 'second' way in which one can understand Caribbean 'identity': while a first perspective thinks about it in terms of 'the common historical experiences and shared cultural codes which provide us, "as one people", with stable, unchanging, and continuous frames of reference and meaning', the second view of identity 'recognizes that, as well as the many points of similarity, there are also critical points of deep and significant *difference* which constitute...—since history has intervened—"what we have become"'.[9] Díaz's recognition of the instability of the category of 'Caribbean' or 'Dominican' is reflective of the burden of a traumatic history that continues to 'intervene' in the everyday lives of the De León family and the wider Dominican(-American) community around them.

In her history of the conditions that helped to feed the myth of Dominican singularity during the Trujillato, Lauren Derby describes how 'everyday forms of domination' consolidated into a 'culture of compliance' during this period.[10] While Díaz constructs a complex geography of the Dominican Republic that stretches well beyond the borders of the nation located in

---

[8] Meghan O'Rourke, 'Questions for Junot Díaz: an interview with the Pulitzer Prize-winning author', *Slate Magazine* (8 April 2008), <http://www.slate.com/id/2188494/> [1.5.2011].

[9] Stuart Hall, 'Cultural Identity and Diaspora', in Jana Evans Braziel and Anita Mannur, eds., *Theorizing Diaspora*, Oxford: Blackwell, 2003, pp. 233–246, at 236.

[10] Lauren Derby, *The Dictator's Seduction: Politics and the Popular Imagination in the Era of Trujillo*, Durham NC: Duke University Press, 2009, p. 7.

Hispaniola, his decision to produce a fragmented novel that reflects the current state of Dominican-ness has everything to do with the silences or 'blank pages' [*páginas en blanco*] (149), in Yunior's words, of the island nation's recent history. For Díaz, the caesuras that emerge in the retelling of the Trujillato have much to do with a larger, more 'hemispheric' (as he calls it), power relation, the consequence of which has been mass diaspora. When asked how the story of Oscar, a Dominican-American living in Paterson, New Jersey connects with a novel about Trujillo, he replied: 'I guess the question for me is, how are they not related? It's like the history of the Dominican Republic. You can't tell the history of the US without the history of the Dominican Republic, and yet people do so all the time. Oscar ... is one of Trujillo's children'.[11] In this case, the Dominican 'history' that Díaz is telling recalls the long-standing complicity between the USA and the Trujillo regime. Rather than echoing the myth of a consolidated nation that the dictatorship so jealously guarded (and the USA supported from the sidelines), he accentuates the end result: a fissured diasporic nation and geography. It is therefore literature's task to address the silences and fragmentations provoked by the regime.

But, to Díaz, the interrelation between Dominican and wider American histories dates back to earlier times. This is evident in the novel's prologue, which opens with the episode of Christopher Columbus's landfall in the island of Hispaniola, the moment in which America was branded the 'New World':

> They say it came first from Africa, carried in the screams of the enslaved; that it was the death bane of the Tainos, uttered just as one world perished and another began; that it was a demon drawn into Creation through the nightmare door that was cracked open in the Antilles. *Fukú americanus*, or more colloquially fukú—generally a curse or a doom of some kind; specifically the Curse and Doom of the New World. Also called the fukú of the Admiral because the Admiral was both its midwife and one of its great European victims ... In Santo Domingo, the Land He Loved Best (what Oscar, at the end, would call the Ground Zero of the New World), the Admiral's very name has become synonymous with both kinds of fukú, little and large ... (1)

Indeed, the '*fukú americanus*' curse that befalls Dominicans and (ultimately) Oscar has two figureheads: Columbus and Trujillo. In this prologue, Díaz forcefully articulates his concerns with the cultural and historical

---

particularity of the Dominican Republic, and its centuries of troubled history. He negotiates both local and global histories, moving from a consideration of the nation's twentieth-century political trajectory to a wider contemplation of its position at/as the cataclysmic centre of the New World.

Importantly, the prologue makes a quick transition from the term 'New World' to Oscar's later nomination of Santo Domingo, the first landfall, as 'the Ground Zero of the New World'. This marks a departure not only from the narrative of Columbus 'discovering' America, but also from any other attempt to appropriate this denomination for an autochthonous project of self-definition, in the way that, for example, the Latin American *mundonovistas* rethought the hemisphere from the late nineteenth century until the mid-twentieth century.[12] In this sense, Díaz complements Glissant's effort to expose the fallacy of addressing the Caribbean region and the Americas as 'new'. Oscar's final realisation about the significance of Santo Domingo indicates the implosion of that concept of utopian novelty. The protagonist's late twentieth-century revision takes into account the series of dramatic events that followed Columbus's discovery. Instead of recreating Columbus's narrative of wonderment, however, Díaz's novel begins on a note of deep disenchantment, as it casts a backward glance on Dominican history. As the prologue continues, Yunior explains how, in the twentieth century, fukú found a second emissary in the figure of Trujillo. The prologue moves quickly from the curse of discovery to the curse of ruthless modern-day dictatorship: in just seven pages, the narrator offers his version of past events by continuously referring back to fukú's overwhelming tutelage, even linking Trujillo (the 'Curse's servant or its master', 2–3) to John F. Kennedy's death in 1963. But rather than taking the fukú's history towards a more traditional historicisation of Dominican history, Díaz uses science-fiction references to illustrate the depths of the curse's vicious machinations: 'like Darkseid's Omega Effect … it always—and I mean always—gets its man' (5). These allusions to monstrous comic-book characters like Darkseid will resonate in different ways: while one kind of reader will need to acquaint her/himself with the provenance of the name 'Darkseid', for anyone who is at all familiar with the science-fiction canon (the science-fiction aficionados that will read the novel as well as those with more informal knowledge of the genre),[13] the sci-fi references fully convey the narrator's point about the

---

[12] We can identify the emergence of a *mundonovista* literature in novels by *costumbrista* (local colour) authors from the 1920s, such as José Eustasio Rivera and Rómulo Gallegos. In their work, these authors revisit and subvert colonial forms of travel writing, for example, as a way of symbolically appropriating the native landscape.

[13] Purist science fiction and fantasy followers have given Junot Díaz's novel mixed

breadth of Trujillo's trail of corruption. Science fiction allows Díaz to set the tone of hyperbolic strangeness, and ultimately estrangement, for the rest of the novel. In the prologue, he moves the more folkloric, legendary idea of fukú towards an alignment of Dominican history with the science-fiction genre. And, in the example of the footnote in which Glissant meets Uatu the Watcher, two discourses that are so profoundly engaged with narrating forms of alienation—Caribbean discourse and science fiction—are brought into dialogue.

To begin answering the question about the applicability of science fiction to a narrative history of the Dominican Republic, we should think about the genre's own trajectory. Arguably dating as far back as Mary Shelley's *Frankenstein* (1818), science fiction's flourishing is commonly understood as a late nineteenth-century North Atlantic phenomenon.[14] Fredric Jameson, for one, argues that the conventional birth of the genre is 1895, when H. G. Wells published *The Time Machine*.[15] As would be expected, there are multiple theorisations of science fiction and the limits of the genre have been hotly debated since the first efforts to discuss it as an academic object of study emerged in the mid-twentieth century. One general explication about the imaginations of science fiction's multiple practitioners is that they take technological progress as their principal inspiration. An advocate of this theory is Roger Luckhurst, who categorically describes science fiction as

---

reviews. Henry Wessells, who wrote on the novel in the *New York Review of Science Fiction*, notes that while, '[i]n one sense', the novel 'is written within the genre, for there are frequent allusions to science fiction and fantasy beyond the named appearances', Díaz ultimately manipulates the genre 'for purposes outside of the literature' of science fiction and fantasy. On top of this, Wessells criticises the way in which Oscar's affinity with these genres is represented as modes of escapism. Henry Wessells, 'A Short and Contentious Note about *The Brief Wondrous Life of Oscar Wao* by Junot Díaz', *The New York Review of Science Fiction* 20, no. 243 (2008), pp. 10–11, at 10.

[14] Kingsley Amis offered some of the first surveys of science fiction in a series of lectures he gave at Princeton University, which are compiled in his *New Maps of Hell*, London: Victor Gollancz, 1961. One of his introductory remarks about the genre was a delineation of its geographical limits: science fiction, he says, is a 'characteristically American product with a large audience and a growing band of practitioners in Western Europe, excluding the Iberian peninsula and, probably, Ireland' (p. 17). For a brief revision of the geography of science fiction's emergence, see Roberto de Sousa Causo, 'Encountering International Science Fiction through a Latin American Lens', in James Gunn, Marleen S. Barr, and Matthew Candelaria, eds., *Reading Science Fiction*, New York: Palgrave Macmillan, 2009, pp. 142–156.

[15] Fredric Jameson, *Archaeologies of the Future: The Desire of Utopia and Other Science Fictions*, London: Verso, 2005, p. 56.

'a literature of technologically saturated societies'.[16] However, as Luckhurst also notes, the genre's visions of science do not always result in descriptions of a confident technological age. Instead, a considerable portion of science-fiction texts deal with the disenchantment brought on by such markers of modernity, because they imagine the fallout that arrives when industrialisation, scientific experimentation, and evolution have run their course. In this sense, science fiction fluctuates between utopian and dystopian depictions of our world and others.[17] As well as commenting on scientific invention, science fiction can provide a larger commentary on the societies that inhabit these ultra-technological universes.

If science fiction belongs to 'technologically saturated societies', as Luckhurst points out, it is important to keep in mind the social groups that are at a disadvantage in the face of this kind of innovation. Writing specifically about this issue, John Rieder stresses nineteenth-century science fiction's historical indebtedness to colonialism, and specifically the European colonisation of America and Africa. Rieder remarks on the imbalances that surface when, employing their magnificent 'gadgetry', the travellers of classic science fiction (for example, in the novels of Jules Verne) come into contact with and ultimately colonise their Others:

> Verne's marvelous journeys do not simply penetrate space, but rather the travel gains its interest by consistently defying political boundaries and threatening to render them meaningless ... The advent of the spectacular invention therefore inevitably invokes that embracing pattern of uneven economic and cultural distribution, colonialism, and with it arises the specter of those encounters between cultures with wildly different technological capabilities that produced during this period some of the most one-sided armed conflicts in human history ...[18]

The combination of discovery and technological prowess in works of classic science fiction never fails to echo the first encounters between Europeans and the populations in other continents like Africa and America. Here, Rieder is offering us a view from the side of those who are 'discovered' and

---

[16] Roger Luckhurst, *Science Fiction*, Cambridge: Polity Press, 2005, p. 3.
[17] See Peter Fitting, 'Utopia, Dystopia and Science Fiction', in Gregory Claeys, ed., *The Cambridge Companion to Utopian Literature*, Cambridge: Cambridge University Press, 2010, pp. 135–153.
[18] John Rieder, 'Science Fiction, Colonialism, and the Plot of Invasion', *Extrapolation*, 43, no. 6 (2005), pp. 373–394, at 377.

who come into brutal contact with the tools of colonisation. Science fiction can highlight the disconnections inherent in over- and underdevelopment. The gap or disconnection in time and place that is felt by those who are 'discovered' or disadvantaged within this scene of encounter becomes an important feature of Díaz's use of science fiction in *Oscar Wao*.

The encountered subjects in this genre are commonly described as aliens, a word that takes on a number of meanings and implications in *Oscar Wao*. 'If the rocket ship is the basic icon of science fiction', writes Thomas M. Disch, 'the genre's primal scene is first contact with an alien'.[19] More often than not, science fiction contains scenes of contact between travellers and subjects from other worlds or cultural backgrounds. As the genre has continued to evolve, the stories of encounter, discovery, and colonisation have moved towards representations of other types of aliens, the 'resident aliens', which Disch (echoing Kipling) describes as 'that lesser breed before the law' and that reflect science fiction's engagement with contemporary national politics.[20] US government discourse and the genre even share the same term ('resident alien') to describe those who cross the border to live in the USA. In Díaz's novel, aliens come to mean both the creatures that occupy Oscar's adventures in reading science fiction and the Dominican population that comprises the 'Diaspora' in the USA. Yunior describes the scene of this kind of alienation in his portrayal of Belicia's flight from Santo Domingo to New York City:

> Her dreams are spare, lack the propulsion of a mission, her ambition is without traction. Her fiercest hope? That she will find a man. What she doesn't yet know: the cold, the backbreaking drudgery of the factorías, the loneliness of Diaspora, that she will never again live in Santo Domingo, her own heart. (164)

The unadorned prose style in this passage could be said to echo the technical precision of sci-fi writers like Philip K. Dick. The short clauses, which move across temporalities and emotional states, are arranged paratactically, without any conjunctions to allow for a softer description of Belicia's sentimental state as well as the future that awaits her. This passage reduces the different emotional effects of Belicia's journey away from Santo Domingo to a list of contained events of defamiliarisation, which are not allowed to exceed their own ordered position within the parataxis. The short clause that

---

[19] Thomas M. Disch, *The Dreams Our Stuff Is Made Of: How Science Fiction Conquered the World*, New York: Touchstone, 2000, p. 185.

[20] Disch, *The Dreams*, p. 188.

closes the passage ('her own heart') may seem the most personalised, yet because of its grammatical positioning it sounds like a shard that survives the original impact of her experiences, but remains an emblem of the loss she continues to undergo. To add to the resonances of a science-fiction idiom in this passage, the narrator describes Belicia's journey away from the island using the language of 'missions' and mechanical 'traction'.[21] Returning to the idea of the alien and alienation, it is not difficult to imagine how these shared terminologies collapse to form Díaz's (and Oscar's) understanding of the diasporic Dominican community as a nation of aliens. Díaz's capitalisation of the word 'Diaspora' describes another country (or even planet) that ceases to be defined by the borders of the Dominican nation, but instead by the individual experiences of expectation, fear, and disillusionment of all those who leave their homes behind. But Díaz points to a discrepancy between each generation's assimilation of the experience of exile. Belicia's generation seeks to forget the pangs of exile and ultimately to erase the previous home. As Yunior explains, she '[e]mbraced the amnesia that was so common throughout the Islands, five parts denial, five parts negative hallucination. Embraced the power of the Untilles' (258–259).[22] If, for Belicia, the' Un-' in 'Untilles' signifies a removal of the 'Islands' from her immediate memory, for Oscar and his sister Lola it is closer to the preposition of expectation ('until') in the sense that the family's past becomes a question that continuously awaits resolution. In addition, for this generation which is once removed from the extreme event of exile felt by Belicia, alienation (here, the feeling of being an alien) can also describe the experience of being an outcast within the communities of ethnic others in the USA.

Science fiction offers Oscar a universe of aliens that allows him to reflect on his own cultural condition as a child raised under the circumstances of diaspora. This is evident in one of Yunior's footnotes in which he asks: 'You really want to know what being an X-Man feels like? Just be a smart bookish boy of color in a contemporary US ghetto ... Like having bat wings or a pair of tentacles growing out of your chest' (22n6). Identity is complex within the country called 'Diaspora', the collective of subjects whose lives have been transformed by departure. Yunior observes that, in the neighbourhoods

---

[21] Freedman uses the phrase 'technology of emotion' to describe the way in which Dick intercalates the language of technology with the description of sentimental states (*Critical Theory and Science Fiction*, p. 32).

[22] This line is reminiscent of Derek Walcott's assessment of the Antilles in his 1992 Nobel Prize Lecture: 'All of the Antilles, every island, is an effort of memory; every mind, every racial biography culminating in amnesia and fog' (*The Antilles: Fragments of Epic Memory. The Nobel Lecture*, London: Faber and Faber, 1993, p. 27).

where many of these subjects settle, a sign of particularity or difference within a community that is itself defined by its otherness in terms of ethnicity and class, entails a further and dramatic level of self-alienation. As Díaz explains in an interview with Haitian-American novelist Edwidge Danticat:

> There are … certain kinds of people that no one wants to build the image of a nation around. Even if these people are in fact the nation itself … In the Dominican culture that I know, a character like Oscar was not going to be anyone's notion of the ideal Dominican boy. In the Dominican culture I know, someone like Oscar would not be labeled Dominican, no matter what his actual background was.[23]

Oscar's affinity with the outcasts from the *X-Men* series (a Jack Kirby/Stan Lee creation) translates this multilayered sense of difference within the communities that seek to forge a specific mode of unity and 'nation' within their new environments.

Rather than simply describing the feeling of being different, however, science fiction also becomes a particular mode of reflection about personal and national history. As Freedman has argued, science fiction has had a long relationship with twentieth-century Marxist, or historical-materialist, thought. This particular interpretation of science fiction describes the genre's inherent critique and deconstruction of (mostly North Atlantic) historical processes. In this line of thinking, science fiction tends towards an inspection of rationalism and Enlightenment that, according to Jameson, studies 'all the constraints thrown up by history itself—the web of counterfinalities and anti-dialectics which human production has itself produced'.[24] (To name but one classic example of sci-fi's musings about these historical 'constraints', Dick's *The Man in the High Castle* [1962] imagines a long World War II that is won by the Axis powers.) Thus, the science-fiction canon provides examples of some of the most reflexively critical modes of writing that we possess. This is precisely the reason behind Freedman's alignment of the genre with critical theory: the two forms of discourse, according to him, depend upon a 'dialectic standpoint' that insists upon notions of 'historical mutability, material reducibility, and, at least implicitly, utopian possibility'.[25] This particular fascination with casting a critical glance at man-made world

---

[23] Edwidge Danticat, 'Junot Díaz (interview)', *BOMB*, 101 (Fall 2007) <http://bombsite.com/issues/101/articles/2948> [1.5.2011].

[24] Jameson, *Archaeologies*, p. 66.

[25] Freedman, *Critical Theory*, p. 32.

events—the propensity to spin history's master-narratives in different ways in order to question humanity's possible evolutions—returns us to Díaz's strategic use of science fiction in *Oscar Wao*. Díaz deploys the storylines of science fiction and the so-called 'Genres' (20) as analogies for the events and personages of the Trujillato (for example, the comparison between the Dominican dictator and the evil Sauron character from the *The Lord of the Rings* trilogy—see 2n1).[26] On a different level, Díaz is also interested in describing the living subcultures of science fiction through his character-isation of Oscar. In the opening pages of the novel, the narrator explains that Oscar's understanding of the world was filtered through his 'hardcore' reading habits. The protagonist's career as a reader of these 'Genres' provides the perspective and sensibility from which Oscar's story will be told. The most remarkable element of Díaz's inventive assimilation of his native country's local history and the Dominican diaspora is precisely how he simultaneously describes science fiction as both a practice and a theory of reading.

Although his real name is Oscar De León, the nickname 'Oscar Wao' emerges from the Dominican-Spanish pronunciation of 'Oscar Wilde'. Yunior teasingly compares the protagonist to the Anglo-Irish writer when Oscar dons a Doctor Who outfit (the time-travelling humanoid at the centre of a long-running BBC series that is not as widely known among US television audiences) one Halloween while at university.[27] This etymology of the name already points to a richly transnational 'canon' that describes a sentimental

---

[26] By 'Genres', Díaz means the 'speculative genres', a concept that, as Ingrid Thaler explains, is 'an umbrella term for all kinds of fantastic genres, including utopian and science fiction, which deliberately and explicitly disturbs mimetic notions of "realistic" representation' (*Black Atlantic Speculative Fictions: Octavia E. Butler, Jewelle Gomez, and Nalo Hopkinson*, New York: Routledge, 2010, p. 2). In terms of Oscar's canon, the 'genres' are more specifically related to science-fiction literature (novels, films, and comics) and fantasy literature (for example, Tolkien).

[27] Yunior narrates: 'Halloween he made the mistake of dressing up as Doctor Who, was real proud of his outfit too. When I saw him on Easton [at Rutgers University, New Brunswick, New Jersey], with two other writing-section clowns, I couldn't believe how much he looked like that fat homo Oscar Wilde, and I told him so. You look just like him, which was bad news for Oscar, because Melvin [another Dominican-American university student] said, Oscar Wao, quién es Oscar Wao, and that was it, all of us started calling him that …' (p. 180). Since the *Doctor Who* debut in 1963, there have been eleven generations of Doctors, all of whom have worn different costumes. Oscar dressed as Doctor Who at some point between 1988 and 1992, his university years (p. 167), and it is likely he took his inspiration from earlier Doctors who wore fin-de-siècle-inspired outfits, such as the one played by William Hartnell in the first series (1963–1966).

education and also allows the characters to relate through literary allusions. The transnational readerly practice is set into dialogue with the physical diasporic movement of the De León family. The young characters in the novel (Yunior, Oscar, and his sister Lola) enter the subcultures of the USA full-force while inhabiting the Latino enclaves of the New York tri-state area, while their parents bear the physical and emotional wounds of an exile brought on by the violent Trujillato. In a detailed description of Oscar's career as a 'young nerd', Yunior notes that:

> Back when the rest of us were learning to play wallball and pitch quarters and drive our older brothers' cars and sneak dead soldiers from under our parents' eyes, he was gorging himself on a steady stream of Lovecraft, Wells, Burroughs, Howard, Alexander, Herbert, Asimov, Bova, and Heinlein, and even the Old Ones who were already beginning to fade—E.E. "Doc" Smith, Stapledon, and the guy who wrote all the Doc Savage books—moving hungrily from book to book, author to author, age to age. (It was good fortune that the libraries of Paterson were so underfunded that they still kept a lot of the previous generation's nerdery in circulation.) ... Could write in Elvish, could speak Chakobsa, could differentiate between a Slan, a Dorsai, and a Lensman in acute detail, knew more about the Marvel Universe than Stan Lee, and was a role-playing game fanatic ... Dude wore his nerdiness like a Jedi wore his light saber or a Lensman her lens. Couldn't have passed for Normal if he'd wanted to. (20–21)

This passage offers an insight into the alternative education that Oscar received through a transnational science-fiction canon. His knowledge of the genre begins with literature, moving from early twentieth-century novels by the cult writer H. P. Lovecraft and E. E. Smith (the so-called father of the space opera) to the mid-century 'hard' science-based fiction of Asimov and Heinlein.[28] In his list of Oscar's tastes in science fiction, Yunior is intent on giving us a clear sense of his friend's archive in terms of a material history of reading: here, the passion for the science-fiction classics is linked to the outdated collection of a regional library serving a multicultural readership. His career as a science-fiction aficionado opens up, in Oscar's experience, to more intense *performances* of science fiction and fantasy, from role-playing

---

[28] According to Edward James, 'hard' science fiction was more interested in issues of 'technology, physics, and space exploration' than in 'psychology', 'sociology', or 'pure literary experimentation' (*Science Fiction in the Twentieth Century*, Oxford: Oxford University Press, 1994, p. 178).

to learning fictitious languages like Tolkien's Elvish or Frank Herbert's Chakobsa (from the *Dune* series).

The narrator continues trying to make sense of Oscar's relationship with the Genres in an accompanying footnote:

> Where this outsized love of genre jumped off from no one quite seems to know. It might have been a consequence of being Antillean (who more sci-fi than us?) or of living in the DR for the first couple of years of his life and then abruptly wrenchingly relocating to New Jersey—a single green card shifting not only worlds (from Third to First) but centuries (from almost no TV or electricity to plenty of both). After a transition like that I'm guessing only the most extreme scenarios could have satisfied. Maybe it was that in the DR he had watched too much *Spider-Man*, been taken to too many Run Run Shaw kung fu movies, listened to too many of his abuela's spooky stories about el Cuco and la Ciguapa? Maybe it was his first librarian in the U.S., who hooked him on reading, the electricity he felt when he touched that first Danny Dunn book? ... Or was it something deeper, something ancestral?
>
> Who can say? (21–22, n6)

In this footnote, which contains the rhetorical question that motivates my essay, Yunior sets his description of Oscar's preferences as a reader alongside his reality as a Dominican-American subject who appears to be mediating different levels of cognition. The more science fiction he reads, the more Oscar employs the texts in this genre to comprehend the distance between his situation as one of many Dominicans living in the USA, and the strange, often hallucinatory, progress of Antillean and Dominican history that provoked this journey away from the homeland in the first place. In addition, science fiction allows Oscar to account for the ways in which the everyday elements of his family's and his native country's circumstances that are (supposed to be) familiar often appear outlandish, as if they belonged to an altogether different world. In the passage above, Yunior reflects on the reasons why Oscar, a child of diaspora, should find a home and (to a great extent) a philosophy and way of life in the 'Genres', the canon of books, comic books, and films that he acquired in the North. The narrator's first theory is perhaps the most baffling, because it depends on what could be understood as an essentialist alignment of the Antilles and science fiction. He then moves on to an explanation that is more descriptive of the classic scenarios of science fiction: the 'alien's' journey to different worlds, the encounter with the other culture, as well as the recognition of technological incompatibility between those two cultures. To Oscar, science fiction is the expressive machine that best represents his particular experience of cultural displacement, which is felt as both a disjuncture of time (the feeling that the Dominican Republic lags 'centuries' behind the ultra-technological USA) and space (the 'shift' from 'Third to First' World).

Yunior's hesitations about the reasons for Oscar's almost total identification with science fiction (expressed in the line 'Who can say?') move across the fields of aesthetics, ethnogeography, and history. Yunior presents the possibility that this affinity is deeply ingrained in Oscar's cultural background, his being 'Antillean'. Moreover, he hypothesises that it may have something to do with a collective past, with 'something ancestral'. Yunior thus aligns the idea of an Antillean identitary essence—the cultural sense of consolidated 'oneness' (to quote Hall)—with the adjective 'sci-fi'. This genre, intent on 'historical mutability', as Freedman terms it, in turn corresponds with Díaz's effort to depict the delusion of trying to reclaim an authentic and stable sense of Antillean selfhood.[29] Somewhere in this movement between essence and mutability we find Oscar's own experience. Yunior implies that this fluctuation between the two offers an interpretation of the larger picture of Antillean diaspora. Writing about how one uses the term '*diaspora*', Brent Hayes Edwards suggests that it does not 'offer the comfort of abstraction, an easy recourse to origins', nor does it provide 'a foolproof anti-essentialism'. Instead, Edwards offers the notion of '*décalage*', which is '... either a difference or gap in time (advancing or delaying a schedule) *or* in space (shifting or displacing an object)'.[30] The *décalages* of the diasporic experience in Díaz's novel are felt in Oscar's and Yunior's reflections on how each arrival to either home (the Dominican Republic or the USA) constitutes a deferral of complete belonging. In *Oscar Wao*, we see how *décalage* finds its aesthetic form in a genre replete with temporal and spatial displacements, which enables the protagonist to question what makes him part of the Antillean 'us'. In this sense, science fiction becomes a form of critical reflexivity that allows the perceptual and existential impasses of diaspora to surface.

We can gather that, to the narrator and Oscar, the science-fiction genre is part of a process, an acquired experience of transculturation, a long history of reading, and an accumulation and mediation of what Yunior calls the 'extreme scenarios' (22n6) of cultural displacement.[31] It is imbricated

---

[29] Freedman, *Critical Theory*, p. 32.

[30] Brent Hayes Edwards, *The Practice of Diaspora: Literature, Translation, and the Rise of Black Internationalism*, Cambridge, MA: Harvard University Press, 2003, p. 13. Edwards adapts the term originally coined by Léopold Senghor.

[31] I am using Fernando Ortiz's definition of 'transculturation', which refers to

with his family history, and becomes a trope with which to negotiate the different shocks of the new that emerge when revisiting the *heres* and *theres* of diaspora—the home where Oscar is an outsider and the 'ancestral' land where he is considered a 'gringo' (278). Here, sci-fi shifts into a new realm of meaning, as it points to localised ancestry and a multicultural reading experience. Put differently, Oscar's canon of texts, which range from a variety of national traditions and periods, determine his perception of contemporary Dominican identity. In Oscar's experience as a first-generation Dominican-American, we could therefore argue that sci-fi can describe the hyper-assimilations that are the product of diaspora: the child of immigrant parents emerges from hyphenated cultural status (he is Dominican-American) to become the subject of a particular rendition of what it means to belong—where belonging is paradoxically constituted from experiences of the familiar rendered strange. For Oscar, belonging lies somewhere between imagined community and a continued reflection on difference.

Science fiction's reflections on difference entail a constant transformation of the categories of the known and the unknown. The most effective science-fiction texts seek to question the histories, identities, and cultures that were previously thought unshakeable. In his seminal essay 'On the Poetics of the Science Fiction Genre' (1972)—which is arguably the inauguration of a narratology of science fiction—Suvin proposes that this is a '*literature of cognitive estrangement*'.[32] From the outset, according to Suvin, the worlds created in science fiction should maintain an intimate dialogue with the world that we know through a relationship of estrangement—a notion that has its original inspiration in the Brechtian *Verfremdungseffekt*. As Edward James has noted, Suvin favours a definition of science fiction as a form of literature that is 'intended primarily to comment on our own world, "through metaphor and extrapolation"'.[33] Central to his argument is his adaptation of Ernst Bloch's concept, the '*novum*', which Suvin defines as science fiction's invocation of 'a strange newness'.[34] In the best of sci-fi cases, the novum describes a compellingly complete geography and history. As Patrick Parrinder explains, 'estranged fiction needs to change our view of our own condition, and not simply to momentarily dazzle us with

---

the 'different phases of the process of transition from one culture to another' (*Cuban Counterpoint: Tobacco and Sugar*, trans. Harriet de Onís, Durham, NC: Duke University Press, 1995, p. 102).

[32] Suvin, 'On the Poetics', p. 372.

[33] James, *Science Fiction in the Twentieth Century*, p. 111.

[34] Suvin, 'On the Poetics', p. 373.

a superficially unfamiliar world'.[35] Ideally, then, science fiction has the capacity not only to address possible futures, but also 'naturalistic' presents and the 'historical past', without resorting to an aesthetic that betrays any unnecessary frivolities.[36]

In subsequent revisions of his theory of the novum, Suvin explains this concept as a correspondence of ethics, history, and form. In his *Metamorphoses of Science Fiction* (1979), he explains that '[a]n aesthetic novum is either a translation of historical cognition and ethics *into* form, or ... a creation of historical cognition and ethics *as* form'.[37] For Suvin, the novelty of a science-fiction text—which should always remain cognitively valid through the careful description of a '*specific* time, place, agents, and cosmic and social totality'—emerges from what he calls a 'reality displacement'.[38] A reader's reality comes into contact with another set of circumstances (for example, a new social order in a faraway planet), which can nevertheless be assimilated as conceivable. The relationship between estrangement and the novum is thus the mediation between the aesthetic development of an understanding of a place, and a simultaneous invocation of a feeling of strangeness inherent to the observation of that place. The cognition of a sci-fi novum mirrors the open-endedness of reality—what Suvin describes in a later text as a 'more mature polyphony' of different futures and outlooks.[39] Importantly, the novum is dependent upon the idea of seeing a different place in order to see one's own environment *differently*, and to give this new perception a viable form. The novum concept thus abandons any hint of stability in our conception of temporal or spatial perceptions. Instead, it offers what Jameson (in an active dialogue with Suvin) calls the 'shocked renewal of our vision [of culture and its institutions] such that once again, and as though for the first time, we are able to perceive their historicity and their arbitrariness'.[40] The novum in Díaz's novel emerges in Oscar's 'shocked' reassessments of Antillean history and a changing Dominican geography. Díaz aligns the encounter with the novum (the bewilderment followed by recognition) with Oscar's and Yunior's realisations about the way events have transpired in the

[35] Patrick Parrinder, 'Revisiting Suvin's Poetics of Science Fiction' in Parrinder, ed., *Learning from Other Worlds: Estrangement, Cognition and the Poetics of Science Fiction and Utopia*, Liverpool: Liverpool University Press, 2000, pp. 36–50, at 40.
[36] Suvin, 'On the Poetics', p. 378.
[37] Darko Suvin, *Metamorphoses of Science Fiction: on the Poetics and History of a Literary Genre*, New Haven, CT: Yale University Press, 1979, p. 80.
[38] Suvin, *Metamorphoses*, p. 80, 71.
[39] Darko Suvin, *Positions and Presuppositions in Science Fiction*, Basingstoke: Macmillan, 1988, p. 83.
[40] Jameson, *Archaeologies*, p. 255.

Antilles in the past five centuries, and the development of diasporic nations emerging from these islands. In Díaz's construction of the Antilles, the shock of renewal is intensified, given that what he is proposing is that the region and its history are subjected to a double vision that refracts the empirical into the seemingly untenable. In this respect, Díaz's novel constitutes a link within an evolution from the concept of 'New' World to a more accurate perception of the region's condition as 'Novum' World.

Díaz is far from oblivious to how the Antillean region has been both theorised and fictionalised in the twentieth century. Among his many theoretical and literary allusions, for example, is a mention of Ortiz that allows Yunior to illustrate the ethnographic aspirations of the generation of men to which Oscar's grandfather, Abelard, belonged. In addition, Díaz opens *Oscar Wao* with an epigraph from Derek Walcott's 'Schooner Flight'. The stanza from the Walcott poem follows a first epigraph—a quote from a 1966 *The Fantastic Four* number: 'Of what import are brief, nameless lives ... to Galactus??'—another instance in which Díaz pairs an Antillean writer with science-fiction greats. One person that Díaz does not mention in *Oscar Wao*, however, is Alejo Carpentier. Yet, the rhetorical similarity between Díaz's line 'who more sci-fi than us?' and Carpentier's '¿Pero qué es la historia de América toda sino una crónica de lo real-maravilloso?' ['After all, what is the entire history of all America if not a chronicle of the marvellous real?'] in the prologue to *El reino de este mundo* proves intriguing.[41] The rhetorical questions by Díaz and Carpentier seem similar: both attempt to align a specific geographical location with an ontological or aesthetic category. There are some indissoluble differences, however. While Carpentier uses the expansive term 'América' for his question, Díaz limits himself to the Antilles. And, importantly, while Carpentier's 'lo real maravilloso' is not straightforwardly a literary genre—despite the multiple genealogies that trace magical realism back to Carpentier's prologue— science fiction is. Rather than slip into the inaccurate interchangeability of Carpentier's category with magical realism, or mention the ways in which

---

[41] Alejo Carpentier, *El reino de este mundo* [1949], Barcelona: Seix Barral, 2005, p. 12. While Carpentier's novel was first published in 1949, the essay that would become the novel's prologue appeared in *El Nacional* (Caracas) on 8 April 1948, under the title '"Lo real maravilloso en América" (prólogo del libro inédito *El reino de este mundo*)'. The English version is taken from a translation of Carpentier's longer version of this essay from 1964, 'On the Marvelous Real in America', trans. Tanya Huntington and Lois Parkinson Zamora, in Lois Parkinson Zamora and Wendy B. Faris, eds., *Magical Realism: Theory, History, Community*, Durham, NC: Duke University Press, 1995, pp. 75–88, at 88. All subsequent quotations from Carpentier's essay are taken from Zamora and Faris's edition with page references included after quotations.

Díaz uses magical realism as a strategy, let us think of Carpentier's 'lo real maravilloso' as a complicated category that exceeds aesthetic form.[42] Despite the absence of an actual acknowledgment of Carpentier in *Oscar Wao*, Díaz's question 'who more sci-fi than us?' is influenced by Carpentier's own question about regional exceptionality, as it endeavours to find a working perceptual model to define regional 'oneness', if we return to Hall's analysis. Both questions entail a certain critical reflexivity towards the authors' native lands or continents. Díaz's question, however, represents a dramatic overhaul of Carpentier's in that it introduces a sense of contemporary history. Throughout his 1949 prologue, as in his further revisions of the concept of 'lo real maravilloso', the Cuban author casts a backward glance at American history, and limits his description of the mid twentieth-century regional scene as one that simply 'present[s] us with strange occurrences every day'.[43] Díaz reopens the style of rhetorical question that Carpentier introduced in 1948, but he complicates the Cuban author's model by emphasising the effects of diaspora on Antillean history and geography.

As Carpentier would have it, 'lo real maravilloso' is a state of being (what he calls the 'extreme state' [*estado límite*], 86) that is evident everywhere in the American 'ontology', its 'virgin[al] landscape', racial miscegenation ('fecund racial mixing'), and the 'revelation constituted by [the] recent discovery' of the continent (88). Amaryll Chanady explains 'lo real maravilloso' as a 'territorialization of the imaginary', or 'a particular manifestation' of an avant-garde perspective that is 'ascribed to a particular continent in an act of appropriation'.[44] For our purposes, let us think of Carpentier's conception of American exceptionality as a specific revision, but not a condemnation, of the idea of America as the 'New World'. Unlike later critics (including

---

[42] When asked in an interview why he 'makes fun of magical realism' in *Oscar Wao*, Díaz replied: 'I don't think I make fun of MR any more than I make fun of hip hyper-realism. For the record I've got nothing against magical realism. It's a narrative strategy. A tool. Like all tools, useful in the right hands. I just don't believe in hewing to any one strategy or one tool. To approach this world you need all strategies, all tools'. See Rosa Cao, 'In the Sandbox: An Interview with Junot Díaz', *The Tech*, 28, no. 27 (6 June 2008), <http://tech.mit.edu/V128/N27/diaz.html> [2.5.2011]. For a discussion of the magical realist elements in *Oscar Wao*, see Hanna, 'Reassembling the Fragments'.

[43] Carpentier, 'The Baroque and the Marvelous Real', trans. Tanya Huntington and Lois Parkinson Zamora, in Zamora and Faris, eds., *Magical Realism*, pp. 89–108, at 107.

[44] Amaryll Chanady, 'The Territorialization of the Imaginary in Latin America: Self-Affirmation and Resistance to Metropolitan Paradigms', in Zamora and Faris, eds., *Magical Realism*, pp. 125–144, at 131. As Chanady also notes, Carpentier uses the more specific term 'baroque' to designate the aesthetic expression that can best illustrate the more expansive category of 'lo real maravilloso' ('Territorialization', p. 133).

Díaz) who would reject the idea that Columbus had in fact discovered a new world, Carpentier's work represents an earlier episode in the transitions within post-colonial thinking in Latin America and the Caribbean. He appropriates this terminology for his own purposes, as part of his call for a revamped native appreciation of America. This locates Carpentier at a climactic end of a spectrum of the *mundonovista* tradition of thinking in the late nineteenth and first half of the twentieth century. *Mundonovismo* repudiated the centuries of essentialist European interpretations of Latin American and Caribbean reality through a self-articulation that came from within this so-called new world. Carpentier's 'lo real maravilloso' becomes the circumstance through which subjects can themselves begin to recognise their home as a new world. However, as Antonio Benítez-Rojo has argued, Carpentier does not fully shed the persona of the discoverer that post-colonial critics would later shun. Benítez-Rojo offers a biographical explanation for Carpentier's location between European exoticist discourse and late twentieth-century post-colonial thought. He notes that Carpentier is caught between his European and American parentages: stemming from his bicultural heritage, he approaches the 'islands and rain forests' of this continent in the manner of one who discovers—that is, as one who paradoxically discovers, according to Benítez-Rojo, 'a world that he has already conceived, that was *his*, and that has been thought up, imagined, and desired ahead of time by Europe'.[45] Ángel Rama has succinctly described this as the 'self-discovery [*autodescubrimiento*] of Antillean idiosyncrasy'.[46] Within the scenes of encounter in Carpentier's description of 'lo real maravilloso' we recognise the performance of a curious type of spatial and temporal displacement. Carpentier essentially has it both ways: he attempts to erase and in many ways condemn the centuries-long European claim of having discovered America through a process of discovery of self and continent, but does so in a manner that could be said to resemble the European tradition of awe and wonder that he wants to invalidate.

Carpentier's formulation involves a further paradox, which makes his particular description of 'lo real maravilloso' sound rather more noticeably 'sci-fi'. To discover one's own place again as *new* would first involve a

---

[45] Antonio Benítez-Rojo, *The Repeating Island: The Caribbean and the Postmodern Perspective* [1989], trans. James E. Maraniss, Durham, NC: Duke University Press, 1996, p. 183. In the second edition of *Imperial Eyes: Travel Writing and Transculturation* (New York: Routledge, 2008, p. 229), Mary Louise Pratt goes as far as saying that what Carpentier accomplishes is the recolonisation of America by a 'white, creole' perspective.

[46] Ángel Rama, *La novela en América Latina*, Montevideo: Fundación Ángel Rama, 1982, p. 196.

process of estrangement. Put differently, to claim that a native geography is unfamiliar or new requires a certain level of alienation together with a dramatic overhaul of one's faculties of perception. The *mundonovismo* of Carpentier thus entails a performed return to the *wonder* of discovery, followed by the expansion of a poetics of encounter that can be employed to narrate everyday experience. In this sense, Carpentier's 'real maravilloso' shares a number of qualities with Suvin's ideas of 'cognitive estrangement' and the 'novum' so crucial to science fiction. Carpentier signals that the primary problem we face as readers of this region is how to *commence* a relationship of new perceptivity with the locality of his America: he writes, 'If our duty is to depict the world, we must uncover and interpret it ourselves. Our reality will appear new to our eyes'.[47] 'Lo real maravilloso' and 'cognitive estrangement' are both categories that combine levels of empirical appreciation of a given geography (the 'real' in Carpentier and the 'cognitive' in Suvin) with a particular readerly conduct, which is itself characterised by the constant movement between recognition and non-recognition. This allows for an understanding of Carpentier's concept of 'lo real maravilloso' as the necessary effort made by the native reader to assess the intersection of literary aesthetics and geographical representation throughout American history.

Carpentier's imagination of 'lo real maravilloso' is dependent on a dynamic movement throughout history to arrive at an essence of what makes the continent so strange and, in his view, remarkably distinct. The longer version of Carpentier's essay on 'lo real maravilloso' (1964) is organised according to a journey that takes the author from China, the 'world of Islam' (77), and Prague back to his native Latin America. It is through different experiences of estrangement that he begins to understand where he comes from: 'The Latin American returns to his own world and begins to understand many things' (83). Keeping in mind how important the voyage is to a comprehension of one's provenance, let us return to Díaz and his representation of the new Dominican geography that has been so vastly changed by diaspora. Despite the similar impetus behind their questions about Antillean and American exceptionality, there are clearly profound differences between Díaz's and Carpentier's visions of history, let alone cultural and ethnic identity. Whereas the wonder inherent in Carpentier's rediscovery of the New World is at least partially dependent on a rehearsal of the dream of utopia of the Europeans who arrived in America in the fifteenth century, Díaz's conjugation of doom and discovery from the very first page of *Oscar Wao* sets the tone for a distinctly dystopian vision of the Antilles.

---

[47] Carpentier, 'Baroque', p. 106.

In Díaz's novel, things have dramatically accelerated from Carpentier's 'marvellous reality'. A history of diaspora, to recall Hall, has 'intervened' into Carpentier's New World. And there are other significant differences between the two authors. Whereas Carpentier describes an America that is on the whole perceived as *home*, Díaz's sci-fi Antilles presupposes a continuous journeying between the new home in the north to the 'Islands' that have been left behind: 'Every summer Santo Domingo slaps the Diaspora engine into reverse, yanks back as many of its expelled children as it can ... Like someone had sounded a reverse evacuation order' (271). Even after the event of diaspora occurs, the departure continues to be re-enacted with every visit back to the Dominican Republic. This episode from *Oscar Wao* leads us back to Hall's observation that the New World 'stands for the endless ways in which Caribbean people have been destined to "migrate"; it is the signifier of migration itself—of traveling, voyaging, and return as fate, as destiny'.[48] For Díaz as for Hall, the term 'New' has undergone a radical revision that elides all aspirations of stability. In their understanding of diaspora as constant transformation, they ask us to rethink completely the Antilles as a geography that begins with the principle of mobility and change. This is why the comparison with Carpentier proves important: America in Carpentier's conception is a stable signifier, constantly awaiting its (re)discoveries. For Díaz, the Antilles and the Dominican Republic are relentlessly changing, and their meaning (if there is one) is elusive, shifting with every departure and every arrival.

Science fiction narratives imagine a multiplicity of experiences of displacement and strange encounters. Díaz uses this genre in *Oscar Wao* as a prism through which to begin to comprehend Antillean diaspora. On one level, it becomes a way to illustrate not only what the Antilles, and specifically the Dominican Republic 'have become' (if we recall Hall's assessment). On another level, science fiction allows the reader to reflect upon what the inhabitants of the new country called Diaspora are still in the process of becoming. In his use of the 'sci-fi' adjective to talk about the Antilles and the string of suggested resemblances between historical figures and science-fiction characters, Díaz invokes the genre metaphorically. As we have seen, this provides him with a compelling means of comparison between a specific literary realm and the complexities of contemporary Antillean geography. Science fiction becomes a perspective through which to assess and reassess the shocks of departure, arrival, and the consequent experiences of displacement that are part of everyday life for diasporic subjects. By locating the science-fiction genre within the Antilles and the Dominican

---

[48] Hall, 'Cultural Identity', p. 243.

Republic, he offers his reader a transformed and transforming portrait of these geographies. From within the country of Diaspora, reading science fiction entails a practice that allows the subject to come to terms with the dispersals that have defined the Dominican nation, and the Antillean region as a whole. By calling Antilleans 'sci-fi', Díaz is not introducing a particularly innovative manner to describe, or for others to perceive, this region. Instead, he offers the tried and tested genre of estrangement *par excellence* as a tool to frame the ethnic and social geography that preoccupies *Oscar Wao*. In this novel, Díaz provides a perspective of the Antilles as a region that has ceased to be local, and that is no longer ensconced in the cartography of the Caribbean basin. Much like the evolution of the science-fiction genre itself, the 'Antilles' have become an expanding concept, enmeshed as they are in myriad perceptions of displacement and narratives of estrangement. In Díaz's formulation of the Antillean geographical experience, there is not one new world, but many strange new worlds that emerge with each journey between the old and new home. Within each of these continued movements between cognition and estrangement, we find Oscar, a reader with a will to reassess what it means to be Antillean, who is constantly seeking the opportunity to articulate this strange form of belonging.

Inventing Tropicality: Writing Fever, Writing Trauma in Leslie Marmon Silko's *Almanac of the Dead* and *Gardens in the Dunes*

Hsinya Huang

This essay reads the imagined space of the American Topics in Leslie Marmon Silko's novels, *Almanac of the Dead* and *Gardens in the Dunes*, against the European Enlightenment configuration of racialised bodies and disease.[1] For European colonial invaders, the lands surrounding the present-day USA-Mexico border invoked images of the tropics. And yet calling this (in fact sub-tropical) part of the globe 'the tropics' was a way of defining a culturally alien and environmentally distinctive landscape against temperate Europe. As Europeans invented the tropicality of the Americas, they did not turn them into tropical Edens, as they presumed they would. The Americas became the 'diseased' lands, the tropical Inferno: since the colonial contact, pestilence, treaties, removal, forced relocation, and other expulsions of Native Americans from their homelands combine to result in what David E. Stannard would call 'the worst human holocaust the world had ever witnessed.'[2] Environmental heat was transformed into the body heat of Native American sickness and became an appropriate metaphor for Silko to disclose the bitterness and poignancy of Native American traumatic history.

Indeed, within a few decades of European arrival in the New World, Native American populations were reduced by about ninety per cent by

---

[1] A partial version of these readings appeared in *Tamkang Review*, 35.3–35.4 (2005), pp. 155–205.

[2] David E. Stannard, *American Holocaust: The Conquest of the New World*, Oxford: Oxford University Press, 1992, p. 146.

epidemics of smallpox, measles, and other fatal European diseases.[3] These epidemics are now believed to have contributed at least as much as Spanish arms to toppling the Aztec and Inca Empires, destroying the indigenous populations with infections to which the conquerors were largely immune. Disease was also a potent factor in the European conceptualisation of Native American society: that the indigenous population contracted fatal diseases was considered evidence of their racial and physical inferiority. This was especially so by the close of the nineteenth century, when Europeans prided themselves on their scientific understanding of disease causation and mocked what they saw as 'the fatalism, superstition and barbarity of indigenous responses to disease.'[4] Fostered by the growing understanding of disease aetiology and transmission in the late nineteenth century, Europeans took great pride in their innate racial and physical 'superiority'.[5] This belief, in turn, legitimised (in the minds of the colonisers, at least) Euro-American colonial expansion. The destruction of indigenous societies by 'germs' helped to fulfil what white colonists regarded as their manifest destiny.

In his 1754 version of 'Of National Characters', David Hume states, 'I am apt to suspect the negroes and in general all other species of men (for there are four or five different kinds) to be naturally inferior to the whites. There never was a civilized nation of any other complexion than white'.[6] He further contends that the characters of men depend on their air and climate, and that the degree of heat or cold should naturally be expected to have a strong influence. This understanding led Hume to conceive of all people that 'live beyond the polar circles or between the tropics' as inferior to the rest of the species, and 'incapable of all the higher attainments of the human mind'.[7]

People beyond the polar circles or between the tropic zones are indeed more vulnerable to the diseases of Europe's temperate zone. The alleged superiority of the temperate climates, a dominant theme in much environmentalist writing from the seventeenth century,[8] was duplicated in the

---

[3] Kenneth F. Kiple, 'The Ecology of Disease', in W. F. Bynum and Roy Porter, eds., *Companion Encyclopedia of the History of Medicine*, New York: Routledge, 1994, vol. 1, pp. 357–381, at 367–369.

[4] David Arnold, 'Introduction: Disease, Medicine and Empire', in David Arnold, ed., *Imperial Medicine and Indigenous Societies*, Manchester: Manchester University Press, 1988, p. 7.

[5] Arnold, 'Introduction: Disease, Medicine and Empire', p. 8.

[6] David Hume, 'Of National Characters', in *Race and the Enlightenment: A Reader*, ed., Emmanuel Chukwudi Eze, Oxford: Blackwell, 1997, pp. 30–33, at 33.

[7] Hume, 'Of National Characters', pp. 32–33.

[8] For further details of Western environmentalist writing, refer to Richard Grove,

colonial thesis: the contrast between the temperate homeland and tropical colony sets up the latter as a 'frontier' that awaits 'benevolent transformation' by the white race.[9]

Medical practices based on this understanding of climate and the racialised body therefore seemed to legitimise the superior political, technical, and military power of the West, and hence constituted a celebration of imperialism itself. Medicine gave expression to Europeans' faith in their innate superiority, their mastery over other races as well as over nature. Medicine, as David Arnold points out, registers the imperial determination to reorder the environment and refashion indigenous cultures, histories, and societies in light of their own priorities.[10] Indeed, the term 'tropical' suggests a uniform natural environment in which scientific expertise can be readily deployed and transferred. In many ways, European colonisers saw the indigenous population as a part of the landscape itself. The places where millions of Natives lived for centuries in settled communities are described, by such eminent historians as Oscar Handlin and Bernard Bailyn, as 'empty spaces', 'wilderness', 'virgin land', 'unopened lands', 'void', and 'a vast emptiness' that blissfully await white cultivation, and where the indigenous inhabitants are conceived of as 'a part of the landscape', living like other 'lurking beasts' in a sort of 'trackless wilderness'.[11]

Native American communities were indeed removed to make the space empty for the colonial settlement. The removal of Native American people from their lands gathered massive momentum when Thomas Jefferson made the Louisiana Purchase in the early nineteenth century by buying the homelands of several hundred tribes, ironically not from the tribes themselves, but from France. Jefferson considered it degrading for Indians and whites to live in close proximity, and believed that the only remedy was to remove the Indians. Jefferson's idea was drafted into law as the

---

Green Imperialism: Colonial Expansion, Tropical Island Edens and the Origins of Environmentalism, 1600–1860, New York: Cambridge University Press, 1995, Eze, ed., *Race and the Enlightenment: A Reader*, and Roxann Wheeler, *The Complexion of Race: Categories of Difference in Eighteenth-Century British Culture*, Philadelphia: University of Pennsylvania Press, 2000.

[9] David Arnold, 'Medicine and Colonialism', in Bynum and Porter, eds., *Companion Encyclopedia of the History of Medicine*, vol. 2, pp. 1393–1416, at 1395.

[10] David Arnold, 'Introduction: Tropical Medicine before Manson', in Arnold, ed., *Warm Climates and Western Medicine: The Emergence of Tropical Medicine, 1500–1900*, Amsterdam: Rodopi, 1996, pp. 1–19, at 17.

[11] For bibliographical detail concerning how the American historical textbooks have (mis)represented the Americas as lands of vast emptiness, see Stannard, *American Holocaust*, p. 288, notes 17–20.

Removal Act of 1830, under the stewardship of white supremacist John C. Calhoun, and was implemented by Andrew Jackson.[12] The Act gave the federal government power to remove all Native Americans from their lands east of the Mississippi River to territories west.

While Euro-American expansion accomplished its fullest result through law and treaties that forced Native populations to cede tribal land to the US government, destructive epidemics, warfare, and forced expulsion resulted, in effect, in a Native American holocaust. The brutal acts that aimed to exterminate Native people were written out of official history, and Native American deaths were attributed largely to the epidemics that spread throughout the continent. Disease became a metaphor of imperialism, a smoke screen by which European invaders covered their slaughter of Native peoples and exploitation of the land. Disease lies at the intersection between colonialism and racism: 'The depopulation of the Americas was not ... solely an ecological accident ... It was also the outcome of Europeans' racial contempt, brutal economic policies, and their lust for land and riches.'[13]

Time and the diseased body in *Almanac of the Dead*

Leslie Marmon Silko's *Almanac of the Dead* chronicles the course of these epidemic diseases. The novel spans five hundred years, and takes an ancient almanac as its pivotal text. The first accurate year of the almanac is 1560, the year in which colonial disease made its appearance: 'The year of the plague—intense cold and fever—bleeding from nose and coughing, twisted necks and large sores erupt. Plague ravages the countryside for more than three years. Smallpox too had followed in the wake of the plague. Deaths number in the thousands.'[14]

More gruesome examples follow: '1590—In the sixty-seventh year after the alien invasion, on 3 January 1590, the epidemic began: cough, chills, and fever from which people died" (*A*, 577); '1617–24—Smallpox'; '1621— ... the

---

[12] Paula Gunn Allen, Introduction, in Gunn Allen, ed., *Spider Woman's Granddaughters: Traditional Tales and Contemporary Writing by Native American Women*, New York: A Fawcett Book, 1989, pp. 1–26, at 11–12. During the brutal winter of 1838–1839, about 4000 Cherokees died as a result of the removal. The route they traversed and the journey itself became known as 'The Trail of Tears' or, in a direct translation from Cherokee, 'The Trail Where They Cried' [Nunna daul Tsuny].

[13] David Arnold, *The Problem of Nature: Environment, Culture and European Expansion*, Oxford: Blackwell, 1996, p. 85.

[14] Leslie Marmon Silko, *Almanac of the Dead*, New York: Penguin, 1991, p. 577. Further page references are included parenthetically in the text with the abbreviation *A*.

plague began to spread' (*A*, 578); 'The Great Influenza of 1918' (*A*, 579). Yoeme, keeper of the sacred almanac, who is about to be put to death, records in her notebook:

> The day before my execution the news reaches town. At first the officials refuse to believe the reports of so many sick and dead. Influenza travels with the moist, warm winds off the coast. Influenza infects the governor and all the others. The police chief burns to death from fever. (*A*, 579–580)

Instead of following the chronological progression of events, Silko represents time through lands and bodies, both of which are 'dis-eased' and share eerily similar markings.[15] While the year 1560 is identified through the wasting of bodies, 1566 is noted for the eruption of land: 'between one and two in the afternoon an earthquake caused great destruction' (*A*, 577). Land erosions alternate with epidemic outbreaks as the Native body suffers. Erosion and suffering are reflected in the fragmentation of characters, the rupture of lands, and the fevers of bodies. *Almanac of the Dead* echoes Michel de Certeau's alignment of the '*tortured* body' with 'another body, *the altered earth*.'[16] Thus, drought and famine accompany fever: there is 'mourning for water, there is mourning for bread. Bloody vomit of yellow fever' (*A*, 575).

Disease becomes dis-ease; fever and drought—the dis-eased body and land—are the inscriptions of colonialism. In tracing the epidemics, *Almanac of the Dead* intertwines feverish bodies with dry lands. Indeed, fever travels with tropical heat: 'the news reaches town ... Influenza travels with moist, warm winds off the coast' (*A*, 580). In the old wing of the El Paso Veterans Hospital lie soldiers of the First World War and the Spanish and Mexican wars, who contracted 'tropical fevers' and lung diseases as a result of El Paso's dry climate; Silko describes these men as having 'been dead for years—worse than dead to their families' (*A*, 351). Fever becomes a feature of the tropical, as do drought and heat. Drought has left the lands devoid of green. In the dust-haze, lawns that were once alive and green are now indistinguishable from the cement of buckling sidewalks:

> Even the so-called desert 'landscaping' was gaunt; the prickly pear and cholla cactus had shriveled into leathery, green tongues. The ribs of the

---

[15] Lidia Yuknavitch, *Allegories of Violence: Tracing the Writing of War in Late Twentieth-Century Fiction*, New York: Routledge, 2001, p. 108.

[16] Michel de Certeau, *Heterologies: Discourse on the Other*, trans. Brian Massumi, Minneapolis: University of Minnesota Press, 1986, p. 227 (italics in the original).

giant saguaros had shrunk into themselves. The date palms and short Mexican palms were sloughing scaly, gray fronds, many of which had broken in the high winds and lay scattered in the street. (*A*, 63–64)

Ironically, there used to be plentiful fresh water in Tucson, which is what the word *tucson* means in the Papago language (*A*, 190). The character Leah plans a dream city modeled on Venice that 'revolve[s] around water, lake after lake,' with 'each of the custom-built neighbourhoods linked by quaint waterways … Leah's "someplace" for obtaining all the cheap water she wanted would be from the deep wells she was going to drill' (*A*, 375). Unfortunately, the arrival of white settlers and subsequent colonial exploitation, whose effects are represented in Leah's drilling for cheap water, entail drastic change. Epidemics, drought, and death befall this border city and its inhabitants, which Native Americans understand as 'The Reign of Fire-Eye Macaw':

> Some knew it as 'The Reign of Fire-Eye Macaw', which was the same as saying 'Death-Eye Dog' because the sun had begun to burn with a deadly light, and the heat of this burning eye looking down on all the wretched humans and plants and animals had caused the Earth to speed up, too—the way the heat makes turtles shiver in a last frenzy of futile effort to reach shade. (*A*, 257)

Silko links the narrative of disease and colonial encounters to the Mayan calendar, the source of the indigenous conception of the Earth, which is endowed with the powers of convalescence. Karl Taube suggests that the Mesoamerican calendar is concerned with 'the definition of space as well as time'.[17] Each of the twenty-day months in the 260-day Mayan calendar is oriented to a particular direction, passing in counter-clockwise succession from east to north, west, and finally south (*A*, 13). Unlike the modern Western calendar, which informs people of the present year and date, the Mayan almanac also chronicles changes in the landscape, maintaining regularity across generations by documenting the changes of the earth.

In depicting the devastating effects of the year of dry winds and sunlight, Silko represents Native American trauma through diverse metaphors of heat: 'The Reign of Fire-Eye Macaw'; 'a deadly light'; 'this burning eye'; and 'fire-eye.' Heat is understood in accordance with a mythic prophecy found in the almanac. As feverish diseases spread across the continent, there is an

---

[17]   Karl Taube, *The Legendary Past: Aztec and Maya Myths*, London: British Museum Press, 1993, p. 13.

accompanying '[t]wenty-year drought: the hooves of the deer crack in the heat; the ocean burned so high the face of the sun was devoured; the face of the sun darkened with blood, [and] then disappeared' (*A*, 576). While it is variously represented in the novel as a commodity (*A*, 661), a site of war (*A*, 656), sacred tradition (*A*, 762), and an allegory for Mexico (*A*, p650, 661), Tucson is predominantly a place of heat.[18] Heat seems to accumulate and evolve from the slaughter that takes place in and near Tucson—warfare, murders, exploitation, smuggling of drugs and illegal organs, all chronicled as the heat of lands and bodies. The almanac records time by relentlessly referencing lands and bodies in a symbiotic relationship: 'Twisted necks and large sores' are conflated with 'ravaged countryside'; earthquakes and coughs and chills alternate on 'the surface of the Earth'.[19] *Almanac of the Dead* gives voice to diseased bodies and ravaged lands in this tropical inferno.

Fevers and droughts register more than just physical suffering. The history of America after the coming of Spaniards entails 'death and decay.'[20] Silko chose to set her novel in Tucson, a 'ghost city', where numerous innocent Indian women and children were murdered by settlers over the period of colonisation (*A*, 661). The characters Mosca and Rose claim to see ghosts; the spirits of the dead can never rest but are seen wandering across the land. The US-Mexico border becomes the 'space of death', where 'torture is endemic and where the culture of terror flourishes', to borrow Michael Taussig's words.[21] Tucson, a border city, where historical killings have been buried but where the ghosts of the departed remain, is the centre around which the narrative revolves.

Indeed, *Almanac of the Dead* provides a history of Native American slaughter, which is spatially indicated on a map, entitled 'Five-Hundred Year Map' of the Americas, within the outside covers of the novel. As the map suggests, the novel recounts five hundred years of missing history when millions of Native Americans died. The character Angelita La Escapia, who intends to initiate a revolution against the white US government, gives the numbers of the dead, slaughtered by colonial invaders:

1500—72 million people lived in North, Central, and South America.
1600—10 million people lived in North, Central, and South America.
1500—25 million people live in Mexico.

---

[18] Yuknavitch, *Allegories of Violence*, p. 109.
[19] Yuknavitch, *Allegories of Violence*, p. 108.
[20] Leslie Marmon Silko, *Conversations with Leslie Marmon Silko*, ed., Ellen L. Arnold, Jackson: University Press of Mississippi, 2000, p. 129.
[21] Michael Taussig, *Shamanism, Colonialism, and the Wild Man: A Study in Terror and Healing*, Chicago: University of Chicago Press, 1987, p. 4.

1600—1 million people lived in Mexico. (*A*, 530)

This calculation corresponds to figures in David E. Stannard's *American Holocaust* and Ward Churchill's *A Little Matter of Genocide*. By the end of the nineteenth century, writes Stannard, Native Americans had undergone the 'worst human holocaust the world had ever witnessed, [...] consuming the lives of countless tens of millions of people.'[22] According to Angelita's research in *Almanac of the Dead*, epidemics brought by Europeans account for the deaths of many Native Americans (*A*, 527–530). And yet, the historical slaughter due to the colonists' racial brutality resulted in even more deaths. For Angelita, American colonial history is a history of crime, which Europeans need to face (*A*, 527).

Silko puts together the history of the genocide of the Native peoples of America. Native Americans, for their part, can never forget the slaughter. As Chief Seattle proclaimed, 'the white man will never be alone ... Let him be just and deal kindly with my people, for the dead are not powerless. *Dead, did I say?—There is no death, only a change of world.*'[23] Despite the pain of historical loss, *Almanac of the Dead* suggests that those who died in the past do not actually pass away; their souls simply appear in different shapes. Five hundred years of slaughter have produced lands ravaged by souls that can never rest. As Sharon Patricia Holland points out, in Silko's hands 'the Americas become a territory ravaged by centuries of genocide—it is a narrative told from the eye view of native peoples—when death and destruction are not part of a hidden past but are on the brink of engulfing [us].'[24] Indeed, *Almanac of the Dead* is haunted by disquieting spirits; these even have 'weight', and thus can 'make a wagon heavier for the horses to pull' (*A*, 191). As the character Mosca warns, 'You can hear them ... because the dead souls are out on cloudy days to bring rain ... Dead souls stay near us, but they don't break the silence' (*A*, 603). Such souls can never rest but must keep 'running away ... thinking they are escaping the slaughter' (*A*, 190). Mosca and other white characters suffer from nightmares of wandering ghosts, and frequently claim to see devils.

---

[22]   Stannard, *American Holocaust*, p. 130.

[23]   This version of Chief Seattle's speech has appeared in anthologies of Native American literature and oratory, but most do not identify its source. The main source is a 1932 pamphlet by John M. Rich, copies of which are located at the Seattle Historical Society and at the Library of Congress. For further details, see Jerry Clark, 'Thus Spoke Chief Seattle: The Story of An Undocumented Speech', *Prologue: Quarterly Publication of the National Archives and Records Administration*, 18, no.1 (1985), pp. 58–65.

[24]   Sharon Patricia Holland, 'Telling the Story of Genocide in Leslie Marmon Silko's *Almanac of the Dead*', in her *Raising the Dead: Readings of Death and (Black) Subjectivity*, Durham: Duke University Press, 2000, pp. 68–99, at 70.

Silko sees contemporary reality as according with the prophecy of the ancient almanac, which predicted the New World catastrophe: '11 AHU was the year of the return of fair Quetzalcoatl. But the mention of the artificial white circle in the sky could only have meant the return of Death Dog and his eight brothers: plague, earthquake, drought, famine, incest, insanity, war, and betrayal'; consequently, 'the deer die: drought' (*A*, 572, 574). Kept intact by its keeper Yoeme, and later by her two granddaughters, the almanac contains a living power that predicts future occurrences.[25] Drought, illness, and colonial invasion are closely associated in a mythic vision of ancient wisdom: 'Dog = rainless storms. The dog carries a lighted torch: drought, great heat, heaped-up death' (*A*, 574). Yoeme declares, 'The old-time people [have] warned that Mother Earth would punish those who defile and despoil her ... Fierce, hot winds would drive away the rain clouds; irrigation wells would go dry; all the plants and animals would disappear' (*A*, 632). Drought and death are nature's retribution, while fever is an acting-out of internal inflammation as resistance to colonial exploitation. Yoeme proclaims that the veins of silver have dried up because the mining engineers have ravaged them, but the white invaders also suffer: 'Years of dry winds and effects of the sunlight on milky-white skin had been devastating... . The white man had violated the Mother Earth' (*A*, 120–121).

The mining of toxic chemicals that occurs in the novel precipitates further disaster for Native American lands. Tribal lands have long 'suffered from the polluting effects of heavy industry, toxic dumping, contamination of air and drinking water from off-reservation sources, and from fallout from nuclear testing and arms production'; in particular, 'they have been damaged by the impact of mining operations on reservations'.[26] Across the

---

[25] Silko's almanac is a prophecy, much like the Mayan codices, and connects the ancient Mayas to the tribe's present and future, which the almanac foretells. The almanac in the novel predicts a revolution beginning in Chiapas moving from south to north to reclaim Native American lands. The actual revolution took place on 1 January 1994, when the Zapatista National Liberation Army [*Ejército Zapatista de Liberación Nacional*] declared war on the government of Mexico. For detail, refer to Leslie Marmon Silko, 'An Expression of Profound Gratitude to the Maya Zapatista', in her *Yellow Woman and a Beauty of the Spirit: Essays on Native American Life Today*, New York: Simon & Schuster, 1996, pp. 152–154; Debora Horvitz, 'Freud, Marx and Chiapas in Leslie Marmon Silko's *Almanac of the Dead*', *Studies in American Indian Literatures*, 10, no. 3 (1998), pp. 47–64; and Joni Adamson, *American Indian Literature, Environmental Justice, and Ecocriticism: The Middle Place*, Tucson: University of Arizona Press, 2001.

[26] Jace Weaver, 'Triangulated Power and the Environment: Tribes, the Federal Government, and the States', in Weaver, ed., *Defending Mother Earth: Native American Perspectives on Environmental Justice*, New York: Maryknoll, 2001, pp. 107–121, at 109.

Southwest, uranium mine waste and contamination from nuclear tests have ruined dwindling supplies of fresh water, while chemical pollutants and heavy metals from abandoned mines leak mercury and lead into aquifers and rivers.[27] Silko identifies the site of uranium mining at Paguate, one of seven villages on the Laguna Pueblo reservation in New Mexico. In Navajo cosmology, Beautiful Lake is where mortals emerge as living souls from the Fourth World. The lake disappears when the tribe cannot stop the mining; so too do orchards and fields of melons. Nearly all the lands to the east and south of Paguate are swallowed by the mine; its open pit gapes within two hundred yards of the village.[28]

Silko focuses on colonial land usurpation to delve into devastating acts perpetrated against Native environments. With the expansion of colonial sovereignty, the best land allotments went to the colonisers: 'The whites came into these territories. Arizona. New Mexico. They came in, and where the Spanish-speaking people had courts and elected officials, the *americanos* came in and set up their own courts—all in English. They went around looking at the best land and where the good water was' (A, 213).[29] Silko contests how capitalists have polluted and exploited the land while turning a blind eye to their own greed. Capitalists as land-destroyers are exemplified in the character of Leah Blue, a real estate tycoon who proposes to recreate Venice in the Arizona desert. In her plan for the Blue Water Development Corporation, Leah describes how she will change the desert landscape by drilling water from underground, to build more golf courses (658). The drilling, however, destroys 'foothill paloverde trees all across the valley', rendering indigenous lands 'pumped dry' (A, 651).

Silko highlights the environmental depredation through her narratives of the climate change that transforms the forest into an earthly inferno in the torrid borderlands between the USA and Mexico. This drastic climate change, as she puts it in the novel, has been prophesied in the almanac as 'the Reign of Xolotol, the Death Dog', when the earth becomes barren and dry. Indigenous people across the Mexico-USA border believe that the epoch of Death Dog has been in place during the five hundred years of colonial rule: 'the sun had begun to burn with a deadly light, and the

---

[27] Leslie Marmon Silko, *Sacred Water*, Tucson: Flood Plain Press, 1993. Above ground atomic testing took place between 27 January 1951 and 11 July 1962. For further details, refer to Carole Gallagher, *American Ground Zero: The Secret Nuclear War*, Boston: MIT Press, 1994.

[28] Leslie Marmon Silko, 'Fifth World', in *Yellow Woman*, pp. 126–127.

[29] For the character Zeta, the US government is a ridiculous entity, because 'no legal government could be established on stolen land' (p. 133).

heat of this burning eye looking down on all the wretched humans and plants and animals had caused the Earth to speed up, too—the way the heat makes turtle shiver in a last frenzy of futile effort to reach shade' (*A*, 257). The colonialists continue to stray from valuing the interconnectedness of lives in an ecosystem, hence the devastation of the American continent. As a matter of fact, Silko relies on not only indigenous tribal almanacs for prophecies of destructive colonisation but also sections of old colonial American almanacs, added freely by the keepers, where tribal and colonial histories intertwine (*A*, 570). While 'sections of late seventeenth-century American almanacs [...] employ earth mother imagery in profusion' and advise colonial farmers about 'how to make healing herbal remedies', sections of late eighteenth- and early nineteenth-century almanacs kept by the twin sisters, Lecha and Zeta, 'advise colonists to see the Earth as commodity and to master nature's processes for profit [...]; they show how European consciousness about nature has been deliberately constructed over time to support colonialist objectives'.[30] European-Americans have since suffered from 'a sort of blindness to the world', and failed to recognise the complexity of non-human beings in world ecology (*A*, 224).

Gardens in the Dunes

In the modern world, imperial commercial and militant agendas continue to sacrifice indigenous cultures and lands, and Silko's Native characters feel the loss of spiritual identity to technology and prejudice. In 'America's Debt to the Indian Nations: Atoning for a Sordid Past', Silko quotes a report issued by the US Commission on Civil Rights:

> Indian water rights to the Colorado, Rio Grande, San Juan, Gila, and Salt Rivers will have far-reaching effects on the growth and quality of life in Los Angeles, Phoenix, Tucson and El Paso. Indian tribes control 3 percent of the total national oil and gas reserves and 7 to 13 percent of US coal deposits. Indian tribes control a large number of extensive uranium deposits.[31]

Elsewhere, the report accounts for the federal policy of relocating 'the Indians' around the Colorado River, to remove the 'impediment to Amer-European

---

[30]   Joni Adamson, *American Indian Literature, Environmental Justice, and Ecocriticism: The Middle Place*, Tucson: University of Arizona Press, 2001, p. 143.

[31]   Silko, *Yellow Woman*, pp. 75–76.

designs on the continent'.[32] As Silko relates in an interview concerning the writing of *Gardens in the Dunes*:

> I had this idea about these two sisters, and I knew right away that they weren't Pueblo people. I knew that they were from the Colorado River. There are some Uto-Aztecan groups mixed in with the Yuman groups over there. These were some of the people that lived in some of the side canyons on the Colorado River. *So many of the cultures along the Colorado River were completely wiped out. There's no trace of them left.* And it was done by gold miners and ranchers. They didn't even have to use the Army on them. Just the good upstanding Arizona territory, the good old boys, slaughtered all these tribes of people that are just gone forever. So *I decided that my characters would be from one of these remnant, destroyed, extinct groups. They'd be some of the last of them.*[33]

Silko commences *Gardens in the Dunes* with an account of the last Native survivors to the west of the Colorado River. The text recalls Louise Erdrich's pronouncement in *Tracks* of 'the last buffalo ... *the last* bear ... *the last* beaver ... *the last* birch ... *the last* Pillager'[34]: 'The Sand Lizard people were never numerous, but now Grandma, Mama, and baby Sister [Sister Salt] were the lonely Sand Lizard people living at the old gardens'.[35] Surviving Native people have difficulty believing the stories of bloodshed and cruelty attributed to white strangers, but the reports are true: 'This happened long, long ago but the people never forgot the hunger and suffering of that first winter the invaders appeared. The invaders were dirty people who carried disease and fever (*GD*, 15). As she does in *Almanac of the Dead*, to chronicle the Native struggle against invading armies and diseases, Silko begins *Gardens in the Dunes* with fever, famine, and drought. The tropical land acts out its trauma in diverse forms of storms and disease, reminiscent of the tribal etiology: the invaders' violation of the spiritual law leads to disharmony nation- or world-wide, which then works its way among the populace as disease. The sentence that immediately follows the opening catastrophe of

---

[32] Jace Weaver, *That the People Might Live: Native American Literatures and Native American Community*, Oxford: Oxford University Press, 1997, p. 17.

[33] Silko, *Conversations with Leslie Marmon Silko*, pp. 163–164; italics added.

[34] Louise Erdrich, *Tracks*, New York: Henry Holt, 1988, p. 2; italics added.

[35] Leslie Marmon Silko, *Gardens in the Dunes: A Novel*, New York: Simon & Schuster, 1999, p. 17. Further page references are included parenthetically in the text with the abbreviation *GD*.

hunger and disease, bloodshed, and cruelty suggests a journey of return to the original home, 'the old gardens' (*GD*, 15).

Silko sets her novel on the late nineteenth-century frontier, less than a decade after the 1890 Wounded Knee Massacre, when white colonists were expanding their territory. In a brief temporal shift, Silko describes an earlier period, hundreds of years prior, when the Sand Lizard people lived peacefully in their gardens, but we soon learn that in the novel's main time period, 'a gang of gold prospectors surprised them; all those who were not killed were taken prisoner. Grandma Fleet lost her young husband to a bullet; only the women and children remained, captives at Fort Yuma' (*GD*, 16). There are, in effect, only four survivors: Grandma Fleet, Mama, Sister Salt, and Indigo.

If *Almanac of the Dead* emphasises the horrifying plagues and endless drought of the post-Columbian era, *Gardens in the Dunes* dramatises Native American catastrophe as a heat over the lands. The origin of bodily disease and land dis-ease lies in the violation of spiritual law; Native people regard fever and drought as an acting-out of disharmony on all scales—among humans, and between humans and nature. Indeed, throughout *Gardens in the Dunes*, colonialists exploit a nature they consider to be a subjugated biosphere, with man in charge. The white colonist Edward, for example, is 'amazed to read about a three-thousand-pound remnant of a meteor discovered in Indian ruins' (*GD*, 403). He can hardly control his excitement as he analyses the most recent sample taken from the test hole, which proves it to 'be almost pure cadmium with platinum, and traces of iridium, and palladium studded with white and black diamonds of industrial quality' (*GD*, 404). The old gardens are finally abandoned not only due to the outbreak of epidemic disease, but the subsequent famine and drought, an acting-out of tribal trauma in the land itself.

Consequently, the days become longer and 'the desert heat [gathers] in the Earth, day after day, swelling larger, filling [peoples'] lungs with heat until there [is] no space for oxygen' (*GD*, 45). Delicate sand food plants disappear as the days become warmer, and the Sand Lizard people eat the last of the dried dates. Grandma Fleet 'ration[s] the dry meat and the dry apples' (*GD*, 36), and explains these casualties as a tribal cosmic pattern: '"You never know", she says, "some years the rains will come late but other years the summer rains will not come at all"' (*GD*, 47).

The catastrophe begins with the disappearance of a giant snake. Grandma Fleet relates the tribe's drastic conditions through a mythic vision of 'the big snake ... almost as old as she was, and the spring belonged to him' (*GD*, 36). For Grandma Fleet, all desert springs have resident snakes. If people kill the snakes, precious water disappears. She insists, 'whatever you do, don't offend the old snake who lives at the spring' (*GD*, 36). The mythic serpent is the fountain spring of all interconnected lives. Using Mayan, Aztec, and Pueblo (Navajo) myths, Silko identifies the archetypal snake as the source of water and life, a creature that suggests a certain cultural homogeneity to the American indigenous traditions.[36] For the Pueblo people, 'the Giant Plumed Serpent, messenger spirit of the underworld, [comes] to live in the beautiful lake … near Kha-waik', where the Pueblo believe mortals emerge from the Fourth World and where Silko herself was raised. A 'great misfortune' comes upon tribal people because the greedy colonists destroy the lake, and 'all the water [is] lost. The giant snake [goes] away after that. He has never been seen since. That [is] a great misfortune for the Kha-waik-meh' (*A*, 577).

And yet, *Gardens in the Dunes* never fails to portray tribal life before white exploitation. Silko reveals a garden with abundant water for enrichment. As Sister Salt calls Indigo to come outside,

[the] rain smelled heavenly. All over the sand dunes, datura blossoms round and white as moons breathed their fragrance of magic. Indigo came up from the pit house into the heat; the ground under her bare feet was still warm, but the rain in the breeze felt cool—so cool—and refreshing on her face. She took a deep breath and ran up the dune, where Sister Salt was naked in the rain. (*GD*, 13)

In contrast to the dry, outlandish existence after white colonists destroy the ecosystem,[37] Silko depicts a tribal garden with deep sand that still holds

---

[36] The symbols and meanings of snakes in Pueblo and Mesoamerican myths are numerous; see Taube, *The Legendary Past*, and Paula Gunn Allen, *The Sacred Hoop* [1986], Boston: Beacon Press, 1992, pp. 127–128. Silko conflates myth with tribal reality as she relates an actual experience in 1979 when she was at Laguna visiting the locations of the old uranium mines. She heard about the giant stone snake that had appeared near the Jackpile uranium mine. She saw the snake, which had by then become a religious shrine. Rumour had it that the snake's appearance was a sign that the uranium mine had won, and the snake was pointing at the next mesa the open pit would devour. But the next thing she heard was that the Jackpile Mine had closed because of a worldwide uranium glut; that meant the rumour about the miners winning had been wrong (Silko, 'Notes on *Almanac of the Dead*', pp. 138–139). Silko once painted the mythic snake in her mural and above the snake she painted words in Spanish 'as if they had blossomed out of the flowers and plants that grew around the giant snake'. The words say: 'The people are hungry. The people are cold. The rich have stolen the land. The rich have stolen freedom. The people demand justice. Otherwise, Revolution' (p. 144), which perhaps best indicate Silko's motives for recreating tribal snake myths in her novels: to resist colonial usurpation and exploitation of tribal lands, with which the mythic serpents are closely connected.

[37] *Gardens in the Dunes* also relates the tribal catastrophe to the dam construction

tight 'precious moisture from runoff that nurtured the plants; along the sandstone cliffs above the dunes, dampness seeped out of cracks in the cliff' (*GD*, 14). Amaranth grows profusely at the foot of the dunes. When there is nothing else to eat, there is amaranth; every morning and every night Sister Salt boils up amaranth greens just as Grandma Fleet taught her to do. Usually, '[a]fter the rain, they [tend] the plants that [sprout] out of the deep sand; they each [have] plants they [care] for as if the plants were babies' (Ibid.). Grandma Fleet tells them, 'the old-time people found the gardens already growing, planted by the Sand Lizard, a relative of Grandfather Snake, who invited his niece to settle there and cultivate her seeds'. (*GD*, 14–15)

As the tribal people inhabit the Sand Lizard's gardens, they call themselves the 'Sand Lizard's children'. The gardens epitomise the deep connections between animate and inanimate things, and among living beings. The Sand Lizard does not own the garden, but teaches her children how to tend it:

> The first ripe fruit of each harvest belongs to the spirits of our beloved ancestors, who come to us as rain; the second ripe fruit should go to the birds and wild animals, in gratitude for their restraint in sparing the seeds and sprouts earlier in the season. Give the third ripe fruit to the bees, ants, mantises, and others who [care] for the plants. A few choice pumpkins, squash, and bean plants [are] simply left on the sand beneath the mother plants to shrivel up dry and return to the Earth. Next season, after the arrival of the rain, beans, squash, and pumpkins [sprout] up between the dry stalks and leaves of the previous year. (*GD*, 15)

Sand Lizard's teachings illustrate the mutual and regenerative relationships among all living creatures: each contributes to the regenerative circle and should therefore be respected. As the Sand Lizard and her children cultivate their gardens, herbs become medicine for survival in addition to food. During years of little rain, tribal people count on amaranth and sunflowers. For times of drought, they gather succulent roots and stems growing deep beneath the sand. Later in the novel, the narrator reflects on a time when

---

projects of white settlers. The novel narrates how after the river's course is diverted, Sister Salt is much saddened to 'find silver-green carp belly-up, trapped in water holes in the empty riverbed': 'She trie[s] to care for the datura plants and wild purple asters on the riverbank suddenly left high and dry. She call[s] them her flower garden, but the asters [die] and the datura [wilt] if she [does] not carry them buckets of water every day' (p. 212). Sister Salt's futile efforts to sustain life in the riverbed, along with the environmental casualties caused by the digging of the channels and diversion of the river, create a vivid contrast of two different value systems.

Sister Salt suffered from 'ghost sickness, and the school staff feared typhoid, though she had no fever. The twins [Maytha and Vedna] brought her the fresh datura root she requested, and she rubbed it against her cheeks and forehead to ask its help' (*GD*, 203).

From time to time, Grandma Fleet still visits the old house to feed the ancestral spirits, where, '[i]n time of emergency, the old gardens [can] be counted on for sanctuary' (*GD*, 15). The Sand Lizard people are able to remain peacefully at the old gardens, because the invaders '[fear] the desert beyond the river' (*GD*, 16). As instructed by Grandma Fleet, they continue to cultivate their tropical gardens that are not inflicted, and plant and gather herbs there.

Grandma Fleet's teaching, however, can hardly prevail once the white invaders dominate their lands. By the time whites have expanded their reach, there are numerous occasions when herbs are abused to reap capitalistic benefits. Edward, for instance, '[makes] it his practice to collect samples of local and regional agriculture', as he knows the Natives 'possess unknown medicinal plants with commercial potential ... He purchase[s] bunches of mysterious dried flowers beneficial for weak hearts and bald heads; he [finds] strange roots in the shape of a baby's fingers, said to aid in digestion. He methodically peer[s] into the stalls and shops that [are] closed lest he miss some unusual item' (*GD*, 86). Edward is obsessed with the classificatory system of botany, and sees himself as 'a man of science' (*GD*, 77). Using Edward's notes and maps, a work party 'retrace[s] his steps to collect vast quantities of specimens needed for the displays at the Centennial Exposition' (*GD*, 92), where 'the focus of the exhibit [is] to be commerce, industry, and natural history of the Gulf and the Caribbean Sea' (*GD*, 91). Soon after, white brokers come upriver and demand the tribe's entire stock of a particular herb to corner the market: 'Indians who did not cooperate were flogged or tortured' (*GD*, 133).

Colonial geographical exploration of the New World included the appraisal of natural resources, surveys, and the collection of flora and fauna. Old World medicine constantly turned to the American pharmacy for cures. Indeed, the American continent came to represent a laboratory for modern science in Europe. Throughout European expansion, colonists could test their scientific hypotheses about nature's regularities over vastly larger and more diverse terrains than those of Europe. They mined indigenous societies for knowledge and resources that could benefit their scientific enterprises, and incorporated them into European science. Native informants taught colonists about local flora and fauna, minerals and ores, climate, diseases, and pharmacological remedies. Western medicine today thus incorporates many elements from the New World tropics.[38] But while colonists freely pillaged Native pharmacies in search of suitable drugs (along with other 'useful' plants and minerals), they also exploited the ritual traditions and earth held sacred by Native tribes. This is a matter not of disparate regional perspectives, but rather of different worldviews. The transition from the healing herbs of the tribes to the potent drugs of modern science parallels the transfer of power from the red (tribe) to the white (State), and the eradication of the sacred worldviews from which tribal healing evolved.

Medicine became, in a sense, the patient in need of treatment, failing to function 'within a diseased (and infectious) world'.[39] *Almanac of the Dead* interrogates the profit motive in selling medicine. Its narrator notes that tribal sorcerers become rich by 'making up and selling various odd sorts of alleged "tribal healing magics" and assorted elixirs, teas, balms, waters, crystals, and capsules to the city people, mostly whites [who] anxiously purchased indigenous cures for their dark nights of the soul on the continents where Christianity had repeatedly violated its own canons' (*A*, 478). Silko vividly illustrates how white invaders coarsely interpret tribal healings, abusing Native medical knowledge for the commercial exchange of herbs and medicines: 'Money was changing hands rapidly; fifties and hundreds seemed to drop effortlessly from the white hands into the brown and the black hands. Some bought only the herbs or teas, but others had bought private consultations which cost hundreds of dollars' (*GD*, 719). As they collect materials to add to their almanac, Lecha and Zeta discover that patent-drug companies have proliferated ancient farmers' almanacs, while medicine shows give away almanacs as promotional gimmicks. For Lecha and Zeta, not even the fragments of ancient paper could be trusted, for they

---

[38] European colonialists in the Americas, despite their disregard for the indigenous cultures, adopted a number of Native American herbal remedies, including the use of cinchona as a febrifuge. It is now widely known that Native American herbs have been appropriated by Western medicine to enhance its pharmacology. The most evident fact is that more than two hundred drugs that were used by Native Americans have become official in the *US Pharmacopeia* for varying periods from the first edition of 1820 and in the *National Formulary* since it began in 1888. For details, refer to Virgil Vogel, *American Indian Medicine*, Norman: University of Oklahoma Press, 1990, and Jack Weatherford, 'The Indian Healer' and 'The Drug Connection' in his *Indian Givers: How the Indians of the Americas Transformed the World*, New York: Fawcett Columbine, 1988.

[39] Ann Folwell Stanford, '"Human Debris": Border Politics, Body Parts, and the Reclamation of the Americas in Leslie Marmon Silko's *Almanac of the Dead*', *Literature and Medicine*, 16, no. 1 (1997), pp. 23–42, at 27.

bear all 'clever forgeries, recopied, drawn, and coloured painstakingly' from the colonial script (*GD*, 570).

Indeed, tribal medicine becomes inextricably bound to the colonial enterprise of domination, appropriation, and abuse. In *Gardens in the Dunes*, Native survivors lament the loss of their ancient garden; only dry lands remain, which no longer produce healing herbs. The land remembers its muted history, however, and bears unspeakable pain, sometimes even responding to white invasion: 'The brief twilight of the tropics began to give way to darkness and Edward felt a growing panic that sent him walking faster and faster until he was running for the riverbank' (*GD*, 134). 'Where are your gardens?' Edward asks, addressing the question to a tribal woman. The woman points at the hills above the beach, where Edward sees only weeds and shrubs.

Regeneration and resistance

In *Almanac of the Dead*, the ancient almanac not only chronicles the disease and dis-ease that ravage the Earth but also offers the hope of universal regularity: a time of rain and recovery will eventually follow the reign of Xolotol (Death Dog) in the number of Eight. It is the period when the '[r]ain god sits on coiled snake enclosing a pool of water; the number nine is attached. Nine means fresh, uncontaminated water' (*A*, 574). The rain will nurture lands that have been barren. Silko reminds us that 'the almanac ha[s] living power within it, a power that would bring all the tribal people of the Americas together to retake the land' (*A*, 569). *Almanac of the Dead* involves many important and varied voices: Sterling, a Laguna native; Seese, a white woman; Yoeme, a Yaqui; Root, of Spanish descent; Rose, a North Native American; Tacho, a mestizo; Clinton, the first black Indian; Angelita, a Mayan; Awa Gee, an Asian. Although they are 'scattered in all directions', together they comprise a tribal force that recognises the Earth as home (*A*, 702). As Joseph Epes Brown points out, '[t]he land nurtures the people by sharing its power, giving songs for ceremonies, herbs for healing, and visions for strength. In turn, people honour the land by treating it with respect, performing ceremonies, and singing songs of thanks'.[40]

Indeed, as Silko claims, 'The ancient Pueblo people called the Earth the Mother Creator of all things in this world'.[41] For Native Americans, all beings in the universe are integral to the spirit of Mother Earth and

---

[40] Joseph Epes Brown, *Teaching Spirits: Understanding Native American Religious Traditions*, New York: Oxford University Press, 2001, p. 24.

[41] Silko, 'Interior and Exterior Landscapes', p. 4.

form an interconnected web.[42] Physical substances, animals, humans, and non-humans all contain a living power that resonates with the Earth. Silko thus depicts a rock, a cottonwood tree, a lizard, and a bird as having their own spirits (*A*, 224, 117, 593). Throughout Silko's novels, Mother Earth is a living character endowed with powers of healing. She contains the living spirits that exist in Native medicine. For example, coca leaves are governed by the deity Mama Coca, who 'had loved and cared for the people for thousands of years' and 'had taken away the[ir] pains' (*A*, 502). For Native Americans, the Earth offers the necessary medicine for survival and brings both spiritual and physical healing. As Donald L. Fixico notes, Native Americans 'found themselves constantly dependent upon their natural environment ... Plants and herbs provided them with medicine ... Such plants and herbs had spiritual powers to help the people'.[43] Humans constitute just a small portion of this network of living power. As Paula Gunn Allen writes, the 'sacred power' of the Earth and medicine are related terms, since the power of sacred healing lies in the 'force' of the Earth to purify evil.[44] Without the Earth, as a Chippewa-Cree tribal leader says, 'Our medicine, ceremonies, prayers [would be] ineffective'.[45]

Thus, in contrast to the disease and dis-ease that befall indigenous people and lands, both novels envision an indigenous force that continually gathers strength for the Earth's reclamation and healing. 'The land of the dead is a land of flowers and abundant food' (*A*, 572), as Silko affirms in *Almanac of the Dead*, where the crowded and decaying notebooks of the almanac bear witness to indigenous curative energies. The almanac predicts that the forces of the Earth will work for Native Americans. For, 'the land of the dead' is also 'a land of flowers and abundant food'. Earthquakes, floods, and famines lead to 'civil strife, civil crisis, [and] civil war' (*Almanac*, 765); nonetheless, there are chances for uprising or change. Storms bruise the land, and earthquakes and floods 'leave scars we might ordinarily associate with a human immune system under attack'.[46] While the human exploitation of lands is always accompanied by natural disasters—plague, starvation, famine, drought, and cholera—these are symbols of invasion and occupation. The human immune system, aligned with the Earth, will eventually fight against disease and dis-ease.

---

[42] Silko, 'Interior and Exterior Landscapes', p. 6.
[43] Donald L. Fixico, 'The Struggle for Our Homes: Indian and White Values and Tribal Lands', in Weaver, ed., *Defending Mother Earth*, pp. 29–46, at 34.
[44] Allen, *The Sacred Hoop*, pp. 72–73.
[45] Quoted in Brown, *Teaching Spirits*, p. 32.
[46] Yuknavitch, *Allegories of Violence*, p. 109.

The old almanacs do not just tell 'when to plant or harvest' (*A*, 137), but also prophesise cures. While the open-pit uranium mine has been closed for years in *Almanac of the Dead*, the character Sterling knows that 'the buffalos [are] returning to the Great Plains' as he draws near to the mine's former site (*A*, 758). The almanac is said to have 'living power within it, a power that would bring all tribal people of the Americas together to retake the land' (*A*, 569). While the discovery of the Americas is described as violence through robbery (*A*, 576), the almanac also contains materials that should be read as a form of resistance.[47] Its guardians are charged with finding and recording those fragments of history before they disappear. To combat disease/dis-ease, Native Americans seize hold of a memory that is essential for their survival, as it 'flashes up in a moment of danger'.[48] Without the almanac, the tribal people 'would not be able to recognise the days and months yet to come, days and months that would see the people retake their land' (*A*, 570). As the prophecy realises itself at the end of the novel, tribal people rejoice at the reappearance of the stone snake: 'The snake didn't care about the uranium tailings ... Burned, radioactive, with all humans dead, the Earth would still be sacred. Man was too insignificant to desecrate her' (*A*, 762).

Here, Silko refers to Quetzalcoatl, the plumed serpent of Aztec myth, who is widely identified with water, fertility, and, by extension, life itself. As his name suggests both the sky (*quetzal*, meaning bird) and the Earth (*coatl*, meaning serpent),[49] Quetzalcoatl is credited with the power of 'restoration of the sky and Earth'.[50] He slays the monster that brings drought and disease, transforming himself into a tree to connect with the sky and bring rain to the lands. One aspect of Quetzalcoatl, Ehecatl, is the god of wind, who appears in the breath of living beings and in the breezes that bring fructifying rain clouds. Finally, Quetzalcoatl represents the deity who goes to the four worlds below, recreating humanity from the dead. The almanac contains fragments regarding these dead spirits: 'Dead souls travel branches and roots of the ceiba trees to reach the land of the dead' (*A*, 572). A benevolent god, Quetzalcoatl 'gathered the bones of the dead, sprinkled them with his own blood, and recreated humanity' (*A*, 576). If the disappearance of the snake indicates loss of water and subsequent misfortune, the reappearance of the giant stone snake indicates a rebirth, suggesting a cycle of destruction and regeneration that

---

[47] Yuknavitch, *Allegories of Violence*, p. 104.

[48] Walter Benjamin, 'Theses on the Philosophy of History', in his *Illuminations*, trans. Harry Zohn, New York: Schocken Books, 1969, pp. 253–264 at 255.

[49] Neil Baldwin, *Legends of the Plumed Serpent: Biography of a Mexican God*, New York: Public Affairs, 1998, p. 12.

[50] Taube, *The Legendary Past*, pp. 36–37.

accords with a natural rhythm: 'The snake was looking south, in the direction from which the twin brothers [Tacho and El Feo] and the people would come' (*A*, 763).[51] Silko assures us that '[t]he rain will follow the Twin Brothers with the sacred macaws and the thousands of people walking North'.[52]

In an essay titled 'Fifth World: The Return of Ma Ah Shra True Ee, The Giant Serpent', Silko refers to the mythic serpent as an actual occurrence during the colonial exploitation of Native American lands. She describes the discovery of 'a giant stone snake formation ... one morning in the spring of 1980 by two employees of the Jackpile uranium mine'.[53] This event frightened the white miners, but 'there was a great deal of excitement among Pueblo religious people because the old stories mention a giant snake who is a messenger for the Mother Creator'.[54] The myth of the giant serpent seems to have become reality, and Native people were encouraged by 'the sacred messenger spirit/ from the Fourth World below'.[55] They chanted, '*Ma ah shra true ee*, the sacred messenger, will appear again and again. Nothing can stop that. Not even a uranium mine'.[56]

Thus, fever and drought should be read as forms of *resistance* to disease, the 'affection of life striving to break away from death'.[57] Fever has a salutary value: it is an excretory movement, purifying in intention as its etymology shows—*februare* is to ritually expel the shades of the dead from a house.[58] Disease carries potential for salvation. In *Gardens in the Dunes*, plague 'fever' is transformed into pledged 'fervour' for the rebirth of the Earth, while the land is an animate 'Mother' (*GD*, 625). This is embodied in the performances of the Ghost Dance that bookend the novel:

> If the Paiutes and all the other Indians danced this dance, then the used-up land would be made whole again and the elk and the herds

---

[51] *Almanac of the Dead* predicts a revolution beginning in Chiapas moving from south to north to reclaim Native American lands under the leadership of Sterling and the twin brothers, Tacho and El Feo. For this indigenous revolt in *Almanac of the Dead*, see Silko ('An Expression of Profound Gratitude'), Horvitz ('Freud, Marx and Chiapas'), and Joni Adamson, *American Indian Literature, Environmental Justice, and Ecocriticism: The Middle Place*, Tucson: University of Arizona Press, 2001.

[52] Coltelli, '*Almanac of the Dead*: An Interview with Leslie Marmon Silko', p. 132.

[53] Silko, 'Fifth World', p. 126.

[54] Silko, 'Fifth World', p. 126.

[55] Silko, 'Fifth World', p. 127.

[56] Silko, 'Fifth World', p. 134.

[57] Quoted in Michel Foucault, *The Birth of the Clinic*, trans. Alan Sheridan, New York: Vintage Books, 1975, p. 178.

[58] Foucault, *The Birth of the Clinic*, p. 179.

of buffalo killed off would return. The dance was a peaceful dance, and the Paiutes wished no harm to white people ... If they danced the dance, then they would be able to visit their dear ones and beloved ancestors. The ancestor spirits were there to help them ... They all were happy and excited because they had seen the Earth reborn. (*GD*, 23–24)

Spirits and spectres return not to haunt but to help. The dancers are careful to drag their feet lightly along the ground to keep in touch with Mother Earth. They move from right to left, because that is the path followed by the sun. Native bodies correspond with the Earth body in a cosmic harmony that has long been disturbed by white invasion. Only by dancing can they call forth the Messiah, who will bring with him beloved family members and friends, those who moved on to the spirit world when '[t]he invaders made the Earth get old and want to die' (*GD*, 26). Silko identifies this Messiah as 'Jesus Christ of the Americas',[59] and uses her novels to foretell a Native return to the Americas, 'because [they] are all the children of Mother Earth' (*GD*, 32).

It is in the bodily practice of the Ghost Dance, a dance attuned to cosmic rhythms, where the past is retrieved and the mundane conflated with the sacred. The prophecy of a Messiah had been reported 'six or seven years before, [when] newspapers reported the Indians claimed to have a Messiah, a Christ of their own, for whom they gathered to perform a dance' (*GD*, 262). In the Ghost Dance, this prophecy is represented ritually to evoke the joining of the individual, tribe, and Earth. Wovoka, the Ghost Dance leader, says it is done 'to repel diseases and sickness, especially influenza' (*GD*, 32). Healing and redemption are expressed through gestural relations between the indigenous body and Mother Earth. The tortured body that suffers from detention, dislocation, hunger, and disease is joined by another body, the altered Earth, and returns to be reborn.

That Silko opens and closes *Gardens in the Dunes* with the Ghost Dance is thus a deliberate response to the threat to tribal survival. While performance of the Ghost Dance led to the Wounded Knee Massacre in 1890, Silko represents this historical incident as a demand for justice and 're-membering,' to put back together what has been fragmented by colonial history. In her ritual account, the dance is the bodily performance of ancient belief regarding returning the dead to life. The Ghost Dance is far from what Edward, in a wisecrack, refers to as 'religious hysteria' (*GD*, 320), or

---

[59]   Ellen L. Arnold, 'Listening to the Spirits: An Interview with Leslie Marmon Silko', in Arnold, ed., *Conversations with Leslie Marmon Silko*, Jackson: University Press of Mississippi, 2000, pp. 162–196, at 164.

what federal officials see as 'a secret army in disguise' (*GD*, 45); it is instead an act of survival, representing the joint will of the tortured body and the altered Earth to be reborn.

Consequently, material life is highly charged with a spiritual energy that circulates within and nurtures the cosmos. While the garden is a prominent metaphor, representing Native American historical paradigms, cultural systems, and concepts of thinking, Grandma Fleet cultivates the old gardens in a very pragmatic manner. The more strange and unknown the plant, the more interested Grandma Fleet is in it. She loves to collect and trade seeds: 'Others did not grow a plant unless it was food or medicine ... Grandma said they never found a plant they couldn't use for some purpose' (*GD*, 83–84). She is the tribal gatherer, according to Paula Gunn Allen's definition:

> Gathering is a discipline that requires respect on a primary spiritual level. It develops refined powers of observation and discernment in the ritualist and extensive knowledge of seasons, weather, astronomy, and healing, conferring on its devotee a degree of mental sophistication that rivals that of physicians, scientists, computer experts, or metaphysicians.[60]

Silko constantly recalls the Native American garden of blessed subsistence, vividly pictured in Grandma Fleet's efforts to transform the desert into a tropical garden as their home. The character Indigo endeavours to sustain and transmit the tribe's garden legacy. When Indigo receives a package 'that held a small silk-bound notebook where Aunt Bronwyn hand-printed the names (in English and Latin) of medicinal plants and the best conditions and methods to grow them,' she realises that '[a]ll the other pages in the green silk notebook were blank, ready for [her] to draw or write anything she wanted. Bundled on top of the notebook with white ribbons were dozens of waxed paper packets of seeds wrapped in white tissue paper' (*GD*, 267). With seeds to be planted and blank pages to be filled in, Indigo is on her way to becoming not only a writing subject, but an historian and physician with the power to recall her tribal culture and populace from extinction, to 'return the dead to life', so to speak. The simplest tool for achieving this is a pencil:

> [Indigo] took the little pencil that belonged with the notebook and practiced copying the Latin names and the English names on a blank page: monkshood, wolfsbane, aconite, *Aconitum napellus* ... Below

---

[60] Allen, *The Sacred Hoop*, p. 12.

the picture she copied its medicinal uses from Aunt Bronwyn's list: anodyne, febrifuge, and diuretic. Hattie added these words to her spelling list, so Indigo wrote their definitions right beside them. 'Anodyne' is Greek for 'no pain'; 'febrifuge' she remembered as 'refuge from fever'. Hattie told her the English word 'febrile' came from the Latin *febris*, for 'fever'; 'diuretic' was from the Greek for 'urine'. (*GD*, 282)

Indigo works with women of different ethnic origins to complete her medicine book. It is a hybrid text, combining the pre-modern and the tribal to combat the modern tyranny of science, capitalism, and colonialism. Before any tribal medicine is actually re-inscribed or memory transmitted, Silko closes the novel with a return to the old gardens. Privileging a down-to-earth practicality, she depicts women planting seeds, gathering flowers, and sharing a connected consciousness. The end meets the beginning: it is Grandma Fleet's tribal way that prevails after all.

Conclusion

If *Almanac of the Dead* chronicles tribal history (time) through metaphors of feverish bodies and dry lands, *Gardens in the Dunes* maps tribal geography (place) through curing herbs and healing rituals. Whereas *Almanac of the Dead* depicts disease and dis-ease, *Gardens in the Dunes* focuses on healing and cure. They should be read as twin texts, and twins are in fact recurrent prototypes in Native American writings. *Gardens in the Dunes* commences and ends with the Ghost Dance. Through the metaphor of the garden, it rejuvenates the exploited dry lands with moisture-bearing herbs and plants. Grandma Fleet sorts her collection of seeds, and has everything prepared by the time the rain comes, so they can sow them into the damp earth promptly. She becomes lively 'as she [sings] out a welcome to the [rain] clouds' (*GD*, 47). She explains 'the differences in the moisture of the sand between the dunes ... some of the smaller dunes were too dry along their edges and it was difficult to grow anything there; in marginal areas like these it was better to let the wild plants grow' (*GD*, 47). Rain and herbs are charged with sacred spirituality as Grandma Fleet 'greet[s] the clouds with tears in her eyes', thinking of 'their beloved ancestors return[ing] to them as precious rain' (*GD*, 47–48).

Different plants, trees, and herbs permeate *Gardens in the Dunes* as Silko's characters cultivate gardens of semi-tropical vegetation. Silko privileges tropicality, writing against the colonial depiction of the tropical as inferior. In *Gardens in the Dunes*, therefore, heat no longer conveys infectious germs but curative energies. On the highest dune, near the spring, Grandma Fleet digs herself a little pit house where she plants apricot seeds. She arranges 'willow branches in a latticework to support more willow branches so as to form a roof over the dugout' (*GD*, 50). Passages concerning planting, flowers, and herbs are the threads that tie characters intimately together. After the first beans and squash are harvested, Grandma Fleet leaves her shelter by the peach seedlings less and less often. The girls help her walk through the gardens, where she surveys 'the sunflowers, some small and pale yellow, others orange-yellow and much taller than they were; then she examined the brilliant red amaranth ... The gardens were green with corn and bush beans' (*GD*, 50–51). And Indigo dreams she comes back home to the old gardens, 'where the sunflowers and corn plants and squash' once grew (*GD*, 304).

As the twins Maytha and Vedna arrive at the garden, even from a distance 'the bright ribbons of purple, red, yellow, and black gladiolus flowers were impossible to miss, woven crisscross over the terrace gardens, through the amaranth, pole beans, and sunflowers' (*GD*, 474). The twins take delight in the 'speckled corn' effect that Indigo makes with the gladiolus, which she plants in rows to resemble corn kernels. Maytha favours 'lavender, purple, white, and black planting', but Sister Salt and Vedna prefer the dark red, black, purple, pink, and white planting. In the morning sky, 'blue morning glories wreathed the edges of the terraces like necklaces' (*GD*, 476). Down the shoulder of the dune to the hollow between the dunes, silver-white gladiolus with pale blue and lavender glows among the dark jade datura leaves. 'Just wait until sundown—the fragrance of the big datura blossoms with the gladiolus flowers [will] make them swoon', Indigo promises (*GD*, 476).

In their gardens, the material meets the sacred. While Indigo dreams of the big rattlesnake (*GD*, 304), the snake actually returns to the old garden to greet Sister Salt (*GD*, 477). *Gardens in the Dunes* ends where it begins, with the tribal sisters gathering stones to build 'the spirit house of the Lord' (*GD*, 454). Others join the sisters in dance, and as the drum calls them to the spirit house, they sing the new songs, each in a different language—Sand Lizard, Paiute, Chemehuevi, Mojave, and Walapai—'because in the presence of the Messiah, all languages [are] understood by everyone' (*GD*, 465). This political coalition, as de Certeau points out, is triggered through an alliance between the '*tortured* body and another body, *the altered Earth*',[61] with the will for rebirth and power. They dance slowly and carefully, trailing their feet gently to caress Mother Earth, as they watch the storm clouds move on (*GD*, 465–466).

---

[61] De Certeau, 'Politics of Silence', p. 227; italics in original.

Lecha in *Almanac of the Dead* conceives of illness as arising from human separation from the Earth: 'They all had given the loss different names ... but Lecha knew the loss was their connection with the earth' (*A*, 718). Addressing Buffalo as their 'slain sister' and Condor as their 'slain brother' (*GD*, 467), Silko's characters in the Ghost Dance connect the dead and the living, human and nonhuman, spiritual and physical to rejuvenate the Earth. By inscribing what was in actuality a traumatic historical event that led to the Wounded Knee massacre, Silko represents the performance of indigenous bodies as attuned with the altered Earth body and exploited lands. Silko assures us, 'The Ghost Dance has never ended, it has continued, and the people have never stopped dancing' (*A*, 724): 'Rejoice! Mountains and valleys! The mighty river runs free once more! Rejoice! We are no longer solitary beings alone and cut off. Now we are one with the Earth, our mother' (*A*, 733). The ritual becomes the locus for representing the hidden past and repressed memory, invoking individual, tribal, and Earth bodies as places of vibrant connection, historical memory, and tribal knowledge. Both novels elaborate on diseases that paradoxically 'unify' people, tribe, and Earth. Finally, as Gerald Vizenor suggests, Native American works themselves can be seen as the literary equivalent of a Ghost Dance, creating 'a literature of liberation that enlivens tribal survivance'.[62]

Silko's deployment of Native American counter-discourses of history and place in *Almanac of the Dead* and *Gardens in the Dunes* contests Euro-American epistemologies and their entrenched colonial relations of power and knowledge. The destruction of body and land coincides in history. While history becomes our illness, as the almanac shows, in water there dwells a regenerative, life-giving power. Fever and drought give way to the healing power of rain clouds, semi-tropical gardens, and flora and fauna of enormous curative energies. In fever and drought, therefore, is contained a living power, a potential for salvation, for the Earth as well as the body.

---

[62] Gerald Vizenor, 'Native American Indian Literature: Critical Metaphors of the Ghost Dance', *World Literature Today*, 66, no. 2 (1992), quoted in Edward Huffstetler, 'Spirit Armies and Ghost Dancers: The Dialogic Nature of American Indian Resistance', *Studies in American Indian Literatures*, 14, no. 4 (2002), pp. 3–18, at 9.

Imperial Archaeology:
The American Isthmus as
Contested Scientific Contact Zone

Gesa Mackenthun

Panama—Potsdam

In the summer of 1847, while the US armies of Zachary Taylor and Winfield Scott were on their way to conquering Mexico City, the US adventurer and proto-archaeologist John Lloyd Stephens, famous 'discoverer' of many Maya ruins, joined the first US steamship voyage from Boston to Bremerhaven, being the official representative of the Ocean Steam Navigating Company, to whom the ship belonged. Although the steamer was beaten by its British rival, the Britannia, Stephens landed safely in Bremen, attended official dinners in celebration of the revolutionary technology that would introduce a new age of transportation, and went on a one-day trip to Berlin before continuing his journey to the river Rhine. As he writes, he only had one purpose in Berlin. With a written recommendation from the former Prussian minister to Washington in his pocket, he passed through the Brandenburg Gate and travelled on to Potsdam, where he heard to his chagrin that the object of his detour, the 78 year-old Alexander von Humboldt, was indisposed and would not receive anyone. Stephens left his card nevertheless, upon which he was instantly called into an adjoining apartment where Humboldt greeted him, saying that no introduction would have been necessary.[1] Stephens, the expert at discovering the monuments

---

[1] The summary of Stephens's visit to Humboldt is based on his own account, 'An Hour with Alexander von Humboldt', *Little's Living Age*, 15 (1847), pp. 151–153, and on Victor von Hagen's additional information in *Maya Explorer: John Lloyd Stephens*

of American antiquity, compares the aged aristocrat-scholar himself with
a monument:

> He was recorded in the annals of a past generation. Indeed, his reign
> had been so long, and his fame went back so far, that until I saw him
> bodily, I had almost regarded him as a part of history, and belonging
> to the past; even then, alone and in the stillness of the palace, I could
> hardly keep from looking at him as something monumental, receiving
> the tribute of posthumous fame.[2]

Humboldt's manner of speech, rather than his mild accent, reminded
Stephens of the American senior scholar Albert Gallatin, 'who was an old
personal friend' of Humboldt, 'and to whom he wished to be remembered'.
    What Stephens expresses here is more than just the reverence paid to an
elderly scholar. Having been a model for a whole generation of scientists,
Humboldt, at mid-century, stood for a 'romantic' scientific approach to
nature that was gradually being replaced by more positivistic, less aesthetic
attitudes. With the growing specialisation and institutionalisation of the
sciences of man and nature and the waning of an Enlightenment, holistic
approach inspired less by commercial interest than by a lingering spiritual
reverence for creation, the Humboldtian model was going out of fashion
along with the type of the aristocratic gentleman-scholar able to dedicate
all his money and time to his chosen scientific project. That Stephens, as
we will see, belonged to the new time is properly symbolised by his chosen
means of transportation. Alongside searching for unknown Maya ruins
in the forests of Central America, he had made himself renowned as an
engineer who was in 1847 actively contributing to the construction of the
Panama railway that was to connect the two oceans and greatly enhance
global commerce.
    During their meeting in Potsdam, the two men of science concentrated
on the themes offered by the new age. Their conversation circled around
technological inventions and politics: the situation of political unrest in
Europe on the eve of 1848, and the US war against Mexico—the country
outside Europe which seems to have interested Humboldt most. Praising
Prescott's book on the Spanish conquest of Mexico, Humboldt 'was full of
our Mexican War'. This certainly was a difficult topic for Stephens, as the
general attitude in Europe—and that of a minority in the USA—was not in

---

and the Lost Cities of Central America and Yucatán [1947], San Francisco: Chronicle
Books, 1990, pp. 266–270.
    [2] Stephens, 'An Hour', p. 152.

favour of this imperial aggression (Humboldt's friend, Albert Gallatin, was one of its fiercest antagonists).³ Stephens evades the topic by emphasising the USA's 'Prussian' values: even 'in monarchical and anti-republican countries', he writes, 'a strong impression of our ability and power for war [...] raises us to the rank of a "first rate power", and makes us "respected"'. Humboldt tells him that the Prussian king, together with his military advisors, had gone over all the military moves of the US army and that Taylor's action, 'with a handful of regulars, and a small body of volunteers', had

> struck [them] with admiration at the daring and skill displayed at Buena Vista. [...] Amid the bitterness and malignity of the English press, it [sic] was grateful to hear from such lips, that the leading military men of a military nation did justice to the intrepidity and high military talents of General Taylor.⁴

This short meeting between the 42 year-old Stephens and the Prussian patriarch of natural science is striking on account both of the discrepancy between the Enlightenment ideals and the jingoistic justification of imperial warfare which seem to belong to different epochs altogether, and of the international social network that scientific activity produced. Not space nor language, nor the fact that the two had never corresponded prevented Stephens from being received at very short notice and in spite of Humboldt's indisposition. In addition to their strong cosmopolitan spirit, both scholars were united by their 'planetary consciousness', the term Mary Louise Pratt uses to describe the desire to investigate the depths of the countries and cultures which a previous generation had merely mapped out but left largely unexplored.⁵ But while Humboldt's name generally stands for the utter dissociation between scientific and political pursuits—an attitude that Pratt refers to as 'anti-conquest'—Stephens makes no qualms about his pride in the USA's imperial and expansionist policy. Shortly after the conversation at Potsdam, the territory of the USA was enlarged by a third as a result of the Treaty of Guadalupe-Hidalgo (1848), the military leader Zachary Taylor became President of the USA, gold was discovered in California, and adventurers from the East Coast and Europe mass-migrated to the West Coast, many of them via the new railway line through Panama engineered

---

³ See Albert Gallatin's critical assessment of the war in his leaflet *Peace with Mexico*, New York: Bartlett & Welford, 1847.

⁴ Stephens, 'An Hour', p. 152.

⁵ Mary Louise Pratt, *Imperial Eyes: Travel Writing and Transculturation*, London: Routledge, 1992, p. 15.

by, among others, John Lloyd Stephens. The times of humanistic explorations à la Humboldt seemed to be over.

This essay takes a closer look at what appear to be two distinct scientific approaches to the natural world and to the antiquities of Central America in the middle of the nineteenth century: the Enlightenment natural history approach of Humboldt, and the imperial approach of Stephens. Pratt gives the following description of the difference between them:

> [T]he system of nature as a descriptive paradigm was an utterly benign and abstract appropriation of the planet. Claiming no transformative potential whatsoever, it differed sharply from overtly imperial articulations of conquest, conversion, territorial appropriation, and enslavement. The system created [...] a utopian, innocent vision of European global authority, which I refer to as an *anti-conquest*. The term is intended to emphasize the *relational* meaning of natural history, the extent to which it became meaningful specifically in contrast with an earlier imperial, and prebourgeois, European expansionist presence.[6]

This raises the general question of whether it is really possible to define the two attitudes ('imperial' and 'anti-conquest') as oppositional paradigms or place them on a chronological scale. A look at the entanglements between science and imperialism in the nineteenth century, illustrated by the encounter in Potsdam, suggests that the natural history approach, rather than being a temporary phenomenon—a politically innocent episode that preceded the more durable imperial paradigm—was in fact coterminous with and dialectically related to imperialism.

While we may hesitate to agree with Pratt as to the general innocence and disinterestedness of natural history—some of the most representative expeditions of this kind (such as the Cook voyages or the Charles Wilkes expedition of the 1840s) were financed by imperial governments who assigned political and economic value to their scientific exploits—the name of Alexander von Humboldt may indeed seduce us into believing that the production of knowledge about the world served no interests except those of human curiosity. What follows will explore some effects of the contemporaneity of these two paradigms or moral systems, and consider some of the complexities and intricacies that their coexistence produces in textual representations of Central America between the late 1840s and the late 1850s. The period was characterised by revolutionary changes around the Western world, as well as transformations in the various fields of science—from the

---

[6] Pratt, *Imperial Eyes*, pp. 38–39.

improvements in transportation technology to the substantial intellectual shock waves caused by the publication of Charles Darwin's *On the Origin of Species* (1859).

It was also a period of informal imperialism with regard to Central America. The focus here is on the ways in which the imperial rivalry between the USA and Britain on the Gulf Coast affected the production of archaeological and other knowledge about the region of Yucatán, Honduras, El Salvador, and Nicaragua. While textual examples taken from the writings of John Lloyd Stephens, Ephraim George Squier, and the Austrian scientific traveller Carl Scherzer belong to the 'imperial' discourse, the 'natural history' approach is represented by a little-known travelogue of the French scholar, Chevalier Arthur Morelet, whose style seems remarkably archaic and quaint compared with that of the other texts. The textual geography to be explored is both transnational and transoceanic.

John Lloyd Stephens's hidden Maya city

John Lloyd Stephens's travelogues, *Incidents of Travel in Central America, Chiapas, and Yucatan* (1841) and *Incidents of Travel in Yucatan* (1843), had opened up the world of science to the ancient Maya ruins of which Stephens made precise descriptions and measurements while his British partner, the painter Frederick Catherwood, skillfully copied the hieroglyph-covered steles and bas-reliefs. Himself the typical polytropic Yankee of the post-Jacksonian age of US expansion, Stephens was not content in laying bare ancient ruins: besides his endeavours for the advancement of scientific exploration, he also laid the groundwork for successive attempts to engineer a crossing through the isthmus of Central America. His first vision (before he began constructing the Panama railway) was that of a canal through Nicaragua. In his description of this transoceanic water route of the future, his vision of international commerce converges with his half-satirical praise of the area as a site of luxury tourism:

I am persuaded that the time is not far distant when the attention of the whole civilized and mercantile world will be directed toward it; and steamboats will give the first impulse. In less than a year, English mailboats will be steaming to Cuba, Jamaica, and the principal ports of Spanish America, touching once a month at San Juan and Panama. To men of leisure and fortune, jaded with rambling over the ruins of the Old World, a new country will be opened. After a journey on the Nile, a day in Petra, and a bath in the Euphrates, English and American travellers will be bitten by moschetoes on the Lake of Nicaragua, and drink Champagne and Burton ale on the desolate shores of San Juan on the Pacific. The random remarks of the traveller for amusement, and the observations of careful and scientific men, will be brought together, a mass of knowledge will be accumulated and made public, and in my opinion the two oceans will be united.[7]

A few years after Stephens's suggestion, the tycoon Cornelius Vanderbilt would begin exploring Nicaragua for the possibility of constructing a canal. The project misfired in the end, but US attempts to gain control of the isthmus crossing continued. Stephens's texts combine a pragmatic, scientifically informed and future-oriented strand with a residual romanticism. They abound with tales from the Spanish conquerors as whose modern successor Stephens liked to regard himself.[8] The legends of old join the interests of the expansionist present in the theory of the cultural homogeneity of the whole indigenous population of America that Stephens shares with a series of contemporary experts, craniologist Samuel G. Morton among them. This conviction of the fundamental identity of all Indian groups throughout the hemisphere, as well as his additional conviction that the pre-Columbian civilisations of America migrated from north to south, underwrite Stephens's frequent inclusion of Central American antiquities and aboriginal inhabitants into the collective property of the USA: he transports steles—and intends to transport whole Mayan cities—from Honduras and Yucatán to New York assuming that they 'belong of right to us' (*ITCA*, I, 115–116). Morton's analysis of skulls which Stephens dug up from Indian graveyards convinces him of the 'physical conformation with all the tribes of *our continent*' (my emphasis) which proves to him that

these crumbling bones declare, as with a voice from the grave, that we cannot go back to any ancient nation of the Old World for the builders of these cities; they are not the works of people who have passed away,

---

[7] John Lloyd Stephens, *Incidents of Travel in Central America, Chiapas and Yucatan.* [1841], 2 vols., New York: Dover, 1969, I, p.418. Hereafter cited in the text as *ITCA*.

[8] Stephens's travelogues have recently been analysed by Bruce A. Harvey, *American Geographics: US National Narratives and the Representation of the Non-European World, 1830–1865*, Stanford: Stanford University Press, 2001; R. Tripp Evans, *Romancing the Maya: Mexican Antiquity in the American Imagination 1820–1915*, Austin: University of Texas Press, 2004; and Steve Glassman, *On the Trail of the Maya Explorer*, Tuscaloosa: University of Alabama Press, 2003. See also Gesa Mackenthun, 'The Conquest of Antiquity: The Travelling Empire of John Lloyd Stephens', in Susan Castillo and David Seed, eds., *American Travel and Empire*, Liverpool: Liverpool University Press, 2009, pp.99–128.

and whose history is lost, but of the same great *race* which, changed, miserable, and degraded, still clings around their ruins.[9]

In rejecting then circulating theories about the Egyptian or other Old World origins of ancient American civilisations, Stephens simultaneously includes the aboriginal groups of Mesoamerica in a continentalist notion of territorial and cultural identity that is in full accordance with the dominant Monroe Doctrine. Having been officially sent as an envoy of the van Buren government to enter into negotiations with the various post-colonial governments in Central America, Stephens here merely voices the official political ideology in scientific terms.

However, as his words also suggest, his continentalist narrative is peppered with romantic tales of the survival of remnants of the ancient indigenous cultures. In his first travelogue Stephens tells of his and Catherwood's encounter with the cura of Santa Cruz del Quiché in Guatemala, an illustrious and humorous priest who tells them of the areas never conquered by the Spaniards:

and at this day the northeastern section, bounded by the range of the Cordilleras and the State of Chiapas, is occupied by Candones or unbaptized Indians, who live as their fathers did, acknowledge no submission to the Spaniards, and the government of Central America does not pretend to exercise control over them.

But what 'roused' the explorers most was the report of a 'living city' situated on the other side of the sierra, 'large and populous, occupied by Indians, precisely in the same state as before the discovery of America'. The cura had heard of this city many years before and was told

that from the topmost ridge of the sierra this city was distinctly visible. He was then young, and with much labor climbed to the naked summit of the sierra, from which, at a height of ten or twelve thousand feet, he looked over an immense plain extending to Yucatan and the Gulf of Mexico, and saw at a great distance a large city spread over a great space, and with turrets white and glittering in the sun. The traditionary account of the Indians of Chajul is, that no white man has ever reached this city; that the inhabitants speak the Maya language, are aware that a

---

[9] John Lloyd Stephens, *Incidents of Travel in Yucatan* [1843], 2 vols., New York: Dover, 1963, I, pp. 167–168. Hereafter cited in the text as *ITY*.

race of strangers has conquered the whole country around, and murder any white man who attempts to enter their territory. (*ITCA*, II, 195–196)

In his second travelogue Stephens adds further information on the unbaptised Indians called Lacandones who inhabited the undiscovered wilderness surrounding Lake Petén in Guatemala—a 'mysterious city', he adds, 'never reached by a white man, but still occupied by Indians precisely in the same state as before the discovery of America' (*ITY*, II, 128).

The story of the mysterious 'living' Maya city nicely rounds off Stephens's 'post-heroic'[10] archaeological vision in conjuring up a notion of legitimate succession between the surviving remnant of the Maya and the US-Americans who, according to Stephens, seem to be the only ones prepared to turn the area of 'failed states' into a commercial and touristic hub of the future. According to his continentalist theory of geographical determinism, Mesoamerica was the 'rightful' possession of the USA anyway.[11] To his account of the hidden city he adds a series of speculations as to how to make contact with its inhabitants, some of whom may even know how to read the ancient inscriptions on the steles he has found throughout the country. But his projected strategy wavers between imitating the Spanish *conquistadores* by taking the city by force (which Stephens considers, for some inexplicable reason, to be more justifiable than the Spanish conquest itself) or making time-consuming attempts at patient reconnaissance with the shy natives by studying their language and culture. Not surprisingly, Stephens avoids the dilemma by not even trying to get a view of the city (*ITCA*, II, 196–198).

Imperial science at the American Isthmus

The rumoured hidden city—reminiscent of Sir Walter Ralegh's narrative about the empire of Manoa, or El Dorado—is constantly evoked in Stephens's text although, like Ralegh before him, he never produces any hard evidence for its existence. It continued its ghostly presence in the texts of another US

---

[10]   Harvey, *American Geographics*, p. 160.

[11]   This continentalist theory of rightful possession can be traced back to Jefferson, who likewise regarded the European settlers as legitimate heirs of the 'vanishing' indigenous population. In the age of westward expansion, the argument of geography, according to which Central America was a 'natural' extension of the United States, was very influential. The British argued similarly in legitimating their occupation of Belize (in their view a geographical extension of Jamaica) and in attempting to expand their sphere of influence to Honduras. On the US theory of 'geographical predestination' see Albert K. Weinberg, *Manifest Destiny* [1935], Chicago: Quadrangle, 1963, chapter 2.

citizen whose scientific writings, in spite of adhering to current style and method, bear a political subtext inspired by their author's position as US Chargé d'Affaires to the republics of Central America, first in Honduras and then in Nicaragua. Like Stephens, Ephraim George Squier, the renowned scholar of American antiquities, evokes the deeds of the Spanish invaders as the history of an heroic age, recently narrativised in romantic fashion by William Prescott in 1843. Arriving in Nicaragua in 1849, one year after the Treaty of Guadalupe-Hidalgo, Squier geared his activities and writings at securing US control of the isthmus and fending off British rivals. The story of the hidden city, which is widely circulated throughout Squier's writings of the 1850s, may be seen in conjunction with the British policy of gaining control of the Bay of Honduras (the entrance to the projected railway) by establishing an indigenous puppet government called the 'Kingdom of Mosquitia' to be run by Mosquito (Miskito) Indians and considered as a British protectorate. As James Dunkerley describes in some detail, the policy of both Britain and the USA was rather contradictory, with local agents acting in stark discordance with official agreements between the two governments.[12] Suffice it to say that dashing 28 year-old Squier cared little about the orders from Washington and entered into contracts with local governments in the name of the USA which were subsequently repealed by Washington.[13] Like Stephens before him, Squier was a great champion of US expansionism. As he wrote in his first book based on his sojourn in Central America and in the light of the recent victory against Mexico:

> The fortune of war has planted our eagles on the Pacific: across the entire continent [...] our Republic is supreme. Our trim built ships of the deep [...] sweep in the trade of Europe on one hand, and on the other bring to the mouth of the Sacramento the treasures of the Oriental world [...] To gird the world as with a hoop, to pass a current of American Republicanism [...] over the continents of the earth, it

---

[12] For a full account, see James Dunkerley, *Americana. The Americas in the World, Around 1850*, London: Verso, 2000, pp. 561–590.

[13] According to his own account, Squier in 1850 negotiated a treaty with El Salvador which 'secures to the citizens of the United States all the rights, privileges, and immunities of citizens of San Salvador in commerce, navigation, mining, and in respect of holding and transferring property in that state' (*The States of Central America: Their Geography, Topography, Climate, Population, Resources, Production, Commerce, Political Organization, Aborigines, etc., etc.*, New York: Harper and Brothers, 1858, p. 313. Hereafter cited in the text as *States*.) In fact, Squier's private policy, unendorsed by Washington, amounted to an act of filibustering quite similar to William Walker's concurrent actions in Nicaragua.

needs but one small spot should be left free from foreign threats and aggression.[14]

With a remarkable sweep, Squier's imperial vision moves from the newly extended national territory of the USA to an embrace of *all* continents—and from jingoistic aggression to the notion of the freedom of world trade to be benevolently defended by the USA against the threats of 'foreigners'. The diplomatic correspondence suggests that Squier did not limit the voicing of his opinions to his 'scientific' texts. In order to avoid further irritation of the British representatives in Belize, US Secretary of State Clayton withdrew Squier from the scene in June 1850. Yet in 1853 Squier returned to Central America, again on an official mission, this time to Honduras, in order to draw up the plans for the interoceanic railway planned there.[15] In addition to two major books on the history and archaeology of the states of Central America, very much based on the findings of Stephens (who had died of fever in New York in 1852), Squier also wrote a series of polemics against the British presence on the isthmus and on what he regarded as the fake kingdom of Mosquitia.[16] The polemic particularly fed on Squier's description of the Miskitos as an abominable, hybrid, and degenerate race of 'Sambos'—a description that fully exploited the scientific racism en vogue in the USA at the height of expansionism (for example in the work of Nott, Tyler, and Morton).[17] In his book *The States of Central America* (1858), Squier distinguishes the mixed-bloods in league with the British from three further groups of natives, at least one of which may turn out to be useful for the USA in the future. The first of these groups are the 'Caribs', remnants of the 'aboriginal inhabitants of San Vincent'. In 1796, they had been carried to

---

[14] Ephraim George Squier, *Nicaragua: Its People, Scenery, Monuments, and the Proposed Inter-Oceanic Canal*, New York, 1852); quoted after Harvey, *American Geographics*, p. 179.

[15] As well as the long quotations from Squier's diplomatic correspondence provided by Dunkerley, Squier's career is also described by Estuardo Núñez Hague, 'Diplomat on the Trail of the Incas. Ephraim G. Squier, US Envoy Extraordinary', *América*, 13, no. 4 (1961), pp. 3–7; Terry A. Barnhart, *Ephraim George Squier and the Development of American Anthropology*, Lincoln: University of Nebraska Press, 2005, chapters 7, 8, and 9: and Harvey, *American Geographics*, chapter 4.

[16] See, for example, Ephraim George Squier, 'Our Foreign Relations: Central America–The Crampton and Webster Project', *Democratic Review*, p. 31 (1852) and 'The Mosquito Question', *American Whig Review* (February 1850), pp. 188–208, and (March 1850), pp. 235–268. See also Harvey, *American Geographics*, p. 178.

[17] Squier gives a historical account of the 'Mosquitos' cum 'Sambos' in *The States of Central America*, pp. 228–231.

the island of Roatan, off the coast of Honduras, by the British, after which the displaced tribe founded new settlements on land granted them by the Spaniards near Truxillo. Though also racially mixed like the Mosquitos, Squier views the Caribs in a much more positive light, mainly because they are known as good labourers, having long specialised in the cutting of mahogany (*States*, 232–234). Being skilled in the use of the axe, they already possess 'some knowledge of the building of roads and bridges'. In addition, they are '[f]rugal, patient, and docile' and 'have many of the best qualities of a valuable laboring population'. In short, 'they must prove of the greatest service in the future development of the vast resources of that country [Honduras], and of the utmost importance in the construction of the proposed rail-way between the seas'. He is convinced that about 3,000 labourers may be 'procured for a reasonable compensation' (*States*, 234–240). By 1858, Squier had exchanged his promotion of a canal route through the Lake of Nicaragua for an intercoeanic railway leading through Honduras, which he develops at length in a separate document, *Honduras Interoceanic Railway*.[18]

While Squier's interest in the Caribs is of a very pragmatic nature, his scientific imagination is aroused by his discovery of various indigenous groups in Nicaragua and neighbouring states which he believes to be of Aztec stock. Although he propounds the theory that Yucatán was the original cultural centre from which all of Mesoamerica was peopled (*States*, 315), he also speculates, on the basis of linguistic evidence gathered through his own conversations with natives and in the Spanish chronicles, that the Nahua speakers of Nicaragua and San Salvador were the remnant of former 'colonies' of the Aztecs, about 2000 miles distant from their imperial center, Anahuac (*States*, 318). In spite of the spuriousness of his sources (few of the Spanish chroniclers had a sufficient knowledge of Mesoamerican languages, let alone the methodological support of empirical linguistics), he authoritatively states that '[t]he science of ethnology is now happily so far advanced as to require a closer authentication of the facts upon which it proceeds than can always be derived from the vague and frequently obscure allusions and statements of the ancient chroniclers' and he claims to have found more recent evidence in a few towns near Sonsonate whose inhabitants seem to

---

[18] By the time of its publication, and in response to a rather ineffective truce between Britain and the USA concerning the Mosquito question in 1850, Squier had ended his previous Anglophobia and now offered his services to the British. His proposal for the Honduras railway is preceded by a motto from Lord Clarendon and was published in London: *Honduras Interoceanic Railway. With Maps of the Line and Ports*, London: Trübner & Co., 1857.

have retained ancient Aztec customs and racial integrity (*States*, 319). Squier provides a more extensive discussion of his thesis of the Aztec remnant in Nicaragua in his essay 'Observations on the Archaeology and Ethnology of Nicaragua' (1853), where he states that

> this continent has not been exempt from those migrations, corresponding to the currents and tides of the ocean, which have earlier or later, swept over every part of the Old World, and affected so remarkably, by intermixture and change of soil and climate, the conditions and relations of its inhabitants. [...] We have then presented to us the extraordinary phenomenon of a fragment of a great aboriginal nation, widely separated from the parent stock, and intruded among other and hostile nations.[19]

As evidence Squier refers to a 'tradition' among the Nahua speakers of having once migrated south because they had been overpowered by a hostile nation. They refer to their land of origin as 'Ticomega Emeguatega'—a name that, Squier has to admit, 'corresponds to none with which we are acquainted'.[20] In the absence of evidence that would conform with his scholarly criteria quoted above, Squier resorts to some 'obscure allusions and statements of the ancient chroniclers' and finds corroboration for a tribe having migrated south in the early history of the Aztec rule in Mexico in the historical work of Juan de Torquemada. According to this early seventeenth-century creole chronicler, the said tribe was well received in the area of Nicaragua but soon began to overpower the neighbouring nations.[21] This is not precisely empirically acceptable evidence but circumstantial evidence combined with guesswork at best. What is striking about Squier's migration theory is its close resemblance to the story of the Puritan migration, an analogy evoked by the naturalised image of the 'ocean' as the agent of global migration. Like Squier's Nicaraguan Nahua speakers, the Puritans mutated from a persecuted group to become themselves invaders. The history of migration, according to Squier, is one of violent clashes between powerful rivals, not of peaceful interaction. The climate and soil may mix, 'colonies' of pure-blooded 'parent stocks' don't. Sure enough, the Mexican chronicles which Squier uses to substantiate his case are full of migration stories,

---

[19] Ephraim George Squier, 'Observations on the Archaeology and Ethnology of Nicaragua', *Transactions of the American Ethnological Society*, 3, no. 1 (1853), pp. 84–158, at 115.

[20] Squier, 'Observations', p. 115.

[21] Squier, 'Observations', p. 116.

that of the Chichimecas, the later Aztecs, being the most significant one.[22] But literary analogy cannot replace scientific proof. Perhaps sensing that more evidence is needed, Squier then places the migration of the assumed Aztec tribe within a global context of world-historical migrations caused by 'persecution'—the 'Mormons in the Valley of the Salt Lake, and that of the Jews in Palestine'.[23] Like many of its historical siblings, this migration, too, was 'undertaken in consequence of persecutions, through the midst of intervening nations—an armed migration, giving war to the weak and the hostile, and negotiations with the friendly'.

Increasingly echoing the rhetoric of the originator of the concept of 'manifest destiny', John L. O'Sullivan, Squier uses the naturalising imagery of irresistibly moving population masses to put his theory into world-historical perspective: 'The descent of the Germans on Rome was no migration', yet 'it was the eddy, the outward flow of the great current, which afterwards swept over the ocean barrier, traversed a new world, and is now gathering its volumes on the golden shores of the Pacific'.[24] Empire, having moved west since the times of Constantine, in America tends to move south as well—or at least there is a 'tradition' of powerful nations in the north establishing colonies in the south. Clearly, the theory of the Aztec 'remnant' inhabiting San Salvador and Nicaragua functions rhetorically as a historical precedent for the present activity of US settlers, filibusters, and other privateering citizens who encroached on Mexico and Central America after the acquisition of Texas—William Walker's occupation of Nicaragua being the most glaring example.

Next to Carib labourers to build the canal and pure-blooded Nahua speakers to guarantee an aristocratic and heroic lineage far beyond the cultural centres of Mesoamerica, Squier mentions a third group of natives who, as described by Stephens, may yet inhabit the unexplored regions of Petén as the last survivors of the ancient Maya.[25] The Guatemala chapter of *The States of Central America* includes a long description of the district of Vera Paz, which,

---

[22] As we now know, the Aztecs came to power by way of cultural and linguistic adaptation and by intermarriage into the remnant of the ancient Toltec dynasty.

[23] Squier, 'Observations', p. 117.

[24] Squier, 'Observations', p. 119.

[25] In *States* (p. 327), Squier mentions the tribe of the Pipiles who, according to Herrera, spoke (at the time Herrera was writing) the Mexican tongue but also had a language peculiar to themselves. Although the Mexican empire never extended to San Salvador or Nicaragua, it may be possible that Nahuatl was used as a lingua franca for trading, which would explain the bilingualism.

containing in its midst the celebrated yet mysterious lake of Itza, or
Peten, [...] has the interest of an unsolved problem to geographers.
Nor has it fewer claims upon the ethnologist and antiquary. Within
its fastnesses, with habits, religion, and laws unchanged, still exist the
remnants of the indomitable Lacandones, who figure so largely in the
story of the Spanish Conquest, the cruel Itzaes, and the warlike Chols
and Manches. Its forests hide numberless monuments of ancient art
and superstition, and within their depths, far off on some unknown
tributary of the Usumasinta, the popular tradition of Guatemala
and Chiapa places that great aboriginal city, with its white temples
shining like silver in the sun, which the Cura of Quiché affirmed to
Mr. Stephens he had seen with his own eyes from the summits of the
mountains of Quetsaltenango. (*States*, 532)

The text subsequently summarises a host of accounts to verify the existence
of the rumoured city 'with large edifices, and many cattle in the pastures',
according to one version; a city inhabited, according to another, by the
friendly and peaceful Itzas who are the 'terror of the frontier Spanish
provinces'—apparently Squier's free translation of the account of the
chronicler Juarros which also translates the Itzas of Guatemala into the
'domestic' (US-expansionist) language of frontier warfare (*States*, 532, 545,
548–549). The nature of the Itzas changes according to the source quoted,
but ultimately the representation of them as cruel idolators predominates.
Deviating from his Spanish sources, Squier claims that the Itzas were recent
intruders to the Lake Petén area, 'colonists from the seats of the Mayas in
Yucatan [...] at the period of the Conquest' (*States*, 550).

Due to Squier's habit of ignoring the impact of historical power on the
lives of cultures other than European—a frequent tendency in early (and
some contemporary) ethnographical writing—the identity of the natives
does indeed become mysterious. The Itzas of Lake Petén, subdued by the
Spaniards in 1698, are mixed together with the Lacandones of the recent
Caste War and declared a Maya remnant, analogously to the Nahua-speaking
inhabitants of Nicaragua and San Salvador.[26] Their 'mystery' is merely the

---

[26] The Caste War of Yucatan consisted of a series of violent uprisings by the Lacandon
Indians against the Creole colonial power. Military action lasted from 1848 to about
1855, but the largely unexplored area of Petén remained a territory of insurgents until
the end of the nineteenth century. Incidentally (or not), the Zapatista movement of the
1990s has one of its roots in Lacandon country. The most comprehensive treatment of
the Caste War is Nelson Reed, *The Caste War of Yucatan*, Stanford: Stanford University
Press, 1964.

result of their semantic and ideological double-inscription as both savage and civilised which could answer to two requirements at once: a colonial discourse of the 'natural' eradication of savagery by the powers of civilisation, and a romantic (yet no less colonial) discourse of exotic splendour and civilisational continuity: a *translatio imperii* among noble races.

The legend of a Maya remnant still existing in the limitless forests of Guatemala or Yucatán recurs in Squier's novel *Waikna, or, Adventures on the Mosquito Shore*, published under the pseudonym Samuel A. Bard in 1855. The novel, which must be seen as part of Squier's above-mentioned anti-British campaign, at the same time expresses his racist views, cast in a battle of pure against impure blood, with the wretched 'Mosquitos' (also called 'Sambos') representing the latter and threatening to overrun the former.[27] As is revealed at the end of the book, amid ancient ruins, the US narrator's indigenous servant, Antonio, is a descendant of the ancient Maya nation who once ruled over this region. Written in the light—or rather the shadow—of the Caste War which shook all Yucatán at the time, Squier imagines Antonio to be part of a 'secret organization' of Indian nations

which all the disasters to which they have been subjected, have not destroyed. It is to its present existence that we may attribute those simultaneous movements of the aborigines of Mexico, Central America, and Peru, which have, more than once, threatened the complete subversion of the Spanish power.[28]

Antonio, whose features are identical with those Bard finds on a bas-relief in the ruined city, is resolved to join the rebellion, as his own father 'had gathered the descendants of the ancient Caziques amid the ruins at Chichen-Itza, and there they had sworn, by the heart of Beelam Votan, to restore the rule of the Holy Men, and expel the Spaniards from the Peninsula'.[29] The novel ends in a state of political stasis—the Indian rebellion begins but encounters failure—and with the narrator plunging, Natty Bumppo-like, into the 'untracked wilderness' of Petén in order to accompany his former servant Antonio, now 'the dreaded chieftain and victorious leader

---

[27] For a discussion of the racial, as well as colonialist, discourse of the novel, see Harvey, *American Geographics*, pp. 180–189.

[28] Samuel A. Bard [Ephraim George Squier], *Waikna. Adventures on the Mosquito Shore* (1855), Gainsville: University of Florida Press, 1965, p. 258.

[29] Bard, *Waikna*, p. 330.

of the unrelenting Itzaes of Yucatan', to gather new strength at the 'lake of the Itzaes'.[30]

Squier's literary production of a mythical remnant of the Maya nation, which further develops the rumour found in Stephens's travelogue, may be seen to answer to the ideological requirements of both imperialism—in constructing an indigenous ally in full possession of ancestral rights and ready to fend off not only Spanish but also British imperial rule—and of romanticism, in adding one more item to the impressive stock of late imperial romances à la Rider Haggard: stories of hidden ancestral treasure and powerful ancient dynasties secretly surviving in remote places and subterranean palaces but equipped with powers of biblical dimension.

Translating the anti-conquest

One last, and from a transnational perspective most interesting, example for Squier's ideological campaign in justifying a US presence at the Isthmus is the translation of a French travelogue which he organised, engaging his multilingual wife as translator and peppering the text with his own comments. Pierre Marie Arthur Morelet is today remembered as a naturalist specialising in molluscs, many of which still bear his name, as does a crocodile, *crocodylus morelitii*. Having taken part in a scientific expedition to Algeria in 1839, he subsequently collected specimens in Spain and Portugal and became one of Europe's best-known experts in the field of conchology. In 1846 and 1847 the aristocrat undertook a self-financed voyage to Yucatán whose scientific results he readily published for the Académie des Sciences in Paris. It was only in 1857 that he could be prevailed upon to also publish a narrative of his journey addressed to a broader readership. His *Voyage dans l'Amérique centrale, d'Ile de Cuba, et le Yucatan* sparked Squier's interest because Morelet had travelled to precisely the unexplored regions of the Petén district which so much preoccupied Squier's imagination. In fact it seems that Squier, in his description of the Lacandones in *The States of Central America*, had made use of information he found in Morelet's account. But the textual borrowing went in both directions.

By the time he published the English translation of Morelet's narrative under two different titles in 1871, *Travels in Central America, Including Accounts of Some Regions Unexplored since the Conquest* and the more sensationalist one, *Itza, or the Unexplored Regions of Central America*, Squier had made his truce with the British. In fact, he had offered his advice and expertise to the British government for building a railway line

---

[30] Bard, *Waikna*, p. 332.

across Honduras, printed with the same London publisher as the Morelet translation in 1857. The English version of Morelet's text, cut by several chapters (on the Atlantic crossing, on Cuba, on the route between the Pacific coast and Belize), is accompanied by Squier's introduction, which expresses his major reason for making this text available for an English-speaking public:

> Whoever glances at the map of Central America will observe a vast region, lying between Chiapas, Tabasco, Yucatan, and the Republic of Guatemala, and comprising a considerable part of each of those States, which, if not entirely a blank, is only conjecturally filled up with mountains, lakes, and rivers. It is almost as unknown as the interior of Africa itself.[31]

The proto-Conradian beginning quickly merges into an evocation of the well-known 'remnants of the ancient Itzaes, Lacandones, Choles, and Manches' who have so far resisted colonisation and still live according to the style of their ancestors. Within the depths of this untrodden region, Squier continues, only slightly modulating the text of his 1858 book,

> the popular tradition of Guatemala and Chiapas places that great aboriginal city, with its white walls shining like silver in the sun, which the cura of Quiché affirmed to Mr. Stephens he had seen, with his own eyes, from the tops of the mountains of Quesaltenango.
>
> It is a region, therefore, of singular interest, appealing equally to the geographer, the student of natural history, the antiquary and the ethnologist. And lying, moreover, almost at our own doors, rich in its resources and tempting in its natural wealth, it must soon appeal to that restless spirit of enterprise and commercial activity which, not content with its past triumphs, long for new conquests and a wider field of exercise.[32]

Momentarily forgetting that the volume is published with a British press, Squier continues to describe the various attempts of the Spaniards to subdue the Itzaes, their success in doing so in 1698, and accounts of their descendants haunting the region ever since. '[O]nly the vaguest notion exists

---

[31] Ephraim George Squier, 'Introduction', in Arthur Morelet, *Travels in Central America, Including Accounts of Some Regions Unexplored since the Conquest*, trans. Miriam Squier, London: Trübner, 1871, p. xi. Hereafter cited in the text as *Travels*.

[32] Squier, 'Introduction', in Arthur Morelet, *Travels*, p. xii.

of the remote district of Peten, and of the great Lake of Itza' and of the former 'metropolis of the Itzaes'.[33] He describes the natural surroundings as a hostile '*terra incognita*' awaiting to be brought 'within the circle of modern knowledge' by foreign exploration.[34] As a reason for his publication of Morelet's narrative he declares the strong 'appeal' it has 'to American interests', too strong indeed to be 'allowed to remain in the comparative obscurity to which the mistaken delicacy of its author would condemn it'.[35] Less delicately, Squier himself bans to obscurity the chapter referring to Cuba—another interest zone of the USA—as being of 'subordinate importance'.

A comparison with the French original shows that Squier tampered relatively little with the text in detail. In the beginning, long narrative sections are replaced with Squier's summaries and additional information. At the end of the second volume the reasons given for Morelet's hasty departure upon receiving news from home that demanded his instant return in 1847 somewhat differ from the original.[36] More interesting is the mutual traffic that took place between the texts of the two travellers. Having finished his account of his journey across Guatemala, Morelet, in the French original, abandons his usual narrative style and, jumping ahead of time (a practice found nowhere else in his 600-page tome), gives a highly tendentious account of the British activities at the Mosquito Coast taken straight out of Squier's anti-British writings—both a précis of his position published in Paris in 1856 and longer passages taken from his sensationalist novel, *Waikna* (*Voyage*, II, 300–306). Without being able to verify the impact that Squier had on that part of Morelet's text, it is interesting to note that just these passages are missing from the British version of 1871. Since 1860, the diplomatic

---

[33] Squier, 'Introduction', in Arthur Morelet, *Travels* , p. xiv.

[34] Squier, 'Introduction', in Arthur Morelet, *Travels* , p. xv.

[35] Squier, 'Introduction', in Arthur Morelet, *Travels* , p. xvi.

[36] Without explaining what precisely demanded his return, the social unrest preceding the *annus mirabilis* 1848 is referred to in both texts: while Squier reminds his readers of the remote events ('the flight of King Louis Philippe, [...] which [...] made the year 1848 one of the most memorable in history', *Travels*, p. 413), Morelet more explicitly articulates the sentiments of his own class. 'Enfin, nous arrivâmes en France, le 22 février 1848, au début de cette révolution inouïe qui mit les destinées d'un grand pays entre les mains d'une poignée de conspirateurs et de factieux' ('We finally arrived in France, on the 22nd of February 1848, at the beginning of that unheard of revolution which put the destinies of a great country into the hands of a handful of conspirators and insurgents'). Arthur Morelet, *Voyage dans l'Amérique Centrale, l'Île de Cuba et le Yucatan*, Paris: Gide et J. Baudry, 1857, 2 vols., II, p. 307. Hereafter cited in the text as *Voyage*.

relations between Britain and the USA with regard to the isthmus area had developed into a collaborative effort to build a railway through Honduras or Nicaragua.[37] Apart from this anachronism, Morelet's text offers little to substantiate Squier's greatest desire—proof for the existence of living Maya in Petén. Although the French traveller gives a detailed account of his journey to Flores, the district town located at the site of the ancient Itza, as well as lengthy summaries of all the knowledge he can find on the wild Lacandones and on ancient ruins nearby, he is ultimately unable to find out more due to the secretiveness of the local population and due to a prolonged fever which had bound him to his hammock while at Flores. On account of the natural spatial limitations of Flores he denies the possibility that this could ever have been an important establishment (or 'metropolis', as Squier has it). Directly addressing the local legend that migrates through the texts of Stephens and Squier, he adds:

> As to the existence of a mysterious city, inhabited by the Indians who still live in the centre of Peten, as they did of old, pursuing all their ancient habits and practices—this is a notion which must take its place among the fancies of the imagination. This tale originated in Yucatan, and travelers in relating it, have given it far too great prominence. The Indian villages of the district of Peten are small and squalid. The inhabitants are subject to the laws of the country, and if a few tribes escape from the Spanish jurisdiction, it is only at the price of dispersion and poverty that they enjoy their independence. (*Travels*, 242–243)

Although Squier adds a long footnote referring to yet more local legends about Itza, Morelet has with one stroke disproven Squier's fantastic claim; moreover, having been to the place himself, he also shows that there is nothing mysterious or inapproachable about it: Flores is a remotely located, underdeveloped, and boring district town, fortunately—for Morelet the naturalist—surrounded by interesting fauna and flora, which he describes at length.

Yet, as neither Morelet apparently knew in 1846 nor Squier in 1871, a gigantic *ruined* Maya city *had* been found just a three-day journey away from Flores. The expedition to the ruins of Tikal, one of the largest sites of the pre-classical period (c.600 BC–c.600 AD), had started on its search in February 1848, just a few months after Morelet had left the area, and concurrently with the outbreak of the Caste War. The expedition was led by Modesto Méndez, the *corregidor* of the district of Petén in Guatemala. The

---

[37] Dunkerley, *Americana*, p. 611.

party started from Flores on 23 February and reached Tikal after a three-day journey on foot. The members of the party undertook basic measurements of the buildings, caused some destruction while trying to break through a wall in search of treasure, enjoyed the view from the high towers of Tikal, copied some of the glyphs and images they found on bas-reliefs, found footprints and arrows of the Lacandones, and took possession of the ruins in the name of the Republic of Guatemala by inscribing their names on the walls. One of the indigenous officials, governor Tut, promised to show Méndez a stone engraved with the image of a bull some three leagues distant, which, they conclude, must be evidence that the ancient Maya did domesticate cattle.[38] The report was printed in the newspaper *Gaceta de Guatemala*.[39] The discovery became known outside of the Spanish-reading world through the publication of Méndez's report in German translation in the first edition of the *Zeitschrift für allgemeine Erdkunde*, edited by the famous German geographer Carl Ritter in 1853. In the German edition, it is accompanied by explanatory remarks and an appendix that betray a remarkable knowledge of the history and present exploration of ancient sites in Mesoamerica. While the 'Geh.[eimer] Finanzrath Hesse', the royal Prussian agent for Central America, demonstrates his expertise on both the history and the present state of the area, the appendix, written by the German-Baltic traveller Jégor von Sivers, summarises all the relevant sources on Yucatán, from Villagutierre, Juarros, and Herrera to Waldeck, Kingsborough, and Stephens, and his US epigone, Benjamin Moore Norman.[40] His report, which takes most of its information from Stephens's two travelogues, unsurprisingly ends with an account of the defeat of the inhabitants of Itza in 1698 and with a reference to Stephens's as well as Squier's accounts of the living city. He also mentions that Squier, in a publication on the antiquities and linguistic situation in Nicaragua, writes of having sent a native pioneer to find out more about the ancient yet still inhabited Maya city. The man, according to von Sivers, confirmed the rumours of a *ruined* city, 'thereby depriving the ghost of that ancient and allegedly still independent and inhabited city of its credibility'.[41] The authors of these texts deem it likely that the rumours

---

[38] Modesto Méndez, 'Ueber neue Entdeckungen und Beobachtungen in Guatemala und Yucatan', *Zeitschrift für allgemeine Erdkunde*, 1 (1853), pp. 61–68.

[39] Robert C. Aguirre, *Informal Empire. Mexico and Central America in Victorian Culture*, Minneapolis: University of Minnesota Press, 2005, p. 90, 178, n. 74. The Spanish text was reprinted in *Anales de la Socieded de geografía e historia de Guatemala*, 7, no. 1 (1930), pp. 88–94.

[40] Jégor von Sivers, 'Yucatan, seine Literatur und seine Alterthümer', *Zeitschrift für allgemeine Erdkunde*, 1 (1853), pp. 79–93.

[41] '[...] wodurch das Gespenst jener alten angeblich noch frei bewohnten Stadt immer

spread by Stephens, Squier, and others refer to Tikal, the 'ghostly' metropolis which had been deserted for centuries even when the Spaniards arrived and whose very name had fallen prey to historical oblivion—'Tikal' simply means 'ruined palaces'.[42]

It seems that the year 1848 was rich in ghosts—be it spectral Maya cities or the spectre of communism. As Robert Aguirre shows, the discovery of Tikal also became known to the masterminds of empire in London, either through the German translation or through direct information sent to the Foreign Office from Belize together with reports on the Caste War.[43] Aguirre also shows that Britain was interested in acquiring one of the ancient Maya cities in order to transport its remains to London. The scheme failed partly because of the difficulty in removing the ruins and partly because of an excess of communication and the resulting inertia of the British colonial bureaucracy.[44] John Lloyd Stephens was engaged in a similar run on the treasures of American antiquity—only that the US invention of a national past was coupled with aspirations to a continentalist future, based on the logic of geographical determinism and territorial adjacency.[45]

What's more interesting in our context, however, is the 'translation' of knowledge on the fabled Maya city between Guatemala, the USA, France, Great Britain, and Germany. The fact that the scholars involved were multilingual (or, as in Squier's case, had a multilingual wife) did not prevent the partial blockage of important knowledge on some of the transnational information channels. Squier was apparently unaware of the German translation of the Tikal report, even though he was very much aware of the work of the editor of the journal in which it appeared: he had even dedicated his 1855 book *Notes on Central America* to Carl Ritter. The list of references appended to his introduction to his wife's translation of Morelet's *Voyage* contains several German texts (both in translation and in

---

mehr an Glaubwürdigkeit verliert' (Sivers, 'Yucatan', p. 192).

[42] Modesto Méndez and Finanzrath Hesse, 'Erläuternde Bemerkungen zu den Federzeichnungen der Monumente von Tikal und Dolores', *Zeitschrift für allgemeine Erdkunde*, 1 (1853), pp. 170–175, at 175.

[43] Aguirre, *Informal Empire*, p. 178, n. 73.

[44] Aguirre, *Informal Empire*, pp. 88–97. Two other candidates for removal were Quiriguá and Copán.

[45] Stephens articulates a need for national comparison when he asserts that '[t]he casts of the Parthenon are regarded as precious memorials in the British Museum, and casts of Copán would be the same in New-York', *ITCA*, I, pp. 115–116. See Evans, *Romancing the Maya*, and Mackenthun, 'Conquest of Antiquity'. For 'geographical determinism' and 'adjacency' see Weinberg, *Manifest Destiny*, chapter 2.

the original) by writers such as Carl Scherzer, Moritz Wagner, and Julius Froebel.[46]

In fact, the vicinity of the names of Carl Ritter (1779–1859), the founder of modern geography in the German lands, and Carl Scherzer (1821–1903), the Austrian scientific traveller and propagator of emigration, stresses the division that runs through the whole discourse on Mesoamerica—and scientific discourse generally—at the time. While Ritter's geographical vision was strongly indebted to the holistic and humanistic approach of Humboldt (1768–1859) and even carries significant theological overtones, Scherzer represents the very opposite approach: as a representative of the imperial Austrian government he was seeking to lay the ideological groundwork for mass emigration and colonisation of the states of Central America, as well as the exploitation of their products, with apparently few qualms about legal or moral complexities. His two-volume report on his circumnavigation on board the imperial Austrian ship *Novara* in 1857–1859 gives evidence of this new taxonomic and economic mentality, completely devoid of romantic residues such as Stephens's and Squier's hidden city. Scherzer collects all available information on the size, number, and frequency of ships passing the isthmus, as well as all available and commercially useful data on the products of the countries he visits—just as Squier did when he made a proposal to the British for the joint construction of a railway across Honduras.[47]

This is a far cry from the philosophical approach to nature represented by Carl Ritter, to whom Squier surprisingly dedicated one of his books. Working as a school teacher most of his life, Ritter, inspired by and collaborating with Pestalozzi, made significant contributions to the reformation of school teaching, especially in the fields of geography and history. Dedicated to the holistic Humboldtian view, Ritter set out to write a definitive work on the geographical composition of the world, but he did not get beyond Africa (one volume) and Asia (20 volumes). Contrary to most of his contemporaries,

---

[46] Squier, 'Introduction', in Morelet, *Travels*, p. xvii.

[47] Squier, *Honduras Interoceanic Railway*; Carl Scherzer, *Wanderungen durch die mittel-amerikanischen Freistaaten Nicaragua, Honduras und San Salvador. Mit Hinblick auf deutsche Emigration und deutschen Handel*, Braunschweig: Georg Westermann, 1857, Karl von Scherzer, *Reise der österreichischen Fregatte Novara um die Erde in den Jahren 1857, 1858, 1859 unter den Befehlen des Commodore B. von Wüllerstorf-Urbair*, 2 vols., Wien, 1865. Scherzer's activity falls into the imperial post-Habsburgian period when Austria was involved in various international conflicts, including the Crimean War. Infected with the germ of scientific racism, he praises the great advantages of a 'nordic emigration' to Mesoamerica, and en passant he mentions that the Nicaraguan lead, gold, and gem mines are all controlled by US companies (Scherzer, *Wanderungen*, p. 170).

Ritter did not subscribe to the doctrine of nationalism but viewed the spatial order of the world in terms of the 'lawful order between space and the history of its populations'.[48] Retaining a pietistic sense of creation as the work of a divine intelligence, Ritter sought to reconcile the notion of the shaping impact of the natural environment on human action with the idea of man's freedom of decision. In this he was, in the words of Büttner and Hoheisel, 'a real possibilist'.[49] Like many of his contemporaries, he regarded North America as the place where human civilisation would realise its best potential.

Not surprisingly, knowledge of Ritter's work faded shortly after his death in 1859—the year that so shattered the Bible-based view of natural history. But while his ideas seemed antiquated in nationalist and industrialising Europe, they fell on fertile ground in the USA, especially through the impact of his pupil Arnold Guyot. This Swiss intellectual refugee of 1848 spread Ritter's geographical ideas during a celebrated lecture tour in Boston and other parts of New England and the subsequent publication of *Earth and Man* (1849), which would run through numerous editions in the USA for decades to come.[50] Obviously the difference in reception is related to the different reaction to—that is, rejection of—Darwinism in the USA. Ritter's and Guyot's concept of an organic unity between man and creation was doubtlessly favoured by an intellectual world strongly influenced by the very similar ideas of transcendentalism, the USA's secular religion at mid-century.

As the circulation of knowledge about the expedition to Tikal, and Squier's dedication of his work to Ritter suggest, the discourse about Central America and Yucatán in the mid nineteenth century must be seen as a complex translational space, not only in the sense of literal translation but also as a site of travelling knowledges, whose significance changes according to the discursive context in which they are used. In such a situation, anachronisms and ideological inconsistencies are predictable. Like Carl Ritter, Arthur Morelet belongs to that group of writers whose approach to nature and its

---

[48] Manfred Büttner and Karl Hoheisel, 'Carl Ritter (7. August 1779 bis 28. September 1859)', in Manfred Büttner, ed., *Carl Ritter. Zur europäisch-amerikanischen Geographie an der Wende vom 18. zum 19. Jahrhundert*, Paderborn: Schönigh, 1980, pp. 85–110, at 96.

[49] Büttner and Hoheisel, 'Carl Ritter', p. 102.

[50] Büttner and Hoheisel, 'Carl Ritter', p. 104. In going to the USA, Guyot followed the call of his compatriot Louis Agassiz who had already left in 1846 and who introduced Guyot into the American scientific community. On Guyot's influence in the USA, see Richard Harthorne and Klaus D. Gurgel, 'Zu Carl Ritters Einfluss auf die Entwicklung der Geographie in den Vereinigten Staaten von Amerika', in Manfred Büttner, ed. *Carl Ritter*, pp. 201–219.

beings is still guided by a humanistically-inspired reverence for creation that has, in Pratt's words, a 'utopian, innocent vision of European global authority'.[51] These qualities are readily, and very competently, translated by Miriam Squier, not without adding a moralising twist here or the full text of a psalm there.[52] Though taking a scientific approach to American nature, Morelet's vision completely differs from the utilitarian (ir)rationality of Ephraim Squier. While spending a fortnight in the ruins of Palenque, together with his French servant Morin and the dog Fido whom they had picked up in the nearby village, Morelet is enraptured by the sights and sounds of the surrounding nature:

> When night fell, [...] the ruins appeared to be enchanted, and I can well conceive that the superstitious terrors of the Indians would prevent their remaining here in the darkness. They imagine that the place is haunted by the spirits of its early occupants; that by moonlight the bas-reliefs become invested with life, and that the warriors step out of their stone frames and stalk through the sombre galleries.
>
> For my own part, although without fear of these nocturnal visitors, there were times when I could not avoid some little superstitious emotion. Tiny, winged lamps seemed floating in the atmosphere, first with the brilliancy of a spark, then with a fugitive brightness which lost itself in a train of light; at the same time undefinable sounds seemed to proceed from all parts of the woods—not terrific [...] but soft and sweet like the music of birds, and as mysterious as the accents of an unknown tongue. I seemed to detect life in all things around me; the plants, the trees, the old walls themselves, appeared imbued with its spirit, and to speak a language of their own. [...] Now it was like the silvery tinkle of

---

[51]   Pratt, *Imperial Eyes*, pp. 38–39.

[52]   When Morelet philosophically writes, 'Les ruines de Palenque nous présentent, par le mystère impénétrable dont elles sont enveloppées, un exemple saisissant du néant de l'humanité' (*Voyage*, I, pp. 273–274), Mrs. Squier supplements the reference to the 'nothingness of humanity' with a remark on the 'vanity of man's attempts to perpetuate his own glory' (*Travels*, p. 98)—a remark that may be read as a critique of her own husband's jingoistic pursuits (she would force a divorce trial two years later). Morelet finishes his text with an evocation of God's grandeur: 'l'image du créateur m'est apparue dans toute sa majesté, et [...] je me suis écrié avec le Psalmiste: 'Seigneur, je vous louerai parce que votre grandeur a éclaté d'une manière étonnante; vos ouvrages sont admirables, et mon âme en est pénétrée' (Ps. 138)' (*Voyage*, II, p. 307). The translation contains the whole psalm (*Travels*, p. 414). For a summary of the public scandal that Squier's private life caused, see Terry E. Barnhart, 'Epilogue. Insanity and the "Eclipse of Genius"', in *Ephraim George Squier*, pp. 317–332.

a little bell, or a plaintive voice calling in the distance, then a rustling sound, and next a sob from the interior of the ruins. Again, it was like a thousand gentle whispers, a thousand little cadences, celebrating, in a universal concert, the coolness and magnificence of the night. At one time I surprised a frog on the staircase, whose croakings had mystified us, from its resemblance to the barking of a dog. Even Fido had been equally deceived with ourselves, and during our first night in the ruins had kept up a reciprocal chorus with this inhabitant of the stream. (*Travels*, 100–101; *Voyage*, I, 274–275)

The French original continues to describe the author's feeling of speechless awe: 'le trouble inexprimable dont mon âme était agitée, en présence de ces débris sans nom et de cette nature inconnue, s'associaient à une admiration respectueuse pour l'intelligence toute-puissante, qui semblait tirer du néant un monde que j'avais ignoré' (*Voyage*, I, 276). Yet, being a naturalist intent on advancing the knowledge of the world by defining new species, Morelet excitedly leaves the ruined city the next morning and follows the sounds of a rare bird whose song, he writes, was 'clear, limpid, and full of cadence, such as those produced by a musical box. [...] I shouldered my gun with the liveliest satisfaction, and started in pursuit of the unseen musician' (*Travels*, 101–102). Paying little attention to land marks, he follows the enchanting bird farther and farther into the wilderness. But instead of getting a shot at it, he soon finds himself lost in the intractable forest. After several minutes of fearful paralysis, he musters his wit and begins to systematically explore the surroundings, always keeping his point of origin in sight and backtracking when the direction proves wrong. As the day moves toward dusk, having bruised his knee with a pointed rock during a fall, and beginning to seriously suffer from thirst, Morelet finally finds his way back to Palenque just before nightfall. His servant Morin, 'in his anxiety for me, had forgotten to prepare supper, and as a crowning misfortune, Fido, disgusted with so long a fast, devoured greedily the collection of birds and insects which had cost me so dear' (*Travels*, 107). He never hears the sound of the wonderful bird again, but the next morning he re-establishes his collector's ego by killing 'a superb *hocco* (*crax alector*, L.)'.

Morelet offers several more entertaining anecdotes of picaresque adventures whose literary effect is heightened by the frequent inclusion of dialogues with his uneducated but witty companions—his French servant and native guides. His text also offers serious and extremely well-written descriptions of the natural world he encounters, which betray his scholarly expertise. What the text does not contain, however, is hard evidence for the existence of Stephens's and Squier's living Maya city. Rather the opposite:

Morelet, who has spent several weeks in Flores due to a prolonged fever, knows for sure, from frequent conversations with the locals, that there is no such city nearby. Neither is there anything mysterious about the Lake Petén or the location of Itza, the site having been renamed Flores by the Spanish conquistadores after its destruction in 1698. It is now the seat of the district government of Vera Paz. He regrets not having been able to go and explore the surroundings of Flores himself due to his illness, thus not being able 'to add any information to the knowledge which we possess concerning the antiquities of the country. [...] May some more fortunate traveller profit by my hints and fulfill the task which I had marked out, and save from oblivion [...] the last vestiges of Maya civilization in these regions' (*Travels*, 241; *Voyage*, II, 65–66).

Though much more indebted to the romantic tradition of natural history than either Stephens or Squier, Morelet provides information that definitely transports their mysterious city to the world of colonial fairy tales. Yet, it is strange that Morelet seems to have heard nothing about the existence of Tikal which, as mentioned above, is located only three days from Flores. Perhaps anticipating the consequences of divulging their knowledge to strangers, the natives of Petén knew how to keep their secret about their ruined palaces with tops as high as to allow views of such faraway places as the Bay of Belize.

Neither is Morelet more successful in discovering durable evidence of the existence of survivors of the ancient Maya. He makes occasional contact with Caribs and Lacandones, without clearly distinguishing between the two groups (*Travels*, 155). While underway by boat he and his Indian guides encounter a canoe occupied by one of 'the independent or unconquered Indians'. Being 'deeply interested' in having 'a nearer sight of this child of nature', he orders to give chase. Having captured the man Morelet explains to him that he 'had no hostile designs, but, on the contrary', wanted to 'elevate him to the dignity of our pilot, with liberal recompense for his services'. He notices, however, that his captive did not share his fondness for this plan, neither does he give away any useful information when asked. But the rum they give him to drink

> acted at the same time upon his brain and the muscles of his tongue, which at last began to perform its functions. I questioned him concerning the ancient ruins which have been (erroneously I think) described as existing near this locality. Our Indian confirmed what I had previously heard at Tenosique, namely, that no ruins are to be found here. Perhaps the castellated rocks which I have before mentioned, have led to this error, and credit has thus been given to human industry

for a simple freak of nature. It would indeed be astonishing if there existed ruins of importance on the upper course of the Usumasinta, since the annals of the new world do not mention any civilization or culture in all the mountainous region to the east of Peten. (*Travels*, 155; *Voyage* I, 317–318)

And he mentions, as he would again later, that 'these unexplored Cordilleras' were inhabited by 'poor, inoffensive savages' who avoid contact with the Spaniards and only occasionally come to the settlements for the purpose of trade. Not content with this sparse information, Squier adds two long footnotes referring to other reports, one of which does mention large ruins in the very region visited by Morelet while the other emphasises the unexplored state of that region, which 'is at present as little known as the interior of Africa'. He adds a long description of the Lacandones by the illustrious 'Count' Jean Frédéric Maximilien Waldeck, who had spent some time living in the ruins of Palenque in 1832–1833 and published his widely read account of his journey in 1838. Waldeck, of course, had never been near Petén (*Travels*, 155–157).

Having questioned his prisoner, Morelet and his companions prepare for the night. After a rather comic dialogue assessing the dangers of a Carib attack, they decide to place their prisoner between them. On the next morning, the prisoner is gone, together with his boat (*Travels*, 158).

Topographies of deep space

Squier's attempt to adapt Morelet's travelogue to his ideological narrative about the existence of a hidden Maya city in the unexplored depths of Yucatán or Guatemala may be regarded as a leftover from his earlier massive campaign in favour of an American intervention in the isthmus region in the 1850s. Since the conquests of Mexico and Peru, the lure of secret civilisations and secret treasure has, after all, been one of the motors of the mythology of adventure and consequently of imperial expansion.

The ideology of adventure celebrated one of its peaks in the romantic historiography of the nineteenth century. The economic and political activities of the USA in Mesoamerica in the 1850s were strongly aided by the circulation of Prescott's romanticised versions of the Spanish conquest of Mexico and Peru, which raised Hernán Cortés to the quintessential model of heroic imperial action.[53] In the context of modern global capitalism,

---

[53] Martin Green names the deeds of Cortés as one of three models for modern adventure literature, Robert Clive's battles in India in the 1750s and Napoleon's march

adventure fictions, mixing the medieval knight and the early modern military leader with the contemporary figure of the adventure capitalist, mercenary, or (as in Poe and Verne) scholar, provided the ideological imaginary for an expansive transnational merchant empire. In the hands of Squier, owing to his strong emphasis on racial degeneration, romantic mystery is shot through with what Brantlinger has called the imperial gothic[54]—a lingering anxiety about the success and permanence of imperial control, as well as about the danger of cultural disintegration through biological degeneration. In fact, the fear of racial amalgamation was perhaps the major argument against a straightforward conquest of Mesoamerican states.[55]

Yet, as Bruce Harvey suggests, the fascination with hidden ancient civilisations—the desire for authentically pre-modern or non-modern geographical realms untouched by telegraph and steam power—also reflects a scientific interest in 'deep spaces', usually in combination with the notion of 'deep time'. This scientific discourse of depth is best evidenced in the burgeoning field of geology and (one should add with regard to

---

on Egypt in 1798 being the other two (*Dreams of Adventure, Deeds of Empire*, New York: Basic Books, 1979, chapter 1).

[54] Brantlinger regards the imperial gothic as expressing 'anxieties about the waning of religious orthodoxy, but even more clearly it expresses anxieties about the ease with which civilization can revert to barbarism or savagery and thus about the weakening of Britain's imperial hegemony'. The principal themes of the imperial gothic are 'individual regression or going native', the 'invasion of civilization by the forces of barbarism', and the 'diminution of opportunities for adventure and heroism in the modern world' (Patrick Brantlinger, *Rule of Darkness. British Literature and Imperialism, 1830–1914*, Ithaca: Cornell University Press, 1988, pp. 229–230).

[55] Jefferson's famous evocation of a hemispheric Anglo-Saxon empire (in a letter to James Monroe, 1801) is coupled with the fear of racial mixture: 'However our present interests may restrain us within our own limits, it is impossible not to look forward to distant times when our rapid multiplication will expand itself beyond those limits, and cover the whole northern, if not the southern continent, with a people speaking the same language, governed in similar forms, and by similar laws; nor can we contemplate with satisfaction either blot or mixture on that surface' (quoted in Frederick Merk, *Manifest Destiny and Mission in American History* [1963], Cambridge MA: Harvard University Press, 1995, p. 9). The annexation of Texas in 1845 was applauded because the Mexican territory had been taken over by 'Anglo-Saxon' settlers coming from the USA. The Mexicans were regarded as a mongrel race, indolent, irrational, and Catholic. The admission of such a population, it was believed, might endanger the principles of democracy just as it would threaten the racial integrity of the USA. Thus the fear of racial hybridisation—the loss of Anglo-Saxon features due to racial amalgamation—inflected the desire for territorial expansion. Ironically, the major ideologemes of American imperial expansion, racial supremacy and quasi-religious civilisational mission, tended to impair each other out of a fear of racial amalgamation.

Mesoamerica) vulcanology. Harvey reads this, especially with reference to Melville's obsession with metaphors of depth, as part of an aesthetic of the sublime in response to religious disenchantment—the loss of a sense of a beginning and an end to natural history: 'The paradox of the empirical uncovering of strata' suggests that 'even as sacred history was replaced by the evidence of the rocks, the geological images of stratification or a succession of limits ultimately suggested a limitless, open-ended sublimity, a horror vacui'.[56] In the field of archaeology, the desire to lay open ruined cities may be viewed as part of the same desire to know and expose to view the 'antique and exotic haunts of time', not just of European, Christian time but also of the inscrutable temporality of other cultures. The ruined cities of Mesoamerica confronted Western travellers and scholars with the challenge of an 'other' temporality in the first place. While the language of racial savagism, deployed in descriptions of Mesoamerica's indigenous and black populations, fundamentally denied any historical coevalness between them and Western cultures, the encounter with illegible but apparently complex chronicles carved into ancient monuments of unknown age seriously threatened this cultural self-image. Ancient certainties about the extent of space and time evaporated in the light of new scientific discoveries. Like Rider Haggard's Ayesha, surviving since time immemorial to threaten the British Empire with her knowledge and occult power, the story of the hidden Maya city raised the spectre of a culture whose secret knowledge may threaten all of modernity's grandiose inventions with sacerdotal superiority.

Panama—Petersburg

In February 1850, a young merchant from Petersburg (but actually born in Mecklenburg) left from Liverpool on the steamer *Africa* for California in order to claim the inheritance of his dead brother who had followed the lure of gold but lost his life to the typhoid fever. After a most enjoyable time in New York our entrepreneur, according to his diary, paid his respects to President Fillmore, who introduced him to Mr. Webster, Mr. Clay, and other leading politicians. We now know that this part of his diary, like some others, was invented. As it is, our traveller passed the isthmus on Stephens's Panama railroad with some effort and was amazed at the improvised state of the infrastructure. He claimed his brother's money in Sacramento and

---

[56] Bruce Harvey, 'Melville, Deep Time, and the World in Ruins. Or, Digging toward Eternity', in Gesa Mackenthun and Sünne Juterczenka, eds., *The Fuzzy Logic of Encounter. New Perspectives on Cultural Contact*, Münster: Waxmann, 2009, pp. 207–227, at 221, 217.

increased it by way of intelligent loaning and speculation, being an expert in this field. 'My purchases', he writes, 'go for the most part to the house of Rothschild at London, whose branch-establishment at San Francisco supplies me by every night's steamer with the necessary Coin'. His bank 'is from early till late constantly jammed, crammed and rammed full of people from all nations and I have to speak all the day long in 8 languages. In fact if I knew a hundred languages it would not be sufficient to speak to every one in his native tongue'. In spite of his huge financial success he decides to return to Petersburg out of fear of being robbed and out of homesickness. He nearly dies of fever and hunger during the return journey (the Panama rail link still being very unreliable), but returns to Petersburg a rich man, and increases his wealth by trading in colonial products before and during the American Civil War, especially in cotton, sugar, and indigo. Having amassed a significant fortune by way of 'original accumulation', trade in the slave-based Atlantic economy, and speculation, our modern adventure capitalist decides to give up the nerve-wrecking merchant life in favour of a life for the sciences. He returns to a childhood dream of a fabled ancient city whose location is unknown and thought to be purely poetic. He takes the account of Homer literally and discovers the remains of Troy in 1871–1873.[57] John Lloyd Stephens and Heinrich Schliemann may have met, as Victor von Hagen claims,[58] or they may not—there is no mention of a meeting in Schliemann's travel diary. The co-presence of these two early archaeologists at the site of capitalism and tropical fever exquisitely illustrates the elusiveness and unpredictability of imperial science's mythical geography. The story of the imperial topography of archaeology has only just begun to be written.

---

[57] The summary and quotations above are taken from Heinrich Schliemann, *Schliemann's First Visit to America, 1850–1851*, ed., Shirley H. Weber, Cambridge, MA: Harvard University Press, 1942, pp. 21–82; quotations at pp. 66, 67, 68. For a good summary of Schliemann's early career, see Justus Cobet, *Heinrich Schliemann. Archäologe und Abenteurer*, München: C. H. Beck, 1997, pp. 30–54.

[58] Von Hagen, *Maya Explorer*, p. 296.

Space Age Tropics

Mimi Sheller

Bulldozers uproot ancient rainforest and the sacred mountains of indigenous tribal peoples, explosives blast away the outer crust of earth and giant trucks move in, digging their claws deep into the exposed bauxite ore. A reddish dust fills the air, eventually settling on every leaf, roof and lung for miles around. The bauxite ore is washed, strained, baked and dried into a fine powdery dust. Poured into the deep holds of ships, the alumina crosses the world in search of cheap electricity, drawn to the raging rivers and geological forces that have been tamed to feed the smelters. Into the mile-long lines of smelter pots it pours, where a jolt of electric current awakens the secretive metal from its oxide slumber. Electrons jump to order, molten shining metal forms like lava around the cathode of a carbon crucible. The alchemical forces of the universe are unleashed, setting in motion an alluvial flow of aluminium. Out of the pots, presses and rollers, a tidal wave of castings, forgings and sheets of metal enter the factories of the world to be turned into finished goods like car parts and airplane fuselages, cans and wrappers, kitchenware and foil, chairs and satellites.

All of the airplanes, computers, satellites and communication systems that keep our world moving owe their existence to aluminium. Many technologies associated with mobility not only depend on this light metal, but also depend more deeply on the *idea of mobility* that aluminium enabled. We get so used to the powers and possibilities of aluminium that we take it for granted and begin to forget it is there. A multitude of metal products travels around the world, passing through our hands, lifted to our lips, lifting us off our feet—lightweight cans, food packaging, trains and planes, and the orbiting satellites that connect our phone calls. Light, fleet, it makes us feel like we can fly. Aluminium creates the invisible metallic infrastructure of modernity that puts people and things in motion. Meanwhile, far up in space a ring of satellites and space debris circles the Earth like an aluminium halo, echoing Space Age fantasies of mobility and connectivity and Cold War fears of global destruction, as it drifts amongst a light haze of aluminium dust left from the trails of rocket fuel.

A good portion of the world's alumina-bearing bauxite ore was first wrested from the tropical earth of Suriname and Jamaica. Just as anthropologist Sidney Mintz showed in his classic study *Sweetness and Power* how the modern Atlantic world was built upon Caribbean plantations and European sugar consumption in the age of slavery, we could say that bauxite/ aluminium offers a successor to that story, a re-working of the material relation between Northern urban metropoles and Caribbean peripheries of modernity.[1] The emergence of industrial-scale smelting in the 1890s updated the asymmetric global relations of Empire by recombining the emerging technologies of mobility, speed, and flight in the North, with the heavier, slower technologies of mining, labour exploitation, and resource extraction in the American Tropics.

This essay draws on my work in progress, *Aluminum Dreams: Lightness, Speed, Modernity*, which traces the silvery thread of aluminium across time and space back to its source in the tropics. It is a little known tale that encapsulates the making of global modernity, the creation of multinational corporations, the rise of the USA as a world power, the modernisation of warfare, the invention of 1950s suburbia and the American Dream—but also many other Aluminium Dreams around the world. Especially pertinent here are those of the Caribbean nations, on the verge of independence, pursuing the 'lift-off' of modernisation as described by W. W. Rostow in his 1960 classic *The Stages of Economic Development*, a bitter fledgling experience out of which would emerge not a flight toward economic modernity, but a sharpening of Caribbean theories of underdevelopment and dependent development.[2]

There are two faces to aluminium—the ethereal lightness of modernity's dreams of mobility, speed, and faster communication, on the one hand, and the heavy burdens of modernisation on the other: the gritty labour of mining, the waste of open-cast mines and mud lakes left behind, and the destructive power of explosives and weaponry it makes. These are the counterpoints of the Space Age Tropics. Like fleet-footed Mercury, the messenger of the gods, locked in brotherhood with Vulcan, 'a god who

---

[1] Sidney Mintz, *Sweetness and Power: The Place of Sugar in Modern History*, New York: Penguin Books, 1986.

[2] W. W. Rostow, *The Stages of Economic Growth: A Non-Communist Manifesto* [1960], Cambridge: Cambridge University Press, 1990; Brian Meeks and Norman Girvan, eds., *Caribbean Reasonings: The Thought of New World, The Quest for Decolonisation*, Kingston: Ian Randle, 2010.

does not roam the heavens but lurks at the bottom of craters, shut up in his smithy, where he tirelessly forges objects …'; Italo Calvino reminds us that 'to Mercury's aerial flight, Vulcan replies with his limping gait and the rhythmic beat of his hammer'.[3] Lightness and weightiness, beautiful arts and destructive weaponry, flight through the air and descent into the dark depths of the earth, are all part of aluminium's meaning and impact. And like West Africa's Ogun (or Haiti's Ogou), the god of iron-forging, weaponry, and technology—who was carried over to the Americas in Haitian Vodou—metallic modernity bears a two-edged sword of creativity and destruction.[4]

If the aluminium of the twentieth-century USA came largely from the bauxite mines of the Caribbean, how does the age of aluminium look from its sites of production in the Caribbean? What other modernities exist behind its shiny surface, underpinning the erstwhile sci-fi futures of the metallic metropolis and the domestic dreams of post-War suburbia? Perhaps the machinery of modernity looks more ominous from the other side of the bulldozers, freighters, conveyor belts, and power lines that ceaselessly suck aluminium from the earth's bauxite ores. We can reconnect the iconic objects of American modernism with the places in which their core material was produced through a close look at the visual images of the Caribbean circulated by aluminium producers themselves; the texts, musical recordings, and touristic practices that accompanied those images; and the counter-struggles of Caribbean people to exercise sovereignty over their own lands, resources, and self-representations.

Bauxite mining underpins a crucial connection between the production of the material culture and visual image of modernity in the USA in the age of aluminium, the parallel consumption of raw materials and visual images of tropical backwardness in the Caribbean, and the counter-production of a Caribbean modernity based on notions of national independence and resource sovereignty. In the North, the Caribbean has long served as a site of tropical semi-modernity, set apart from metropolitan modernity through forms of colonial exploitation and imperialist exotification of its 'colorful' people, 'vivid' nature, and 'dream-like' landscapes.[5] This essay will explore how the transnational aluminium industry contributed to producing these

---

[3] Italo Calvino, *Six Memos for the Next Millennium*, Cambridge MA: Harvard University Press, 1988, p. 55.

[4] Sandra T. Barnes, ed., *Africa's Ogun: Old World and New*, 2nd ed., Bloomington: Indiana University Press, 1997.

[5] Mimi Sheller, *Consuming the Caribbean: From Arawaks to Zombies*, London: Routledge, 2003; Krista Thompson, *An Eye for the Tropics*, Durham: Duke University Press, 2006.

divergent modernities. While the aluminium industry took off by promoting a gleaming aerodynamic modernism in its primary consumer markets in the USA, it simultaneously benefited from, and reproduced, a very different image of tropical temporal suspension in the Caribbean, which supported not only the projects of transnational mining companies from the 1920s to the 1970s, but also their offshoots into cruise tourism in the 1940s and 1950s.

The cool space-age futurism of aluminium modernity had to be purposefully and consciously constructed via its contrast with a backward world that was projected as a fascination with the steamy jungles of the tropics, the hybrid races of the Caribbean, and the pulsing music of the islands. This patronising imagery of the region as primitive, backward neighbours, which anthropologist Michel-Rolph Trouillot calls 'the Savage Slot', depended on the erasure of the very mining and processing industries that made modern technology possible.[6] The aesthetics of the age of aluminium were produced out of the exploitation of tropical lands and Caribbean peoples, an exploitation twice over as the under-developed tropics were geologically mined and visually represented as a tourist paradise to be consumed in images, music, and literature. And these physical and visual geographies of the twentieth century feed into contemporary debates over modernisation and development in the Caribbean today, in which bauxite and tourism remain key economic sectors, and 'representation' remains both a political problem and an issue central to Caribbean literary and artistic practice.

The material flows of mining and the mobility of light metals is intimately linked with the visual circulation of images of the Caribbean, and the embodied practices of tourism that connected the Caribbean and the USA. Here I offer a brief overview of the history of the aluminium industry in the Caribbean, then focus on reading a striking series of luxury magazine advertisements promoting the Caribbean cruises of the Alcoa Steamship Co. from 1948 to 1958. In this period Alcoa became the biggest producer of aluminium while Jamaica and Suriname became the two largest exporters of bauxite in the world. I explore how tropes of mobility and modernisation set the USA apart from the Caribbean, at the very moment when Caribbean colonies were attempting to assert resource sovereignty and new forms of political and cultural self-representation.

---

[6] Michel-Rolph Trouillot, *Global Transformations: Anthropology and the Modern World*, New York: Palgrave Macmillan, 2003.

Alcoa in the Caribbean: Suriname and the
Saamaka Maroon Territories

While the USA had some bauxite mines in Arkansas and Tennessee, Caribbean bauxite became the key source for US aluminium smelters throughout the mid-twentieth century. From early on in the expansion of the industry, the Aluminium Corporation of America, or Alcoa, 'went to the British and Dutch Guianas to explore their rich bauxite lands, and in December 1916, Alcoa organised the Surinaamsche Bauxite Maatchappij. Thereafter, all significant additions to Alcoa's bauxite reserves would come from overseas.'[7] US military might stood behind Alcoa's expansion into the region: 'In its search for new bauxite reserves, the aircraft industry made large investments in Suriname', according to Sandew Hira. 'A massive import of capital was accompanied by the stationing of a large and highly paid American army unit to protect the interests of … Alcoa.'[8] Alcoa first mined bauxite in Suriname in 1917, and later began producing alumina (the middle-stage in the process, which was then shipped to smelters in the USA) there in 1941. The Second World War created a worldwide surge in demand for aluminium, and Suriname remained the largest exporter of bauxite up until the 1960s, when it was surpassed by Jamaica.[9]

Military power enabled the USA to commandeer Caribbean resources, and no one consulted local people, especially indigenous people and Maroons, on the use of their lands. 'By far the largest development project ever carried out in Suriname was the construction of a hydroelectric dam and an artificial lake in order to generate electricity for an aluminium smelter' in 1966–1967.[10] The reservoir created by the hydroelectric dam effectively blasted a hole through Saamaka Maroon territory, covering the great rapids of Mamadan and some 43 villages, decimating a traditional culture that was highly place-based. Alcoa financed the Affobakka dam and the smelter at Paranam, while the Surinamese government agreed to relocate

---

[7] George D. Smith, *From Monopoly to Competition: The Transformation of Alcoa, 1888–1986*, Cambridge: Cambridge University Press, 1988, p. 98.

[8] Sandew Hira, 'Class Formation and Class Struggle in Suriname: the Background and Development of the Coup d'Etat', in Fitzroy Ambursley and Robin Cohen, eds., *Crisis in the Caribbean*, New York: Monthly Review Press, 1983, pp. 166–190, at 166.

[9] For a general history of Alcoa, see Charles C. Carr, *ALCOA: An American Enterprise*, New York: Rinehart & Co., 1952; and Smith, *From Monopoly to Competition*.

[10] Ellen-Rose Kambel, 'Land, Development, and Indigenous Rights in Suriname: The Role of International Human Rights Law', in Jean Besson and Janet Momsen, eds., *Caribbean Land and Development Revisited*, New York: Palgrave Macmillan, 2007, pp. 69–80, at 72.

the Saamaka Maroons whose territory was unilaterally appropriated. In the 1959 Brokopondo joint venture between the Government of Suriname and Alcoa, the Government agreed to give Alcoa exclusive rights to 'exploration for bauxite in a zone which is bounded by the Atlantic Ocean on the north, by the Fourth Parallel on the south, the Marowijne River on the east, and the Suriname River on the west'. They in return agreed to build a hydroelectric plant involving several dams and a reservoir predicted to rise 50 meters over the existing river elevation.[11]

Besides electricity generation and bauxite mining, the foreseen benefits of the project for Suriname included not only road construction that would make the region of the upper Suriname River more easily accessible, but also: 'Social Sector—Transmigration of native hinterland population ["bosland-bevolking"], including thereunder education, hygiene, medical attendance, intensifying agricultural and town-planning at Paranam. Recreation and Tourism—Along the edge of the lake and the nearby mountain-ranges'.[12] Thus the removal of the 'boslandbevolking', or people of the woodland, that is, the Maroons, was actually seen as one of the benefits of the project, as was the opening up of the interior to development and the potential for tourism. From the start tourists took to the ships making their way up the Suriname River (see Figure 1):

> For the tourist, there can be few thrills equal to that of winding for 10 to 12 hours between two constantly narrowing walls of jungle greenery, broken only occasionally by primitive Djoeka villages, until the tree branches actually scrape the sides of the vessel, and then suddenly and unexpectedly bursting out upon the spectacle of a colorful and modern industrial community in the heart of the jungle.[13]

A modern industrial community in the heart of the jungle would be the promised reward for modernisation, brought thanks to Alcoa.

---

[11] Richard Price, *First-Time: The Historical Vision of an Afro-American People*, Baltimore: Johns Hopkins University Press, 1983; and see Richard Price, *Travels with Tooy: History, Memory, and the African American Imagination*, Chicago: University of Chicago Press, 2008, pp. 174, 398, fn 5.

[12] Alcoa Archives, MSS 282, Subseries 6: Suriname Bauxite Company, Suriname, 1929–1973, Box 18, Booklet: 'BROKOPONDO joint venture SURINAME-SURALCO', stamped 1 October 1959 [Contract in Dutch and English], pp. 39, 41.

[13] *SURINAAMS BAUXIET / SURINAME BAUXITE: A Story of Cooperation in the Development of a Resource*, Paramaribo, Suriname: Suriname Bauxite Co., 1955 [in Dutch and English, published on the occasion of the first ever visit to Suriname by a Sovereign of the Kingdom of the Netherlands, Her Majesty Queen Juliana], p. 112.

Figure 1   A photographic view of a presumed Djoeka (Maroon) village from the
Suralco Freighter on the Suriname River (1955).

The gates of the dam were first closed off in February 1964, and the
flooding of the Suriname River reached its full height in July 1971, which
in fact ended up 80 meters above the original level.[14] According to Richard
Price, pre-eminent anthropologist of the Saamaka Maroons, 'approximately
half of traditional Saamaka territory was flooded in order to produce cheap
electricity for Alcoa's new smelter near the capital. Six thousand people
were forced to leave their homelands, some settling in special "transmigration villages" to the north of the [artificial] lake, others establishing
villages near its southern border'.[15] The transmigration villages lacked basic
facilities, including electricity, while the power lines to Alcoa's smelter ran
nearby. They were also not given secure land tenure. Price bitterly describes
the mid-twentieth century in Suriname in these terms: 'The colonial state

[14]   Alcoa Archives, MSS 282, Subseries 6: Suriname Bauxite Company, Suriname,
1929–1973, Box 17, Folder 5, Fact Sheet: Suriname Aluminum Company.
[15]   Price, *First-Time*, front matter.

and Alcoa get tough and unilaterally appropriate one-half of Saamaka territory for a hydroelectric dam and lake. There is no international outcry (from anthropologists or anyone else)—only a feel-good project to save the displaced animals'.[16]

In planning for Suriname's independence between 1975 and 1980,[17] further development plans called for 'the building of a huge hydroelectric station in the west of Suriname, for an alumina and aluminium plant and for a city on the site of the present Indian village of Apoera. The plan revolved around the mining and processing of the enormous bauxite reserves in the Bakhuys mountains in the south-west of the country', considered one of the world's largest reserves at the time.[18] The plan, however, never came to fruition, although Alcoa and other companies remained involved in negotiations with the government to revive the 'West Suriname Project' for the development of a new hydroelectric dam and bauxite-mining region up until quite recently.[19] In 1998 the US State Department called alumina exports 'the backbone of Suriname's economy'. 'The preeminence of bauxite and Alcoa's continued presence in Suriname is a key element in the U.S.-Suriname economic relationship', according to a 1998 State Department briefing.[20]

In addition to controlling bauxite mines, Alcoa and BHP Billiton also share (55/45%) operations at the Suralco 1.7 million ton alumina refinery in Paranam on the Atlantic coast. Alcoa continues to expand Suralco's activities today, at the expense of Saamaka people and the ecology of the region. Since the 1990s the problems faced by these Maroon communities have continued:

These once forested communities now live in a moonscape, surrounded by blasted rock, covered in dust and debris from blasting and are

---

[16] Price, *Travels with Tooy*, p. 174.

[17] Dutch Guiana became the independent Republic of Suriname in 1975, but about 40 per cent of the population chose to emigrate to the Netherlands prior to independence. 'Within five years, the political system had totally collapsed, and the country was under martial law between 1980 and 1988', and continued to be ruled by army commander Lt. Col. Desire Bouterse for many years: see Franklin W. Knight, *The Caribbean: The Genesis of a Fragmented Nationalism*, New York: Oxford University Press, 1990, p. 327.

[18] Hira, 'Class Formation and Class Struggle in Suriname', p. 176.

[19] 'Maroon Community Petitions Suriname Government about the Operations of a US-owned Bauxite Mining Company', Forest Peoples Programme, 17 September 1998.

[20] Bureau of Inter-American Affairs, 'Background Notes: Suriname', US Department of State, March 1998, cited in *Behind the Shining: Aluminum's Dark Side*, IPS/SEEN/TNI report, 2001, <http://countrycurrents.blogspot.com/2009/09/behind-shining-aluminums-dark-side.html> [28 June 2010].

subjected to high intensity lights that allow mining to take place 24 hours a day, seven days a week. Adjoemakondre is an extreme example of the impact of Suralco's activities. It is presently surrounded by three active concessions and mining is taking place less than 200 meters from the village itself. Much of the community's agricultural and hunting lands, and in some cases houses, have been destroyed and the river that runs through the village has turned brown-orange due to run off from the mining areas. Community members also allege that their health has suffered as a consequence of environmental contamination caused by Suralco's activities.[21]

Price goes on to describe the twenty-first century in scathing terms:

In Suriname, there are yet more blatant attempts to abrogate unilaterally the eighteenth-century Maroon treaties. The government in Paramaribo cuts up the bulk of Saramaka territory into parcels and leases them to Chinese, Indonesian, Canadian, American, and other multinational logging and mining companies. Logging roads are cut through [historic] First-Time village sites; game, birds, and fish disappear; vast expanses of red mud and white sand replace tropical forest; thousands of tons of cyanide- and mercury-laced gold-mining slag bury watercourses.[22]

The Association of Saamaka Authorities, representing the interests of the Maroons, filed a suit before the Inter-American Court for Human Rights 'seeking collective title to the lands on which Saramakas have lived, farmed, and hunted since the eighteenth century'.[23] The Saamaka people won their case in 2007/2008, but it remains to be seen whether the landmark ruling against the Government of Suriname, recognising their collective land rights and right to self-determination, will be enforced.[24] I return to their story below, but first will turn to Jamaica, where US aluminium transnationals also made inroads in the post-War period.

---

[21] *Behind the Shining.*
[22] Price, *Travels with Tooy*, p. 175.
[23] Price, *Travels with Tooy*, p. 175.
[24] Richard Price, *Rainforest Warriors: Human Rights on Trial* (Philadelphia: University of Pennsylvania Press, 2011).

Alcoa in the Caribbean: Jamaica

The successful expansion of the US market for aluminium in the 1930s and 1940s, and even more so into the 1950s, required a steady supply of high-quality bauxite, which was running low in Alcoa's home-based mines in Arkansas and Tennessee. The threats posed by German U-boats to trans-Caribbean shipping during the Second World War prompted an interest in securing steady supplies closer to the US mainland, including Jamaica, where bauxite ore was discovered only in the 1940s, as well as some smaller mines in the Dominican Republic and Haiti. The increased demand for aluminium during the Second World War, the emergence of the USA as the world's largest aluminium producer, and the dangers of wartime shipping all led to the emergence of Jamaica as the primary supplier of bauxite to the US aluminium companies.[25]

The system of Allied collaboration known as 'Lend-Lease', along with the September 1940 destroyers-for-bases agreement, also enabled the USA to provide aluminium to British wartime industries (whose European sources of bauxite and power had been seized by Germany) in exchange for air bases in British colonies, including Jamaica, Trinidad, and British Guiana.[26] These new military bases embodied the waning of Britain's power in the region and gave the USA a valuable military foothold just as the US multinationals were engaging in bargaining over access to resources, preferential tariffs, and deals for low taxation.

Kaiser Aluminium (which benefited from the breakup of Alcoa's monopoly after the Second World War) based its new mining operations in Jamaica, and the US mining companies acquired up to 142,000 acres of agricultural land for mining exploration, while Reynolds Metals gained exclusive access to 206,000 acres of Crown Land in British Guiana.[27] The following advertising campaigns are situated in this context of bargaining between multinational corporations with strong financial (and ultimately military) backing from the US government and a weak post-War British colonial state under pressure from economic stress at home as well as local social mobilisations in its colonies.

---

[25] Carlton E. Davis, *Jamaica in the World Aluminium Industry, 1838–1973*, vol.1, Kingston: Jamaica Bauxite Institute, 1989.
[26] Davis, *Jamaica in the World*, p. 54. And see O. Nigel Bolland, *The Politics of Labour in the British Caribbean*, Kingston: Ian Randle and London: James Currey, 2001, p. 443.
[27] Gerald Horne, *Cold War in a Hot Zone: The United States Confronts Labor and Independence Struggles in the British West Indies*, Philadelphia: Temple University Press, 2007, p. 160.

In a striking series of luxury magazine advertisements, the Alcoa Steamship Company promoted its Caribbean cruises from 1948 to 1958. The Alcoa Steamship Company played a special role in the Caribbean, not only shipping bauxite and some alumina to the USA, but also carrying cruise ship passengers, commissioning artists to depict Caribbean scenery, selling recordings of Caribbean music, and even sponsoring the Caribbean Arts Prize in the 1950s. The company operated three 'modern, air-conditioned ships', each carrying 65 passengers, which departed every Saturday from New Orleans on a 16-day cruise, making stops in Jamaica, Trinidad, Venezuela, Curacao, and the Dominican Republic. The cruise ships stopped in the ports of Kingston, Curacao, La Guaira, Puerto Cabello, Guanta, Port of Spain, and Ciudad Trujillo. They also ran several freighters out of New York, Montreal, and New Orleans, which carried 12 passengers and made longer, slower trips; these ships delivered bauxite for Reynolds and Kaiser as well as for Alcoa.[28]

The same economic, political and spatial arrangements that locked in huge market advantages for transnational aluminium corporations simultaneously opened up Jamaica for tourism mobilities. Tourism then instigated the circulation of new visual representations of movement through the Caribbean. While Alcoa promoted novel products, modern skyscrapers and metallurgical research and development in the USA, the company envisioned the Caribbean as a source of bauxite, a potential market for 'superior' American products, and a timeless destination for tourists travelling on its modern ships to safely step back into the colourful history, exotic flora, and quaint folkways of diverse Caribbean destinations. While these modes of imaging are not surprising (and continue in other ways today), what is striking is the degree to which they diverge from the futuristic images of super-modernity that were simultaneously being promulgated in the US consumer market for aluminium products. The images seamlessly meld together tourism, business travel, bauxite shipment, and cultural consumption, yet carefully detach the American Tropics from modernity in the USA.

---

[28] The three ships, the Alcoa Corsair, Cavalier, and Clipper, were built in 1946, costing about $2,250,000 each, and were in service until 1960, at which point they were decommissioned largely because the company could save millions of dollars by switching their shipping operations to Liberian flags of convenience using non-American seamen. (Alcoa Archives, MSS 282, Box 11, Internal Correspondence, 22 September 1960, From F. A. Billhardt, Alcoa Steamship Company, Inc., New York Office To: Mr. L. Litchfield Jr., Pittsburgh Office, Re: Economic Study of Passenger Ships, Alcoa Steamship Company, Inc.)

The first series of ads, which ran from 1948–1949, was created and signed by the graphic artist Boris Artzybasheff. A Russian émigré to the USA, Artzybasheff was most wellknown for his cover portraits for *Time* magazine, his colourful series of Shell Oil ads, and his surreal drawings of anthropomorphic machines. For Alcoa he produced an unusual series of portraits of Caribbean people, each surrounded by a gorgeous tapestry of flowers, fruiting plants, and native fauna. The overall impression is a storybook land of diverse exotic races, colourful landscapes, and romantic adventure. A Carib mother and child, for example, are depicted as timeless primitives, holding up fruit and peering out from dark eyes and exotically painted faces (Figure 2). Although the images appear at first to promote cultural encounter and ethnological curiosity within touristic contact zones, such typifying images circulate within a long lineage of tropicalising representations of Caribbean islands and people.[29]

The text of the Artzybasheff series emphasises the swashbuckling and colonial history of the Caribbean, which marked the region with diversity: 'if you look carefully you'll see how the distinctive architecture, languages and races of this area have been blended by centuries into interesting new patterns'. Each image represents an example of racial blending or distinctiveness, portraying a male or female racialised persona in typical costume, including Carib Indians, various types of Afro-Caribbean or mixed race individuals, East Indian Hindu, East Indian Muslim, and various types of whites of Spanish, Dutch, or Anglo-Caribbean origin. Each image also includes a distinctive flower, foliage, and often a typical bird or butterfly, suggesting a kind of natural history that conjoins island people and wildlife, naturalising races through attachment to specific places.

In line with other visual representations of the Caribbean, black men are portrayed only in safely 'civilized' roles, including as a bewigged Judge and as a white-uniformed policeman. Pinned down like tropical butterflies, women of colour appear in typical poses such as 'Dark-eyed senoritas, descended of conquistadores of old' or a stereotypical Creole belle, wearing a madras head-tie and gold jewellery. Hindus and Muslims appear in unusual hats in

---

[29] W. J. T. Mitchell, *Landscape and Power*, Chicago: University of Chicago Press, 2002; Richard Grove, *Green Imperialism: Colonial Expansion, Tropical Island Edens, and the Origins of Environmentalism, 1600–1860*, Cambridge: Cambridge University Press, 1995; Candace Slater, 'Amazonia as Edenic Narrative' in William Cronon, ed. *Uncommon Ground: Rethinking the Human Place in Nature*, New York: W. W. Norton, 1996; Sheller, *Consuming the Caribbean*; David Arnold, *The Tropics and the Traveling Gaze: India, Landscape and Science, 1800–1856*, Seattle: University of Washington Press, 2006.

Figure 2   Fanciful depiction of "Carib Indians" by Russian graphic artist Boris Artzybasheff for the Alcoa cruise line's advertising in the U.S. holiday market (1948).

front of their exotic temples, while a Dominican sugarcane-cutter appears as noble worker with the tools of his trade in hand. The images paper over the ethnic, class, and colour hierarchies that fanned political unrest throughout the post-War Caribbean; they offer not only a visually flattened perspective, but also a historically and socially flattened one. Ironically, in

Figure 3   Another of Boris Artzybasheff's series produced in the 1940s promoting Alcoa cruises, this image is the only one to introduce elements of modernity: oil rigs in the background and the industrial worker holding a heavy wrench.

this very period Alcan's DEMBA mine in British Guiana (part of Alcoa when built) was using racial and ethnic divisions of labour to reinforce the occupational and political divisions between Guyanese of African and East Indian descent, and the class hierarchies between black and white. The picturesque racial and ethnic diversity of the Caribbean was also a useful tool in corporate hands.[30] The US bases of the 1940s brought with them

---

[30]   An interesting account by a former mine worker is provided by Odida T. Quamina, *Mineworkers of Guyana: The Making of a Working Class*, London: Zed Books, 1987; on the history of class and ethnic divisions in British Guiana, see Walter Rodney, *A History of the Guyanese Working People, 1881–1905*, Baltimore: The Johns Hopkins

deep-seated conflicts with their host countries over Jim Crow segregation, blatant racism, and extensive prostitution.

In one Alcoa ad depicting a Venezuelan oil worker (Figure 3), even oil derricks become part of the picturesque scenery. A wrench-wielding worker is enfolded in delicate pink flowers and lush foliage:

> Thanks to this liquid asset, and to picturesque forests of oil wells, Venezuela is today one of your best foreign markets. It is fast-developing, nearby, has ready cash, and is *hungry* for American-made products— and all that their superiority represents. [...] VISIT THE MAGIC CARIBBEAN, where business is easily dovetailed with a relaxing, tropical vacation.

This ad positions Latin Americans as 'hungry' for the superiority of US products, the epitome of modernity. These ads appeared in the post-war period when American production capacity, inflated for wartime, outstripped domestic consumer markets. Thus they allude to the Caribbean and Latin America not only as tourist destinations but also as potential markets for US goods. Another image of a modern-looking Venezuelan man points out that:

> His native land is a tourists' paradise of tropical mountains and romantic beaches. But to businessmen visitors, with an eye for more tangible assets, his country also is one of vast progress and thriving markets. It buys its manufactured products largely from the U.S.A.— sends us valuable raw materials we need. Linking together these good-neighbor countries—transporting cargo, carrying passengers, are the fast, modern ships of Alcoa's fleet.

Here we see the direct linkage of tourism and US export markets via the Alcoa fleet. It suggests that business can be combined with a tropical vacation, positioning the Caribbean as a place outside of modernity where relaxation reigns supreme. The ad alludes to the government's post-war 'good neighbor' policy, which promoted US business interests in Latin America and the Caribbean. Tourism, along with bauxite mining, both enabled and masked the economic and political processes that transmuted tropical lands, bauxite ore, and the labour of Caribbean workers not only into futuristic aluminium appliances, light-weight vehicles, and bombers, but also into

University Press, 1981; and on ongoing tensions see Brackette Williams, *Stains on My Name, War in my Veins: Guyana and the Politics of Cultural Struggle*, Durham: Duke University Press, 1991.

backwards islands for relaxing tropical holidays. Connectivity was also a form of disconnectivity, and modernisation for the North was a form of de-modernisation for the Tropics.

Caribbean responses: national resource sovereignty

Access to oil and bauxite, more than romantic tourism or opening new markets, were the main reasons for US businesses and military bases to be in the region. The Guyanese left-wing labour leader Cheddi Jagan noted in 1945 that wages for workers were 'only one-third to one-quarter of comparative wages in bauxite and smelting operations in the USA and Canada', and he dreamed of an independent nation with its own aluminium industry.[31] The Caribbean Labour Congress [CLC] was formed in 1945 and from 1947, under the leadership of communist Richard Hart, vigorously promoted the formation of a self-governing West Indies Federation with Dominion status. Both Guyanese and Jamaicans in the labour movement struggled to shift the terms of their enrolment in the world economy and transform the ways in which their natural resources (and labour) were being mobilised for the benefit of others.

When the devaluation of the British pound in 1949 reduced the Jamaican bauxite royalty to US 14 cents a ton, and the Korean War along with US stockpiling led to increasing demand for bauxite in the early 1950s, Jamaica's opposition People's National Party [PNP] began calling for a higher royalty. Yet with the weakened British state powerless to stop the US corporations, and some Jamaican elites eager to modernise their industrial and transportation infrastructure, Jamaica remained an attractively cheap destination for both mining companies and tourists.

The second series of Alcoa Steamship ads, published in 1951–1952, depicts botanical paintings of tropical flowering trees by the respected botanical illustrators Harriet and Bernard Pertchik. These images tap into a long tradition of botanical collection and illustration of tropical plants by colonial naturalists, who collected material in the Caribbean and incorporated it into systems of plant classification and medical knowledge.[32] Botanical collection is linked to forms of colonial control over nature and an imperial gaze that merges the picturesque with the pragmatic use of natural resources

---

[31] Horne, *Cold War in a Hot Zone*, p. 160.
[32] David P. Miller, 'Joseph Banks, Empire, and "Centers of Calculation" in Late Hanoverian London', in *Visions of Empire: Voyages, Botany, and Representations of Nature*, eds., David Philip Miller and Peter Hanns Reill, Cambridge, Cambridge University Press, 1996, pp. 21–37.

and uses both as a justification for imperialist 'improvement'; this imperial gaze was later reinvented as a key constituent of 'the tourist gaze'.[33] These ads reiterate a kind of visual nostalgia for colonial botanising and natural history, while also including in their lower corner small sketches of white tourists relaxing on board the cruise ships, suggestive of the contrasting modernity and luxuries of the leisure class who can enjoy a cruise through the tamed islands of the Caribbean. It is US tourists who move, while the islands and Caribbean coastal countries are collected, catalogued, and made known as sites of natural beauty, even as their interior forests were being cleared, flooded, and strip mined for the precious ore below them, leaving behind lakes of toxic 'red mud' and land useless for agriculture.

Recent studies in visual culture show how painted and photographic images of the Caribbean constantly re-inscribe picturesque island landscapes, romantic tropical nature, and hybrid mixtures of exotic races. Such images have frequently been used to market the region to both business investors and tourists. They have also had an impact on re-shaping the built environment and natural landscape to fit external expectations and serve the needs of both local elites and foreign corporations. As Krista Thompson has shown in her study *An Eye for the Tropics*, photographic images of the Caribbean produced for tourist markets in the early twentieth century tropicalised nature by emphasising lush and unusual plants, exoticised local people by showing them in rustic and primitive settings, and erased signs of modernity such as electric power lines or new urban areas. National elites had an interest in furthering these projects of self-exotification for the tourist market, just as they had an interest in encouraging foreign investment, whether in agriculture or mining. And it was often the same corporations involved in both sectors: the same ships that were laden with bananas or bauxite on the way to North America or Britain carried passengers on the return journey, while businessmen interested in investing in the region stayed at hotels owned by the multinationals.[34]

At the same time, the Caribbean claims one of the most mobile working classes in the world, but its patterns of mobility were tightly channelled and controlled. It was foreign corporations who governed the patterns of labour migration whether to work on the sugar plantations of other islands, the banana plantations of Central America, or in the building of a trans-isthmus railway and the Panama Canal. Nevertheless, this mobile working class was at times highly politicised, cosmopolitan, and critical of the world

---

[33] John Urry, *The Tourist Gaze*, London: Sage, 2002; Arnold, *The Tropics and the Traveling Gaze*; Sheller, *Consuming the Caribbean*, pp. 36–70.
[34] Krista Thompson, *An Eye for the Tropics*.

economic system. Ideologies such as Garveyism, pan-Africanism, Socialism, and Communism circulated amongst them, and between the Caribbean and its US outposts in places like Harlem.[35] The most organised workers in the region were the stevedores and other port workers who, along with sugar plantation workers, led the major strikes or 'labor rebellion' of 1937–1938.[36] As Jamaica adopted universal enfranchisement in the 1940s and moved towards self-government in the 1950s, thanks in part to this major labour uprising, there was 'an increasing sense of nationalism and concern for the protection of national resources', especially among the labour parties of the left.[37] Out of the labour movement arose a generation of nationalist leaders who pushed the British West Indies towards independence, and towards democratic socialism.

The US aluminium corporations, however, continued to present an image of docile Caribbean labour and amenable lands (even as they broke the resistance of the seamen's unions, as noted above, by resorting to flags of convenience). California-based Kaiser Aluminium ran an advertisement in the *Saturday Evening Post* in 1953 portraying a monolithic Jamaican miner standing with a lump of red ore in one hand, a shovel resting in the other, and the word "BAUXITE" emblazoned across him (Figure 4). The text reads:

IN OUR NEW BAUXITE MINES in Jamaica there is enough rich aluminium bearing ore to last more than half a century. Our increased supply of bauxite is only part of our vast expansion. This year our many plants will turn out over 25% of all the aluminium made in this country. This is twice as much as the whole industry produced before World War II. We are proud of the leading part we are playing in the most vital and exciting of all American industries today. For, aluminium is not only revolutionizing American manufacturing—it is revolutionizing American living. In thousands and thousands of useful products, aluminium is taking the place of other metals—making

---

[35] Cedric J. Robinson, *Black Marxism: The Making of the Black Radical Tradition*, Chapel Hill: University of North Carolina Press, 2000.

[36] Ken Post, *Arise ye Starvelings: The Jamaican Labour Rebellion of 1938 and Its Aftermath*, The Hague: Martinus Nijhoff, 1978.

[37] Davis, *Jamaica in the World*, p. 135. There were few strikes or 'unrest' associated with the Jamaican bauxite mines, largely because they employed a relatively small number of workers, these workers were relatively well paid compared to other local industries, especially agriculture, and were thus easily replaceable. See Bolland, *Politics of Labour*; Evelyn Huber Stephens and John Stephens, *Democratic Socialism in Jamaica: The Political Movement and Social Transformation in Dependent Capitalism*, Princeton: Princeton University Press, 1986, p. 27.

THE SATURDAY EVENING POST

BAUXITE

IN OUR NEW BAUXITE MINES in Jamaica there is enough rich aluminum bearing ore to last more than half a century.

Our increased supply of bauxite is only part of our vast expansion. This year our many plants will turn out over 25% of all the aluminum made in this country. This is twice as much as the whole industry produced before World War II.

We are proud of the leading part we are playing in the most vital and exciting of all American industries today. For, aluminum is not only revolutionizing American manufacturing—it is revolutionizing American living. In thousands and thousands of useful products, aluminum is taking the place of other metals—making these products better—and cheaper.

Because of aluminum, a brighter future lies ahead. We are continuing to expand—and to work with manufacturers to turn aluminum's unlimited opportunities into realities.

Kaiser Aluminum

America's fastest growing major producer of aluminum

Figure 4   Advert from 1953 showing a Jamaican bauxite worker towering above the landscape like a colossal statue. He holds up a lump of ore whose colour matches his skin perfectly.

these products better—and cheaper. Because of aluminium, a brighter future lies ahead.

The text slides easily from bauxite to finished aluminium products, and from Jamaica to 'American living'. It makes no allusion to the Jamaican worker it portrays or whether he is to be included in the brighter future ahead; but it does allude to the company's remarkable degree of access to Jamaican resources, made possible in large part by the US government's breaking up of Alcoa's monopoly to the benefit of Kaiser, the US military power stationed in the Caribbean during and after World War Two, and the favourable 1947 tariff deal. The miner's powerful stillness and reddish brown hue, matching the lump of bauxite ore and the ground beneath his feet, set Caribbean people apart from the futuristic mobility so heavily promoted in US consumer markets.

The year is significant, because it was in October 1953 that the British government, with US support, forcibly suspended the constitution of Guyana and deposed the labour-left government of Cheddi Jagan, elected by a majority under universal adult suffrage, which had threatened to take back mineral resources and move the colony towards independence.[38] Coming just as the government was in the process of passing a Labour Relations Bill that would have protected unions and labour rights, the coup nipped in the bud Jagan's longer-term plans to create forward linkages through locally-based aluminium smelters and fabrication plants using the country's significant potential for hydropower. Bolland argues that the 'consequences of the suspension of Guyana's constitution and subsequent British actions were devastating for the development of politics in the colony', leading to a deep racial split within the People's Progressive Party, and long-lasting racial polarisation between Afro-Guyanese and Indo-Guyanese.[39] The year 1953 also marks the collapse of the CLC under pressure of Cold War anti-communist campaigns, ending the hopes for an independent pan-Caribbean labour movement. These events make evident the power of colonial governments and transnational corporations to break the strength of the labour movements in the region, and suggest the degree to which nascent nationalist movements and soon-to-be independent governments would not be allowed to assert resource sovereignty.

The move towards political and visual self-representation

The third Alcoa Steamship Co. series, which ran from 1954 to 55, is a striking set of folkloric portrayals of musical performances, parades, or dances, both religious and secular, by the graphic illustrator James R. Bingham. Readers are encouraged to write in to purchase 45 rpm recordings of the music that accompanies some of the dances, including the Banda dance of Haiti, the Joropo of Venezuela, the Merengue of the

---

[38] Bolland, *Politics of Labour*, pp. 617–621. The British sent two frigates from Bermuda, a cruiser from Jamaica with 500 troops, and were prepared to support them with a second cruiser and an aircraft carrier stationed in Jamaica.
[39] Bolland, *Politics of Labour*, pp. 624–625.

Dominican Republic, and the Beguine of the French West Indies. Other ads represent the Pajaro Guarandol 'folk dance of the Venezuelan Indians', the steel pan and 'stick dance' of Trinidad, the 'Simadon' harvest festival of Curacao, the folk dance of the Jibaros of Puerto Rico, and the John Canoe dancers of Jamaica whose costumes date back to the eighteenth century and possibly to West Africa. This series connects touristic consumption of musical performances from across the Caribbean with an almost ethnographic project of investigation of traditional cultures and people who again seem outside of modernity, but available for modern cruise tourists to visit. Yet the potential circuits of travel of the musical recordings and dance styles also hint at the powerful cultural currents emanating out of Caribbean popular cultures and circulating into US urban culture via Caribbean diasporas. However primitive or traditional these dances appear, the vivid forms of dance and music also attest to a kind of cultural vitality that could quite literally *move* people in unexpected (and possibly dangerous) ways.

The Alcoa Steamship Company also adjusted its cultural strategy in this period, and began to sponsor the Caribbean Art Competition in 1954–1955 (Figure 5). This led to a show of 127 paintings by Caribbean artists (selected from 'nearly thirteen hundred entered', which toured the region in 1956, with exhibitions in Puerto Rico, the Dominican Republic, Trinidad, Jamaica, Haiti, Venezuela, British Guiana, Suriname, Antigua, Curaçao, and Barbados. The exhibition opened at the National Arts Club in New York, where it was judged by a panel of 'three eminent New York judges' and cash prizes of $10,000 were awarded. Alcoa also 'announced that it has purchased a number of the paintings, and these are being used in the Company's national colour advertising during the next two years', such as the image by Haitian painter Castera Bazile in Figure 5.

The artwork also was reproduced on 'travel folders and direct mail brochures for travel agents and the general public throughout North America'.[40] Thus one can begin to see a move towards Caribbean *cultural* self-representation, paralleling the strengthening movement for independent self-government and resource sovereignty that emerged in this period. Yet, in parallel to the limited control over minerals and metals, Caribbean self-representation was negotiated in relation to foreign corporate sponsorship and tourist markets for art and music.

In 1956, changes in the internal and external political situation led into

---

[40] 'Alcoa's Caribbean Find [sic] Art Exhibition', *The Barbados Advocate*, 29 September 1956, p. 11. Many thanks to Leah Rosenberg for locating and providing this article to me.

Figure 5   Winner of Alcoa's Caribbean Arts Prize in 1958, the painter Castera
Bazile of Haiti is lauded in the text as having "caught much of the color and
warmth of a Caribbean village on a lazy Sunday afternoon".

a new conjuncture for bargaining between the state and the transnational
corporations. A major renegotiation of the terms of royalty payments and
taxes was undertaken by PNP Chief Minister Norman Washington Manley
(one of the founding fathers of Jamaican independence) in 1956–1957, based
on the principle that 'Countries in the early stages of economic development
ought to derive the largest possible benefits from their natural resources.
They ought not to be regarded merely as sources of cheap raw materials

for metropolitan enterprises'.[41] Following tough negotiations, the 1957 agreement re-set the royalty for 25 years at four shillings (US56c) per ton on the first million tons, three shillings (US42c) per ton where production exceeds one million tons but is below two million, two shillings (US28c) per ton on any excess over two million tons.[42] In October 1957 the Soviet Union launched the first Sputnik satellite, a small aluminium orb that triggered the Space Race with the USA. A British West Indies Federation was also created in 1957, but the most influential political leaders in Jamaica (Norman Manley and Alexander Bustamante) and in Trinidad (Eric Williams) refused to stand as candidates in federal elections, and when Jamaica pulled out altogether in 1961 it fell apart.[43] The Korean War made aluminium an even more crucial 'strategic material', and the US government began stockpiling it. This led to a substantial increase in revenues to the Jamaican government, contributing more than 45% of the country's export earnings by 1959. Jamaica moved from supplying about one quarter of all US bauxite imports in 1953 to over one half in 1959, with 40% of total shipments of crude bauxite and alumina between 1956 and 1959 going into the US government stockpile.[44]

In 1959 the Cuban Revolution carried Fidel Castro into power, and the Cold War went into full swing in the Caribbean. Jamaica achieved independence in 1962 and by the 1960s 'was the world's largest producer of bauxite' according to historical sociologists Evelyn Huber Stephens and John Stephens: 'In 1965, the country supplied 28 per cent of the bauxite used in the market economies of the world ... [and] bauxite along with tourism fueled post-war Jamaican development and the two provided the country with most of her gross foreign exchange earnings'.[45] In 1967 the major copper-producing countries of Zaire, Zambia, Chile and Peru moved partially to nationalise foreign copper mines and formed a cartel, the Conseil Intergouvernemental des Pays Exportateurs du Cuivre (CIPEC). Then the socialist government of newly independent Guyana nationalised the Demerara Bauxite Company in 1970 and took a 51% stake in Alcan's DEMBA subsidiary.

The New World Group of economists at the University of the West Indies

[41] Norman Washington Manley to Kaiser Bauxite Company, 23 May 1956, cited in Davis, *Jamaica in the World*, pp. 189–190. Davis offers a detailed account of the negotiations, having himself played a major part in the later 1974 negotiations as a technical advisor to the PNP's Bauxite Negotiating Team and as Executive Chairman of the Jamaica Bauxite Institute from its inception in 1975.

[42] Davis, *Jamaica in the World*, p. 229.

[43] Knight, *The Caribbean*, p. 303.

[44] Knight, *The Caribbean*, p. 251.

[45] Stephens and Stephens, *Democratic Socialism in Jamaica*, p. 26.

(including Lloyd Best and Norman Girvan, in particular, leading members of the Caribbean 'dependency school' of economic theorists) published many critiques of foreign capital and the economic underdevelopment of Jamaica and began to call for the nationalisation of the Jamaican bauxite industry in the early 1970s.[46] It is in the context of the bauxite industry that these radical Caribbean economists first elaborated theories of 'dependent development', and socialist post-independence nationalist leaders such as Prime Minister Forbes Burnham of Guyana and Michael Manley of Jamaica tried to stand up to the multinationals and the International Monetary Fund by nationalising the bauxite industry in the 1970s.[47]

In 1973 Prime Minister Michael Manley's People's National Party government, which was trying to implement democratic socialism in Jamaica, 'opened negotiations with the aluminium TNCs on acquisition of 51 percent equity in their bauxite mining operations, [...] acquisition of all the land owned by the companies in order to gain control over the bauxite reserves, and a bauxite levy tied to the price of aluminium ingot on the US market'.[48] In March 1974, inspired by the success of OPEC, a bauxite producer's cartel known as the International Bauxite Association [IBA] was set up and was quickly able to double the price of bauxite on world markets. The Jamaica Bauxite Institute was also formed to gather information on the industry both locally and internationally and thereby increase state capacity for regulation of the mining sector and for bargaining with transnational corporations.

Initially these new Caribbean leaders held no enmity towards the USA. Indeed, they arguably desired to escape their colonial past in order to embrace exactly the kind of modernity that US technology promised. They shared the dreams of the Space Age and the light modernity that aluminium could bring to their countries too. However, Manley's socialist rhetoric, friendship with Fidel Castro, and support for African liberation movements such as the MPLA in Angola did not endear him to the USA,

---

[46] Meeks and Girvan, *Caribbean Reasonings*; Norman Girvan, *Foreign Capital and Economic Underdevelopment in Jamaica*, Mona: University of the West Indies, Institute of Social and Economic Research, 1971; Norman Girvan, *Corporate Imperialism: Conflict and Expropriation*, New York: Monthly Review Press, 1976.

[47] Evelyne Huber Stephens and John D. Stephens, 'Bauxite and Democratic Socialism in Jamaica', in Peter Evans, Dietrich Rueschemeyer and Evelyne H. Stephens, eds., *States versus Markets in the World System*, Beverly Hills: Sage Publications, 1985.

[48] Evelyne Huber Stephens, 'Minerals Strategies and Development: International Political Economy, State, Class, and the Role of Bauxite/Aluminum and Copper Industries in Jamaica and Peru', *Studies in Comparative International Development*, 22, no. 3 (1987), pp. 60–102, at 63–64.

or to the transnational corporations. In response, American aluminium companies 'doubled their bauxite imports from Guinea in 1975, [and] they reduced their Jamaican imports by 30 per cent ... Jamaica's share of the world market for bauxite plummeted'.[49] This was a dramatic period in Global South self-assertion, yet they ultimately failed in their struggle to gain control over their own resources as mining investments shifted to countries like Australia and Guinea.

The corporate powers that controlled the global aluminium industry would never allow developing countries, especially socialist ones, to wrest control over their own resources. The bauxite taken from the Caribbean allowed the USA to build a material culture of light aluminium, unquestionable military air power, and space-age mobility. At the same time, the terms of oligopolistic international trade and market governance that allowed this transfer of resources to take place helped to lock in place structures of global inequality that prevented Caribbean countries from exercising true sovereignty or benefiting from their own resources.[50] Today, the region remains a major producer of bauxite, through companies that are partly state-owned and partly owned by major transnational corporations such as Alcoa, Alcan, and Rusal. In Guinea too, one of the poorest countries in the world, people live in abject conditions right next to the largest bauxite reserves in the world. Like Jamaicans in earlier generations, Guineans have recently participated in their first democratic elections as an unstable military government promised to bring democracy and, at last, modernisation. Yet the hasty contracts with huge Chinese and Russian mining corporations who are vying for control over Guinea's untapped metals and minerals do not bode well for the future.

Conclusion: the Caribbean as Space Age Tropics

The Caribbean appears as an afterthought in the gleaming Age of Aluminium as imagined in the USA. In 1962, coincidentally, not only did Jamaica achieve independence, but the 50-foot antenna of the American Telstar satellite, which used 80,000 pounds of aluminium, beamed the first satellite television pictures back to a transmission station in Maine. Also that year the first

---

[49] Clive Y. Thomas, *Dependence and Transformation: The Economics of the Transition to Socialism*, New York: Monthly Review Press, 1974, p. 83.

[50] For an argument against the Caribbean's capacity to 'reach out beyond the extractive stage of production', see Sterling Brubaker, *Trends in the World Aluminium Industry*, Baltimore: The Johns Hopkins Press, 1967, sponsored by the Ford Foundation-funded non-profit Resources for the Future, Inc.

two Americans to orbit the earth, John Glenn in the craft Friendship 7 and Scott Carpenter in Aurora 7, happened to splash down in their aluminium capsules and space suits in the Atlantic Ocean close to the nearby Turks and Caicos Islands, and were brought to the US Air Force Base on Grand Turk for debriefing and meetings with US Vice President Lyndon B. Johnson. One imagines the top-secret spacecraft washing up on a remote coral cay like something out of a James Bond novel. After all, Ian Fleming wrote twelve of the Bond stories at Goldeneye, his plantation retreat in the hills above Kingston, and his hero was named after the respected ornithologist who had authored the first authoritative field guide *Birds of the West Indies*. Amidst the dying embers of the British Empire, Fleming conjured up the juxtaposition between super-modern Agent 007's extreme forms of light, fast, mobility and the sinister tropical profusion, ancient Voodoo rituals, and racial/sexual intrigue of the 'primitive' Caribbean.

The fast metallic contours of Bond's line of Aston Martin cars, beginning with the 1965 model and up to the most recent DBS and DB9, were built on aluminium frames, embodying his technological prowess and suave lightness. All the more so set against the Caribbean backdrop. By the time of the first human landing on the moon in 1969, Neil Armstrong and Buzz Aldrin could step out of their aluminium landing craft onto the Sea of Tranquillity while the mother ship Columbia orbited the moon, just as the Saamaka lands in Suriname were being drowned under 80 meters of flood water. The curious Caribbean footnotes to modernity's outer space achievements ought to draw our attention back down to the ground of Suriname, Guyana, and Jamaica, where an analysis of the mobile *and* immobile material cultures afforded by aluminium can elucidate not only the cultural history of technology, design, and popular culture, but also the broader currents of global inequality and relative positioning which shaped the American Tropics.

As this essay has noted, bauxite mining is linked to the displacement of historically unique Maroon communities in Suriname, as well as tribal peoples in Australia and India, with the 2008 ruling of the Inter-American Court of Human Rights setting a new standard of protection of their rights. Bauxite mining causes ecological damage in the form of forest clearance, lakes of red-mud, water and air pollution, and negative health effects on workers and nearby populations. The Caribbean today remains active in plans for the expansion of aluminium production. New bauxite mines are controversially being planned in the forests of Suriname and in the Cockpit country of Jamaica, while the building of new smelters in Guyana, Suriname and Trinidad remain hotly contested. Throughout the world people are protesting against the multinational mining corporations, from the Rights

Action Group in Trinidad, to the Naxalite rebels in India, who in July 2009 briefly overran the largest bauxite mine in Asia, taking 150 people hostage and escaping with a bounty of mining explosives, which they use to make bombs and landmines.

Ironically, many Saamaka Maroons displaced from their homelands have ended up in the neighbouring French territory of Guyane, a former penal colony known for its brutal and deadly prisons, but where the capital Cayenne is now the location of the European Space Programme.[51] The modernising society of Guyane 'is trying so hard to replace its image as a penal colony with that of gleaming Ariane rockets', writes Price, as two modernities again converge at a crossroads of sharp contrasts.[52] Thus it seems fitting that in March 2008 the first European Space Agency Automated Transfer Vehicle was launched on an Ariane 5 rocket from Kourou, in Guyane—appropriately, it is named 'Jules Verne', after the science fiction writer who first recognised aluminium's potential to get us to the moon, when it was still a rare precious metal in 1865. Gazing towards the heavens an observer of the historic launch might not have noticed the displaced Saamaka Maroons living as non-national migrants on the fringes of the former French penal colony of Cayenne, nor that they had just won a landmark human rights case.

The flooded ancient homelands of the Saamaka are cast into the shadows by the towering launch pads and aerodynamic rockets of the European Space Program. Global viewers lift their gaze away from the disturbed jungles and displaced Maroons of the interior, following the rockets up towards the high-tech heavens where the aluminium-light 'Jules Verne' capsule has been successfully attached to the International Space Station. Modernisation has not brought the Caribbean the space age future promised by the acolytes of the age of aluminium. Yet the Caribbean remains an active scene of contention over the future of the aluminium industry and the self-determination of the people living there.

The emergence of aluminium-based practices of mobility, alongside modern ideologies and representations of that mobility, pivoted on the co-production of other regions of the world as backwards, slow, and relatively immobile—'bauxite-bearing' tropical regions that would be mined by multinational corporations for the benefit of those who could make use of the 'magical metal' to become modern. Such relative mobilisations and

---

[51] For a fascinating account of contemporary French Guiana, see Peter Redfield, *Space in the Tropics: From Convicts to Rockets in French Guiana*, Berkeley and London: University of California Press, 2000.

[52] Price, *Travels with Tooy*, p. 194.

demobilisations, modernisations and de-modernisations, are constitutive of the connections and disconnections between North America and the Caribbean that allow discrepant or disjunctive modernities to exist side by side. If the metallic sheaths of our 'featherlight aluminium' notebook computers (like the MacBook Air, which symbolically dissolves into the ether) best represent the speed and lightness of the messenger Mercury today, then we would do well to remember the mines, the forges, and the weapons of Vulcan/Ogou, for the two brothers move in parallel through the world, above and below the American Tropics.

Black Jacobins and New World Mediterraneans

Susan Gillman

We all recognise the back-handed compliment of one of the most familiar formulas for comparison: so and so (fill in the name of a national patriot/founding father of another nation) is the George Washington of his country. Who can miss the assumption of superiority in the presumed equal sign? The equation puts the second term, the other, first but doesn't fool anyone in the process. No spectres shadow these comparisons, at least not with the subtle kind of haunting that Benedict Anderson finds in José Rizal's (first great novelist and founding father of the modern Philippine nation) famous Filipino nationalist novel *Noli Me Tangere* (1887), when the young *mestizo* hero views the botanical gardens in colonial Manila and sees the shadow of their European sister gardens. No spectres on the order of that double vision, because when Rizal is lauded as the Filipino George Washington, as he so often was by the Americans who 'liberated' the Philippines from Spain at the end of the Spanish-American War, the spectre is right there on the surface, transparent if not visible. The comparative formula that equates Rizal with the first founding father assumes the originality and primacy of Europe and Euro-America and the imitative second-order of all the modernising societies in the other Americas, Asia, and Africa that follow.[1]

Perhaps less familiar is Melville's comic take in *Moby-Dick*: 'Queequeg is George Washington, cannibalistically developed', a sardonic reformulation

---

[1] Anderson makes Rizal a focal point at various key junctures in his work: see *Imagined Communities: Reflections on the Origin and Spread of Nationalism*, London: Verso, 1983; 1991; 2006; *The Spectre of Comparisons: Nationalism, Southeast Asia and the World*, London: Verso, 1998; *Under Three Flags: Anarchism and the Anti-Colonial Imagination*, London: Verso, 2005.

of the comparative equation that mocks its assumed hierarchies. Less familiar still, or perhaps just not as obvious *as* formulas are 'Black Reconstruction', 'Black Jacobins', and other such titles that nod to and riff on their own founding fact of comparison. Classics of revisionist historiography, W. E. B. Du Bois's *Black Reconstruction* (1935) and C. L. R. James's *The Black Jacobins* (1938) were published only three years apart. Just a few years later, in 1949, Cuban novelist Alejo Carpentier coined his 'Caribbean Mediterranean' (see the prologue to *El reino de este mundo* [*The Kingdom of this World*]), using the ancient Mediterranean, oceanically transferred to an imagined modern Caribbean based in the revolutionary sensibility and history of Haiti. All three, Du Bois, James, and Carpentier, point at once to the silent presence of comparison looming as a *raison d'être*.

In the case of *Black Reconstruction* and *The Black Jacobins*, the comparative mode is foundational to the histories they narrate. Written explicitly from within an orthodoxy of the 'failure' of Reconstruction and the primacy of the French Revolution, both books signal the aim to produce a corrective historical narrative named as 'black'. Behind them, verging on an infinite regress, is a long line of very different variations on the theme, including among James's sources Percy Waxman's *The Black Napoleon* (1931) and, translated from the Russian, Anatolii Vinogradov's *The Black Consul* (1935). While James dismisses both books in his annotated bibliography, along with most of the biographies of Toussaint, as 'poor', their titles are clearly linked to his study (one of his chapters is even titled 'The Black Consul'). Another example is 'Black Spartacus', a formulation that James adapts and incorporates along with the others for his revisionist history of the Haitian Revolution.

When James uses the term 'black' (and 'Negro', as in *A History of Negro Revolt* [1938]), he brings up the historical legacies and meanings of blackness in the Caribbean and the USA, Europe and Africa. James was a consistent advocate in the struggle for black self-determination and a consistent critic of the 'particular burden which is the special inheritance of the black skin'.[2] 'I am Black European', he said in conversation during the late 1960s, 'that is my training and outlook', a comment that John Bracey, one of his interlocutors, took as cautionary in several senses, speaking both *of*

---

[2] Quoted in Glenn Richards, 'C. L. R. James on Black Self Determination in the United States and the Caribbean', in Selwyn R. Cudjoe and William E. Cain, eds., *C. L. R. James: His Intellectual Legacies*, Amherst: University of Massachusetts Press, 1995, pp. 317–327, at 317; see also Brett St. Louis, *Rethinking Race, Politics, and Poetics: C. L. R. James's Critique of Modernity*, New York: Routledge, 2007, pp. 38–42, on black political identity, class consciousness, and the pedagogy of race.

the weight of European intellectual and cultural baggage and *for* Europe's multiracial and multicultural history.[3] In the context of *The Black Jacobins*, James introduces blackness as a comparative measure to assess Toussaint's leadership: if, on the one hand, 'Toussaint L'Ouverture [was] one of the most remarkable men of a period rich in remarkable men', and moreover 'between 1789 and 1815, with the single exception of Bonaparte himself, no single figure appeared on the historical stage more greatly gifted than this Negro, a slave till he was 45', then it must also be said that 'Toussaint was no phenomenon, no Negro freak. The same forces which molded his genius had helped to create his black and Mulatto generals and officials'.[4] Here James alludes to key conceptual issues in his thinking on the relations between race and revolutionary leadership, the role of the leader and the 'masses' in developing revolutionary strategies, and ultimately the political formation of the black Jacobins as a modern people and modern subjects in the New World. The last question is a special one for historians, literary critics, and Marxist theorists in that it has implications for the choice of sources and archival research. In what forms does the individual, defined both collectively as the 'mass' and singularly as the leader, speak? James was out to demonstrate that black people collectively had a history, a world history, 'and in that history there were men who were fully able to stand comparison with great men of that period', he later explains.[5] Thinking with and through comparison here, James outlines the defensive limits and offensive possibilities of using blackness as a conceptual and revisionist resource for constructing world history.

So, despite its discontents, the comparative imperative is fundamental to James's historical project in *The Black Jacobins*. Rather than avoid Benedict Anderson's spectres of comparison, James courts and manages them. Anderson's image for the machinery of comparison is the 'incurable doubled vision' of a telescope, which he traces to Rizal's fictional hero, and by extension to all colonials, who see themselves automatically (Rizal says *maquinalmente*) as though from the end of an inverted telescope. In contrast to this fixed ('incurable') doubled vision, James actively summons and

---

[3] See John Bracey, 'Nello', in Scott McLemee and Paul Le Blanc, eds., *C. L. R. James and Revolutionary Marxism: Selected Writings of C. L. R. James 1939-1949*, Atlantic Highlands, NJ: Humanities Press, 1994, pp. 53–54, at 54.

[4] C. L. R. James, *The Black Jacobins: Toussaint L'Ouverture and the San Domingo Revolution*, 2nd ed., rev., New York: Vintage/Random House, 1963, Preface to the First Edition, p. x, p. 256 (references, hereafter abbreviated *BJ*, are cited parenthetically in the text).

[5] C.L.R. James, "Lectures on *The Black Jacobins*," *Small Axe*, 8 (September 2000), 65–112 (p. 84).

exorcises the spectres. The title *The Black Jacobins* alone establishes that fact. More than a literal parallel but less than a metaphor, it looks back and forth, not directly or automatically but by implication and association, from the vantage points of both the Old and New Worlds. Like the comparative logic of the title, both direct and implied, fundamental and assumed, unspoken and taken for granted, the comparative thinking in the book itself—as we shall see—is most present subtextually on the margins, grammatically in various comparative structures and modes, and paratextually in the prefaces and appendix that frame the whole. As a result, comparativism saturates the deep structure of the book but goes largely unsaid at the level of the spoken argument.

James's foundational statement of the when, where, how, and why of *The Black Jacobins* comes not in the text 'proper', neither the 1938 nor the 1963 version, but at the opening of the preface to the 1963 Vintage edition, where he starts by looking immediately at the appendix at the end of the book. 'The Appendix, "From Toussaint L'Ouverture to Fidel Castro"', he says, 'attempts for the future of the West Indies, all of them, what was done for Africa in 1938' (*BJ*, viii). Following James's logic and looking to the appendix, we find a parallel line, oft-quoted, that pinpoints the location and time of the historical conjuncture of his project. 'What took place in French San Domingo in 1792–1804 reappeared in Cuba in 1958' (*BJ*, 392). Together, these two paratextual statements, from the 1963 preface and appendix, establish the founding comparative credentials of the Black Jacobins project and underline the relevance to it of the text's publication history. Linking 1938 and 1963 as well as the beginning and ending of his book and its own history, James bookends both his text and the contexts that it inhabits and conjures in a notably open-ended way, opening out the historical perspective to a desired future.

First published simultaneously in London by Secker and Warburg and by Dial in New York, *The Black Jacobins* as a text has both a deeply comparative architectural structure and publication history. James's book appeared in 1938 and in 1963 a revised edition was issued in the USA by Vintage, with a new preface, appendix, and several footnotes. David Scott, who calls the 1963 edition 'an event', is one of a handful of critics who focus on the texts as a series of changing 'translations', in response to different historical moments, both of themselves and of the Haitian Revolution itself.[6] I will return at the end to the question of translation in James, the multiple acts of translating

---

[6] David Scott, *Conscripts of Modernity: The Tragedy of Colonial Enlightenment*, Durham: Duke University Press, 2004; Kara M. Rabitt, 'C. L. R. James's Figuring of Toussaint Louverture: A Reassessment of C. L. R. James's Interpretation', in Selwyn

that constitute *The Black Jacobins*, including his adaptations of the sources, some already in translation (and hence already adapted), but for now let us note that the link between comparative study and translation, not as a metaphor but as a material practice, grounds James in, and identifies him with, a particular multilingual and transnational practice of black history.

As a work of self-translation, *The Black Jacobins* includes not only the two editions, the double preface, the added appendix, and an updated bibliography but also passages in the revised text, usually in footnote form, where James comments self-consciously on his perceptions of history and his own process of writing ('This statement has been criticized. I stand by it. C. L. R. J.' [*BJ*, 88]). The paratexts lay out the history of both the Haitian Revolution and the book itself. This chronology has multiple layers and dimensions: the two prefaces, one dated 4 January 1962 and entitled the 'Preface to the Vintage Edition', and the other, undated 'Preface to the First Edition'; the 'Prologue' to the 1938 text that starts with the period when 'Christopher Columbus landed first in the New World at the island of San Salvador'; the 'Bibliography', annotated to reflect James's continuing research in and assessment of the historical and critical sources; and finally, the 'Appendix', entitled 'From Toussaint L'Ouverture to Fidel Castro', famous in its own right as an extended essay. The timeline of 1938–1963 (roughly the same period that the Cuban Carpentier's Caribbean Mediterranean is circulating in various forms and languages) also reaches out to related texts, including James's play, *Toussaint L'Ouverture*, produced in 1936 with Paul Robeson in the lead and revised by James in the 1970s as *The Black Jacobins*, and James's 1971 'Lectures on *Black Jacobins*', a Summer Research Symposium at the Institute of the Black World in Atlanta. As well as 'How I Wrote *The Black Jacobins*' and 'How I Would Rewrite *The Black Jacobins*', those lectures include a third, '*The Black Jacobins* & *Black Reconstruction*: A Comparative Analysis'. The lectures show James as an active and activist comparator of his own work and of his work in relation to others'.[7]

All of the comparisons are notably time-bound. Were he writing a book more suited to 1971, James says, he would not have described the slaves from the outside but would have found the evidence in the documents

---

R. Cudjoe and William E. Cain, eds., *C. L. R. James: His Intellectual Legacies*, Amherst: University of Massachusetts Press, 1995, pp. 118–135.

[7] James's lectures were published as "Lectures on *The Black Jacobins*," in *Small Axe*, 8 (September 2000), 65–112; references hereafter cited parenthetically in the text. Although few historians and critics do more than to note the contiguity of James's and Du Bois's books, for an extended critical comparison of *The Black Jacobins* and *Black Reconstruction*, see Anthony Bogues, *Black Heretics, Black Prophets: Radical Political Intellectuals*, New York: Routledge, 2003, pp. 69–93.

('they would be around, you have to look for them', 'the evidence is *there*, I know it is there', [Lectures, 100]) to let them speak for themselves, as Du Bois did in 1935, showing how all revolt against constituted authority 'has to begin from below' by 'the people down below' (105), the 'obscure creatures', obscure not only in San Domingo but also in Watts, Detroit, Cleveland, and Harlem (106), the 'two thousand leaders' (108) who, in addition to Toussaint, had to be conquered. Comparing his book to Du Bois's as well as 1935 to 1971 puts into context the achievements of James's *Black Jacobins*—in Robin Blackburn's apt formulation, 'both the book and the historical force that it named'.[8]

Since the time when James delivered those three lectures in Atlanta in June 1971, there has emerged a distinguished record of revisionist scholarship (Blackburn, Du Bois, Fick, Geggus, Trouillot) countering the dominance of the French Revolution, viewed both as prior and causal, bigger and more influential. Yet even now historians, perhaps inadvertently, keep alive the ghosting comparison. 'Compared to the Russian or Chinese Revolution, or the French Revolution with which it was intertwined, the revolution that two hundred years ago created Haiti was a small-scale affair', writes David Geggus in the preface to his 2001 collection on the impact of the Haitian Revolution in the Atlantic World.[9] This is most visible in the well-known historiography of the 'silencing' of the past, where Michel-Rolph Trouillot says that the Haitian Revolution 'entered history with the peculiar characteristic of being unthinkable even as it happened'.[10] Some scholars have also challenged the absolutism of Trouillot's silencing thesis, stressing instead, as historian Ada Ferrer does, how the archive contains traces of the conflicts between competing histories, their would-be tellers, and which narratives would dominate in which national and transnational memory circuits.[11] While Ferrer succeeds in getting inside and moving beyond Trouillot's claim, Geggus more tentatively notes that even if the Haitian Revolution was not quite an 'unthinkable event',

---

[8]   Robin Blackburn, 'The Black Jacobins and New World Slavery', in Selwyn R. Cudjoe and William E. Cain, eds., *C. L. R. James: His Intellectual Legacies*, Amherst: University of Massachusetts Press, 1995, pp. 81–97, at 83.

[9]   David P. Geggus, ed., *The Impact of the Haitian Revolution in the Atlantic World*, Columbia, SC: University of South Carolina, 2001, p. ix.

[10]   Michel-Rolph Trouillot, *Silencing the Past: Power and the Production of History*, Boston: Beacon, 1995, p. 73. Trouillot's title omits the name of Haiti, which provides the major examples in two central chapters.

[11]   Ada Ferrer, 'Talk about Haiti: The Archive and the Atlantic's Haitian Revolution', in Doris L. Garraway, ed., *Tree of Liberty: Cultural Legacies of the Haitian Revolution in the Atlantic World*, Charlottesville: University of Virginia Press, 2008, pp. 21–40.

nothing like it had happened before. Haiti was, Seymour Drescher similarly concludes, both 'unforgettable and unrepeatable', a spectral event with no past and no future.[12]

In contrast, James seizes upon the 'Black Jacobins', both the book and the historical force, as themselves neither unthinkable nor unrepeatable but rather inescapably comparative. The text's own bookends, the preface and appendix to the revised second edition of 1963, in themselves a self-reflexive comparative ensemble, establish initially how the story of Haiti could not be told without making comparisons of various kinds, in multiple spheres, both spatial and temporal, textual and contextual. Writing first in 1938 and then rewriting in 1962, James confirms the necessity not so much to bring Haiti out of the shadow of the French Revolution but rather to court and incorporate the spectral relations that connect them. 'It is impossible to understand the San Domingo Revolution', James says twice, both times paratextually, once in the bibliography and again in 'How I Wrote *The Black Jacobins*', 'unless it is studied in close relationship with the Revolution in France' (*BJ*, 383; Lectures, 76). Then, amplifying the Haiti-French revolutionary comparison of the past, which occupies the great bulk of the book, demonstrating that black people have a specific historical past, at the very end there is another comparison, to a very different place and time, between Haiti and what was 'bound to happen' in Africa in the future (Lectures, 73).

Here, in the very last pages of the book, James makes the critical move linking his own time of writing in the 1930s to the Haitian revolutionary moment of the 1790s. 'Finally', he says—signalling that we have arrived simultaneously at the end of the book and the beginning of a new argument, requiring comparison to another time and place—'despite the temporary reaction of Fascism, the prevailing standards of human liberty and equality are infinitely more advanced and profound than those current in 1789. Judged relatively by these standards, the millions of blacks in Africa ... are as much pariahs in that vast prison as the blacks and Mulattoes of San Domingo in the eighteenth century' (*BJ*, 375–376). What is the point of these comparisons, the 'more than' and 'as much as'? In the rest of the passage, an oft-quoted section that starts with 'the imperialists [who] envisage an eternity of African exploitation', James unfolds a series of temporal relations that challenge the assumption of an imperialist eternity. Comparative grammatical structures allow James to speculate further, via a series of doubled 'if ... then' analogies, that Toussaint and all the others

---

[12] Geggus, *The Impact*, p. xi; Drescher, 'The Limits of Example', in Geggus, *The Impact*, p. 13.

in 1790s Haiti are 'symbols of the future' (*BJ*, 377). The time of that future, however, is a moving target:

> If in 1788 ... these fine [white French] gentlemen had been told that in three years the blacks would shake off their chains and face extermination rather than put them on again, they would have thought the speaker mad. While if today one were to suggest to any white colonial potentate that among the blacks whom they rule are men so infinitely their superior ... that in a hundred years' time these whites would be remembered only because of their contact with the blacks, one would get some idea of what the Counts, Marquises, and other colonial magnates of the day thought of ... Toussaint ... when the revolt first began. (*BJ*, 376)

It takes two conditionals, expressed in the subjunctive mood through two different past tenses, past perfect and future perfect, moving time backward one and two steps, to express the hypothetical, a set of alternative futures, three years from 1788 and one hundred years from today, that define James's account of the Black Jacobins.

So it is clear, starting right from the 1938 edition, that what James had in mind with *The Black Jacobins* was to write proleptically and comparatively about the 'San Domingo Revolution' as the 'preparation for ... the revolution in Africa' (Lectures, 72). Whereas in 1938 he makes this point directly only at the very end of the text, it becomes increasingly prominent in the subsequent paratexts, written between 1962 and 1971, which confirm and deepen the original claim. The 1963 revised version makes a point of keeping unchanged the predictive and contested nature of the Haiti-Africa comparison. 'I have retained the concluding pages', James writes in the preface to the revised edition, 'which envisage and were intended to stimulate the coming emancipation of Africa' (*BJ*, vii). 'I wrote my book with the African revolution in mind', James reiterates in his 1971 Atlanta lecture, 'How I Wrote *The Black Jacobins*': 'It seems that those who come from a small island always think of a revolution in very wide terms ... You can't begin to think of a little revolution in a small island' (Lectures, 74). Playing with scale and scope here, James widens the historical perspective both spatially and temporally, in a way that mocks the concept of Haiti as, in Geggus's words, a 'small-scale affair' and the unexamined equation between size and power that undergirds such claustrophobic (self-enclosed, self-confirming, self-limiting) comparisons.

As a revolutionary event, James's Haiti appears not only inescapably but also multiply comparative, anchoring a circuit pointing from the Caribbean to Africa and back to the West Indies. *The Black Jacobins* initially positions Haiti in relation to France as well as vice versa, tracking the 'reciprocal radicalization' of the two revolutions in the Caribbean and the metropolis, and moving back and forth, backward and forward, in both space and time from the Americas to Europe and Africa. Then in yet another oceanic transposition, one of those shifts through which his history of Haiti always points elsewhere, James asserts in the 1963 appendix that 'what took place in French San Domingo in 1792–1804 reappeared in Cuba in 1958'. Making this single, massive space-time shift moves us deeper into the comparative vein. 'Castro's revolution is of the twentieth century as much as Toussaint's was of the eighteenth. But despite the distance of over a century and a half, both are West Indian … West Indians first became aware of themselves as a people in the Haitian Revolution' (*BJ*, 392). The conjuncture that James sets up here in the space and time of the 'West Indies' reminds us why comparison was unavoidable, given that there was no reasonable way to claim that Africa-in-the-1930s or 1960s is part of the same conjuncture as Haiti in 1800. Africa-in-the-1960s must be brought in through a non-conjunctural link, while Africa-in-the-1930s is the imminent, still 'bound-to-be' decolonised and Africa in the 1970s raises a missing archive (the voices 'from below' of the 'masses' themselves in this account told from the 'outside', the literary voices of the appendix). Therefore *The Black Jacobins* is pressed into the service of a different conjuncture: Africa-of-the-present, both the 1930s and 1960s, is the object.

Part of what makes *The Black Jacobins* an exemplary and lasting work of historical criticism, then, is the self-consciousness with which James connects the story of Toussaint to the emerging, still-unfinished stories of his own times (the post-war decolonisation of Africa, the sixties spread of radicalism and revolutionary consciousness around the world), and by extension to our time—as well as times yet to come. This view, expressed by Scott and endorsed by many others, confirms that the Black Jacobins, both the book and the force it names, produced and were the products of a complex set of space-time shifts and transferences.[13] The most striking space-time transposition is the famous claim at the opening of the appendix, which could be a signature refrain for *The Black Jacobins* as a whole: 'What took place in French San Domingo in 1792–1804 reappeared in Cuba in 1958' (*BJ*, 391).

---

[13] See Scott, *Conscripts*, p. 10.

When and where was the Haitian Revolution?

To thus incorporate on so many levels the spectres of comparison has far-reaching consequences for the spatio-temporal relation fundamental to comparative thinking. Where and when was the Haitian Revolution? Here are some preliminary answers, via James, to a deceptively simple question.

The 'where' introduces all those place names, in all those languages, not only the Spanish Santo Domingo, French Saint Domingue, and the indigenous 'Haiti', but also all the other terms for the region as a whole, then and now, including West Indies, Greater or circum Caribbean, Nuestra América, the Other America, Black Atlantic, New World Mediterranean— and American Tropics. James's own shorthand 'San Domingo', which he uses rather than the French Saint Domingue and sometimes produces what sounds like a misnomer (French San Domingo), brings up the issue of translatability of terms (which I will address at the end of the essay). The 'when' brings in the different timelines of the 'Haitian Revolution', some starting as early as the 1750s with the maroon resistance and execution of Mackandal, others with the 1789 fall of the Bastille, others with the 1791 mass slave uprising (the legendary meeting of 22 August in Bois Cayman) and burning of Le Cap Français led by the Jamaican Boukman, still others (James among them) with the 1792 decree of the French National Assembly giving freedom and citizenship to France's slaves, and some ending in 1803 with the death of Toussaint, the temporary triumph of Napoleon's forces and the restoration of slavery, or in 1804 with the establishment of the independent Haiti by Jean-Jacques Dessalines. The point is not which is the correct alternative, but how revealing is the unexamined use of such varying dates and names for events and figures. The names themselves point to the shifting setting of *The Black Jacobins*, located at the confluence of three languages and four empires at different stages of development (France, Spain, Britain, USA). So the space of the Black Jacobins is notably transnational and multilingual while their time is, if anything, even more multidimensional.

The 'where' leads to the when, just as space and time are mutually constitutive. The Caribbean or New World Mediterranean, perhaps least well-known of the names for the region as a whole, echoes Anderson on Rizal and how the spectre of the new is shadowed by the old. Expanding the Mediterranean to include America and the New World underscores how space may have its own temporal dimension.[14] Beyond the obvious new-old relation implicit here is the special problem of comparability in

---

[14] See Johannes Fabian, *Time and the Other: How Anthropology Makes its Object*, New York: Columbia University Press, 1983.

the New World context: not only that the 'new' (of New Canaàn, New
York, Nouvelle Orléans and all the other 'new' New World cities) inevitably
raises, perhaps is haunted, shadowed by, the spectre of the 'old' but also, far
more tellingly, the special nature of that newness itself. Rather than either
genealogical continuity *from* the old *to* the new, or displacement *of* the old
by the new, in the Americas 'new' and 'old' were understood 'synchronically,
coexisting within homogeneous empty time', as a sense of (in Anderson's
words) 'parallelism', 'simultaneity' or 'comparability'. The 'doubleness of the
Americas', where the 'new' is happening not after but coterminous with a
reanimated, relocated 'old', accounts for why the spectre of comparison is
so protean, palpable, and elusive, formative, memorable, and forgettable, in
the Americas context.[15] American exceptionalism is rooted in its special
comparability!

The conditions for the specific newness of New World nationalism, the
sense of simultaneity that imagines New York and all the other New World
cities as existing synchronically alongside their Old World counterparts,
were—oddly enough—met in the Americas 'as they had never been before'.
The 'sublime confidence of novelty' first singled out the American Revolution
of 1776 from all the others in Europe and in the Americas that followed
and then initiated a common pattern.[16] The revolutionary wars of 1776–1825
in the Americas aimed not to overthrow or destroy the old European
counterparts but 'to safeguard their continuing parallelism'—and this despite
the fact that 'the Old Time of European new nationalisms was wholly
foreign to the Americas'. An 'exhilarating doubleness' is thus created by the
difference within American comparability.[17] Like Anderson, James sees the
semi-oxymoron of a pattern without peer in the regional history of the West
Indies imposed by two common factors, 'the sugar plantation and Negro
slavery', which produce 'an original pattern, not European, not African,
not part of the American main, not native in any conceivable sense of that
word, but West Indian, *sui generis*, with no parallel anywhere else' (*BJ*,
391–392). Both Anderson and James point to the doubleness of the Americas,
a set of regional imaginaries, grounded in reciprocal apprehensions of
time and space, that are characterised by the contradictions of a special
(in)comparability. American newness is unparalleled, newer than any other.

Both Anderson and James may thus inadvertently be subscribing to the
'myth' or the 'trap' of the 'two Americas', what Peter Hulme calls 'that
dangerous continental divide' between North and South America. The

---

[15]   Anderson, *Imagined Communities*, pp. 187, 191.
[16]   Anderson, *Imagined Communities*, p. 188.
[17]   Anderson, *Imagined Communities*, p. 195.

intellectual problem with the idea of the two Americas is what happens to 'the bits in the middle', the regions known as Central America and 'all those islands', usually referred to as the Caribbean, the West Indies or the Antilles.[18] The idea of the two Americas, North and South, José Martí's 'Our America' and 'the America which is not ours', creates a critical political division with unintended negative geographical consequences, leaving out the key region known as the Caribbean. Some Caribbean intellectuals have responded with a different, more openly comparative terminology that looks elsewhere in space and time and thus sidesteps or perhaps neutralises the trap of the two Americas. Carpentier, we remember, is known for his 'Caribbean Mediterranean', the location he credits as inspiration in the prologue to his novel on the Haitian Revolution *El reino de este mundo* [*The Kingdom of this World*] as well as for his 1962 novel *El siglo de las luces* [*Explosion in a Cathedral*]. It should not be surprising, critic Michael Dash comments, that the idea of an 'Antillean identity' should re-emerge (as always, after Martí, whom Carpentier credits as the originary inventor of the tradition) in the 1940s in the concept of a New World Mediterranean proposed by a Cuban writing about Haiti. Carpentier needs the 'binomial Mediterranean Caribbean', Roberto González Echevarría says, to represent temporally the revival of a world that Europe has left behind and spatially the locus where Europe's Mediterranean origins are replayed in the Caribbean.[19]

All these formulas combining the Caribbean and the Mediterranean, historian Gordon Lewis argues, can be read reflexively as an examination of a comparison. Such terminology, defined by different Mediterraneans, ancient, modern, and metaphoric, allows for exploring connections that go beyond the usual pairings of comparative history. In a very real sense (and as geographers use the term), the Caribbean is a mediterranean sea. What's odd about our terminology is that the sea between Europe and Africa has become known as *the* Mediterranean rather than one of a number of mediterranean seas in the world. Both mediterraneans were set apart from Northern Europe: if the Mediterranean world system was as much, culturally and religiously, related to Africa and Arabia as to Eurasia, the Caribbean was as much an extension of West Africa as it was of Elizabethan England. This

---

[18] Peter Hulme, 'Expanding the Caribbean', in Michael Niblett and Kerstin Oloff, eds., *Perspectives on the 'Other America': Comparative Approaches to Caribbean and Latin American Culture*, Amsterdam: Rodopi, 2009, pp. 29–50, at 39, 32.

[19] J. Michael Dash, *The Other America: Caribbean Literature in a New World Context*, Charlottesville: University Press of Virginia, 1998, p. 90; Roberto González Echevarría, *Celestina's Brood: Continuities of the Baroque in Spanish and Latin American Literatures*, Durham: Duke University Press, 1993, p. 183.

explains why for Lewis it is misleading to try to understand the Caribbean simply in European terms—the region's history does not equal the overseas history of France, Spain, England, or Holland. Instead we should approach these historic oceanic societies as themselves twin lodestars of perpetual motion, vast movement of immigrants and emigrants, and racial and cultural intermingling. The Caribbean is a world 'not unlike' the polyglot trading cities of the Mediterranean of the Hellenistic period. It is the world of that period, 'transported to another time and place'.[20] The double negative underlines the kind of comparison, interrupted, uncompleted, and open-ended, that creates the oceanic transposition of the Mediterranean to the Caribbean.[21]

James's 'West Indies' located in the paratexts of the 1963 edition make their own massive moves of oceanic transposition. Beginning with James's preface to the 1938 first edition and ending with the famous appendix to the 1963 second edition, what preserves the relevance, even contemporaneity, of *The Black Jacobins* is the prolepsis characteristic of unfinished or *as yet* unfulfilled history. This conception of history rests on a series of uncompleted comparisons between and among both texts and contexts. Two key framing texts, the 1938 preface and the 1963 appendix, pair James's history of the Haitian Revolution with two distinct moments in his own time, meaning that even as *The Black Jacobins* responded to a historiographic vacuum, it relocated this history. What James emphasises in his 1938 preface are the events that interrupted, animated, and reoriented his work on late-eighteenth-century San Domingo. 'Such is our age and this book is of it, with something of the fever and the fret', (*BJ*, xi) he writes. The 'booming of Franco's heavy artillery' and 'the rattle of Stalin's firing squads' provide the soundtrack for a study that gestures forward to 'the fierce shrill turmoil of the revolutionary movement', with fronts including national liberation struggles in Africa (*BJ*, xi). By 1963 James will return this history to its place of origin, almost, as the diffuse movement of the 1930s converges on a single point of arrival. From Haiti to Cuba, 'From Toussaint L'Ouverture to Fidel Castro', James's black Jacobin is back in the Caribbean but has migrated to the site of a different revolution. The explicit coordinates of this second pairing suggest fulfillment, a history in its 'ultimate stage' (*BJ*, 411). The refrain, 'what took place in French San Domingo in 1792–1804

---

[20] Gordon K. Lewis, *Main Currents in Caribbean Thought: The Historical Evolution of Caribbean Society in its Ideological Aspects, 1492–1900*, Baltimore: Johns Hopkins University Press, 1983, p. 18.

[21] For 'uncompleted', see Anthony Appiah, 'The Uncompleted Argument: Du Bois and the Illusion of Race', *Critical Inquiry*, 12 (August 1985), pp. 21–37.

reappeared in Cuba in 1958' (*BJ*, 391), appears all the more extraordinary in light of the infamy attached to the Haitian Revolution, the defensive efforts throughout plantation America to deny the threat of race war by dismissing the first and only successful slave uprising in the Americas as anomalous and unrepeatable. Made exceptional in its own time, Haiti could be in no way representative of the Caribbean at large.[22] In 1963 James remarks of *The Black Jacobins*, 'I have written about the West Indies in general' (*BJ*, 411), a regional emphasis that would have seemed markedly out of place in the 1938 preface. Where this history leads is made clear in the second half of this claim, which concludes the argument on a note of requisite comparison: 'and Cuba is the most West Indian island in the West Indies' (*BJ*, 411).

So the space of the Black Jacobins, both the book and the force it names, is notably transnational and multilingual while their time is if anything even more multidimensional. Linking the Haitian Revolution and African decolonisation in the 1938 edition and then linking Haiti to the Cuban Revolution in the 1963 appendix, James stresses the disjointed space-time of the 'Caribbean quest for national identity': 'In a scattered series of disparate islands, the process consists of a series of unco-ordinated periods of drift, punctuated by spurts, leaps and catastrophes' (*BJ*, 391). This explains why the Haitian Revolution has produced such a travelling history, and why Haiti poses so insistently the question of why some nations need other nations' histories in order to tell their own. Haiti's 'multifarious' history, as Geggus called it, exported a transnational web of influences and responses, visible and invisible, pro and con, spoken and unspoken, unspeakable and unthinkable, that looms almost larger than the 'event' itself.

Text-networks and comparative strategies

The text of *The Black Jacobins* mirrors this travelling history in that it is both a single celebrated work by James, a textual cluster of different editions, prefaces, and appendices, a play and set of lectures, as well as a wider circle, what we might call *The Black Jacobins*' text-network.[23] 'Text-network' refers to the circulation of a characteristic and central type of Hellenistic world literature, such as the 'Alexander Romance', bodies of prose composition with

---

[22] For invaluable studies of Haitian exceptionalism, see Joan Dayan, *Haiti, History, and the Gods*, Berkeley: University of California Press, 1995; Trouillot, *Silencing the Past*; and Sibylle Fischer, *Modernity Disavowed: Haiti and the Cultures of Slavery in the Age of Revolution*, Durham: Duke University Press, 2004.

[23] For the concept of the text-network, I am indebted to my colleague Dan Selden: see his 'Text Networks', *Ancient Narrative*, 8 (2009), pp. 1–23.

no definitive origin and no telos in their dissemination, no known 'author' and no definitive form; rather they exist only as a multiplicity of different versions, in a wide variety of different languages, re-tailored to fit a host of different cultural contexts, diffused (always in a multiplicity of directions) over much of the Asian-African-European land mass. One way to describe them would be as translations without an original. Taking this lead, we would follow the trail of what could loosely be called *The Black Jacobins'* adaptations, starting historically with the two revolutions, the Haitian and the French, as multi-directional adaptations of one another, and moving to all the 'outsides', textual and contextual, including editions and translations, that constitute the text-network of *The Black Jacobins*. The 'layered nature of the work'—the two editions, the double preface, the added appendix, the updated bibliography—gives a glimpse of 'a multifaceted James', not only his perceptions of Toussaint but also of history and history-writing itself.[24]

While we are reading James's work comparatively, *as* a series of adaptations, what do we find of his strategies for looking comparatively through both ends of Anderson's telescope? The table of contents reads like an outline of the Jamesian adaptive method, enacting and reflecting on his own historical writing practice. The original 1938 chapter titles, which are retained in the 1963 edition, lay out the objects of study as well as the space-time frame of the study in strikingly comparative terms. Chapters come in pairs; some focus on interrelated actors, such as Chapters I and II, 'The Property' and 'The Owners', while others link these groups to temporal processes of action. Chapter IV, 'The San Domingo Masses Begin', is followed by Chapter V, 'And the Paris Masses Complete'. 'The Rise of Toussaint' (VI) leads to 'The Mulattoes Try and Fail' (VII) and 'The White Slave-Owners Again' (VIII). The table of contents 'zigzags' from 1789 (the date that opens the 1938 preface to the first edition), backwards to Christopher Columbus at the start of the 1938 prologue to the first edition, and then returns to 1789 at the opening of Chapter I. This is James's version of Anderson's 'chain of zigzags', the strange pattern of space-time shifts produced in the late nineteenth-century 'era of early globalization' by the eruption of insurrectionary violence through the three worlds of José Rizal: those of Europe, the Caribbean and USA, and the Far East.[25] Finally, moving forward to the 1963 appendix, we find the signature massive space-time transference: 'What took place in French San Domingo in 1792–1804 reappeared in Cuba in 1958' (*BJ*, 391). Starting off as a history from Columbus to Toussaint (the 1938 prologue opens with

---

[24] Rabbit, 'C. L. R. James's Figuring', p. 119.
[25] On 'the zigzag of insurrectionary explosions in the metropole and in the colonies', an 'interactive zigzagging', see Anderson, *Under Three Flags*, pp. 81–82.

Columbus landing in the New World, and the thirteen chapters of the text proper focus for more than 300 pages on Toussaint) and ending with the appendix 'From Toussaint L'Ouverture to Fidel Castro', the text-network as a whole looks from Columbus to Castro. Expressed mathematically: from Columbus to Toussaint + from Toussaint to Castro = from Columbus to Castro. The total evokes a strikingly open-ended comparative history that outdoes even Eric Williams's book of the same title, *From Columbus to Castro: The History of the Caribbean, 1492–1969*, that would not appear until 1970.[26]

The comparative approach is key to the kind of unfinished, provisional history that James favours. This may be surprising, given the critical shibboleths that have dominated the comparative study of slavery and emancipation, a tradition to which James might nominally belong.[27] But while he is never considered a comparative historian, James relies strikingly often on comparative terminology and constructions to make his main arguments. These comparative modes range from relational terms that bring together unlike elements through degree (greater, less than, or equal to) and similitude ('like' and 'as'), to conditional, counterfactual, and speculative relations (expressed in 'if … then' constructions and hypothetical statements using subjunctive conditionals in various tenses). Many of the most quoted and debated passages of *The Black Jacobins* depend on thinking and working comparatively in all of these ways.

Writing as 'a highly trained Marxist' ('that is the person who wrote *The Black Jacobins*'), James famously compares slaves to proletarians and race to class in his assessment of the relative success and failure of the Haitian Revolution (Lectures, 71). Working in 'the huge sugar-factories' of the North Plain, the slaves 'were closer to a modern proletariat than any group of workers in existence at the time, and the rising was, therefore, a thoroughly prepared and organized mass movement' (*BJ*, 86). Assessing Toussaint's failure ('It was in method, and not in principle, that Toussaint failed'), James uses an even more oft-cited set of comparative terms: 'The race question is subsidiary to the class question in politics, and to think of imperialism in terms of race is disastrous. But to neglect the racial factor as

---

[26] See Eric Williams, *From Columbus to Castro: The History of the Caribbean, 1492–1969*, New York: Harper & Row, 1970, and Jaime Suchlicki, *Cuba: From Columbus to Castro*, New York: Scribner, 1974, later, in the 4th edition, revised and updated, retitled *Cuba: From Columbus to Castro and Beyond*, Washington: Brassey's, 1997, 2002.

[27] For a trenchant recent critique of comparative race-slave studies, see Rebecca J. Scott, *Degrees of Freedom: Louisiana and Cuba After Slavery*, Cambridge, MA: Harvard University Press, 2005, pp. 4–6.

merely incidental is an error only less grave than to make it fundamental' (*BJ*, 283). Without commenting in detail on this most debated of James passages, I want simply to note the critical role played by comparative thinking in his articulation of race and class here. James creates a series of weighted relations that do not ultimately align consistently, like an 'if ... then' proposition that does not or will not work: to subordinate race to class in politics is the opposite of elevating race within imperialism, yet the outcome of these assertions is a differently-weighted set of values for race itself, at one extreme (incidental, near-zero) or another (fundamental, near-total). The result is an enigmatic comparative formula that has generated little certainty and much critical disagreement. Finally, equally as cited and debated is James's 'great-men-make-history' line from the 1938 preface. Comparing Toussaint to Bonaparte, James argues, in a famous, unattributed paraphrase of Marx in *The Eighteenth Brumaire* (1852), that 'great men make history, but only such history as it is possible for them to make' (*BJ*, x). Openly alluding to Marx, James's paraphrase of such a well-known line amounts to another comparison, this one assumed and unspoken (it is not necessary to name Marx), through which James raises questions critical to Marxism, about relations between personality and history, leaders and masses, individual creativity and social change, and finally between the roles of art and science in the writing of history. That many of James's sources, including Marx, are translated, by him or others, adds another dimension to the various comparative operations that James works through here.

The best examples of James's comparative thinking, those that combine most or all of the different strategies I have outlined, come, not coincidentally, when he revises the 1938 text in light of the present of the 1960s. Authorial revision, itself a form of comparison, however silent, entails translation and adaptation of both texts and their contexts, both those contexts represented in the texts and inhabited by the texts. In this case revision produced a transparent process of adaptation. It was critical for James to retain in the revised edition the original sense of multilayered, proleptic conditionality embedded in the 1938 ending. Those concluding pages, on the imperialist vision of an eternity of African exploitation, are among the excerpts that James includes in his 1971 lectures, the one from 'How I Wrote *The Black Jacobins*' that I quoted earlier, where he uses those repeated 'if ... then' constructions with verbs in the subjunctive mood and future-past tense: 'If in 1788 anyone had told the Comte'; 'if these fine gentlemen had been told that in three years the blacks would shake off their chains', 'if to-day one were to suggest to any white colonial potentate ... that in a hundred years' time these whites would be remembered only because of their contact with the blacks, one would get some idea of what the Counts ... and other colonial magnates of the day thought of ... Toussaint ... when the revolt first began' (*BJ*, 376). At each signal moment here, James looks forward in time, first three and then one hundred years, producing multilayered relations of past, present, and future that would be repeated in the 1963 edition (not quite one hundred years later).

The layers of time are made even more visible in the footnotes added to the revised edition, which reinforce the conditional prophecy of the original open ending both by retaining and updating it. The additional footnotes confirm and extend, noticeably still at the margins, the closing argument of the first edition, predicting that what happened in Haiti would also happen in Africa. A group of new footnotes (eight in total) comment on the time of the writing, both the first and the revised edition, some noting simply 'written in 1938' (*BJ*, 55, 265) or 'written, it must be remembered, in 1938' (*BJ*, 82), others noting 'Still true, in 1961' (*BJ*, 43), and others explicitly articulating in spatio-temporal terms the significance of this layering of times: 'Such observations, written in 1938, were intended to use the San Domingo revolution as a forecast of the future of colonial Africa' (*BJ*, 18). So what was forecast in 1938 remains present in 1963, still future-facing despite the passage of time, alongside another new forecast, made like the first, at the margins of the text, that 'what took place in French San Domingo in 1792–1804 reappeared in Cuba in 1958' (*BJ*, 391). The effect is to create a series of interdependent conjunctures joined by the anticipatory sense of 'something coming'.[28]

James's footnotes thus mark critical moments of comparison, between and within texts and contexts. In this sense the paratexts, including the prefaces and appendix as well as the footnotes, are not appendages but defining forces within the text-network of *The Black Jacobins*. Only there, only paratextually, are we told the how and why of the whole. 'I have retained the concluding pages', James explains in the preface to the revised edition, 'which envisage and were intended to stimulate the coming emancipation of Africa. They are a part of the history of our time' (*BJ*, vii). 'They', the pages, are part of the history of our time, a speculative, conjectural history that depends on a sense of continuing prolepsis. 'We were all quite certain that after the coming war', James writes in 1971, referring back to the 1930s as though they were yet to happen, 'the African would emerge as an independent force in history'. 'That is why I wrote the book', he reiterates, 'in order that people should think about the African revolution and get their minds right about what was bound to happen in Africa' (Lectures, 72–73).

---

[28] This is Benedict Anderson's term for the future shock of Rizal's proleptic novel *El filibusterismo* (1891): see *Under Three Flags*, pp. 121–122.

'Would emerge', 'should think' and 'bound to happen': the verbs express a counterfactual and hypothetical, an outcome both open and imminent. Rather than revising this central argument of the original, either in 1963 or in 1971, to acknowledge African decolonisation, he lets the prediction stand on its own unfinished terms.

And those terms are also notably comparative. When readers follow the footnote trail and look back to the text that James stresses, in the 1963 preface and the Atlanta lectures of 1971, is retained, unchanged, we find more comparisons, more conditional 'if ... then's, more subjunctive verbs—in short, more of what he calls in the first Atlanta lecture 'speculative thought': 'thinking about what is going to happen as a result of what you see around you' (Lectures, 72). 'But for the revolution', James says in a passage written in 1938, retained and footnoted in the 1963 edition, and reread in his 1971 Atlanta lectures, 'this extraordinary man and his band of gifted associates would have lived their lives as slaves ... standing barefooted and in rags to watch inflated little governors and mediocre officials from Europe pass by, as many a talented African stands in Africa today' (*BJ*, 265). Both the counterfactual verb 'would have' and the comparative simile 'as' preserve the future of the past as it was imagined, still in the conditional, an imperfect and uncompleted action, in 1938. Stressing the significance of that moment, not as fixed or frozen in the past but rather in suspended animation, continuing on into the future, James underlines it three times in 'How I Wrote *The Black Jacobins*', saying of the passage quoted: 'I wrote that in 1938'; 'I was able to say that in 1938', 'Written in 1938'. In so doing he preserves the prolepsis characteristic of *as yet* unfulfilled, or untimely, history. African decolonisation may have occurred but that outcome does not change the urgency of futurity, the 'bound-to-happen'. In 1971, he reaffirms that the book, now revised with the appendix 'From Columbus to Castro', 'was written about Africa. It wasn't written about the Caribbean ... the book has something else in mind than Caribbean emancipation' (Lectures, 73).

Simultaneously, James multiplies the comparative operations that help to produce the history he has in mind, a series of conjunctures in multidimensional time and space, juxtaposing the original pairing of the Haitian-French revolutionary 1790s and the African 1930s with the Caribbean 1960s and 70s. It is no accident that the passage from *The Black Jacobins* that James chooses to quote twice in his 1971 close re-readings appears in the chapter titled (implicitly comparatively) 'The Black Consul', nor that so much of the chapter concerns placing Toussaint comparatively in relation, not only to Napoleon ('With the exception always of Bonaparte, no single figure in the whole period of the French Revolution traveled so fast and so far' [*BJ*, 256]) but also to Spartacus ('No wonder he came in the end to believe in himself as the black Spartacus, foretold by Raynal as predestined to achieve the emancipation of blacks' [*BJ*, 250]). The multiple times and the interrelations among them—the period of the French Revolution, in the end, foretold, predestined—are keyed to an analogous set of comparisons—Raynal's black Spartacus, Toussaint's Bonaparte—which together constitute what James calls (in the 1962 preface) 'the history of our time'. By this James means provisional history, driven by future planning, so that from his perspective in 1971 the important thing about *The Black Jacobins* is that it was written in 1938 and that he made very few changes, 'about eight pages at most', for the 1963 edition (Lectures, 90). 'What I am thinking of is that anything that I write—that anybody writes—in 1971, must have in mind that by 1985 … people will be reading it and will know you see something that matters to them' (Lectures, 90).

What does James have in mind not just with the book but with the whole text-network circulating by the time of the three 1971 lectures? As he works through 'how I wrote' and 'how I would rewrite' *The Black Jacobins*, there is a subtle shift in the nature of the textual timeline. The 'first edition' comes to be characterised most often through the date of its writing, 1938, the 'second edition revised' with the 1960s. If the literary hierarchy split between original and final intention does not quite disappear, it gives way to thinking of books relationally, contextualised through their 'ages', one of James's favourite terms, and the interrelations between the 'different circumstances' in which they are written (*BJ*, xi). Through both the book and the force it names, to use Blackburn's formula one last time, James thinks comparatively and conditionally about 'what I would have written if I were to write it today' (Lectures, 71). The subjunctive conditionals enforce what he calls 'speculative thought', thinking about what is going to happen ('unless, in the words of Hegel, you are doing speculative thought, you are not doing any thought at all') (Lectures, 72, 74). The Hegelian attribution notwithstanding, James's speculative thoughts resemble a cross between Reinhart Kosellek's notion of 'futures past' and what historian Gary Wilder calls Aimé Césaire's 'untimely vision', an imagined future past that never came to pass in Césaire's failed 1946 programme for Antillean independence achieved through French departmentalisation. Wilder underscores the spectral legacy that so many historians have associated with Haiti, by linking Césaire's post-war interventions with the 'spirit' of Toussaint's own failed attempt at decolonisation without national independence (his famously ill-fated reliance on the French). For Wilder, like James, this means that historiography must grapple with the way that the 1790s constituted an immediate historical context for the 1930s and 40s, neither simply an important precedent (though it is that) nor a tragically failed past future, foreclosed once and for all time, but an untimely 'futures past'.[29] 'Untimely' refers to 'practices of temporal refraction whereby people act "as if"': as if they inhabit a different historical moment, as if the future were imminent in the past, as if alternative pasts that never materialised could be reanimated in the present.[30] James's term would be 'the history of our time', of which his book and the (then) 'coming emancipation of Africa' are a part; in 1938 'the history of our time' is produced only by James and associates, those who wrote and spoke 'as if the African events of the last quarter of a century were imminent' (*BJ*, vii).

James's 'as if' is thus nothing more or less than *The Black Jacobins*. This is not just a matter of the ubiquitous conditional verbs and comparative 'if … then' constructions. The whole text-network—the two editions, double preface, added appendix, updated bibliography and footnotes, along with the lectures—confirms and enacts the open-endedness that defines James's 'history of our time'. His speculative thought is clearest in the paratexts, especially the footnotes added to the second edition that underscore—still, submerged, at the margins—the underlying argument of the 1938 edition that what happened in Haiti would—not could but will, the future of the past—also happen in Africa. Just so, the link to Caribbean emancipation, from Haiti in the 1790s to Cuba in the 1960s, is made only in another paratext, the appendix tracing a history 'From Toussaint to Castro'. To preserve and reaffirm this sense of untimely history, James underlines the 1938 proleptic subtext by retaining unchanged the original series of speculative thoughts on the coming emancipation of Africa, leaving them standing, as is, or as was, not updated but simply noted in a parallel series of footnotes. In turn the footnotes neither correct nor revise but underscore, tersely and laconically, the original statements, simply asserting that he stands by them and thus retaining their original controversiality. (In 1938 only James and company thought speculatively, 'as if the African events of the last quarter of a century were imminent'.) In what amounts to a virtual paratextual philosophy, James's third lecture, 'How I Would Rewrite *The Black Jacobins*', stresses that the footnotes in the 1963 edition 'would form an important part' of the first edition, and in fact 'they wouldn't be footnotes if the book were to be rewritten today' (Lectures, 103). Now we are back

---

[29] See Reinhart Koselleck, *Futures Past: On the Semantics of Historical Time*, New York: Columbia University Press, 2004.

[30] See Gary Wilder, 'Untimely Vision: Aimé Césaire, Decolonization, Utopia', *Public Culture*, 21, no. 1 (2009), pp. 101–140; see p. 106 for the 'as if' comment. For another view of James's proleptic thinking, see Kenneth Surin, '"The Future Anterior": C. L. R. James and Going *Beyond a Boundary*', in Grant Farred, ed., *Rethinking C. L. R. James*, Cambridge, MA: Blackwell, 1996, pp. 187–204.

full-circle to the history from below that James would have written today, in the 1970s. But 'poor James, condemned to footnotes', because he doesn't want to change the book too much and 'alter the whole movement of the thing', must thus argue paratextually both for the untimely history and the history from below that he wants to tell (Lectures, 106, 103). The result is either to relegate to the status of a footnote the 'people from below', or to elevate the textual outsides, where the footnotes reside, to full partnership with the rest of the untimely history in and of *The Black Jacobins*.

Provisional conclusions: what was bound to happen in the future

Back to the future: James's appendix famously identifies the Cuban Revolution as both part of the historical conjuncture produced by the Haitian Revolution and part of 'an original pattern, not European, not African, not a part of the American main, not native in any conceivable sense of that word, but West Indian, *sui generis*, with no parallel elsewhere' (*BJ*, 391–392). How can the West Indies be both historically unique and relational? For some, James's model of comparison *is* the problem, imposing the identity of Marx's proletariat on the slaves of New World plantation societies, thus elevating Marxism and relegating to the footnotes the subaltern 'history from below'. In the process, according to this critique, James produces a teleology that minimises Africa and maximises France as 'stages in the development of the West Indian quest for a national identity', and, finally, an articulation of class and racial struggles that translates the specific into the universal (*BJ*, 396). Better yet: mistranslates.

If we look back at all the comparative operations that James works through, thinking of them as a series of changing translations, both figurative and literal, then a pattern of strategic mistranslation emerges: the persistence of incomplete, inconsistent or imperfect translations, such as the misnomer 'French San Domingo', that are only partially acknowledged *as* translations, or transparent translations, such as the many quotations from the sources, that are made entirely silently. The extended passages, for example, that James takes from Pamphile de Lacroix's 1819 memoir of his service in the 1801 French military expedition, headed by Napoleon's brother-in-law Leclerc, are James's own translations into English, only intermittently footnoted. Likewise, James's sources, documented in the footnotes and the bibliography, are predominantly written in French (the rest in English), with excerpts quoted in translations that are generally his own but only rarely noted. (Of the available Toussaint biographies, he comments in the bibliography that he read Anatolii Vinogradov's *The Black Consul* in a 1935 translation from the Russian.) In another variation on the theme of half-spoken or transparent translation, we know that while Marx is evoked, his name is omitted in the celebrated case of 'great men make history', the line in the preface to the 1963 edition noted by Scott and others. Finally, in one more instance, also paratextual, this one from the 1963 appendix, James translates Césaire's poem *Cahier d'un retour au pays natal*, ending with the famous line, 'and no race possesses the monopoly of beauty, of intelligence, of force, and there is a place for all at the rendezvous of victory' (*BJ*, 401). The translation is again James's own, and, notably, he translates Césaire's 'conquête' as 'victory' instead of 'conquest', although Césaire does not use 'victoire' here, and in the previous stanza James translates Césaire's verb 'conquérir' as 'conquer'.[31] However we might read the significance of these anomalies, we cannot miss what they all have in common: a will to open-ended and unfinished translation as yet another manifestation of the speculative history James is writing.

Perhaps what we have here is a strategic failure to communicate. These moments of uncompleted communication are part of the complex act of translation that some critics see as foundational to *The Black Jacobins*, those who follow its paratextual condition, keeping track of the different editions, prefatory and afterword material, and footnotes: a snapshot of a work in all its lives, from past literary and socio-political sources and influences, to contemporaneous texts and contexts of its own present, and finally to its afterlives, including those yet to come. Editions are not just to be cited and done with, and by the same token, footnotes are more than just footnotes, an unofficial running commentary both buttressing and challenging the text, and possibly both creating and revealing a special relation between race and the paratextual condition.[32] The pages themselves, particularly the concluding ones, are part of what James calls 'the history of our time' (*BJ*, vii).

Taking the cue of Shalini Puri, who reviews Scott's *Conscripts of Modernity* as a 'suggestive "translation"' of *The Black Jacobins*, I see James himself through the 'translator's invisibility', his approach to writing the history of the Haitian Revolution as a series of transparent comparisons through which we can see the changing texts and contexts of two revolutions and then more, in response to different historical moments.[33] Throughout James has tried to show, he says in the bibliography, 'the close parallels,

---

[31] On this passage, see St. Louis, *Rethinking Race*, p. 64.
[32] See Beth A. McCoy, 'Race and the (Para)Textual Condition', *PMLA*, 121, no. 1 (January 2006), pp. 156–169.
[33] Shalini Puri, Review of *Conscripts of Modernity* in *New West Indian Guide*, 81, nos. 3 & 4 (2007), pp. 11–14; Lawrence Venuti, *The Translator's Invisibility: A History of Translation*, London: Routledge, 1995.

hitherto unsuspected', between 'two populations so widely separated and so diverse in origin and composition its languages', but the parallels do not consistently align. Rather, James's parallelism allows for the possibility of incomparability, lack of fit between the two histories. This is especially the case when Marxist analysis is brought to bear on what amount to pre-Marxian historical moments. Who but Du Bois in *Black Reconstruction* was thinking in terms of the black worker in 1865, James says, just as he himself was looking for where 'the Marxist analysis could fit' his account of the Haitian Revolution (Lectures, 91). James gives us the text-network of *The Black Jacobins*, encompassing prior texts and future forms as well as the history of the text's multiple presents, all the biographical, socio-economic, cultural, and political contexts in which the work is now and will be read. As translations without an original, they are open-ended, speculative thoughts. Exactly as James would have it: the unfinished, provisional possibilities are tied to the limits of the comparison. Perversely, we conclude that the critical limit is to keep the comparative machinery as he has it, only partially visible, half-spoken, uncompleted.

The Oloffson

Alasdair Pettinger

'It is hard to ignore the hotels', Ian Strachan begins his *Paradise and Plantation*: 'They rise like mammoths of iron and concrete above the homes, the office buildings, the trees of New Providence, island of my birth'.[1] He goes on to argue that Caribbean hotels are modern plantations— locally-run but foreign-owned businesses that create a product for customers overseas, but instead of sugar or tobacco what they offer is a holiday experience in 'paradise'.[2]

The subject of this essay is a rather different hotel. A slightly run-down gingerbread mansion today more likely to find journalists, aid workers, military personnel, documentary film-makers, art collectors, and up-market literary travellers as guests rather than tourists in search of golden beaches. Visitors to the Hotel Oloffson in Port-au-Prince, Haiti, describe it in terms that sharply distinguish it from the towering chain hotels that line seafronts elsewhere in the Caribbean: 'a folly of spires and conical towers' with 'decorative wrought iron and wide verandas' and 'shadowy bohemian interiors'.[3] They invariably refer to its idiosyncratic owner, Richard A. Morse, a Haitian-American with a degree in anthropology from Princeton, founder and lead singer of RAM, commonly described as a 'vodou rock and roots' band, whose political edge has sometimes landed him in trouble with the authorities. They will also remind you that the building was made famous

---

[1] Ian Gregory Strachan, *Paradise and Plantation: Tourism and Culture in the Anglophone Caribbean*, Charlottesville: University of Virginia Press, 2002, p. ix.

[2] Strachan, *Paradise*, pp. 7–11.

[3] Ian Thomson, *Bonjour Blanc: A Journey Through Haiti* [1992], London: Vintage, 2004, p. 20; Brian Thacker, *The Naked Man Festival and Other Excuses to Fly Around the World*, Sydney: Allen and Unwin, 2004, p. 208; Bob Shacochis, 'Haiti', *New York*, 19 April 2004 <http://nymag.com/nymetro/travel/features/situations2004/n_10226/> [29.5.2010].

when it served as the model for the Hotel Trianon in Graham Greene's 1966 novel *The Comedians*.

The essay draws on several travel writers' accounts of the Hotel Oloffson from the last twenty years or so—in other words, the period following the fall of the Duvalier dictatorship, which more or less coincides with the period Morse has run the hotel. I will identify some of the ways in which these writer-guests imaginatively inhabit the various private and public spaces of this particular hotel and its surroundings. And although the Oloffson appears to be an unusual case, I will suggest that there are continuities between it and the 'plantation hotels' invoked by Strachan significant enough to excuse some tentative hypotheses concerning the role of the tropical hotel, the politics of location, and contemporary travel writing.

'I Must Get Back to My Hotel'

Some academics spend a little too much time in hotels, and they are often overly prone, perhaps, to exploiting the hotel's rhetorical possibilities in their writings. As the themes of place, movement, and dislocation hustle for the cultural critic's attention, there always seems to be a vacancy at the hotel, ready to play host to reflections on (or serve as an emblem of) one *zeitgeist* or another.

So, for Siegfried Kracauer, its trivial, superficial, and meaningless interactions make the hotel lobby one of those 'privileged sites' maintained by 'civilised society at the height of its development' that 'testify to its own non-existence'.[4] For Fredric Jameson, the dizzying confusion of the Portman Bonaventure Hotel in Los Angeles signifies 'the incapacity of our minds ... to map the great global multinational and decentred communicational network in which we find ourselves caught as individual subjects'.[5] And for James Clifford, the tourist hotel has taken over from the ethnographer's tent as a more appropriate 'chronotope' of 'culture' as culture becomes increasingly theorised as a site less of residence than of encounter.[6]

Although these three examples might stand for the conceptualisation of the hotel as, in turn, a characteristically modern, postmodern, and

---

[4] Siegfried Kracauer, 'The Hotel Lobby' [1925] in Thomas Y. Levin, ed., *The Mass Ornament: Weimar Essays*, Cambridge, MA: Harvard University Press, 1995, pp. 173–185, at 175.

[5] Fredric Jameson, 'Postmodernism, or The Cultural Logic of Late Capitalism', *New Left Review*, 146 (July–August 1984), pp. 53–92, at 84.

[6] James Clifford, 'Traveling Cultures' [1992], reprinted in *Routes: Travel and Translation in the Late Twentieth Century*, Cambridge, MA: Harvard University Press, 1997, pp. 17–46, esp. 17–25, 30–31.

postcolonial space, they nevertheless share a tendency to treat the hotel primarily as a transit zone, where people are always passing through on their way somewhere else, seeking to orient themselves in much the same way as pedestrians or motorists negotiate a busy junction. The point of view is invariably that of the guests and their fleeting (and often silent) interactions. Accordingly, within the hotel it is the lobby—or, in a more specialised variant, the revolving door—which tends to bear the heaviest figurative load.[7] Even Clifford's careful reflections which go on to warn of the dangers of treating 'the hotel' as a paradigmatic space seem to assume that the hotel must be conceived in this way, and that we are obliged to seek an alternative to the hotel rather than an alternative way of thinking about it.[8]

The representations of the Oloffson considered here rub against this orthodoxy to some extent. As the accounts of (literary) travellers, they still adopt the point of view of the guest—rather than, say, that of the waiter, housekeeper, cook, or driver (whose existence is only obliquely acknowledged). And even Richard Morse—who does make an occasional appearance and is allowed to speak—hardly talks of the business, certainly not the day-to-day business, of running the place. Consequently, this limits the spaces of the hotel which can figure in their narratives. There is no kitchen or laundry or office or staff-room on view here.

But there is much about the hotel that does not conform to the model preferred by the cultural theorists. The reader is constantly reminded of the discomforts and annoyances that preoccupy guests accustomed to more temperate climates and different standards of public health and civic governance. In short the Oloffson is a *tropical* hotel, in which the writer seeks refuge from overpowering heat and buzzing insects, the stress of chaotic streets and pestering street vendors, the fear of robbery or worse. The Oloffson that emerges in these accounts tends to be aligned—more closely than we might have expected—with the all-inclusive resorts and cruise-ships that Strachan describes as 'enclaves' and that Polly Pattullo, in another major study of Caribbean tourism, refers to as 'citadels'.[9] The result is a differently-

---

[7] See Douglas Tallack, '"Waiting, waiting": The Hotel Lobby in the Modern City' in Neil Leach, ed., *The Hieroglyphics of Space: Reading and Experiencing the Modern Metropolis*, London: Routledge, 2002, pp. 139–151; J. Cockburn, 'Simmel, Ninotchka and the Revolving Door' (2005) <http://ro.uow.edu.au/cgi/viewcontent.cgi?article=100 1&context=creartspapers> [29.5.2010].

[8] Clifford, 'Traveling Cultures', pp. 31–36.

[9] Strachan, *Paradise and Plantation*, p. 87; Polly Pattullo, *Last Resorts: The Cost of Tourism in the Caribbean*, London: Cassell, 1996, p. 20. Both these books are excellent studies of the impact of tourism in the Caribbean. See also Mimi Sheller, *Consuming the*

imagined hotel space, one which is less a crossroads (featuring largely polite encounters between fellow travellers) and more a fortress (sealed off from a dangerous and threatening outside world).

This is immediately evident from the proliferating contrasts between what lies within its grounds and what lurks without. On the one hand, there is 'iced tea waiting for me on one of the white wicker tables that lined the verandah', a 'general air of listlessness', 'decadence and lassitude', or more prosaically, the 'excellent restaurant … pleasant pool'.[10] On the other, there is 'the screaming insanity of the Port-au-Prince traffic' or the 'mind-boggling anarchy of Port-au-Prince street life', 'exhaust fumes, burning refuse, the smoke from innumerable charcoal fires', 'the smell of … rotting mangoes, sewage and sweat', 'the sound of mortar fire and automatic rounds' and the sight of the body of a young boy, 'a gaping wound in the back of his head where the bullet had entered'.[11]

The world beyond the hotel seems to be fraught with danger, and when specific threats can be cited they are often quite precisely located in terms of their distance—just up the hill, round the corner, a few blocks away—from the Oloffson, the central point from which all else is measured and judged. In this way the Oloffson plays a similar role to the North American city of departure, which often plays the same anchoring role in the larger travel narrative in which it is embedded. Thus, as one entirely typical scene of arrival in Port-au-Prince has it: 'It really beggars belief that all this exists an hour-and-a-half's flight from glittering Miami, and less than three hours from New York City'.[12]

This stark contrast between inside and outside provides the mise-en-scène

---

Caribbean: From Arawaks to Zombies, London: Routledge, 2003; Landon Yarrington, 'From Sight to Site to Website: Travel Writing, Tourism, and the American Experience in Haiti, 1900–2008', MA thesis, College of William and Mary, 2009.

[10] Kathie Klarreich, *Madame Dread: A Tale of Love, Vodou and Civil Strife in Haiti*, New York: Nation, 2005, p. 88; Thomson, *Bonjour Blanc*, p. 20; Julia Llewellyn Smith, *Travels Without My Aunt: In the Footsteps of Graham Greene*, London: Penguin, 2001, p. 217; Madison Smartt Bell, 'Miroir Danjere', *Hudson Review*, 48, no. 4 (1996) <http://faculty.goucher.edu/mbell/miroir.htm> [10.7.2010]).

[11] Bell, 'Miroir Danjere'; Thomson, *Bonjour Blanc*, p. 23; Smith, *Travels*, p. 212; Klarreich, *Madame Dread*, p. 94, 92. The densest catalogue of images of Port-au-Prince (assaulting the eye, ear, nose, followed by an abrupt shift to the 'utter comfort' of his hotel—though not the Oloffson in this case) is in David Yeadon, *The Back of Beyond: Travels to the Wild Places of the Earth*, New York: Harper Perennial, 1992, p. 49.

[12] David Pratt, 'The Horrors of Haiti', *Sunday Herald*, 22 February 2004. See also Smith, *Travels*, p. 212; Jan Morris, 'Introduction' in Herbert Gold, *Best Nightmare on Earth: A Life in Haiti* [1991], London: Flamingo, 1994, p. x; Gold, *Nightmare*, p. 187; Thacker, *Naked Man Festival*, p. 195.

for the almost obligatory mini-narratives in which the author leaves the safety of the hotel to risk the city beyond and returns, somewhat relieved, usually in the early hours of the morning. Kathie Klarreich, for instance, describes meeting a fellow journalist at the Oloffson who suggests they 'take a drive'. She asks if this is safe. "'Oh, come on", Greg said, "It'll be fine—a lot more interesting than sitting around looking at other journalists who aren't ballsy enough to go out"'.[13] In the course of their tour of the city, they get caught in crossfire at a military checkpoint and notice bodies of murder victims abandoned on sidewalks, untended at State Hospital, gawped at by crowds surrounding a 'bloodied jeep'. Dialogue between the two soon fizzles out as they are rendered speechless by what they see. And if it is only for a moment that Klarreich wonders 'if it wasn't time to retreat back into myself before I drowned in the country's tumultuous sorrow', the episode can only end when they 'walk to my car and once inside locked our doors, rolled up the windows, and drove back to the Oloffson through the deserted silence of the capital's streets'.[14]

In Julia Llewellyn Smith's account, the single outing to and from the Oloffson is replaced by several comings and goings. She arrives at the hotel after a ride from the airport she describes as a 'descent into hell'.[15] Her first venture takes her wandering downtown in the city she describes as a 'ruin' (222) in the company of a guide evidently nostalgic for the authoritarian regime of the Duvaliers and now with 'no hope for my country' (223). This is followed by subsequent encounters with an Arab businessman, a teacher from the USA, a young man offering his services as a guide, and an art dealer; she also attends a 'voodoo' ceremony. Although these encounters take place in a variety of places—from the relatively prosperous suburbs overlooking the city to a 'slum ... on the northern edge of Port-au-Prince' (pp. 234–235)—their mood is dominated by a sense of danger ('We have dozens of weapons stockpiled to protect us from the poor', says the businessman, 228), confusion ('The place hits you like a strobe, all the colour and noise and smells', says the teacher, 229), deprivation ('I haven't eaten in days', says the young man, 232), and irrationality (the art dealer refers to the 'Haitian lack of logic', 247). And although she trivialises the ceremony she attends ('only mildly more exotic than an end-of-term disco'), she insists 'there is an evil side to voodoo' (239–240). Interspersed with accounts of the excursions are scenes in the hotel, where the atmosphere is considerably more relaxed. The hotel

---

[13] Klarreich, *Madame Dread*, p.89.

[14] Klarreich, *Madame Dread*, pp.95–96.

[15] Smith, *Travels*, p.212. Further references are included parenthetically within the text.

plays a crucial role: while Smith confesses to being in love with the city as a whole, she admits this owes something to the charm of the Oloffson (217); and after declaring that she feels 'so happy ... because the Haitians were happy', her only examples of this local contentment are actually hotel staff (the 'girls at reception' and the 'tuxedo'd maitre d'', 242).

The most elaborate excursion is that offered by Ian Thomson—a carefully crafted narrative, owing something perhaps to the 'yuppie nightmare movie' genre popular in the late 1980s, as the narrator soon finds himself in deserted streets on his walk towards the National Palace.[16] The detached tone—that allows him to relish the unexpected pleasure of a conversation in Italian with the owner of a Café Napoli on his first night—soon gives way to impatience, discomfort, and anxiety, as he struggles with unappetising food and finds himself accompanied by Michael, a self-appointed guide, who takes him to a nightclub described as a 'nightmare of swirly multicoloured disco lights' (28), a neighbourhood which 'apparently teems with thieves and ghouls' and allegedly a 'seedbed of AIDS' (29), and finally a brothel where arrangements have been made for him. Thomson announces to Michael that he has had enough and must 'get back to the Oloffson' (30). He eventually walks off in the right direction after paying him (they 'haggled violently over the fee', 30) and—in a resolution more consoling than is usual in the horror film—we next find him back in his room, reading a novel by Ronald Firbank, having more or less regained his composure.

The conventions of mainstream travel literature would normally require that the writer leave the tourist hotel and give the reader an account of the city or countryside that surrounds it, the assumption being that readers would not expect the hotel experience to serve as the primary material for a 'serious' travel book or even article.[17] Indeed, travel writers—especially journalists—often feel compelled to court danger, sometimes competitively, as Klarreich's colleague's reference to those 'who aren't ballsy enough to go out' implies.[18] Or, in Madison Smartt Bell's more sardonic formulation: 'a

---

[16] Thomson, *Bonjour Blanc*, p. 23. Further references are included parenthetically within the text.

[17] But there are notable exceptions, including books such as Matthew Brace, *Hotel Heaven: Confessions of a Luxury Hotel Addict*, London: Old Street, 2008; Sophie Calle, *L'Hotel*, Paris: Actes Sud, 1998; Patrick Boman, *Jakarta*, Paris: Editions Climats, 1992; and Nicole-Lise Bernheim, *Chambres d'ailleurs*, Paris: Éditions Arléa, 1986. See also Richard J. Houk, 'Hotel Terminus: A Farce Without an Ending', *Journal of African Travel-Writing*, 1 (September 1996), pp. 42–51; Chris Epting, 'Let's Spend the Night Together', *Perceptive Travel* (September/October 2007) <http://www.perceptivetravel.com/issues/0907/epting.html> [10.7.2010].

[18] Klarreich, *Madame Dread*, p. 89.

visit to Haiti would not be quite complete without spending at least a few seconds looking down the wrong end of a rifle barrel'.[19]

At the same time, these adventurers always end up 'back' at the hotel, where they will be safe and comfortable, somewhere indeed where they can begin to write up their experiences, which ultimately find their way into print. And, for all the immediacy of the excursion, it can only take shape as a (thrilling) narrative because, crafted in retrospective tranquillity, the survival of the protagonist is assured.

'I must get back to my hotel' (or a variation thereof) marks the turning-point of these mini-narratives, a formulation that alludes both to the danger in which the writers have placed themselves (showing that they have been brave enough to *leave* it) and to the secure vantage point from which the episode can be rendered as an essentially aesthetic experience, sharply bracketed off from the routine of the writer's own life, a life that would not normally have to face the long-term consequences of the chaos, danger, deprivation and so on which the text takes such delight in cataloguing.

In this way, the hotel makes it possible for Port-au-Prince to resemble the classic sources of the romantic sublime, such as overhanging rocks, thunderstorms, raging seas, waterfalls, volcanic eruptions: an object of terror or fear that nevertheless prompts delight because it is enjoyed from a place of safety.[20] This should remind us how much these narratives invest in the dangerous. Whatever the risks the authors take in venturing forth from the hotel, the accounts they produce are overdetermined by their reliance on well-established literary conventions that have figured nature as a site of both terror and wonder, conventions that in the twentieth century were extended in representations of the city and industrialisation in what has been called the 'urban' or 'technological' sublime.[21]

But this aesthetic impulse strikingly (if not knowingly) lends support to a more directly political one. The travel advisories, such as those issued by the US State Department or the Foreign and Commonwealth Office in the UK, have long been the subject of complaint by local tourist operators and other interested parties in Haiti who fight hard to reduce what they see as

---

[19] Bell, 'Kafou Danjere'.

[20] See especially Edmund Burke, *A Philosophical Enquiry into the Origin of our Ideas of the Sublime and Beautiful* [1757, 1759], ed. James T. Boulton, Oxford: Blackwell, 1987, pp. 39–40; Immanuel Kant, *The Critique of Judgement* [1790], trans. James Creed Meredith, Oxford: Clarendon Press, 1952, pp. 110–111. The importance of the safe vantage point is often overlooked by studies of the sublime.

[21] See Christopher Den Tadt, *The Urban Sublime in American Literary Naturalism*, Urbana: University of Illinois Press, 1998; David E. Nye, *American Technological Sublime*, Cambridge, MA: MIT Press, 1994.

exaggerated levels of danger, and suspect that the warnings persist long after the events that prompted them have receded because of pressure from those diplomatic and other workers who receive bonus payments for operating in hazardous conditions.[22]

And while this is no doubt true of many other countries, in Haiti this 'risk assessment' is additionally controversial in that it serves as a major justification for the deployment of foreign military personnel in the shape of the US Marines or the forces deployed by the United Nations Stabilization Mission in Haiti (MINUSTAH) since 2004. The rationale for such interventions presupposes a redefinition of political mobilisation by the mass of the population as essentially a problem of lawlessness.[23]

Particularly contentious has been the MINUSTAH's practice of mapping the city into 'red' and 'green' zones (recommending that NGO personnel avoid the former without armed escort).[24] In 2009 a campaign secured more than 36,000 signatories to a petition to have Bel-Air recategorised from 'red' to 'green'.[25] Richard Morse himself has repeatedly complained that the Oloffson has lost business from being included in the 'red zone', a punishment, he claimed, for his own outspoken views on what he sees as a military occupation.[26] And there is certainly evidence that this zoning prevented essential aid getting through to some of the worst-affected areas in the aftermath of the earthquake of January 2010, leading one observer to remark, 'The false sense of insecurity in Haiti is killing people'.[27]

---

[22] This is a recurring topic of discussion on the Haiti List, an English-language forum moderated by Bob Corbett <http://www.webster.edu/~corbetre/haiti/library/mailing. htm> [10.7.2010].

[23] See, for example, Peter Hallward, 'Securing Disaster in Haiti' (22.1.2010) <http:// www.haitianalysis.com/2010/1/22/securing-disaster-in-haiti> [31.5.2010].

[24] The lead article in *Haiti-Observateur* (9–16 August 2006) on the security situation ('Des lieux dangereux qu'il faut éviter généralement') quotes extensively from a confidential report prepared for MINUSTAH by Control Risks, a risk consultancy based in Mexico City. One of the passages cited from this report refers explicitly to 'the red zone designated by MINUSTAH, an area situated between la Route de Carrefour and the sea' (p. 12).

[25] 'Du rouge au vert', *Le Nouvelliste* (29.7.2009) <http://www.lenouvelliste.com/ articleforprint.php?PubID=1&ArticleID=72534> [30.5.2010].

[26] Richard Morse, 'Haiti: My Experience on the Ground', *Huffington Post* (21.1.2010) <http://www.huffingtonpost.com/richard-morse/haiti-my-experience-on-th_b_431159.html> [30.5.2010]; Richard Morse, 'Haiti: Stealth Zone', *Huffington Post* (16.3.2010) <http://www.huffingtonpost.com/richard-morse/haiti-stealth-zone_b_500585.html> [31.5.2010].

[27] This remark was made as an online comment in response to Andy Kershaw, 'Stop treating these people like savages', *Independent* (21 January 2010) <http://www.

The critic Debbie Lisle has suggested that much contemporary travel writing reproduces 'a problematic geographical imagination that secures the West as safe and civilised and produces the rest of the world as dangerous and uncivilised'.[28] We have seen here that this cartography can be redeployed on a smaller scale between the tropical hotel and its surroundings in a perhaps surprising alliance between romantic aesthetics and imperialist geo-politics.

'Perturbations Pendant La Nuit'

One of the few scholars of travel writing to reflect on the role of the hotel is Mary Louise Pratt, whose remarks on those scenes where the narrator looks out from the balcony on to the Third World city spread below are worth a brief summary here. They are a modern version of the 'Monarch-of-all-I-survey' trope she identifies in those nineteenth-century writings in which European explorers announce their 'discovery' of regions hitherto unknown to their readers in a set piece that describes the panoramic landscape laid out before their eyes, as if it were a large painted canvas.

The view from the hotel inherits the key features of this gaze, so that even while its aestheticisation of the scene may dwell on what is displeasing, rather than pleasing, to the eye or find the landscape denuded of, rather than rich with, 'civilising' or 'modernising' possibilities, the sense of domination—in which the view is assumed to be perfectly framed, as if it includes all there is, designed to be seen from just this vantage point—remains.[29]

Because it foregrounds the relationship between elite travellers and their 'exotic' destinations, this approach seems much more likely to illuminate those accounts in which hotels are figured as secure fortresses rather than busy intersections. And certainly the dynamic of power and pleasure in such balcony scenes would serve well the cynical received wisdom that declares Haiti to be 'the poorest country in the western hemisphere', a 'failed state',

---

independent.co.uk/opinion/commentators/andy-kershaw-stop-treating-these-people-like-savages-1874218.html> [30.5.2010]. The phrase 'false sense of insecurity' was popularised by an influential article warning of the consequences of exaggerating the threat posed by international terrorism: John Mueller, 'A False Sense of Insecurity', *Regulation*, 27, no. 3 (2004), pp. 42–46.

[28] Debbie Lisle, *The Global Politics of Contemporary Travel Writing*, Cambridge: Cambridge University Press, 2006, p. 163. Her remarks are directed at Robert Kaplan in particular, but he is treated as representative of a prevailing trend.

[29] Mary Louise Pratt, *Imperial Eyes: Travel Writing and Transculturation*, London: Routledge, 1992, pp. 201–227.

and insists that any attempt to change this is inevitably doomed. Or, as one traveller puts it: 'The country is, to be perfectly frank, fucked up'.[30]

There are no balcony scenes, however, in the writings on the Oloffson I have examined. The hotel is located on a hill, and certainly from some vantage points one can look out over downtown Port-au-Prince towards the bay beyond. But the fact that it is in its own grounds, set back from the adjacent streets and surrounded by tall trees means that it is not well-suited to such a sovereign gaze.

With hardly a nod to the existence of other areas in which the guests may spend time such as the pool, the bar, even one of the rooms (named after previous celebrated occupants which now, in some cases, include themselves), the literary guests nearly always depict themselves occupying another part of the hotel. 'For my money, the Oloffson's veranda is the supreme hangout in Haiti', declares Shacochis, and his fellow travellers would appear to agree with him.[31] A vantage point to be sure, but unlike Pratt's balcony, a place from which one hears rather than sees. Episodes that take place on the Oloffson veranda are dominated by sounds, reminding us that the ear as much as the eye contributes to the way in which we imagine, inhabit, or orient ourselves in, space.[32]

First of all, it's a place to listen in on conversation while taking breakfast or dinner or sipping the rum punches for which the Oloffson is famous. These of course also offer the writer excellent opportunities to convey the flavour of the clientele. Gold, for instance, reports a parting exchange between a US Episcopalian and a waiter.[33] Smith overhears UN employees discussing 'the best place in town to find Landcruiser parts', quotes an Ozzy Osborne roadie ('Man, once you've seen Ozzy bite the head off a live bat, this voodoo shit don't scare you none'), and cautiously receives at her table the ubiquitous man about town, Aubelin Jolicoeur.[34]

But there are also the sounds from beyond the hotel. 'Beyond the Oloffson's shady gingerbread tracery, the streets were a tumult of shouting, laughing people', writes David Yeadon.[35] It is with such sounds that these writers intensify the mise-en-scène explored earlier. For if the threatening outside can encroach uncomfortably on the safe haven of the Oloffson, it is

---

[30]   Thacker, *Naked Man Festival*, p. 197.
[31]   Shacochis, 'Haiti'.
[32]   See Paul Rodaway, *Sensuous Geographies: Body, Sense and Place*, London: Routledge, 1994, esp. Chapter 6, 'Auditory Geographies', pp. 82–114.
[33]   Gold, *Nightmare*, pp. 320–321.
[34]   Smith, *Travels*, pp. 223–226.
[35]   Yeadon, *Back of Beyond* , p. 57.

most often in this form. Sometimes these disturbances are referred to almost casually, the badge perhaps of the seasoned regular. Shacochis speaks of the veranda as 'the prime venue to eavesdrop on incomprehensible intrigues, slam rum sours with disoriented celebrities, or hunker down when there's gunplay a few blocks over at the National Palace' as if the three activities were equally innocent and diverting.[36] There is something more menacing about 'the helicopters floundering above the Hotel Oloffson' and 'the chopper blades flogging overhead' in Bell's account, though these are mentioned only in passing.[37]

But on other occasions the noise seems to arrest the attention and demand an explanation. Thus Herbert Gold: 'We lounge outdoors at a pool with drinks. When there is a sharp sound it's probably a backfire, not a shot.[38] And Smith: 'We ate lobster and drank champagne. The first thunderbolt of the evening cracked just as a nearby vigilante let out a rat-a-tat-tat of gunfire. I caught Guy's eye. "Don't worry", I lied. "It's just a car backfiring"'.[39] And Thomson, before his venture downtown:

> I sat sipping under the coolness of the fan blades, wondering whether I should stir out alone in Port-au-Prince, when a sudden howling reached me from outside. The barman looked up, bleary-eyed. 'It's Papa Dog', he explained. The hound apparently belonged to the hotelier, Richard Morse, who evidently had an unusual sense of the absurd. Rain began to fall on the wooden roof of the Oloffson, not heavily, but with the carelessness of a leaking basin.[40]

A few pages later, reading in his room after his foray into the city, he is not as sealed off in his novel as perhaps he would prefer: 'I had scarcely begun the tenth chapter … when a sound of machine-gun fire reached me from outside the hotel. It troubled at first, but one got used to it, like the rattle of musketry in a Hollywood epic'.[41]

In each case a potentially disturbing interruption is reassuringly transformed into something harmless—a car backfiring, a domestic pet, an episode in a movie. On other occasions, the response is simply denial. Here is Gold again:

---

[36] Shacochis, 'Haiti'.
[37] Bell, 'Miroir Danjere'.
[38] Gold, *Haiti: Best Nightmare on Earth*, rev. ed., New Brunswick: Transaction, 2001, p. 311.
[39] Smith, *Travels*, p. 249.
[40] Thomson, *Bonjour Blanc*, p. 22.
[41] Thomson, *Bonjour Blanc*, p. 31.

The next night, shots rang out and we looked up from our dinner, stopped our storytelling and waited. Jorgen said, 'Trouble is, we'll never know what that was about'. The strongest description in the newspapers would be 'perturbations pendant la nuit'. So we went on drinking our rum or papaya juice, and then there were more shots, this time closer. We stopped talking. I heard shots and a woman screaming. Then there was silence. 'Well, the lights are still on'.[42]

The next morning: 'Jorgen asked if I had heard the new round of shots, very late, maybe near dawn. "Is that what they were?"'[43]

If the description of the sounds heard on the veranda were an analogue of the sights seen from Pratt's balcony, they would be rendered as the pleasing (or displeasing) strains of a melody or rhythm in an adjectivally dense description that hinted at the possibilities of harmonisation (or confirmed its status as meaningless noise). Doubtless such aural variants of the picturesque may be identified in romantic travelogues (and their successors), but this is not what is heard at the Oloffson.

Instead, we are offered fragments, whose source or meaning tends to be uncertain or ambiguous. As such, the sounds may prompt a certain anxiety. In keeping with the etymology of *eavesdrop*—the term derives from the listener's vulnerability to rainwater dripping from the roof—the vantage point is not that of a sovereign mastery taken for granted but of an explicitly situated insecurity.[44] The potentially threatening nature of these disturbing sounds places them in the realm of the sublime, traditionally as noisy as the picturesque is quiet. But they can only be appreciated as sublime from a place of safety. If one can find sheltered viewpoints from which to enjoy the awesome power and scale of nature, this is perhaps less easy in the case of those noises outside the hotel. The shouts, cries, cracks, explosions are not easily fixed at a comfortable distance but associated with people on the move, and therefore carry with them the possibility that they might enter the grounds and confront the guests. To neutralise them—and restore the security on which the delight in the sublime depends—these fragments are

---

[42] Gold, *Haiti*, p. 292.

[43] Gold, *Haiti*, pp. 292–293.

[44] See Ann Gaylin, *Eavesdropping in the Novel from Austen to Proust*, Cambridge: Cambridge University Press, 2002, pp. 1–25, esp. pp. 17–18. For further insightful reflections on the subject, see Elisabeth Weis, 'Eavesdropping: An Aural Analogue of Voyeurism?' in Philip Brophy, ed., *Cinesonic: The World of Sound in Film*, North Ryde: Australian Film Television & Radio School, 1999, pp. 79–107; Michael Greaney, *Conrad, Language and Narrative*, Cambridge: Cambridge University Press, 2002, pp. 11–26, esp. pp. 25–26.

subjected to reinterpretation, humour, and denial. And this work is never done. 'You feel safe here', writes David Yeadon, 'even though you're only a mortar shot away from the enormous Presidential Palace'.[45] But of course, as soon as you pronounce a place 'safe' you draw attention to the possibility of danger, which no conjunctional phrase can convincingly dispel. Perhaps this is why the brochures for tropical hotels prefer to use the word 'private' instead.

Conclusion: the tropical hotel as heterotopia

Focusing on a single hotel—and a rather idiosyncratic one at that—my sample is hardly enough to formulate even a tentative hypothesis. All I can offer are some initial thoughts on the way a tropical hotel is imaginatively occupied by elite travellers, with particular attention to the veranda as a kind of 'ear of the building'.[46] Like the balcony, it offers a vantage point from which to aestheticise—and depoliticise—both the city or country surrounding it and the narrator's own privileged position and reason for being there. But what is heard from the veranda proves harder to domesticate than what is seen from the balcony, and to that extent may suggest the limits of that pleasure and power more effectively. It certainly makes these narratives more unsettling to read.

In attempting to identify alternatives to the (Western) travel writer's habitual 'cartographies of safety and danger' (to which I referred earlier), Debbie Lisle speaks of 'cartographic inversions' where safe places turn out to be dangerous and vice versa. But what she finds more interesting are the cases in which the distinction itself breaks down, where safety and danger co-exist. Such cases, she argues, are examples of what Michel Foucault has called *heterotopia*, a concept he elaborated in a lecture he gave in 1967.[47]

Given the avowedly tentative nature of his reflections, which he only allowed to be published shortly before his death nearly twenty years later, it is perhaps surprising that they seem to have posthumously been transformed into a blueprint for a new academic specialism. Like utopias, Foucault

---

[45] Yeadon, *Back of Beyond*, p. 55.

[46] Greaney, *Conrad*, p. 26.

[47] Michel Foucault, 'Des espaces autres' [1967], *Dits et écrits*, ed. Daniel Defert and François Ewald, Paris: Gallimard, 1994, vol. IV, pp. 752–762. Translated by Jay Miskowiec as 'Of Other Spaces', *Diacritics*, 16 (Spring 1986), pp. 22–27; and by Robert Hurley as 'Different Spaces' in *Essential Works of Foucault 1954–1984, Vol. 2: Aesthetics, Method, and Epistemology*, ed., James D Faubion, London: Allen Lane, 1998, pp. 175–185. Lisle incorrectly refers to this as a 'late' work, misled no doubt by the date of its first publication (1984).

appears to be saying, heterotopias are spaces that are constituted differently from the spaces that surround them (whose norms they may breach or call into question), but unlike utopias they are real rather than imaginary. In itself this is a rather abstract notion that his bewildering succession of illustrations hardly helps to enrich: brothel, theatre, cemetery, ship, garden, colonial settlement. Some of the 'principles' of heterotopia he offers seem to be somewhat vague or banal: they are found in all cultures but take different forms in different contexts and their functions can change over time.

This conception of heterotopia is in stark contrast to the one he developed in the preface to *Les Mots et les Choses* which was published the previous year.[48] Here, his starting point is a fictional 'Chinese Encyclopaedia' concocted by Jorge Luis Borges, one governed by a number of competing, incommensurable systems of classification that makes the co-existence of the items listed unthinkable (except between the covers of the Encyclopaedia itself). Heterotopia here does not designate a real, social, inhabitable space. On the contrary, it alludes to an impossible space: one that not only does not exist beyond the printed page, but one that is impossible to imagine, and for that reason is likely to provoke uneasy laughter.[49]

At first glance, it would seem that our understanding of the texts devoted to the Oloffson would be better served by the 1967 lecture than the 1966 preface. Firstly, it would be easy enough to add the hotel to the examples Foucault gives us in the lecture. Indeed, the 'honeymoon hotel' is one of them.[50] And secondly, we might (as Lisle does) pay particular attention to Foucault's fifth principle, namely 'Heterotopias always presuppose a system of opening and closing which at once isolates them and renders them accessible'.[51] This would certainly seem to correspond with the experience of guests at the Oloffson, who seek refuge within its walls from the discomforts and dangers of the world outside, and yet continue to hear troubling sounds that remind them of that world from the veranda.

Anyone embarking on a cultural study of a tropical hotel that proceeded from these Foucauldian cues might be expected to attend to its architecture

---

[48] Michel Foucault, *The Order of Things: An Archaeology of the Human Sciences* [1966], trans. Alan Sheridan, London: Tavistock, 1970, pp. xv–xxiv.

[49] Two studies of Foucault's writings on heterotopia I have found particularly useful are Benjamin Genocchio, 'Discourse, Discontinuity, Difference: The Question of "Other" Spaces', in Sophie Watson and Katherine Gibson, eds., *Postmodern Cities and Spaces*, Oxford: Blackwell, 1995, pp. 35–46, and Peter Johnson, 'Unravelling Foucault's "Different Spaces"', *History of the Human Sciences*, 19, no. 4 (2006), pp. 75–90.

[50] Foucault, 'Des Espaces Autres', p. 757.

[51] Foucault, 'Des Espaces Autres', p. 760. My translation.

or its strategic location or its admissions policy.[52] But we could go further and pursue Lisle's attempt to grasp the implications that might flow from thinking of heterotopia less as space (as the 1967 lecture does) than an *ordering* of space (which is the concern of the 1966 preface); specifically, the implication that a single space may be spatially ordered in many different (and inconsistent) ways.

The 'principle' of the six proposed in the lecture that comes closest to the emphasis on proliferation and contestation which one finds in Foucault's preface is the third which declares that 'the heterotopia has the power to juxtapose in a single real place (*lieu*) several spaces (*espaces*), several sites (*emplacements*) that are incompatible with each other'.[53] The use of three separate nouns is perhaps confusing. Edward Casey, for instance, has criticised the lecture for its lack of terminological clarity and is particularly vexed by this passage because of its cavalier attitude to a cardinal distinction of human geography, the distinction between space and place.[54]

Space—according to a standard view—is in itself abstract and devoid of significance for human beings, while place, through being named, mapped, inhabited, is endowed with value and sentiment. Space may be transformed into place, and so the two are often conceived as lying at opposite ends of a continuum. Towards one end we might find the lines and curves and angles studied by geometry and physics. At the other, the world of perception, consciousness and feeling (and its deictic vocabulary of home and abroad, strange and familiar, us and them, safety and danger, and so on).[55]

To the extent that the 'space and place' paradigm tends to assume that the object of study is a single, coherent entity, internally consistent enough to be subsumed by general laws or theorems, or to be imagined and recreated in the mind of an individual or community, it has been criticised for overlooking the fact that places can have multiple identities, which often

---

[52] For studies of hotels on these lines (not all using the term heterotopia), see Zeynep Kezer, 'If Walls Could Talk: Exploring the Dimensions of Heterotopia at the Four Seasons Istanbul Hotel', in Dana Arnold and Andrew Ballantyne , eds., *Architecture as Experience: Radical Changes in Spatial Practice*, London: Routledge, 2003, pp. 210–232; Danny Hoffman, 'The Brookfields Hotel (Freetown, Sierra Leone)', *Public Culture*, 17, no. 1 (2005), pp. 55–74; Gillian Whitlock, *Soft Weapons: Autobiography in Transit*, Chicago: University of Chicago Press, 2007, esp. Chapter 6, 'Embedded', pp. 131–60.

[53] Foucault, 'Des Espaces Autres', p. 758. My translation.

[54] Edward S. Casey, *The Fate of Place: A Philosophical History*, Berkeley: University of California Press, 1997, p. 300.

[55] Yi-Fu Tuan, *Space and Place: The Perspective of Experience*, Minneapolis: University of Minnesota Press, 1977.

conflict with each other.[56] Edward Soja has suggested this requires a new concept of space or type of 'spatial thinking' whose object is neither 'physical form' nor 'mental construct', 'neither a substanceless void to be filled by cognitive intuition nor a repository of physical forms to be phenomeno-logically described'.[57] That Soja takes his cue from Foucault's lecture on heterotopia, and particularly its third principle, suggests that its termino-logical inexactitude is unavoidable, for it is not confusing two categories at all but rather hinting at the need to invent a third (indeed 'Thirdspace' is the name he gives to it). Soja is as comfortable with this 'unsystematic' and 'disorderly' text as Casey is disturbed by it.[58]

Perhaps the most revealing term of Foucault's trio is *emplacement*—a verbal noun which in French is used to refer to the activities of, say, siting a building or positioning a painting. Recalling 'certain aphasics', referred to in the 1966 preface, who fail to arrange 'coloured skeins of wool on a table top ... into any coherent pattern', it foregrounds the idea of heterotopia less as a location than as a practice.[59] The travel narratives examined above, for example, deploy objects and events (mangos, exhaust fumes, a gaping wound, wicker tables, a plate of lobster, rotating fan blades, screams, bangs, and so on) in ways that never quite add up to a coherent whole. The 'Oloffson' that cumulatively emerges from such accounts is fractured, confused, indeterminate. The hotel is coded as simultaneously safe *and* dangerous, evident in the hermeneutic uncertainty regarding the noises beyond the veranda, but also condensed in certain oxymoronic formulations. Bell talks of the Oloffson as being 'in its tactful way a fortress', while Smith compares it to 'Sleeping Beauty's castle'.[60] Both intimidating and protective, impregnable and gentle, the representations of the hotel produce a similar effect to ambiguous patterns such as the Necker cube: one can perceive it alternately as two different three-dimensional objects, but not at the same time. Indeed, we might begin to doubt whether these experiences take place 'in' the same physical or mental space at all. The hotel is real enough, but

---

[56] An argument influentially made by Doreen Massey, 'A Global Sense of Place', *Marxism Today* (June 1991), pp. 24–29.

[57] Edward Soja, *Postmodern Geographies: The Reassertion of Space in Critical Social Theory*, London: Verso, 1989, p. 18, 19.

[58] Edward Soja, *Thirdspace: Journeys to Los Angeles and Other Real-and-imagined Places*, Oxford: Blackwell, 1996, p. 159. See also his 'Heteropologies: A Remembrance of Other Spaces in the Citadel-LA', in Watson and Gibson, *Postmodern Cities and Spaces*, pp. 14–33.

[59] Foucault, *The Order of Things*, p. xviii.

[60] Bell, 'Miroir Danjere'; Smith, *Travels*, p. 217.

its most striking difference from a utopia lies in our inability to create a stable picture of it in our imagination.

This is a consequence of a certain tension within the travel writings discussed in the main body of this essay. But the reason Lisle believes this third principle of heterotopia has a particular resonance within travel writing is because of another—typically keener or more jarring—disharmony, namely, 'the disjuncture between the travel writer's increasingly desperate efforts to contain foreign space within a utopian ideal, and the alternative orderings of space practised by local subjects'.[61]

To be sure, the Oloffson that emerges from the travel texts is also heterotopic, but weakly so. There is a shared consensus of the validity and necessity of the distinction between the 'safe' and the 'dangerous' even if it never quite works. If we attend only to the contradictions *within* the travel writings of foreign visitors we may miss a more striking heterotopia that becomes evident when we also factor in the ways in which the hotel is imaginatively occupied by locals, such as its staff or those living and working nearby.

The testimonies of hotel workers presented in George Gmelch's study of Caribbean tourism offer a good illustration of the way the hotel may be imagined in ways that compete with, and question, the travel writer's habitual cartography that takes such pains to keep the threats and discomforts at a distance. Several of them directly contest the received wisdoms of the guests. For instance, a driver observes that Canada can be just as cramped and dirty.[62] A housekeeper points out that she is the one who must clean up after untidy and dirty visitors.[63] A bartender remarks that 'You'll get mugged here just like you would in a dark alley in New York'.[64] And a head of security insists that the problems he faces (such as drug-use, sexual harassment and theft) are frequently perpetrated by outsiders as well as locals.[65] These employees have often travelled overseas and have a kind of double-consciousness that allows them both to identify with their guests (because it is their job to make them feel comfortable and safe) and to situate their expectations against an alternative standard (that exposes the tourist's assumptions of a clear demarcation between the 'safe' world that is theirs and the 'dangerous' world beyond from which they demand protection).

---

[61] Lisle, *Global Politics*, p. 189, 192.

[62] George Gmelch, *Behind the Smile: The Working Lives of Caribbean Tourism*, Bloomington: Indiana University Press, 2003, p. 60.

[63] Gmelch, *Behind the Smile*, p. 66, 68; see also p. 93.

[64] Gmelch, *Behind the Smile*, p. 73.

[65] Gmelch, *Behind the Smile*, pp. 101–104.

It is quite possible that the staff at the Oloffson, if invited to reflect on these issues, would similarly hint at a hotel imagined and inhabited differently from the one occupied by the guests. The perspectives of people living nearby would no doubt further complicate the picture. I will conclude with some remarks by a resident of Port-au-Prince, the novelist and poet Kettly Mars, in which the Oloffson makes an appearance.

They appear in a short text that belongs to a tradition of what might be called 'travellee writing', in which the host writes about the guest, the local writes about the visitor, converting the latter from observer to observed. It is a tradition perhaps particularly strong in Haiti, whose writers can hardly escape the weight of over two centuries of predominantly negative reportage on the part of European and North American visitors and observers, compelling the targets of such reportage to answer back in various ways.

In 'The Last of the Tourists' Mars describes coming across a backpacker in Pacot, an adjacent neighbourhood. She doesn't speak to him, but from his manner and appearance she guesses he is North American and staying at the Oloffson. 'If you want a taste of the country that's not too artificial, you are in the right place'. She imagines giving him some parting advice: 'Don't stray too far. If things get too heavy, head back to the hotel'. The piece ends with her (silently) bidding him farewell: 'OK, I won't keep you. My work is on the other side of this neighbourhood. It was nice seeing you. Goodbye my friend. *Peace and Love.* Maybe we'll meet again, some day, in Manhattan, why not? We could hang out at Ground Zero and conjugate the verb "imagine"'.[66]

I like to think of this extended apostrophe as a gentle rebuke addressed to the literary guests I have considered in this paper. The last sentence in particular I find suggestive. In proposing the site of the World Trade Center for their next rendezvous, Mars urges us in the strongest terms to question 'the cartography of safety and danger' that places New York and the Oloffson on one side and the streets of Port-au-Prince on the other.[67]

Conjugating verbs (especially the verb *imagine*) is something travel writers could do more often—stuck as they usually are in the first-person singular (extended, occasionally, when holed up in places like the Oloffson, to the first-person plural). If Mars hints at the way she occupies (or orients herself in) Haiti's capital city, she also imagines how the tourist would do

---

[66] Kettly Mars, 'Le Dernier des Touristes', in Thomas C. Spear, ed., *Une journée haïtienne*, Montreal: Memoire d' encrier, 2007, p. 19. Words in italics are in English in the original.

[67] Lisle, *Global Politics*, p. 164.

so. Inviting the tourist to reciprocate, so they can do this together, points towards a more complex, even heterotopic, geography in which the Oloffson may simultaneously figure in radically different, possibly incommensurable, imagined spaces.

Dark Thresholds in Trinidad:
Regarding the Colonial House

Jak Peake

For a man's *house* is his *castle*, et domus sua cuique est tutissimum refugium. (Edward Coke, *The Third Part of the Institutes of the Laws of England*)[1]

For the protection of your person, and of a few feet of your own property, it is lawful for you to take life, on so much suspicion as may arise from a shadow cast on the wrong side of your wall. But for the safety not of your own poor person, but of sixteen thousand men, women, and children ... [and] a province involving in its safety that of all English possessions in the West Indies—for these minor ends it is not lawful for you to take a single life on suspicion, though the suspicion rest, not on a shadow on the wall, but on experience of the character and conduct of the accused during many years previous[?]. (John Ruskin, 'A Speech in London [1866]')[2]

Since the 1970s, scholars have perceived the revolutionary moment in Trinidadian literature as taking place in the 1930s. The *Beacon* group, which emerged from a coterie of 1930s Trinidadian writers, was perceived as an inspired, iconoclastic precursor to the internationally-acclaimed 1950s

---

[1] Sir Edward Coke, *The Third Part of the Institutes of the Laws of England*, London: M. Flesher, for W. Lee, and D. Pakeman, 1644, p. 162. Quoted in Suzy Platt, *Respectfully Quoted: A Dictionary of Quotations Requested from the Congressional Research Service*, Washington DC: Library of Congress, 1987, p. 165.

[2] John Ruskin, 'A Speech in London (1866)', *The Works of John Ruskin*, eds., Edward Tyas Cook and Alexander D. O. Wedderburn, London: George Allen, 1903.

generation of Caribbean writers. Post-1970s research, however, has drawn attention to the *Beacon* group's occasional conservatism, such as Alfred Mendes' devaluation of Africa's cultural wealth.[3] The problematic schisms of the *Beacon* group add extra complexity to the historiography of Trinidadian literature and call for a closer reading of Port of Spain's literary geography. Rather than the monologic imposition of empire or the consistent march of progressive anti-colonialism, such contradictions act as a reminder of the fractious history and geography of the region. Mary Louise Pratt writes of the 'contact zones ... where disparate cultures meet, clash, and grapple with each other, often in highly asymmetrical relations of domination and subordination'.[4] Peter Hulme similarly elucidates, 'no smooth history emerges, but rather a series of fragments, which read speculatively and hint at a story that can never be fully recovered'.[5] Thus colonial and anti-colonial discourses across the American tropics emerge as palimpsests 'made up of a variety of conflicting and contradictory frameworks'.[6] Trinidad in the 1930s was no exception, as Harvey R. Neptune contends, perceiving the colony's emergent nationalist mobilisation as 'strategic, uneven and at times ambiguous'.[7]

This essay aims to investigate one of the lesser explored fragments of 1930s Trinidadian literary geography. The focus of the topo-analysis is the colonial house and its grounds, while the social milieu is that of white, creole elites in Port of Spain—groups generally devoted less attention in literary criticism of 1930s Trinidad. Alongside Alfred Mendes's *Pitch Lake*, a valuable piece of the literary map will be provided by Yseult Bridges's little-known fiction, with particular focus on her debut 1934 novel *Questing Heart*.[8] Though Bridges's memoir *Child of the Tropics* is relatively well-known, her novels

---

[3] That C. L. R. James and Mendes continued to work together, meet socially and refer to each other as friends, highlights the depth to which white supremacy was tolerated and inscribed within the colony. For more criticism on Mendes, see Leah Reade Rosenburg, *Nationalism and the Formation of Caribbean Literature*, New York: Palgrave MacMillan, 2007, p. 125.

[4] Mary Louise Pratt, *Imperial Eyes: Travel Writing and Transculturation*, London: Routledge, 1992, p. 7.

[5] Peter Hulme, *Colonial Encounters: Europe and the Native Caribbean, 1492–1797*, London: Routledge, 1992, p. 12.

[6] This comes from a discussion of Hulme's theoretical outline in Alison Blunt and Gillian Rose, eds., *Writing Women and Space: Colonial and Postcolonial Geographies*, New York: Guilford Press, 1994, p. 31.

[7] Harvey R. Neptune, *Caliban and the Yankees: Trinidad and the United States Occupation*, Chapel Hill: University of North Carolina Press, 2007, p. 20.

[8] Tristram Hill [Yseult Bridges], *Questing Heart*, London: Eldon Press Ltd., 1934 (further references are included parenthetically in the text); Alfred H. Mendes, *Pitch*

have received very scant critical discussion to date.[9] Whether this is due to their having been lost to obscurity or to the fact that it was politically expedient to avoid her work, which exhibits an avidly racist agenda, it is difficult to surmise. Bridges's use of the pseudonym Tristram Hill may be a further contributing factor to the critical silence engulfing her novels. Regardless, these works provide an invaluable insight into the conservatism of the white creole elites of Port of Spain and their imagined and material geography of the island, and particularly western Trinidad.

An investigation into various elites' territorial claims on the land is necessarily linked to the drawing up of plots, boundaries, divisions, and thresholds. From its very earliest usage in Old English in the ninth century, 'threshold' denoted the border or line of crossing into a new region. At the start of the eleventh century, it was used to describe the 'piece of timber or stone which lies below the bottom of a door' and 'crossed in entering a house'.[10] Implicit in its meaning is the notion of crossing and borders, a significant discourse in any discussion of housing and domains in the colonial context, where psychic and social boundaries of race, class and gender have had a dramatic impact on geography.[11]

Territory in the Americas has often been fraught with the contentious associations of land ownership and legal disputes.[12] Where native, slave, and indentured peoples of tropical America have often been symbolically linked to the land as deflowered and exploited, so the spectre of unjust appropriation hovers about the lands and houses owned by the colonial elite. That many of this class, from planters to government officials, saw their presence as strictly necessary to the smooth running of the colonies reveals a self-justificatory circular logic, whereby an air of benevolence and

---

Lake, London: New Beacon Books, 1980 (further references are included parenthetically in the text).

[9] I am aware of only one document which discusses Bridges's fiction critically: see Jennifer Rahim, 'Rising into Artistry and Personhood: Trinidad and Tobago Women's Literature 1900–1990', Ph.D., University of the West Indies, 1992.

[10] Threshold derives from what is literally trampled ('threshed'): the timber beneath the doorframe: see 'Nation', *The Oxford English Dictionary*, 2nd ed. CD-ROM (Oxford: Oxford University Press, 1992).

[11] Malpas stresses that 'the ordering of a particular place ... is not independent of social ordering'. Accordingly the exploration of houses cannot be asseverated from social and psychological considerations: J. E. Malpas, *Place and Experience: A Philosophical Topography*, Cambridge: Cambridge University Press, 1999, pp. 35–36.

[12] Native North American Indians appropriately captured the acquisitive nature of the settlers with the term 'People Greedily Grasping for Land': see Hugh Brogan, *The Penguin History of the United States of America*, London: Penguin, 1990, p. 56.

belief in superior management mask an ideology of colonial dispossession. More often than not, members of an elite—as it must be conceded no one homogenous elite existed—gave credence to the notion that they were themselves the possessors of particularly managerial traits. They reified notions of superiority as an attribute of nature (genetic and racial), culture, nationality and nurture. The word domain derives from the Latin words *dominicus*, 'belonging to a Lord' and *dominium*, the master's property rights.[13] When the word *dominus* ('master') first came to be used in Rome in the third century BC, it meant not merely a property owner of the *domus* ('house') or material possessions but an owner of bodies, a slave master.[14]

The domain, therefore, is particularly apt as a synonym for the tropical American colonial house, where the legacy of slavery, material and corporeal ownership, dominion and domination were and are inextricable from their architectural foundations. 1930s Trinidad was segmented by hegemonic practices that perpetuated the myth of white supremacy in many *domains*. Just as the grandest and most expensive houses lining the Savannah in Port of Spain—which are now known as gingerbread houses and serve as modern-day attractions—belonged predominantly to the white plantocracy or expatriate officials, so the noblest and best traits were often regarded as the innate property of the propertied. Colonial society reified social thresholds through taxonomies which ranked subjects by their degree of both extrinsic and intrinsic 'whiteness'.

Whiteness, in order to maintain the territorial claims of the elite, went beyond the skin deep and was often deemed as synonymous with respectability.[15] In this nexus of psycho-social relationships 'whiteness' could be achieved through conduct: genteel activities such as reading, attending church, and paying deference to social betters. Undoubtedly, such social 'whitening' tactics reified the status quo, leaving the territorial rights of the reigning white elite unhampered. While Trinidadian society was beginning to open apertures of social mobility in anomalous cases for those of darker skin, it did not often do so readily, uniformly, or coherently. Though a master at Queen's Royal College, C. L. R. James was turned down for service in the British army during the First World War on account of his complexion.[16]

[13] Walter W. Skeat, *A Concise Etymological Dictionary of the English Language*, Oxford: The Clarendon Press, 1911, p. 149.

[14] Orlando Patterson, *Slavery and Social Death: A Comparative Study*, Cambridge, MA: Harvard University Press, 1982, p. 32.

[15] Daniel Segal, '"Race and Colour" in Pre-Independence Trinidad and Tobago', *Trinidad Ethnicity*, ed. Kevin A. Yelvington, Knoxville: University of Tennessee Press, 1993, pp. 91–93.

[16] A number of sports and social clubs in Port of Spain prided themselves on certain

Evidently, just as barriers were put in place, thresholds were occasionally crossed. In the period Bridges was writing in the 1930s, Afro-Trinidadian and Indo-Trinidadian intellectuals had begun to permeate many areas of attainment and employment traditionally reserved exclusively for whites.[17] Significantly, in 1929, Vidia Naipaul's father, Seepersad Naipaul, was appointed a columnist for the *Trinidad Guardian*, a newspaper for which Bridges herself published a weekly social column.[18] Bridges's first husband, A. M. Low, mentored Trinidad's first Prime Minister Eric Williams and became C. L. R. James's boss as the principal of Queen's Royal College. In *Beyond a Boundary*, James recalls a remark of A. M. Low's, which he interpreted as having a racial dimension: 'We do our work and in time you people will take over'.[19] In many senses, Bridges's novels can be read as a reaction against such a future, whereby the colonised supplant the colonisers. Though the topic of independence is never explicit in her writing, her negative and stereotypical portraits of black and brown colonials are indicative of her pessimistic view of self-governance in the Caribbean.

Before having read the opening lines of either of Yseult Bridges's novels *Questing Heart* or *Creole Enchantment*, readers will be first alerted by a curious definition of 'Creole' that precedes the foreword: 'The term "Creole" is used in its true sense, meaning a person born in the West Indies but of pure EUROPEAN descent'.[20] This text, which is reproduced almost identically in *Creole Enchantment*, speaks volumes about the social dynamics and potential

---

definitive, occasionally sliding, colour boundaries. According to James, around 1918, the Queen's Park Club was dominated by whites, the Maple Club was predominantly brown-skinned and middle class and Shannon's members were lower middle-class and black. This neat hierarchy was not altogether inflexible however: 'None of these lines was [sic] absolute' (C. L. R. James, *Beyond a Boundary*, New York: Pantheon Books, 1983, pp. 56–57).

[17] A year or two before the publication of Bridges's debut novel *Questing Heart* (1934), C. L. R. James's pamphlets, *The Life of Captain Cipriani* (1932) and *The Case for West-Indian Self-Government* (1933) were published. See C. L. R. James, *The Life of Captain Cipriani: An Account of British Government in the West Indies*, Nelson, Lancs.: Coulton, 1932, and 'The Case for West Indian Self-Government', in *The C. L. R. James Reader*, ed. Anna Grimshaw, Oxford: Blackwell, 1993, pp. 49–62.

[18] Though the exact employment history is unknown, Seepersad Naipaul may have been Bridges's colleague at the newspaper, as she is cited as having kept a weekly social column during her first marriage. Her marriage dissolved in 1928, but it is possible she continued to work at the paper. See the foreword of Yseult Bridges, *Child of the Tropics: Victorian Memoirs*, ed. Nicholas Guppy, London: Harvill Press, 1980, p. 11.

[19] James, *Beyond a Boundary*, p. 37.

[20] See the opening note, preceding the prologue, in Tristram Hill [Yseult Bridges], *Creole Enchantment*, London: Geoffrey Bles, 1936.

uses and appropriations of the word 'creole'. Historically, from its Iberian etymological roots, the term's application was not circumscribed by race or ethnicity. Yet Bridges's usage highlights not a whimsical interpretation, but one designed to demarcate a boundary between European ancestry and non- or miscegenated European ancestry. Mary Gallagher has aptly written of the term 'creole' as perennially at a 'locus of considerable semantic confusion'.[21] Derived from the Spanish *criollo* denoting simply those 'born and raised in the Americas' and not native, and the Portuguese *crioulo*, applied to a slave 'born in his master's house', the term has often been employed by different groups to emphasise variant meanings. Yseult Bridges's term, though perhaps outdated in 1930s Trinidad, harks back to eighteenth- and nineteenth-century French metropolitan usage. Her view is no doubt symptomatic of her elite, Anglo-French heritage. Born in 1888 to a French creole mother and English father, Bridges's formative years can be set against the backdrop of a highpoint in European imperialism.[22] It is likely that her mother's French creole background played a significant role in shaping Bridges's exclusive colonial outlook and trenchant racism.[23] As the product of a Rostant and Maingot union, Bridges's mother Alice was a direct descendant of two large French creole plantation families. Notoriously, French creoles were fiercely protective of their ancestral heritage, rarely marrying outside the exclusive bounds of their ethnic or social milieu. Exogamy was transgressive, leaving 'extensive intermarriage' as the only viable alternative.[24]

---

[21] A 'shifting signifier', according to Bongie, it is both 'slippery' and 'resolutely unstable'. Quoted in Mary Gallagher, 'The Créolité Movement: Paradoxes of a French Caribbean Orthodoxy', *Creolization: History, Ethnography, Theory*, ed., Charles Stewart, Walnut Creek: Left Coast Press, 2007, pp. 220–236, at 225.

[22] Bridges was nine years old in the year of Queen Victoria's Diamond Jubilee (1897), a moment when Britain owned a quarter of the globe and its colonial domination seemed to know no bounds. Eulogies on Great Britannia were hardly lacking, with accolades such as this appearing in *The Times*: 'the mightiest and most beneficial Empire ever known in the annals of mankind' (see Elleke Boehmer, *Colonial and Postcolonial Literature: Migrant Metaphors*, Oxford; Oxford University Press, 1995, p. 31).

[23] Commenting on Bridges's memoir, Bridget Brereton observes that Yseult's mother Alice 'was a domestic tyrant, obsessively critical of her servants' performance (eleven in all, plus sundry less permanent hangers-on), directing their lives with the arrogant self-confidence of a slave-owner's daughter'. Brereton evinces that little seems to have changed 'fifty years after the end of slavery, for a white Creole child in Port of Spain'. Brereton is quoted in Evelyn O'Callaghan, *Women Writing the West Indies, 1804–1939: "A Hot Place, Belonging to Us"*, New York: Routledge, 2004, p. 32.

[24] Bridget Brereton, *Race Relations in Colonial Trinidad, 1870–1900*, Cambridge: Cambridge University Press, 1979, p. 38. Born a year before Bridges in 1887, Frederick

Bridges's curious, somewhat laboured, effort to stress the meaning of the word '"Creole" ... in its true sense', highlights a glaring insecurity on her part: that creoles of European descent have shared habitation with non-Europeans and therefore *may* contain an iota of non-European blood. Genealogy and houses are implicated and *em-bedded* in one another. In the American tropics especially, the history of slave women's unions with plantation owners and the disowned sons of slave masters parallels Bridges's fear of black and white being housed together. Bridges's rather blinkered denotation of the word 'creole'—arguably an attempt on her part to expunge all but 'pure' Europeans from the word's geography—which is neither false, nor fully open to the term's variant meanings, nevertheless is an important one, and of especial relevance to the modern critic, as it offers a sharp jolt to a re-visioning of 1930s Trinidad. It highlights the darker side of white colonial projection, exposing the divisions, schisms, and assumptions of an ethnically diverse but hierarchically rigid society—a society that owes much to its roots in the plantation.[25]

---

de Verteuil writes of French creoles: 'about a dozen families were intimate, the others did not exist'. As late as 1932, a relative of Frederick's, Anthony de Verteuil took pride in his ostensibly pure lineage: 'I am a respecter of the old blood ... I still have that which they cannot buy'. For this circle, as Brereton argues, only those Catholic, aristocratic heirs 'free from the taint of "Negro blood"' were eligible enough: 'intermarriage, social and familial incest, were both a virtue and a necessity'. While Brereton's vivid description captures the ideology of the group, Alice Rostant's and Lechmere Guppy's union highlights the odd discrepancy or tolerance towards outsiders. Though a protestant, he would have satisfied the Rostants on three counts of his wealth, distant nobility and, most importantly, whiteness. In fact, English and French mixing had already proved a success on Bridges's maternal side, as her great-grandfather Leon Toussaint Rostant was lionised by an editor on his death as a pioneer bringing cultivation to the land: 'French blood and English energy created that mixture of kindheartedness and stern resolve, which distinguished most of the old planters who opened up our virgin forests and pushed civilization into the heart of the island' (all quotations here reproduced from Brereton).

[25] In his influential essay 'Plantation America: A Culture Sphere', Charles Wagley defined the 'plantation system with African slave labour ... [as a] fundamental formative' of Plantation-America's 'culture sphere' which Wagley envisaged as spanning from about midway up the Brazilian coast to include parts of tropical Latin America along the Caribbean Coast, the Caribbean, and the Southern United States. The plantation was deemed a spatial, cultural and historical determinant of the societies that grew out of them. Two attributes that Wagley notes of these societies are their rigid class divisions and racial diversity, while 'Caucasoid features' are paid the highest respect. Bridges's and Mendes's novels depict not only worlds founded on the culture of the plantation, but reveal the rigid, hierarchical domesticated worlds that recall that most contentious, anathema and nostalgic of domains: the great plantation

Questing Heart may appear to initially wrong-foot any expectations of white-black segregation by situating its heroine, Christine Bennett, a poor white orphan, as a live-in servant of Mrs Davies, a mixed race woman with 'a touch of the tarbrush' (23). The first impression is a striking one of slavery reversed against the traditional white oppressor: a white woman is the drudge in a house governed by a cruel brown mistress. It is a resonant 'myth of imperial vulnerability' that the would-be oppressors imagine themselves as vulnerable, while positioning the Other as violent and barbaric.[26] Aggressive and bad-tempered, Mrs Davies frequently abuses Christine 'in the foulest language' (50). Likewise Mrs Davies's daughters maltreat Christine, showing her 'contempt and rudeness', while the black servants snub her as a 'poor white' (50). Struggling under the 'vulgarity' and 'libertinism' of such a house, Christine feels ashamed and unclean (50). Every day presents a struggle to keep herself free of the contaminating influence of bad morals and behaviour. The house is inhospitable in the extreme and she its prisoner, economically and psychologically. However, her sexual assault and subsequent physical abuse at the hands of Harry Davies, Mrs Davies's son, and Mrs Davies respectively, culminate in her flight.

The story begins with these events fresh in Christine's mind, having occurred just a few hours earlier. Having fled the nightmare house, Christine sits alone on a park bench on the Pitch Walk encircling the Savannah. She believes her actions are inconsistent with that of a white girl, yet she lacks the luxury of choice afforded the 'respectable inhabitants' of Port of Spain, 'reading on their verandas' or the 'happy people' she observes leaving a cocktail party to return to the sanctity of their own homes (13. 15). Shut out from the sanctuary of a respectable abode, she is in close proximity to the 'night-birds' of the town, a corpus comprising a cosmopolitan group—mixed race, East Asian, and Venezuelan—none of whom are 'pure' Europeans (15). Christine's compartmentalisation of the world into whiteness equals goodness versus non-whiteness as its many-headed repository of evil is Manichean in outlook. Her distrust of darker than white pigmentation is literal, symbolic and ultimately pathological. To be anything other than white is to be swamped in moral darkness. For a brief moment, Christine peers out from her bench at the 'lovely night' and feels she might be able to take great pleasure in it, but for the nagging problem of her security (16).

---

house. See Charles Wagley, 'Plantation America: A Culture Sphere', in *Caribbean Studies: A Symposium*, ed., Vera Rubin, 2nd ed., Seattle: University of Washington Press, 1960, p. 5.

[26] I am grateful to Peter Hulme for alerting me to this notion at Essex. The phrase appears in Norrie Macqueen, *Colonialism*, Harlow: Longman, 2007, p. 94.

For without a house, she cannot be secure and does not have the luxury of privacy. In Mrs Davies's house, she cannot prevent anyone entering her room. She craves not so much a Woolfian 'room of one's own' as a distinctly private space in which intrusion from and contact with the black and brown masses is limited and, quite possibly, prohibited.

At Christine's nadir, Tom Carter, a wealthy businessman, offers her temporary lodging with his children's black ex-nanny, Lizzie Hodge. Pensioned off some years before by Carter, Lizzie lives in Belmonte, a district just east of Port of Spain.[27] Christine promptly accepts the offer, no doubt on account of the fact that Carter is 'white'. His complexion paves the way for Christine's assessment of him as a harmless gentleman with a 'kindliness of manner' and a 'gentleness of voice' (17). Carter is at once elevated to the stature of an 'Arthurian knight' and Bridges does not miss the opportunity for the mock-epic allusion. He is transformed into the questing figure of romance, a knight-errant in white 'shining armour', albeit a duck suit, out to protect a damsel in distress from the monster of Harry Davies (21). In this guise, he initiates a process by which Christine is gradually extricated from her position as a non-owner of property.

Though Christine becomes a lodger in Lizzie's 'cottage', she and Carter tacitly assume the role of superiors towards Lizzie. The cottage serves an interesting purpose here as the signified object, as it has quaint associations in a British context, but bears imperial ramifications in Trinidad.[28] It is suggestive of both a degree of affluence and complicity with the colonial order. As an ex-nurse to Carter's children, Lizzie belongs to the latter camp—her property acquired with certain strings attached. Dismissal of her ex-boss and his companion are out of the question, as she rapidly enters into a role of unpaid service to Christine. Christine cries herself to sleep one night and Lizzie gives her succour. Lizzie's concessions to Christine are subtle, yet diffuse. It is considered natural, for instance, that Christine is seated in Lizzie's best rocking chair when Carter visits (42). Christine's temporary lodging in Lizzie's cottage and its reification of innate white superiority functions as an important stepping stone for Christine, as it prepares her for the proprietary role she will come to fill. The unsuitability of Lizzie's 'noisy, smelly' black neighbourhood, where the 'heat and squalor'

---

[27] Though usually spelt 'Belmont', Bridges adopts this unusual spelling with an added 'e'. See Hill [Bridges], *Questing Heart*, p. 19.

[28] Charles Kingsley devoted an epistolary chapter to his time spent in a Trinidadian cottage. See Charles Kingsley, 'A Letter from a West Indian Cottage Ornée', *At Last: A Christmas in the West Indies* [*The Works of Charles Kingsley*, vol. XIV], London: MacMillan and Co., 1880.

are unbearable and brawls not uncommon, make it expedient, in Carter's eyes, that Christine move (59. 97). The temporary environs of the area, in a house owned by Carter's ex-servant, are not quite fitting. Christine must upscale to bigger and better protection from the invasive forces of the black and brown classes.

The panacea to Christine's social ills and temporal existence, Carter believes, is clear-cut: she must have her own house. If, as Robert Young proposes, to be 'walled' within the city suggested that one was a 'civilized' citizen, as opposed to a 'savage (wild man)' dwelling beyond its realms, the 'walls' of a house might also said to offer a similar ideological and psychological construct.[29] A house's walls can offer sanctuary, but more than this they stand as a symbol of status, social position, kudos and wealth—these latter symbols of the house being especially acute in the colonial Caribbean. Firstly to be housed, as opposed to living in a yard, gave the occupant an entrée into bourgeois, civil and *civilized* society. Distinctions were clearly drawn between overseers' and estate owners' houses, just as they might be between terraced houses and mansions today. The disparity between private housing and communal barrack yards, shanty dwellings, huts, hovels, and street pavements of the homeless—indeed all sites that are not easily subsumed under the category of house—highlight the distinction between the privately owned house and its alternatives. The house acts as a tangible symbol and marker of division in tropical America, attaining a particular colonial resonance.

When Christine comes to occupy her newly built bungalow in Maraval, not only does it stand as a material representation of her newly acquired distinction and innate breeding, as a woman of English birth and parentage, it also signifies her new-found condition of security, psychological dominion and power: it is *her home*—at least it is a home purpose-built for her. Although she does not become the proprietor of the bungalow until after Carter's death, Christine is no longer a guest or itinerant in others' domains. Accordingly, she assumes the role of mistress in the colonial house. To do this, the good house management skills of a colonial disciplinarian must be applied and the Manichean division between 'us' and 'them', white and black, maintained. As colonial manuals on household management often demonstrated, the mistress of the house was often seen as upholding the values of empire. She was often likened to a military leader fronting a campaign, a bastion of domesticity, representing 'the master race' in a land alien to the mother nation.[30] Surrounded on all sides by colonised Others,

---

[29] Robert Young, *Colonial Desire: Hybridity in Theory, Culture and Race*, London: Routledge, 1995, p. 31.

[30] For a general discussion see: Rosemary Marangoly George, *The Politics of Home:*

wicked Calibans and dangerous shades of humanity, she was expected to bring the borders of her home nation to the house.

Christine's expression of pride in being born in England to white parents, as opposed to being creole and, worse still, 'coloured', highlights the hierarchical divisiveness of the society and Christine's position within it: though technically poor, she, as a born Englishwoman, implicitly links herself to the ruling class of British administrators (46).[31] Christine's rise in fortune in light of her ancestry and birth in England—as with Jane Eyre, another unwanted orphan who acquires a fortune after a romance develops between her and her employer—forwards the idea that her innate gentlewomanly status is recognised as she acquires that which ought to be naturally hers.[32] Of the brief narrative sketch that is presented of her parents, her father barely features, while her mother stands out as a spirited, liberal, middle-class woman. Progressive in the sense that she is desirous that Christine have 'a comprehensive outlook upon life', she has home schooled Christine (48). With books evidently abundant, Christine becomes a bibliophile, reading material 'in advance of her years' (48). This apparently felicitous childhood is brought to a swift end with the sudden deaths of her parents, both of whom are hospitalised after a nondescript illness.

Christine's entry into the property-owning class therefore stands as a crucial turning point in which she re-enters the lost social milieu of her childhood. That she becomes a proprietor of a bungalow, a building which it can be inferred she grew up in (playing 'happily with the children from the other bungalows') is significant, suggestive of a mirroring between her past and her present (49). Such mirroring purveys the romantic notion that the unfortunate lapse in-between Christine's two timelines was an unnatural

---

Postcolonial Relocations and Twentieth-Century Fiction, New York: Cambridge University Press, 1996, p. 50. The first chapter of *Mrs Beeton's Book of Household Management*, entitled, 'The Mistress' opens accordingly: 'As with THE COMMANDER OF AN ARMY, or the leader of any enterprise, so is it with the mistress of a house. Her spirit will be seen through the whole establishment; and just in proportion as she performs her duties intelligently and thoroughly, so will her domestics follow in her path' (Isabella M. Beeton, *Mrs Beeton's Book of Household Management*, ed. Nicola Humble, Oxford: Oxford University Press, 2000, p. 7).

[31] Trinidad was no exception to the rule across tropical America that white creoles were perceived by colonial society as one tier below the expatriate class. See: Brereton, *Race Relations in Colonial Trinidad, 1870–1900*, p. 43. For a contiguous portrait of social relations in the Bahamas, see Ian G. Strachan, *Paradise and Plantation: Tourism and Culture in the Anglophone Caribbean*, Charlottesville: University of Virginia Press, 2002, p. 10.

[32] Carter employs Christine for a while as his secretary prior to the development of their romantic attachment.

deviation from her true path. As one of the elite, she must be removed from the common rabble of Belmonte and transplanted to a purlieu in which black and brown colonial subjects—labourers, market-hawkers, and cart-drivers—form a backdrop to the landscape which her bungalow overlooks. Christine has her bed placed so as to observe the vista beyond her veranda and take pleasure in the seemingly paradisiacal scenes of her surroundings:

> She loved the thin stream of life which trickled down her road each morning. Negresses and East Indians, balancing upon their heads trays piled high with vegetables and gaily coloured fruits, passed on their way to the market. The former walked with long strides, swinging hips and straight backs ... chattering and joking at the tops of their voices in a mixture of nigger-English and French *patois*, happy, carefree children of the sun. (107)

What was previously anathema—the sounds, movement and speech of the black, ex-slave community especially—is transfigured through Christine's new location and domain, into a geography of the picturesque and exotic. Topophilia may appear paramount, but it is of a highly conditional kind. For the transformation of the land and its people from the infernal to an Edenic melange of sensuous display, natural beauty, exotic bodies, and aesthetic bodily motion is predicated on Christine's dislocation from the scene in view.[33] She can enjoy the mobile black and brown bodies in a distant scene, unlike when she spent time in 'smelly' Belmonte in close proximity to the principle actors. Tim Cresswell's assertion, 'We do not live in landscapes—we look at them', stresses a significant displacement between the perceived, the perceiver, and the place.[34] Landscape is not lived in, like places, but watched from a location outside the view or frame itself. To be outside the frame can lend a certain safety and unreality to the vision. In Christine's case, her displacement purveys the scene with romance. W. J. T. Mitchell contends that the distinctive traits of a landscape, even when apparently manifest and inherent attributes, are always rendered questionably subjective by their frame and by the person doing the framing: 'even if the features are sublime,

---

[33] I have borrowed the term 'sensuous display' from Edward Casey, 'Body, Self and Landscape', in *Textures of Place: Exploring Humanist Geographies*, eds., Paul C. Adams, Steven D. Hoelscher and Karen E. Till, Minneapolis: University of Minnesota Press, 2001, p. 418.

[34] Tim Cresswell, *Place: A Short Introduction*, Malden, MA: Blackwell, 2005, p. 11.

dangerous, and so forth, the frame is always there as a guarantee that it is only a picture, only picturesque, and the observer is safe in another place'.[35]

The dialectics between the 'artificial' scene which is seen, heard, and ultimately framed, and the real one that is lived, are at play as Christine gazes from her bedroom window. At a remove from the lived and living space of the people on the road, she is nevertheless close enough to receive an 'impression' of the scene. She enjoys consuming the sensuous visual, aural, and mobile scenery. Behind the frame of the narrative, Bridges promulgates the image of the Edenic Caribbean island as an ideal for European occupancy: with colonised lands and people forming a backdrop, the colonial house a sanctuary and a frame, and the European protagonist an occupant, observer, and consumer of all these idyllic scenes.

While distance lends enchantment to the view, Christine's bungalow engenders continual interactions between herself and the darker-skinned. Though no longer living in close proximity to these 'Othered' others, Christine interacts with them as a superior at a remove. Just as the British Empire could be said to have been founded on the political praxis of *divide et impera* ('divide and rule'), so the colonial house represents a microcosm of fractious and divisional hegemonic politics.[36] Christine, however vulnerable and delicate, purveys typically imperialist attitudes in her role as mistress of the house. In her view, the black man is congenitally lazy and must be forced to work for the upkeep and beauty of her garden:

> Christine well knew how quickly the weeds grew, but she also knew that Joseph was no exception to his race. To get work done an eagle eye had to be kept upon him and she thought of the utter futility of the expression 'to work like a nigger'. A nigger never worked unless he were driven to it, and he took little interest and less pride in what he did (142).

Christine's need for surveillance, 'keeping an eagle eye' on Joseph, reveals a panoptic streak in her domination. As Rosemary George writes of the colonial mistress, she 'does not have to keep house as much as supervise the keeping of her house'.[37] Extending this to her grounds and gardens, the mistress is expected to be an imperial manager whose task is not only

---

[35] W. J. T. Mitchell, 'Imperial Landscape', in *Landscape and Power*, ed., W. J. T. Mitchell, 2nd ed., Chicago: University of Chicago Press, 1994, p. 16.

[36] Karl Marx, *New-York Daily Tribune*, 15 July 1857 <http://www.panjab.org.uk/english/KM1WII03.htm> [1.11.2008].

[37] George, *The Politics of Home*, p. 51.

on a par with military leadership, but also plantation ownership. Tellingly, Christine uses the language of the overseer in the plantation field: 'the nigger never worked unless ... driven to it'. Also her presence, command and surveillance are deemed essential to prevent the garden from degenerating into an overgrown tangle of 'weeds'. The Edenic beauty of the garden is reliant on the master class' ability to oversee its cultivation. In this sense, the domestic mistress of the garden and the plantation owner are wedded in their imperial actions and aims: to reap the fruits of others' labour. A belief that the Caribbean colonies' success was entirely dependent on the white class' cultivation, in both the cultural and *agri-cultural* sense, became especially prevalent from the seventeenth century onwards, when buccaneering was gradually supplanted by planting as a more profitable enterprise.[38] The British literary figures of Anthony Trollope, Thomas Carlyle, and James Anthony Froude all perpetuated this belief in the latter half of the nineteenth century with varying degrees of contempt for the Afro-Caribbean. In his essay, 'Occasional Discourse on the Nigger Question', Carlyle wrote of 'Quashee'—a derogatory reference for a black person—as 'growing pumpkins ... for his lazy benefit'.[39] Echoes of Carlyle's Quashee abound as Bridges presents a dual image of the abundantly fertile Caribbean inhabited by the inherently lazy black person. Initially, the free indirect discourse suggests the view of indolent black people is predominantly Christine's, but by the following paragraph, the vision of a tropical cornucopia and the ease of black livelihoods is no longer simply her vision. The perspective is far more impersonal and more heavily steered by the third person narrative, which in turn raises questions about the author's intention:

In a country where there is no winter, where a few saplings driven into the earth and interwoven with strips of bamboo serve as the walls of a house and palm fronds form its roof, where curtains of cheap calico are all that is necessary to veil the open spaces left as doors and windows, where sufficient covering to fulfil the requirements of the law is all the clothing that is needed ... where breadfruit trees flourish in the bush, work can be treated as only an occasional unpleasant necessity. (142–143)

---

[38] See Strachan, *Paradise and Plantation*, p. 33. I have borrowed the term 'agri-culture' from Robert Young, who discusses the etymology of culture as cultivation in some detail: *Colonial Desire*, p. 31.

[39] Thomas Carlyle, 'Occasional Discourse on the Nigger Question' [1849] *Critical and Miscellaneous Essays*, vol. VII, New York: C. Scribner's Sons, 1900, p. 103.

Is this Bridges speaking? Rhetorical as this question may be, there is little to contradict the supposition, as Bridges appears a writer actively engaged in the promotion of imperialist ideology and rhetoric. Equally, this section bears an intertextual relationship with earlier British imperial writing about both Trinidad and tropical America. The ease of tropical life and work is implicitly pitted against the hardship of labour in the North Atlantic world. Trollope believed that black Caribbean labourers were better off than England's labourers: 'In this sense in which they are free, no English labourer is free'.[40] A parallel can be found in Froude, who writes of black Caribbeans accordingly:

> They are perfectly happy. In no part of the globe is there any peasantry whose every want is so completely satisfied as her Majesty's black subjects in the West Indian islands. They have no aspirations to make them restless ... They have food for the picking up. Clothes they need not, and lodging in such a climate need not be elaborate.[41]

Bridges closely re-presents Froude's ideas in *Questing Heart*. Just as Froude considers black subjects to be 'perfectly happy' under the yoke of British rule in their tropical climate, so Bridges's narrative depicts the image of idle blacks living idyllically: 'The lives of the Trinidad blacks are as near happiness as life can possibly be. With few possessions, and fewer wants they are happy, inconsequent creatures, living only to eat and drink and perpetuate their species' (143). Noticeably, both Bridges and Froude combine the happiness of the black person with the simplicity and innocence of a primitive, a being who lives merely for the animal needs and pleasures of eating, resting and procreating. A sense of what Michael Dash dubs 'prelapsarian nostalgia' prevails for the black person, whose wants are less and who is happier without the material possessions or large properties of the whites.[42] Significantly, Bridges draws on the mental image of the black dwelling as one not formally built, bricked or architecturally designed, but one that is wholly constructed from natural materials. Built from saplings, bamboos and palm fronds, the black abode is quite literally a tree house. The implication is that these prelapsarian black people, scantily clad, dwelling in

---

[40] Anthony Trollope, *The West Indies and the Spanish Main* [1860], Gloucester: Alan Sutton, 1985, p. 209.

[41] James Anthony Froude, *The English in the West Indies, or, the Bow of Ulysses* [1888], Marston Gate: Adamant Media Corp., 2005, p. 43.

[42] J. Michael Dash, *Haiti and the United States: National Stereotypes and the Literary Imagination*, Basingstoke: MacMillan Press, 1998, p. 30.

nature, have yet to leave paradise, to know the hardship of labour, disease, and death. They are indivisible from nature, lacking cultivation and culture.

Culture, in its early English usage, related to a process of crop cultivation, tilling the earth and animal husbandry; it connoted the development, improvement, productive use or taming of nature.[43] The first notion of paradise was used by the Greeks and tellingly related to a manmade garden, 'a Persian enclosed park, orchard or pleasure ground'.[44] Helen Tiffin contends that Christianity exported to the Caribbean the 'founding myth' of the 'garden' as an earthly paradise.[45] Paradise and the garden were deeply imbricated with and reliant on cultivation. It was only when nature was left to its own wild devices that paradise might be lost. When the early plantations were developed under Elizabeth I's reign, nature's dangerous potential for overabundance—wilderness and unruly weed-filled gardens—or scarcity—waste, voids, and deserts—were staple images that suggested that to lack cultivation was to founder.[46] In Christine's garden, Joe, the apparently natural black man, is put to work alongside the plants so that the garden will be cultivated. The worry of leaving Joe to his own devices is that nature and the natural man, almost indistinguishable, will overrun the order of the garden, allowing weeds to fester and destroying the paradisiacal haven. Order must be maintained and the colonial black and brown classes regulated stringently.

A series of imagined boundaries are placed between the white proprietor of the brick house and the black owner of the tapia hut, or shanty. John

---

[43] Of the Latin roots for culture, *colere* and *cultera*, it was the former which splintered into a range of meanings: inhabit, cultivate, protect, and honour with worship. From the inhabit root came the Latin *colonus* ('farmer or cultivator') and the derivation 'colony', which denoted in sixteenth-century English, 'a farm, [an] estate in the country; a rural settlement': see Young, *Colonial Desire*, p. 31.

[44] Strachan, *Paradise and Plantation*, p. 5.

[45] Helen Tiffin, 'Man Fitting the Landscape', in *Caribbean Literature and the Environment: Between Nature and Culture*, eds., Elizabeth M. DeLoughrey, Renée K. Gosson and George B. Handley, Charlottesville: University of Virginia Press, 2005, pp. 199–212, at 202.

[46] Notable examples of unruly nature appear in Shakespeare's *Hamlet*, ('tis an unweeded garden / That grows to seed; things rank and gross in nature' [I.II, 135–136]) and *The Second Part of Henry VI* ('Now 'tis the spring, and weeds are shallow-rooted / Suffer them now, and they'll o'ergrow the garden / And choke the herbs for want of husbandry' [III.I, 31–33]) as metaphors of contamination and disease latent within the state. Wilderness and waste had distinct meanings in the Elizabethan era; the former as Keith Thomas asserts was connotative of overgrowth, 'a dense, uncultivated wood', the latter of scarcity, 'land not cultivated or used for any purpose' (quoted in Strachan, *Paradise and Plantation*, p. 21).

Armstrong describes such boundary marking in terms of symbolic 'border guards', who police 'us' and 'them'.[47] As mistress of her bungalow, Christine acts as a 'border guard', deciding both those who can enter her property, who is 'in' or 'out', as well the terms of entry. White people enter the property as friends, acquaintances, lovers and even enemies. Though far from being all equal in Christine's eyes, they are dignified as superior to the black- or brown-skinned, who are only granted access provided they are subservient, ingratiating and, essentially, *know their place*.

What is 'out of place', Mary Douglas suggests, may contaminate, and the colonial house cannot be at risk of such pollution. 'Dirt', writes Douglas, 'is the by-product of a systematic ordering and classification of matter, in so far as ordering involves rejecting inappropriate elements'. The pollution Douglas describes goes beyond the pathogenic and hygienic to the 'symbolic systems of purity'.[48] Black and brown persons who 'fit' the system of classification and ordering in Christine's home, and know their place as inferiors, maintain the status quo and ensure tidiness, cleanliness and order. Indeed their presence in the house as inferiors is vital to the hegemonic foundation of white supremacy. Christine is content to give Lizzie and Myra, whose father is white ('a buckra gen'l'man'), access to her premises because neither openly challenges the codes of white hegemony (110). Lizzie suggests that equality between the races is untenable and lamentable. Slavery recalls a simple, happy time, leaving her nostalgic for its clear lines of segregation: 'Yo' know well dat Lizzie's none of dese new-fashioned niggers what tryin' to set demselves up as white people. Me mudder was born in slav'ry and she tell me how she mudder would not leave de master—not she!' (97). Myra, though not quite as subservient a figure, is ingratiating upon her first call at Christine's bungalow. Myra charms Christine with her promise to call in every day and her compliments as to her well-kept garden and fine house. Myra's good looks and 'more regular features', by which Christine traces some white lineage, highlight how racial taxonomy orders Christine's symbolic placement and perception of her (109). As a woman of 'clear brown skin', Myra appears more beautiful and charming than the darker-skinned Lizzie, and is given to greater liberty within her bungalow (108–109). Significantly, Lizzie is a servant and Myra a market-woman, earning money independent

---

[47] John Alexander Armstrong, *Nations before Nationalism*, Chapel Hill: University of North Carolina Press, 1982, p.6. Quoted in Floya Anthias, Nira Yuval-Davis and Harriet Cain, *Racialized Boundaries: Race, Nation, Gender, Colour and Class and the Anti-Racist Struggle*, London: Routledge, 1992, p.33.

[48] Mary Douglas, *Purity and Danger: An Analysis of the Concepts of Pollution and Taboo*, London: Ark, 1984, p.35.

of a sole mistress and a plantation, as she sells provision ground goods: yams, avocados, and sweet potatoes.

Economically and nutritionally, slave and ex-slave communities thrived on their local produce of root crops and starchy vegetables, diminishing their reliance on imported foods such as saltfish and flour.[49] In Myra's case her 'ground provisions' provide her independence and suggest she is part of the fabric of the natural, pastoral Maraval landscape Christine admires from her bedroom window. Yet in spite of Myra's considerable independence, Christine seems unable to recognise Myra as anything more than a picturesque addition to her two-dimensional, pastoral view. As her loyal devotee, Myra remains, in Christine's eyes, a 'highly diverting', naïve innocent to be petted, encouraged and patronised (111). Christine's patronage extends beyond the economic as she infantilises Myra in the following terms: 'Myra would squat beside her tray and amuse Christine with a queer mixture of Rabelaisian wisdom and childlike innocence. She was very inquisitive, but there was a naïve candour in her questions which robbed them of any impudence' (110).

The infantilisation of black and brown persons in tropical America has a legacy that dates back to its Colombian possession. Just over half a century before Bridges's debut novel was published, Froude wrote: 'these poor children of darkness have escaped the consequences of the Fall'.[50] As innocents, the potential menace of the black and brown races was perpetually mitigated. To think of the ex-slave as an infant, benignly wild and tamable was preferable to the alternative.[51] As an adult capable of open or surreptitious rebellion, the burning down of property, the seizing of existing plantations, and the poisoning of whites, the ex-slave posed too great a threat to the status quo of the colony.

Myra's seemingly fawning behaviour, which can be read with far more ambiguity than Christine and, in all probability, Bridges ascribe, is never shown to be duplicitous or fake. Homi Bhabha suggests 'the *menace* of mimicry' hangs on an ironic or double vision, in which the colonial script is disrupted at the point of disclosure.[52] It is not impossible to read an element

---

[49] The etymology of the provision grounds and starchy vegetables to which they refer—yams, eddoes and sweet potatoes—lives on today as they are still referred to as 'ground provisions' in the Anglophone Caribbean. Sylvia Wynter has distinguished the ex-slave's provision grounds from the plantation: 'Novel and History: Plot and Plantation', *Savacou* 5 (June, 1971), pp. 95–102.

[50] James Anthony Froude, *The English in the West Indies, or, the Bow of Ulysses* [1888], Marston Gate: Adamant Media Corp., 2005, p. 43

[51] I owe the term 'benignly wild' to Strachan, *Paradise and Plantation*, p. 77.

[52] Homi K. Bhabha, *The Location of Culture*, London: Routledge, 2004, p. 126.

of danger and even mockery in what Christine perceives as Myra's 'ingenious impudence', and yet Christine cannot perceive an ulterior, more subversive, script (109). To do so would be to have allowed a white woman to be duped by an inferior and contaminated her home with the touch of a charlatan. The Manichean divisions of the imperial eye allow for no grey areas. If unexceptionable, the black and brown classes are good, servile, docile figures: warm-hearted mammies or avuncular figures like the eponymous protagonist of Harriet Beecher Stowe's *Uncle Tom's Cabin*. If objectionable, they are nefarious, as Fanon contends: the 'quintessence of evil'.[53]

In *Questing Heart*, the Davies family is presented as the embodiment of tropical evil, their house a den of iniquitous dealings. 'An atmosphere of incessant lying, intrigue and illicit love' pervade the Davies's home, where 'Truth and restraint such as her [Christine's] mother taught her' are unknown (50). In this *locus terribilis*, Harry Davies emerges as 'the worst thorn in Christine's side' (51). The reference to St Paul, who receives a 'thorn in the flesh, the messenger of Satan' draws upon the Manichean allegory of good versus evil.[54] Christine, the saintly Christian, her very name charged with metonymic and etymological associations of Christianity, is pitted against Harry, the devil's messenger. The first and most dangerous rupture takes place when Harry kisses Christine, enacting a sexual assault which, Christine's prospective paramour Carter deems tantamount to attempted rape (27).[55] The second major confrontation between the heroine and her nemesis takes place on her veranda. Harry Davies turns up, unannounced, in the hope of extorting money from her or entertaining his friends on her premises at her expense. Though as he states no molestation takes place, his motives are portrayed as both sexual and malevolent: 'He was smiling evilly: his eyes seemed to strip her of her clothes and leave her naked before him' (199–200). Representative of a new psycho-sexual attack, Harry Davies's invasion of Christine's private property re-enacts the events of his

---

[53] Frantz Fanon, *The Wretched of the Earth*, trans. Constance Farrington, London: Penguin Books, 2001, p. 32.

[54] 2 Corinthians, 12:7: Robert P. Carroll and Stephen Prickett, eds., *The Bible: Authorized King James Version*, Oxford: Oxford University Press, 1997, p. 232.

[55] The charge of attempted rape is only ever voiced by Tom Carter. However, the degree to which Davies is guilty of this charge is far more speculative and ambiguous than Carter suggests. Harry is certainly physical, 'hurling himself' on Christine, but the extent to which this is tantamount to attempted rape is uncertain. However Carter's voice is significant here. It recalls the likely outcome, the probably voice, of the verdict if the case ever went to court. For even if Davies were innocent, it is likely in the case of a white woman and a suspected darker-skinned rapist, as with Adela and Aziz in *A Passage to India*, that the latter would be charged.

previous sexual assault. Davies is depicted as the derogatory stereotype of the libidinous, primal Negroid man—a potential rapist seeking a taste of white flesh. Tempted to shoot Harry 'as she would a poison snake', Christine evicts Harry by placing a loaded gun to his head (201). The Edenic symbol reverses the idea of the fallen Eve, leaving her to remain in the prelapsarian home, while the snake, Harry, is banished.

Christine's actions suggest colonial property in the American tropics requires militaristic support, the ability to defend the home turf with firepower from the threat of trespassing aliens. On first registering Harry's presence in her drive, Christine is struck by the 'consciousness of her physical weakness before the brute force of man' (199). Harry's specific embodiment is temporarily sublimated by the impersonal 'man'; he is depersonalised and alien to her femininity, land and house. Though it may seem counterintuitive to consider Harry Davies, a creole of both white and black ancestry, an *alien* in Trinidad, it could be considered a natural corollary of the colonial mindset, which brands subversive subjects aliens and in turn alienates them.[56] The word 'alien', first used in Middle English, initially denoted belonging 'to another person, place or family', as well as its closer modern meaning of strange or foreign.[57] However, it is this former definition which offers a more local definition of alien and it is under this rubric that Harry Davies appears. As a member of another family, social set, and racial ascription, he is effectively an alien invader. It befalls the mistress of the house to follow the call to arms and defend it against attack. The home here is comparable to a fortress, capable of protecting against sexual, physical, and psychic incursion.

In 1604, the significance of the English house passed into common law, as Sir Edward Coke, the Attorney General, ruled: 'the house of every one is to him as his castle and fortress, as well for his defence against injury and violence as for his repose'.[58] It established the legal right of an owner or servant of a house to attack and kill harmful intruders and thieves in protection of themselves or the property.[59] The right to defend property

---

[56] Considering the divisive world of French Algeria, Frantz Fanon writes: 'I owe it to myself to affirm that the Arab, permanently an alien in his own country, lives in a state of absolute depersonalization' (*Toward the African Revolution: Political Essays*, trans. Haakon Chevalier, Harmondsworth: Penguin, 1970, p. 63).

[57] 'Nation', *The Oxford English Dictionary*.

[58] Sir Edward Coke, 2003, Liberty Fund <http://oll.libertyfund.org/title/911/106328> [30.11.2008].

[59] The case also established that the sheriff's men could not force entry into a property without first having a warrant and secondly, identifying themselves. If these procedures where not followed, the property owner was legally entitled to bar his or

again made history when John Ruskin argued in defence of Governor Eyre's actions in the 1865 Morant Bay uprising. Eyre's brutal suppression of an ostensibly peaceful protest resulted in the colonial authority's indiscriminate massacre of over four hundred black and brown Jamaican men, women, and children, the flogging of another six hundred adults and the burning of at least a thousand homes.

In Eyre's defence, Ruskin elicited the example of a case he had read in a newspaper. Spying a drunken man in his garden, the owner shot the trespasser, killing him. The jury found in favour of the homeowner, acquitting him of all charges. On this exemplar, Ruskin built his defence: 'For the protection of your person ... it is lawful for you to take life, on so much suspicion as may arise from a shadow cast on the wrong side of your wall'.[60] Ruskin contended that to take life not merely in defence of the individual, but for 'sixteen thousand men, women, and children ... [and] a province involving in its safety that of all English possessions in the West Indies' was not only legal, but to be commended.[61]

In Ruskin's ominous language, the threat the colonies' darker-skinned masses posed to the colonial house, Anglo-Caribbean possession and, across the Atlantic divide, to the British house is insidious and degenerative.[62] The danger is transnational, the eye of a violent, tempestuous 'contact zone' that refracts and links the contentious issues of property and the sanction of violence and even murder for its defence and upkeep. This has serious implications for the topoanalysis of the house in the American tropics. While the sugar plantation has commonly been perceived as founded, construed, and mixed from and through the blood of slaves, so the colonial house can be

---

her doors to the sheriff's men. See Coke, *The Selected Writings*; and Ronald Hamowy, *The Encyclopedia of Libertarianism*, Thousand Oaks, CA: Sage, 2008, p. 78.

[60] Ruskin, *The Works*, p. 553.

[61] Ruskin, *The Works*, p. 553. The figure of 16,000 may have been a mistaken reference to the number of white people on the island, numbering roughly 13,000 in the 1865 census. They were outnumbered by roughly 350,000 blacks. For more on this see Bernard Semmel, *Jamaican Blood and Victorian Conscience: The Governor Eyre Controversy*, Westport, CO: Greenwood Press, 1976, p. 34. See also Bill Schwarz, *The Expansion of England: Race, Ethnicity, and Cultural History*, London: Routledge, 1996, p. 129. For further surveys of the population, see Arvel B. Erickson, 'Empire or Anarchy: The Jamaica Rebellion of 1865', *The Journal of Negro History*, 44, no. 2 (1959), pp. 99–122, at 100.

[62] Ruskin described himself in opposition to John Stuart Mill and Eyre's other critics, as 'a Re-former not a De-former'. The implication is that he aims to rebuild and reinvigorate society, preventing it from lapsing into cultural entropy: see Ian Baucom, *Out of Place: Englishness, Empire, and the Locations of Identity*, Princeton, NJ: Princeton University Press, 1999, p. 49.

seen to be implicated in this sanguinary process. As a fortress, or possession of higher value than the lives of the colonised, the colonial house represents a site of actual and potential death and bloodletting of poor ex-slave, indentured and labouring classes, while providing security for its owners.

Yet just as the house can be said to provide security, so it is of a speculative, shifting and unstable kind. If the masses are rebellious, then the risk of violent eviction or destruction is high. If it follows that the colonial house's material stability is founded on the subservience of others, so its symbolic association relies on subservience to the master class. It is very telling that Christine is drawn so close to murdering a rebellious, brown-skinned man who threatens to visit her property often and invite his friends. For what is at stake is her reputation. To allow a man of a darker hue to frequent her home with his friends is to invite the terror of housing black, brown, and white under the same roof. It recalls the pre-emancipatory fear that the house operates as a site, to quote Mimi Sheller, of 'dangerous erotics by which the slave is lightened, and the master darkened'.[63] The house stands, therefore, for an array of extrinsic and intrinsic meanings and encodings which not only bear implications with respect to the social standing of the homeowner or dweller, but also vis-à-vis his or her sexual politics, self-projection, and positioning within the community.

*

It is the symbolic and social linkage of houses, reputation, social standing, self, and community which is particularly pertinent to the protagonist of Alfred Mendes's *Pitch Lake*, Joe da Costa. At the opening of the novel, Joe is a bartender of his father's rum-shop in San Fernando. As a family-run business, the shop doubles as both workplace and residence. Though the family home is situated in Port of Spain, Joe's father, 'old' Antonio da Costa and Joe reside in the rooms at the back of the bar. The building is not a house in any conventional sense of the word, but rather a workplace with lodging. It is not the luxuriant or cosy domicile of Christine Bennett's bungalow nor the plantation house, but something closer to a shebeen. In many respects the bar-lodging can be considered the microcosmic component of what Kevin Lynch perceives as the mechanical, 'practical model' of the colonial city. In Lynch's words, this practical, colonial city comprises 'small, autonomous, undifferentiated parts, linked up to a great machine which in contrast has clearly differentiated functions and motions'.[64] As a cog in this colonial

---

[63] Mimi Sheller, *Consuming the Caribbean: From Arawaks to Zombies*, London: Routledge, 2003, p. 118.

[64] Kevin Lynch, *Theory of Good City Form*, Cambridge, MA: MIT Press, 1981,

city-machine, the bar's purpose is entirely functional, to generate money; it is not the family home, thus it is sparse of comforts, décor, and domestic clutter. Primarily, it recalls the imagery and structure of the barrack-yard building. Joe's bedroom, for example, bears closer resemblance to yard dwellers' rooms than it does the bourgeois accommodation of Port of Spain: 'It was a small room with two cots in it, a basin placed on an empty kerosene box, an old dressing-table and a dilapidated wardrobe' (17–18).

It is from these lowly beginnings that Joe seeks escape. As with Christine Bennett, the myth of imperial vulnerability is in operation. Yet where the myth is indivisible from the authorial voice in Bridges's work, Mendes's ironic narrative suggests a distinct separation between the author and protagonist.[65] Joe's vulnerability, as opposed to Christine Bennett's, is perpetually cast in doubt by the narrative's juxtaposition between Joe's life and the lives of characters who are often in far more desperate circumstances. Like Christine, Joe hates his disreputable purlieu, the constant and proximate contact he is brought into with black and brown people and, the final straw, his servitude towards these imagined subordinates: 'common niggers and coolies who were not even fit to tie his shoe-laces' (14). Joe's assumed superiority is the source of both his hatred of others—black, brown, and white—as well as himself. Unlike Christine, his antipathy is not reserved solely for the contemptible: it is all-encompassing. Joe despises his ostensible superiors, the cultured city folk of Port of Spain, his brother Henry, his sister-in-law Myra, and his rich cousins, alongside his supposed inferiors like Maria, his brown-skinned lover. Torn between the two disparate worlds of San Fernando, with its 'mixed rural-industrial' labour force, and the city bourgeois and elites of Port of Spain, Joe chooses the latter.[66]

In San Fernando, the very environment conspires towards Joe's corruption: 'for he was young and plastic, ready to receive the impress of his environment' (14). It is the land and its inherent evil which must be guarded against if he is to avoid becoming 'more vulgar, more coarse' (14). Contamination via the locale and its malign inhabitants is imagined, emblematic, and specular. In the case of Maria, she is partly a projection of

---

pp. 83, 86. See also Spiro Kostof, *The City Shaped*, London: Thames and Hudson Ltd, 1991, and Roy Chandler Caldwell, 'For a Theory of the Creole City', *Ici-Là: Place and Displacement in Caribbean Writing in French*, ed., Mary Gallagher, Amsterdam: Rodopi, 2003, p. 31, fn11.

[65] Mendes's authorial detachment from his protagonist can also be discerned from his autobiography, where he describes the novel as an exploration of 'the destructive force of racial prejudice': *The Autobiography of Alfred H. Mendes, 1897–1991*, ed., Michèle Levy, Barbados: University of the West Indies, 2002, p. 67.

[66] Kenneth Ramchand, 'Introduction', to Mendes, *Pitch Lake*, p. v.

his self-loathing, a hated symbol of his stunted social ambition. In his febrile imagination, even the shop colludes in their egregious union: 'That was another thing the shop had done for him: forced him into a liaison with a barrack-yard girl by bringing him into contact with girls of the barrack-yard type' (20). In Joe's opinion, the shop leaves him and his father vulnerable. 'Stinkin' Po'teegee' is the insult which a black customer shouts at Antonio in the heat of an argument. Though the provocation comes from Joe, who has to be held back from the fray with the customer, it is the locus of the shop that is to blame: 'That was what the rum-shop had done for his father and him and the other Portuguese in the island who owned rum-shops: it had exposed them to the abuse of the labourer, the carterman, the porter' (17). As a consequence, he longs for egress, 'to speed away from this detestable house' (18). In the worst case scenario, he pictures his relocation to the USA, where 'no common black people [are] ready to hurl insults at you' (18).

Aware of his father's affair with an East Indian woman, who has borne his father a child, Joe senses the circularity of events: his affair with Maria might end in children; fear of reiterating mistakes and having the sins of his father repeated abound. He feels he is letting his race down, sliding into degeneracy: 'Was he too unambitious, cheap member of his racial community … helping his acceptance of its standards of living to keep the Portuguese on the bottom rungs of the social ladder?' (25). He envies his rich cousins who have had the advantages of an English education, reside in Port of Spain, are members of the elite St Clair Club, and have now 'turned their backs on' him (25). Initially, he deems them 'snobs', but after some years as a clerk he considers them entirely 'justified in their attitude' (26). To escape and enter the ostensibly civilised society of Port of Spain, he must turn his back on his father's business, San Fernando, and the brown-skinned Maria. For maximum success, he must gain access to the Port of Spain milieu by respectable means. His brother's house presents this opportunity. Therefore it is through property that Joe hopes to gain access to propriety. His thoughts reveal he longs for the kind of exclusive domain where 'acceptance' of racial Others is intolerable, backs are turned on social inferiors, and 'Chinese-Venezuelan Marías' do not pursue him like 'little bitches' (18). Where responsibility is always abdicated and shifted onto Others, even inanimate others, objects, and loci—the house, the bar, the street, the neighbourhood—the individual can only protect himself or herself by ensuring they inhabit, visit and travel in the right or respectable circles. Joe longs for the ideal strictures of the plantation house, the culture of Port of Spain and a house which combines the two: where borders do not require enforcing from within but are maintained from without by rigid social relations and decorum.

At his brother Henry's house, Joe is not disabused of the image of the civil, prosperous, and elite household. He is struck by the 'spaciousness' and 'luxuriance' of Henry's house and its rooms (55). The piano in the drawing room stands as a new accoutrement and sign of Henry's wealth and culture (51–52). Alongside these material and symbolic displays of prosperity, the house also operates along the socio-political lines of the plantation house paradigm. Myra, Henry's wife, behaves like the archetypal plantation house mistress. A difficult, querulous woman with a 'nervous' disposition, she is a despotic ruler of her domestics (323). As mistress, Myra is utterly reliant on her domestics, being easily fatigued by the simplest of chores. In many respects Myra embodies the inherent contradictions Hegel observed in his master-slave dialectic, whereby the master becomes increasingly dependent on the products of the slave's labour.[67] After sacking her maid Iris, Myra cannot function properly: she abhors making coffee herself, finding it almost as fatiguing as 'sweeping' (65). A replacement, Stella, is procured the next day. The motif of expendable black and brown servants is rooted in plantation dynamics. The course is less bloody and violent than in the pre-emancipation era, yet one body easily replaces the next, leaving the master class free from physical toil.

The strictures of Henry's house mirror the thresholds of social tolerance of the great plantation house. Hierarchical racial taxonomy and social categorisation allow only those deemed social equals to enter as guests. The darker-skinned enter only as servants; they are to be seen and not heard, and can be dismissed on the slightest provocation. Endogamy within one's race, class, religion, and social set is rigidly observed. Henry and Myra's union represents a minor crossing of thresholds, as Antonio, a Madeira-born Roman Catholic, objects to Henry's marriage to Myra, a Protestant creole. Henry's desertion represents his entry into the new creole, commercial class. Yet the clash is two-fold. As a member of the new Portuguese club which bars entry to the Madeira-born shopkeeping class, Myra endorses its values and deems those of the shop-keeping class inferior (79). She epitomises the snobbery of the commercial creoles towards expatriate Portuguese where the rule of expatriate elitism, as practised by the British and French, is reversed. As a Madeira-born shopkeeper, Antonio belongs to this supposedly inferior group. This and his prior objection to Henry's marriage explain his rare visits to their house. On the occasion that he does come to the house, Joe is embarrassed by what he perceives as his father's social inadequacies. His behaviour is 'crude' and his English poor (156). Joe fears the impropriety

---

[67]   Regarding the master, Hegel writes: 'What now confronts him [the master] is not an independent consciousness, but a dependent one'. See G. W. F. Hegel, *Phenomenology of Spirit*, trans. A V. Miller, Oxford: Clarendon Press, 1977, p. 117.

of his father meeting Myra's 'nice social set' and is relieved on his leaving (156). The rigid hierarchal structure of plantation culture dominates the nexus of social relations in the house.[68]

Yet it is the rigidity of this plantation culture and legacy which Joe struggles to contend with. As a product of the fraught geographical tensions between rural, south-western Trinidad and the commercial, north-western capital, he is conditioned by a dichotomy of conflicting geographies, contrasting homes, and ambivalent desires. If he were to be diagnosed, it might be termed a form of colonial schizophrenia or psychosis. Throughout, he has two registers of speech, action and thought pattern: one impulse is to be rid of his past, his 'coloured' mistresses, the rum-shop, creolised speech; the other is to have all of the above acknowledged and permitted. The contention is ambivalent, as Joe is perpetually torn between societal acceptance and individualistic desire. In the scene in which Joe intends to dismiss Maria, his sentiment is the obstacle, as he confesses 'he still cared for her' (37). However, another voice of censure can be heard in his internal thoughts: 'his reason warned him, shouted at him that he was making an idiot of himself' (38). Joe is caught between the dualism of his heart and head; his impulse is to pursue Maria, the object of his desire, and admit his 'feelings' towards her; yet the censuring voice of 'reason', that which society may judge, intrudes. Until Joe's murder of Stella, his brother's maid and second coloured mistress, it is the latter—'reason' or fear of social stigma—which wins out. Social ambition thwarts public displays of socially unacceptable behaviour. It is the reason behind the complete contrast of his creolised speech in the San Fernando rum-shop, where he is 'careless with his grammar', and his formal dialogue inside Henry's house (12).[69] The stigma of creolised dialect is such that it must be disowned and denied as the sole, inferior linguistic slippage of lesser classes and races. Joe's perpetual crisis is that he fails to fully adhere to the strictures that the ideal plantation house demands. He is angered on occasions by Myra's social snobbery towards the shop-keeping class and his rural San Fernando origins; likewise Myra's tyrannical treatment of Stella angers Joe (94). At different points in the novel, he is plagued by ambivalent feelings of identification and disassociation towards the underdog. The attraction also works in the same manner towards the elite. The result is perhaps a psychological condition of the *unheimlich*, as Joe is neither at home in the circles of the elite or the inferior, identifying with the opposing group in either instance.

---

[68] Wagley discusses the rigidity of social class in Plantation-America: 'Plantation America', p. 7.

[69] For an example of his formal conversation, see Mendes, *Pitch Lake*, p. 54.

Joe's belief that the life in his brother's Port of Spain house among the higher echelons of society, known as the 'upper ten', will save him is deeply flawed.[70] His belief in an idealised house, run along plantation socio-political lines, is itself problematic. His frustration arises partly from the disjunction between the ideal vision and the reality of such a rigidly run imperial domain. Houses in Port of Spain are very much dominated by women, who are the primary house managers. Both Henry, who regularly retires to the privacy of a bedroom, and Tom Carter, who sleeps in a separate bedroom to his wife, spend much of their working hours in offices only to be ostracised in their respective households. The imperial house in Trinidad is very much a matriarchal site of autonomy in which traditional masculine hegemony is attenuated. Men such as Henry and Carter have financial control, but it is their wives who reign supreme in their domains. It is unsurprising that Joe often pre-empts his actions in relation to Myra's response: in Henry's house, she rules.

Joe overlooks the emasculating world of the Port of Spain house; Henry and Myra often row and respond sarcastically to one another, but it is Henry who retires early to bed or his stamp collection. Furthermore, as Joe embarks on his affair with Stella, he is tortured by his belief in the ideal plantation house. Ironically, his behaviour fits with the reality of the plantation house, where affairs with black and Asian women, in Trinidad and Guyana especially, are common practice. His confusion lies in his inability to sift the mythology of white supremacist values from their commonplace practical application, where apparent loathing cloaks desire. In this respect, Joe, as Cora states, is an innocent, as he cannot fully endorse cynical action. He murders Stella in a fit of passion as he cannot endure the thought of her bearing his illegitimate child and the subsequent fall in his reputation. Yet what he fails to realise, or is perhaps too naïve to contemplate, is the normalisation of such behaviour throughout tropical America. In his typically troubled state during the appearance of his old paramour Maria on Henry's drive, Joe acknowledges that it is common among the men of the community to take a mistress, but considers it his bad luck to get caught: 'every man he knew was doing the same thing—keeping women—but how many were made to suffer as he was being made to?' (217). It is the shame of Stella's giving birth to his illegitimate child which Joe considers insurmountable. Again, the realities of the plantation house tend otherwise. Shame can easily be side-stepped by the semblance of propriety. It is Myra who dismisses Stella and denies the paternity of Stella's child—feigning

---

[70] Mendes, *Pitch Lake*, p. 137. The 'upper ten' referred to the supposed upper ten per cent in plantation society, often at the exclusion of coloureds and free blacks.

ignorance. She also encourages Joe to bribe Stella and 'shut her up', alongside taking her to a doctor who can perform an abortion—illegal at the time (317). Mendes reveals through Myra's behaviour how such cover-ups were carried out. She is even prepared to dissemble to her supposedly good friend Cora to ensure the marriage goes ahead and shame is buried. The house cannot be said to be tainted by the whiff of scandal, and any alternate versions of the house's party line must be quashed.

Though Joe's actions might be deemed autonomous and individual, Myra considers Joe's behaviour—or at least the repercussions—as potentially corrosive to the entire family. The horror that Joe's affair has taken place 'under their [her and Henry's] roof' is that it implicates the house as a source of contamination, tarnishing its residents, guests, and dependents (325). The tone of Myra's responses to Joe's misdemeanours is particularly telling. Sexual promiscuity and interracial sex are perceived as a 'disgrace', yet it is not the immorality of the acts per se which worry Myra, but their social repercussions, their semblance. In the earlier episode in which Maria arrives at the house with her mother Miss Martha, who demands some form of compensation from Joe, Myra's greatest fear is not so much the apparent wrongdoing, but the stigmatisation of having *appeared* to have done wrong:

> 'What an awful business!' Myra moaned, 'and to think this has never happened in this house before, in this whole neighbourhood. That's the worst part, Joe—the neighbourhood. I don't mind so much for myself, but what will the neighbours think? And imagine! Coloured people on either side of us, and we with our white skins'. (221)

In Myra's view, the house's standing is contingent on the neighbourhood's evaluation of it. The etymological roots of 'scandal' can be traced to notions of trapping (to 'snare for an enemy') in Hellenistic literature and 'slander' in Old French.[71] It is this notion of public humiliation which troubles Myra. To be condemned by coloureds is a bridge too far. In Myra's purlieu, the house serves a double purpose: it is a front or façade to be maintained at all costs, with an interior to be concealed from others' view; nevertheless, it possesses an interior world on which the façade of appearances is dependent. In many respects, the house might be conceived of as 'shell-cave' protecting those in its interior from exposure—a place to bury secrets, misdemeanours, and bad news.[72] And yet the potential for 'news' or 'gossip' to travel is

---

[71] 'Nation', *The Oxford English Dictionary*.

[72] I have borrowed the term from Gaston Bachelard, *The Poetics of Space*, trans. M. Jolas, Boston: Beacon Press, 1994, p. 132.

generally contingent on a glimpse or at least a *putative* glimpse of the house's interior world. The house proves vulnerable to both the exterior world—the community—and the interior world of occupants, visitors, and servants, which in turn runs the risk of exposure to the community. In this respect the house, particularly the bourgeois house, might be deemed a disciplinary or panoptic site. It is Joe's constant fear of surveillance and discovery which unnerve him throughout the novel. Indeed, it may be the constraints and pressures of the house itself which drive him to murder.

*

Though a material construct, the house proves to be so much more than mere bricks and mortar. Its psycho-social, symbolic, and tropic functions reveal entire social worlds, in which variant peoples, attitudes, lifestyles are all exemplified. The Trinidadian colonial house, particularly, represents a tropic site of labour division between the master class of owners, residents, and guests, and those on whom the house's functioning survives—servants, groundskeepers, and cooks. That this first group is exclusively white and the second group, for the large part, comprises descendants of enslaved and indentured peoples is illustrative of the Manichean and trenchant divisions rife in 1930s Trinidad. Bridges's and Mendes's fiction reveal a literary geography which conveys not only the symbolic hegemony of the house, but its fault lines. Increasingly the house, in the rigid, hierarchal shadow of the plantocracy and all that this class engenders, appears a burden, circumscribing its inhabitants to prescribed, constrictive roles. Neither Christine Bennett nor Joe da Costa cope well under these strictures. In Christine's case, she is ostracised on account of her previous relationship with Carter, a married man, and her popularity with society men in general. Such is the poor stock of her name, and by association, her bungalow—bought with Carter's money—that removal to England seems the only viable option to ensure her happiness with Alastair, with whom she has fallen in love at the novel's close. In Joe's case, his brother's house appears the catalyst to his nervous breakdown, psychosis, and resultant homicide. Ultimately, the house, in Bridges's and Mendes's treatments, is neither a comfort nor protection against the exterior world; the house and its interiority, it seems, whether glimpsed in actuality or not, are inextricable from, and vulnerable to, the hegemonic narrative of the community. To run against the rules of respectability is to risk a taint which touches the very site the occupant inhabits.

Micronations of the Caribbean

Russell McDougall

Nowhere islands everywhere

A micronation might be located in an apartment, a garden, or a caravan, on a pile of sand or a submerged reef. Some are born of social discontent and idealism; others are created by pranksters, for a laugh; still others from the desire to avoid paying tax; some are fraudulent money-making schemes; and some charge a fee for citizenship, or even a noble title. All are performative fictions—inventions—unrecognised by other 'legitimate' nations. Micronations generally are speculative. The online Invent-a-Micronation Contest organised by BuildingBlog,[1] is dedicated to architectural as well as urban speculation, and to landscape futures. Its 2009 winner was a member of the Barricades Commission, 'an urban micronation made of reclaimed and barricaded space' inspired by the Paris Commune of 1871. Constructed from 'permanently borrowed' materials, it was intended to 'take shape from the wreckage of a world it helps dismantle'. Micronations in this sense might be considered post-colonies—in Achille Mbembe's sense: the 'thing that is, but only insofar as it is nothing'—erupting out of that 'closure of the map' which was the historical result of geographical imperialism, or what Hakim Bey calls 'territorial gangsterism'.[2]

Theorising a related concept—the 'Temporary Autonomous Zone' (TAZ)— Bey deliberately refrained from defining his subject, playfully ('almost' ominously) proposing that it was 'almost' self-explanatory, and that if the

---

[1] Invent-a-Micronation: 2006 Contest Results <http://bldgblog.blogspot. corn/1October2006_bldgblog_archive.html> [24.10.2010].

[2] Achille Mbembe, *On the Postcolony*, Berkeley: University of California Press, 2001, p. 187; Hakim Bey, *The Temporary Autonomous Zone* [1985], New York: Autonomedia, 1991, p. 406.

term were ever really to become current it would be 'understood in action'—
for the TAZ also is a speculative space, 'almost a poetic fancy'.[3] The TAZ is
the equivalent in spatial terms of the forbidden moment, the insurrection
which, unlike the revolution, never finds completion or therefore recognition.
Bey sees the uprising as 'festive', rather than as engaging directly with the
state and leading to violence and martyrdom. Or to put this into Bakhtinian
terms, the TAZ is a carnival space. It is 'a microcosm of that "anarchist
dream" of a free culture'.[4] It is an *event* in cartography, an eruption in the
closed map.

The micronation might be considered as one such form of formlessness:
what Deleuze and Guattari call a 'war machine', a spontaneous uprising
in history (as defined and ordered by the *territorialist* state in its own
image).[5] It is an implication of 'psychic nomadism'—the term coined by
Bey to incorporate a whole battery of allegedly post-ideological concepts
such as 'nomadology' (Deleuze and Guattari) or 'driftwork' (Lyotard and
Van Der Abbeele)—all focused on the de-centring of 'the entire 'European'
project'.[6] Of course, this has been a function of postcolonialism also, now
dissolved into studies of identity-formation and diaspora. But Membe's
post-colony—a 'subjective economy' produced by intense imagination; 'an era
of dispersed entanglements', a unity 'produced out of differences'—is closer
to Bey's notion of the TAZ, having both temporal and spatial dimensions.[7]
Cyber-geography has elaborated a world in which nature seemed no longer to
precede ontologically its technical and scientific elaboration; the idea of the
TAZ clearly derives from this 'new geography', with its spatial perception 'of
things not bounded by rules of proximity'.[8] Such an ontological shift may
be good for the 'subjective economy' of micronations too, which after all
are only *not* nations because they lack recognition, and hardly considered
seriously by any scholarly enterprise. But it is now generally agreed that the
prefix 'cyber' and the descriptor 'virtual' have become redundant, because
the cyber world is really just an extension of the *real* world.[9] Micronations

---

[3] Bey, *The Temporary Autonomous Zone*, p. 402.

[4] Bey, *The Temporary Autonomous Zone*, p. 403.

[5] Gilles Deleuze and Felix Guattari, *Nomadology: The War Machine*, trans. Brian Massumi, Los Angeles: Semiotext(e), 1986; Deleuze, *Negotiations*, trans. Martin Joughin, New York: Columbia University Press, 1997.

[6] Bey, *The Temporary Autonomous Zone*, p. 409.

[7] Achille Mbembe, Interviewed by Christian Hoeller. Africa Dialogue Series, No. 1528. <http://www.utexas.edu/conferences/africa/ads/1528.html> [10.5.2012].

[8] McKenzie Wark, *Virtual Geography: Living with Global Media Events*, Bloomington: Indiana University Press, 1994, p. 1.

[9] Joel Kotkin, *The New Geography: How the Digital Revolution Is Reshaping the*

exist as speculative ventures in time-space both imagined and real, which means they can only be approached by indirection.

The first attempt to survey the global mushroom of micronations, published in 1985—the same year as Bey's rant—was by libertarian science-fiction author, Erwin S. Strauss. Seeking to maximise individual freedoms and minimise or even abolish the power of the state, he gave his book the do-it-yourself title, *How to Start Your Own Country*.[10] Just five years later, Strauss was forced to add a hundred extra pages to the second edition in order to take in the many new micronations that had come into existence since 1979. The multi-authored *Micronations: The Lonely Planet Guide to Home-Made Nations* (2006)[11]—later re-subtitled a *Guide to Self-Proclaimed Nations*—was similarly DIY. But where Strauss's manual was directed at DIY nation-builders, the Lonely Planet guide addresses a readership of DIY travellers—what the travel industry now calls the Free Independent Traveller (FIT). Still, the same principles of autonomy and freedom apply.

Career diplomat James Dobbins's *The Beginner's Guide to Nation-Building*, on the other hand, targets neither FITS nor libertarians but rather political leaders, who may need some assistance with international relations policy, and also citizens who may need help to evaluate their political leaders' performance in this area.[12] Dobbins has mainstream political credibility, having held senior White House and State Department positions under four presidents, and as the director of the International Security and Defense Policy Center (part of the Rand Corporation, which published the book) incorporated to promote 'the public welfare and security of the United States of America'.[13]

Publishers of course are ideologically as well as commercially driven, and the publishing provenance of these titles on micronations is itself an indication of their perspective. The Rand Corporation promotes itself as a non-partisan and non-profit research institution, a global think-tank

---

American Landscape, New York: Random House, 2000.

[10] Erwin Strauss, *How to Start Your Own Country*, Port Townsend WA: Loopmanics Unlimited, 1979. A Chinese-language edition (Taipei: Editions du Flaneur, 2008) is said to explore the development of micronations which were not in existence, or about which Strauss was not aware, when the original book was published, including: Lovely, Atlantium, Molossia, Caux, Elleore, Seborga, Conch Republic, Christiania, Sabotage, and Citynoland.

[11] *Micronations: The Lonely Planet Guide to Home-Made Nations*, Victoria: Lonely Planet Publications, 2006.

[12] James Dobbins, *The Beginner's Guide to Nation-Building*, Santa Monica CA: Rand Corporation, 2007.

[13] Rand Corporation (2011) <http://www.rand.org/about/history/> [10.5.2012].

independent of both political and commercial pressures, with the aim of improving the quality of policy-making across a wide range of areas. But it is US government-funded, its research focus is shaped by US priorities and approximately half of its research involves US national security issues. Hence, despite all its work in social policy, it remains true to its Cold War origins as an instrument for defining US military strategy. In this context, the micronation is a doomsday prophecy of the emerging Third World, which US travel writer and influential foreign affairs analyst, Robert D. Kaplan (advisor to the Bush administration), famously visualised in 1994 as a 'jagged-glass pattern of city-states, shanty-states, nebulous and anarchic regionalisms'— that is, a challenge to democracy.[14] It is the spectre of Third World anarchy, characterised by 'weak central governments' coexisting with the 'personal fiefdoms of charismatic leaders or warlords, or with autonomous regions defined by ethnicity, tribalism, race, or religion'.[15] The micronation, from this perspective, is part of a larger trend that signifies an end to all traditional sources of national cohesion: 'common culture and language, organisation of a coherent national economy, administrative effectiveness, and the ability to provide security'.[16] Steve Metz, of the Strategic Studies Institute (US Army War College), writing at the same time as Kaplan, identified Afghanistan as the key exemplar. So it is no surprise to find Dobbins's latest book, *After the Taliban*, subtitled 'Nation-Building in Afghanistan'.[17]

Strauss's publisher, on the other hand, Loompanics Unlimited—which ceased its thirty-year operation in 2006—specialised in the unconventional, the controversial, the extralegal and the anarchic. I have already characterised Strauss as a speculative libertarian, and his publishing editor, Michael Hoy, shared his opposition to mainstream US libertarian politics, regarding it as generally pro-corporate. The name 'Loompanics', a play upon *National Lampoon*, is a good indication of the publisher's 'festive' character, its preference for the strange but also the useful; in this regard it has much in common with Autonomedia, publisher of Bey's *The Temporary Autonomous Zone*, which advises online that its books exploring 'liberationist' (as opposed to libertarian) politics, art, and philosophy 'may be freely pirated'. Hoy not

---

[14]   Robert D. Kaplan, 'The Coming Anarchy', *Atlantic Monthly*, 28 February 1994 <http://www.theatlantic.com/magazine/archive/1994/02/the-coming-anarchy/4670/> [10.5.2012].

[15]   Steven Metz, 'America in the Third World: Strategic Alternatives and Military Implications', Carlisle, PA.: Strategic Studies Institute, US Army War College, 1994, p. 9. <http://www.strategicstudiesinstitute.army.mil/pdffiles/pub338.pdf> [10.5.2012].

[16]   Metz, 'America in the Third World', p. 9.

[17]   James F. Dobbins, *After the Taliban. Nation-Building in Afghanistan*, Washington, DC: Potomac Books, 2008.

only published but wrote the introduction to Strauss's *The Case Against a Libertarian Political Party*. Their favoured perspective on micronations, the opposite of Dobbins, is one of DIY-anarchism.

The name 'Lonely Planet' originated from its nomadic founding editors' listening to Joe Cocker's live 1970 album, *Mad Dogs and Englishmen*, and mishearing the 'lovely planet' line from the song 'Space Captain'. The album's liner note, proclaiming 'All elements of the Truth are included here', implied that the way to enlightenment was a musical journey of inspired spontaneity; the Lonely Planet guidebooks proposed a style of travel equally rough, ready, and transcendent. Lonely Planet, like Cocker, had the credibility of white soul. But the company is now a good example of what Strauss and Hoy object to: a small and ruggedly independent Australian publisher that grew into a publishing empire, and in 2007—ironically the same year that Lonely Planet released its guide to Afghanistan—literally 'sold out' to the BBC. The Lonely Planet *Guide to Micronations* appeared six years earlier, in the year that gave its title to *2001: A Space Odyssey*, the cult film of the alternative lifestyle generation of 1968, where space travel is offered as a metaphor for the wider exploration of the infinite. No doubt this inspired the timing, but the real harbinger of the Lonely Planet publication was the founding of the League of Micronations on 20 July 2000. Consisting of thirty-five member states, its aim was to strengthen relationships and promote diplomatic relations between micronations, as well as to express the opinion of the members of the inter-micronational community. The League of Micronations was disestablished on 25 August 2007, when it merged with the League of Secessionist States. Lonely Planet's decision in 2000 to diversify aggressively into other product domains coincided with the founding of the League of Micronations; its selling out to the BBC in 2007 coincided with the merger that swallowed the League. The decade prior to that saw the publisher expanding from travel guides into 'travel literature' and also into the digital domain. The book on micronations is one result of this diversification into non-traditional travel spaces, the publisher extending its original baby-boomer 'space' mission—bringing people together, understanding the world, sharing experiences that enrich lives, inspiring people to explore, have fun, and travel. Micronations, from this perspective, constitute one more 'last frontier' of the faraway, the new exotic of the independent space traveller.

Bey was already thinking beyond the old ontologies in 1985 when he took his cue from the title of Bruce Sterling's cyberpunk fiction and gave the many social experiments he saw proliferating under the TAZ umbrella the collective name 'Islands in the Net'. A play upon Hemingway's posthumous title, *Islands in the Stream*, is almost unavoidable. Set primarily in the

Caribbean, Hemingway's islands are like Wordsworth's 'spots of time', isolated moments of stable significance in the flux of a single human life whereas, for Sterling, the seduction of 'Islands in the Net' is the existence of potentially *out-of-control* spaces. For Dobbins these represent opportunities for 'American' nation-building in Iraq and Afghanistan. Yet both Strauss and the Lonely Planet writers propose a number of strategic exclusions from micronation status—like Palestine and Kurdistan—presumably because these are *insufficiently un-recognised*. They also exclude a number of internationally recognised *small* nations—such as Liechtenstein, and Tuvalu—which are *insufficiently speculative*. Whether barely visible or only ambivalently recognised, these kinds of space are neither inherently unstable nor festive. Micronations mostly are like dream worlds, existing on paper, or in the imagination, or in what once was called cyberspace. But there is also a long history of micronations within the region of the American Tropics, and especially in the Caribbean.

The Caribbean—as both geographical and socio-historical space, Marika Preziuso tells us—has been defined by a proliferation of spatial and bio-natural images and tropes.[18] One of these, deeply related to the idea of the micronation, is the sargasso: a place of entanglement, nowhere and everywhere. Physically, the Sargasso Sea lies outside the Caribbean in the Bermuda Triangle and hence in the middle of the North Atlantic Ocean, between the West Indies and the Azores, yet imaginatively it lies at the Caribbean's heart.[19] This is the effect of a very specific literary geography, deriving from Jean Rhys's Caribbean classic, *Wide Sargasso Sea* (1966). But the vortex that sucks that novel's protagonist to her doom is nowhere in the Americas; it is London, England. Still, that aspect of the novel's counter-discourse to colonialism works in part because the *literal* Sargasso Sea has no coastline, and so *it is hard to recognise until you arrive*. It has, in a sense, no definition. Or rather, it has the kind of geographical definition promoted by the cyber-title, 'Islands in the Net', for the Sargasso Sea is bounded by currents instead of shores, a system of currents, in fact, known as the North Atlantic Subtropical Gyre.

The Irish poet, W. B. Yeats, regarded the gyre as a defining image of the cyclical nature of reality, a recurring pattern of growth and decay. But

---

[18] Marika Preziuso, 'Mapping the *Lived* through the *Imagined* Caribbean: Textualities of Space in the Romances by Caribbean Women Writers from the Diaspora', paper given at 'Glocal Imaginaries: Writing/Migration/Place' Conference, Lancaster University, 9–12 September 2009.

[19] Hence the naming of the journal published from the University of Puerto Rico: *Sargasso: A Journal of Caribbean Literature, Language and Culture.*

the logic of the system of currents that defines the Sargasso Sea can also be expressed by a mathematical formula known as the Coriolis effect, which comes into play only when a rotating frame of reference is used. This is an expression of what mathematicians call a fictitious force. That is, it behaves as a real force, but is in fact a consequence of inertia, and so cannot be attributed to the originating body. The North Atlantic Subtropical Gyre, in other words, gives the Sargasso Sea a paradoxical spatial logic for Caribbean history, as *both* mathematically inevitable (*natural*) and *fictional* (artificial), a space that has no origin and comes into being through its own inertia.

Of course, the literary geography of the *sargasso* is not restricted to the Americas. Bernard O'Dowd, apostrophising the emergent nation, 'Australia', on the eve of Federation, imagined it as the 'last sea-thing' to be 'dredged by sailor Time from Space'. Agonising after a shared imagery of community, he asked: 'Are you adrift Sargasso, where the West / In halcyon calm rebuilds her fatal nest?'[20] This was one response to the European closure of the map, the image of the self-proclaimed post-colonial nation as a tangle of weed caught up in the fiction of the fatal nest, like the Caribbean islands. A place 'pregnant with mandrakes', Ezra Pound says, which could give birth only to something that 'never fits or proves useful'. Something, in other words, that is nothing: 'In the whole and all,/Nothing that's quite your own'.[21] Of course, this was always entirely a matter of recognition (or reception). In a New World poetics such as Derek Walcott's, that nothing is paradoxically everything.[22] Or it is Naipaul's despair of the abyss. The spatial field of the Caribbean, according to Antonio Benítez-Rojo, can be modelled in terms of *chaos*, for 'within the (dis)order that swarms around what we already know of as Nature, it is possible to observe dynamic states or regularities that repeat themselves globally', like the sargasso and the micronation: what he calls the 'repeating island'.[23]

Benítez-Rojo defines this field in terms of performance, improvisation, polyrhythm. This is not so far from my own long held view of Caribbean literature as a space where the body disappears into music,[24] especially

---

[20] Bernard O'Dowd, 'Australia', *The Lone Hand*, 4, no. 24 (1909), p. 685.
[21] Ezra Pound, 'Portrait d'une femme', in *Personae: The Shorter Poems*, eds., Lea Baechler and A. Walton Litz, New York: New Directions, 1990, p. 57.
[22] See for example Derek Walcott, 'Nearing La Guaira', in *In a Green Night*, London: Jonathan Cape, 1969, p. 22.
[23] Antonio Benítez-Rojo, *The Repeating Island. The Caribbean and the Postmodern Perspective*, trans. James E. Maraniss Durham: Duke University Press, 1996, p. 2.
[24] Russell McDougall, 'A Casement, Triple-Arch'd. Cultural Kinetics. The Fusion of Music, the Dance and the Word in African and Caribbean Culture', PhD thesis, Queen's University at Kingston, Ontario. 1986; also 'Music in the Body of the Book

when Benítez-Rojo regards the Caribbean performance of identity as a way of sublimating ('defusing') physical violence, which has its roots in the plantation economy of slavery and colonialism. Michael Dash describes the Caribbean subject similarly, as a plenitude wherein the subject is possessed by 'the lost island-body'—a process Wilson Harris calls 're/membering' (a synthesis of memory and imagination).[25]

The repeating island is also a 'floating island' (sometimes called a 'flying island'), seemingly in defiance of gravity: 'like a candle / flame in sunlight, weightless as woodsmoke that hazes / the sand with no shadow'.[26] It occurs naturally but also (increasingly) artificially, coalescing and fragmenting, floating but sometimes sinking, appearing and disappearing. The best-known fictional 'floating island' is Laputa, in Swift's *Gulliver's Travels*, populated by absurdly impractical inventions satirising the Royal Society (which developed out of the Invisible College).[27] A sargasso begins as a number of small 'floating islands', coming together at certain times to form a field, not unlike the idea of the Caribbean (as a field: 'islands in the net').[28]

There has been much debate about the kind of space that Rhys's novel opens up through its articulation of creole character: 'refractive space';[29]

of *Carnival*', *Journal of West Indian Literature*, 4, no. 2 (1990), pp. 1–24; 'Music, Body and the Torture of Articulation in Derek Walcott's "Sainte Lucie"', *Ariel*, 23, no. 2 (1992), pp. 65–83.

[25] Michael Dash, 'In Search of the Lost Body: Redefining the Subject in Caribbean Literature', *Kunapipi*, 11, no. 1 (1989), pp. 17–26. For discussion of the concept of re/memberment, see McDougall, 'Music in the Body'.

[26] Derek Walcott, *Midsummer*, New York: Farrar Straus Giroux, 1984, p. xxv.

[27] A cyber micronation, The Free Republic of Laputa, invented by retired professor of mathematics at the Technical University of Munich, Dr. Werner Heise, is now reportedly located on the fictional island discovered by Lemuel Gulliver. Its origins are purposely shrouded in mist: its internet domain is for sale; digital access to the Union of Sownyet Socialist Republics (USSR)—to which it supposedly belongs—is *verboten*; it has refused to join the League of Secessionist States. Evolving out of the war of fonts which saw Roman Bold triumph over San Seriffe and ascend to the presidency, Laputa's government is a pornocracy apparently modelled on the Saeculum Obscurum of the tenth-century papacy.

[28] Captain C. Dixon told the Royal Geographical Society in 1925 that the Sargasso Sea 'is probably only renewed by the constant addition of plants detached from the shores of the Caribbean Sea' (C. C. Dixon, 'The Sargasso Sea', *The Geographical Journal*, 66, no. 5 (1925), pp. 434–442, at 434.

[29] Keith Russell, '"Now every word she said was echoed, echoed loudly in my head": Christophine's Language and Refractive Space in Jean Rhys's *Wide Sargasso Sea*', *Journal of Narrative Theory* 37, no. 1 (2007), pp. 87–105.

the 'third space of enunciation';[30] non-dwelling space;[31] non-categorical labyrinthine space;[32] dissonant, mutated space—a precursor to the postmodern hyperspace of the bewildered subject of late capitalism;[33] etcetera. It might just as easily be called 'sargasso space'. The sargasso is a continuing trope of digital game cultures too: for example, the crystal sphere of Greyspace[34]—a planetary system of the *Spelljammer* game-universe,[35] with no gravity and no atmosphere—contains a region of 'dead magic' called the Great Sargasso.[36] This is a general reminder of the influence of Caribbean history upon the development of 'outer' space in speculative fiction, beginning perhaps with Isaac Asimov's *Lucky Starr and the Pirates of the Asteroids* (published in 1953 under the pen-name, Paul French).

Experiments are made more possible by islands. Seventeenth-century utopian writing, according to Davis and Faussett, was in part a response to

---

[30] Serena Reavis, "'Myself yet not quite myself'": *Jane Eyre, Wide Sargasso Sea*, and a third space of enunciation; and, "Being herself invisible, unseen, unknown": *Mrs. Dalloway, The Hours*, and the re-inscribed lesbian woman', MA Dissertation, University of North Carolina at Greensboro, 2005.

[31] Andrew Thacker, *Moving through Modernity: Space and Geography in Modernism*, Manchester: Manchester University Press, 2003, p. 193.

[32] Deborah Parsons, *Streetwalking the Metropolis. Women, the City and Modernity*, Oxford: Oxford University Press, 2000, p. 194.

[33] Thacker, *Moving Through Modernity*, p. 220; Fredric Jameson, *The Cultural Turn*, London: Verso, 1998, p. 220.

[34] Greyspace is perhaps a play upon 'dark matter'. In 1993 scientists discovered a cloud of gas approximately 150 million light years from Earth, containing three galaxies, but itself shaped by 'a Sargasso Sea of dark matter'. Douglas Birch, 'UM Students' Curiosity Yields Clue to Birth of Universe', *Baltimore Sun*, 28 January 1993.

[35] 'Spelljammer' is an adventure setting in *Advanced Dungeons and Dragons* (2nd ed.), taking sword-and-sorcery fantasy role-playing into outer space. The popular culture and category-fiction manifestations of sargasso zones and micronations is a subject for another paper. A legendary vessel wandering the spheres, *The Spelljammer* appears indebted, at least in part, to the Robert Louis Stevenson legend of *The Flying Dutchman*, captained by Davy Jones in the *Pirates of the Caribbean* movies, and crewed by the souls of dead mariners.

[36] A 'dead magic' zone is a space where, because of some cataclysmic historical event, magic has ceased to function. More specifically, it is a zone of disabled enchantments, as for example in the fantasy game-world of *The Forgotten Realms*. The historical cause of the nullification in the latter case is an event known as The Arrival (or Time of Troubles). To put this in another way, the dead magic zone is where Prospero's art forsakes him. George Lamming, reclaiming the dead zone through his re-reading of *The Tempest*, discovers what he calls *The Pleasures of Exile* (1960). Rewriting Shakespeare's play in the novel, *Water With Berries* (1971), Lamming presents England as the dead zone for Caribbean artists.

the expanding empire's 'tales of shipwreck and social inversion on far-distant islands'.[37] From Plato's Atlantis to Bacon's New Atlantis, from Sir Thomas More's *Utopia* to Huxley's *Island*, one of the primary drives for inventing your own micronation is utopian, and utopias, being necessarily isolated from mainstream societies, naturally gravitate to islands.[38] This is despite the fact that one *quarter* of the world's sovereign states *consists* of islands or archipelagos, comprising some 600 million people, 10 per cent of the world's population.[39] Islands *do* still offer distinct identities and spaces in an increasingly placeless world, but the island as metaphor, the 'designed island', also tells us something important about the 'art of isolating' in social organisation, which is crucial to all micronations (which are frequently *artificial* islands): the imagining of the island utopia is really the imagining of an in-between space. Utopian fictions of course work 'by indirection, directing the reader's critical gaze away from the society created by the utopian author onto his or her own society'. Their geographical focus, then, is on *interstitial* space. Swift's Laputa coincides with Bacon's New Atlantis: they are one and the same. The literal meaning of the Greek words that Thomas More combined to produce the name of his island, literally the first Utopia, is of course 'nowhere'. Yet by an operation of imagination the Caribbean nowhere is often and at the same time everywhere.

If we ask where *any* micronation is geographically situated the answer is always in one sense going to be 'nowhere'. Yet the technology exists now to situate any place literally anywhere, almost, physically or virtually. It is better to ask, then, what sense of the extended Caribbean, the American Tropics, the variously located 'Islands in the Net' provide.

---

[37] Bridget Orr, *Empire on the English Stage, 1660–1714*, Cambridge: Cambridge University Press, 2001, pp. 188–189, referring to J. C. Davis, *Utopia and the Ideal Society: A Study of English Utopian Writing 1516–1700*, Cambridge: Cambridge University Press, 1981 and David Faussett, *Writing the New World: Imaginary Voyages and Utopias of the Great Southern Land*, Syracuse: Syracuse University Press, 1993.

[38] One among the many unlikely speculations concerning the location of the mythical sunken island of Atlantis, first proposed by Plato in *The Critias*, is that it was located in the Americas and that the Sargasso Sea resulted from its sinking. See particularly the chapter entitled, 'The Sargasso Sea', in Lewis Spence, *Atlantis in America*, London: Ernest Benn, 1925, pp. 186–193.

[39] Godfrey Baldacchino, ed. *A World of Islands: An Island Studies Reader*, Charlottetown, Canada: Institute of Island Studies, University of Prince Edward Island, 2007, p. 1.

Tortuga, pirate 'nation'

The micronation is a phenomenon tied to the development of the idea of the nation-state in the nineteenth century, and the earliest recognisable micronations properly date from that period. But I begin with the seventeenth-century pirate enclave of Tortuga for a number of reasons. First, the inspiration behind Bey's conceptualisation of the TAZ is in fact the 'pirate utopia'; and the first alleged utopia in the Caribbean was the pirate-utopia, founded by the 'Brethren of the Coast' on Tortuga, an island twenty-three miles long and four wide, located seventeen miles off the northwest coast of Hispaniola (*Quisqueya*), Columbus's first landing in America. Today it constitutes what is known as the commune of Île de la Tortue in the Port-de-Paix arrondissement of the Nord-Ouest Department of Haiti.[40] It was also once known as Association Island, one of three English colonies founded on three different Caribbean islands by the Providence Company (or Providence Island Company), the others being Providence and Henrietta (now Providencia and San Andrés, and belonging to Colombia). On Association Island from 1631 to 1635 privateering went hand in hand with plantations, slavery, and the Puritan ideal of a God-fearing commonwealth in the Americas. Here is the second reason for my beginning with Tortuga: it provides a good example of how the kingly states of Europe created their own fictive *dystopia* of the fatal nest, or social sargasso, in the Caribbean. Finally, in the four centuries since its first pirate fame, 'Tortuga' has become a key trope in a transnational discourse of piracy that, while almost seeming to transcend time and place, paradoxically links all piracies back to the Caribbean, including that of present-day Somalia. Tortuga is the very image of an America, utopian and dystopian, in its origins and in its present-day character. In the twenty-first century, while the USA wages war on international piracy (which it equates with terrorism), author Timothy Gatto decries the lead defender of the free world as itself a pirate state.[41] The renewal of US scholarly interest in the Barbary Wars—'America's first confrontation with the Islamic world'[42]—is deeply related to the involvement in the Iraq War. Joshua London proposes that the war against the Barbary

---

[40] Tortuga (Île de la Tortue) should not be confused with Saltatudos (Salt Tortuga) off the coast of Venezuela near Margarita, or with Dry Tortugas near the Florida Keys: see Benerson Little, *The Buccaneer's Realm: Pirate Life on the Spanish Main, 1674–1688*, Washington, DC: Potomac Books, 2007, p. 39.

[41] Timothy V. Gatto, 'The American "Pirate" Nation' (2010) <http://dandelionsalad.wordpress.com/2010/06/13/the-american-pirate-nation-by-timothy-v-gatto/> [10.5.2012].

[42] Christopher Hitchens, 'Jefferson Versus the Muslim Pirates', *City Journal* (Spring

pirates, the first US naval war, not only established its navy but also shaped a nation.[43] And as Frank Lambert argues, 'The Barbary Wars were primarily about trade, not theology'.[44] Tortuga, in this context, is particularly interesting.

In *Terror and Consent: the Wars for the 21st Century*[45] Phillip Bobbitt looks back to the seventeenth-century Caribbean for early evidence of state-sponsored terrorism: the pirates there, he says, were generally in league with one state or another and, like their twentieth-century counterparts, began by attacking the pre-eminent state of the day; they eventually turned their violence against non-combatants and neutrals in the service of their own remarkable political societies which, to summarise briefly the historical evidence, were notable for their ruthlessness, their egalitarianism (much vaunted by some commentators as a precursor for American democracy), their racial and ethnic diversity, and their homosexuality. Pirates, as terrorists of the kingly state, were never confined to the Caribbean, but the popular imagination places them there pre-eminently.[46] Behind the history of Caribbean piracy and pillage, as Peter Galvin has shown, there is a particular geography of easy 'ingress and egress to the Caribbean Sea ... strongly affected by prevailing winds and specific corridors through the West Indies island arc, thereby creating distinct routes and "choke points" of passage' for trade.[47] Literary narratives of piracy remain generally oblivious to the geographical essentials of routes, rendezvous and island strongholds and the spatial strategies associated with locating and holding them. This indifference might almost be seen as a strategy of literary geography, effectively stranding the Caribbean and isolating it from the larger history of the American Tropics. Conversely, a study of 'winds, currents, coastal

2007)   <http://www.city-journal.org/html/17_2_urbanities-thomas_jefferson.html> [16.11.2010].

[43] Joshua E. London, *Victory in Tripoli: How America's War with the Barbary Pirates Established the US Navy and Shaped a Nation*, Hoboken NJ: John Wiley and Sons, 2005.

[44] Frank Lambert, *The Barbary Wars: American Independence in the Atlantic World*, New York: Hill and Wang, 2005, p. 8.

[45] Phillip Bobbitt, *Terror and Consent; the Wars for the 21st Century*, New York: Random House, 2008.

[46] Certainly piracy made no mark on the operations of empire in the western Pacific. (European pirates, that is; Asian ones were very active in the East Indies.) Alan Atkinson *The Europeans in Australia*, vol. 1., Melbourne: Oxford University Press, 1977, p. 29.

[47] Peter R. Galvin, *Patterns of Pillage: A Geography of Caribbean-based Piracy in Spanish America, 1536–1718*, New York: Peter Lang, 1999, p. 184.

features, maritime bottlenecks, historical geopolitics, merchant traffic flow, and the distribution of natural resources reveals *patterns* of piracy that connect the Caribbean Sea to the Gulf of Mexico, Cape Horn, and beyond'.[48]

This is important when one considers, as Nina Gerassi-Navarro has done, that in Spanish America at least, nineteenth-century authors of pirate novels were less interested in accurate representations of the past than in using the genre to discuss the future of Mexico, Colombia, or Argentina.[49] Yet from a US perspective, the Caribbean remains ambiguously outside the nation as a pirate zone. Thus John Wennersten, writing of modern US migration, is able to speak of the founding of micronations in the Caribbean without a trace of irony in terms of 'leaving America', while paradoxically regarding such utopian new-country 'sea-steading' movements as quintessentially American in their quest for a community that 'would go beyond the boundaries of ordinary experience and give dynamic release to the American moral and intellectual imagination',[50] as the Mormons did in Utah and the Mennonites in Nebraska. More succinctly, US playwright, Justin Wells, titles his blistering satire dramatising contemporary cut-throat greed, brutal violence, and global conspiracy hatched in the US boardroom, *Men of Tortuga*—a metaphor apparently un-recognised in Chicago, despite one reviewer commenting in that city's edition of *Time Out*: 'Tortuga gives us savages in suits, drinking good bourbon and plotting destruction'.[51] Tortuga, in this way, gives us corporate capitalist America, piratical in its greed as well as its violence. This is the irony of the contemporary war against pirates on all fronts. As Anne Sweeney, Co-chair of Disney Media Networks and President of the Disney/ABC Television Group, says: 'We understand now that piracy is a business model'.[52]

In the Disney movie series, *Pirates of the Caribbean*, Tortuga is a recruiting ground for pirate captains such as Captain Jack Sparrow. It is on Tortuga, for example, that Sparrow recruits the dwarf pirate who will later voyage

---

[48] Galvin, *Patterns of Pillage*, p. 184.

[49] Nina Gerassi-Navarro, *Pirate Novels. Fictions of Nation Building in Spanish America*, Durham: Duke University Press, 1999.

[50] John R Wennersten, *Leaving America: The New Expatriate* Generation, Westport CT: Praeger, 2007, p. 46.

[51] Christopher Piatt, Review of Jason Wells, *Men of Tortuga*, New York: Samuel French, 2009, in *Time Out Chicago*, 190 (October 2008) <http://chicago.timeout.com/articles/theater/67932/men-of-tortuga-profiles-theatre-theater-review> [21.8.2010].

[52] Katherine Mangu-Ward , 'Pirate Capitalism: Remix Culture Goes Corporate', *Reason*, (May 2008) <http://reason.com/archives/2008/04/09/pirate-capitalism> [5.12.2010].

to World's End to bring him back from the dead.[53] Tortuga here, then, is the origin of salvation. The film reinvents the Brethren of the Coast as the Brethren Court, nine pirate lords from the different seas, something like the ecumenical council of the Vatican, except that the pirates have met twice as many times over the centuries as the bishops. In this US-sponsored pirate fantasy, only the Caribbean sea-lord has any money, which is particularly interesting in view not only of the poverty of the region but also the decline of US tourists there since the films' release.

The inspiration for the films was a Disney theme park ride. This dark ride in Disneyland California is located on New Orleans Square. The USA has made New Orleans the gateway to Caribbean pirate romance. This is a controlled geography, a contained disorder. The 2007 Pirate Convention in New Orleans was organised by a deputy sheriff, and the 750 pirates that took over New Orleans were 'impersonators' carousing through the French Quarter in fancy dress and, instead of pillaging, spending their cash in the city's post-Katrina financially-stressed hotels and restaurants. Still, as one pirate impersonator, identifying as Johnny Redbone from California, said at the time: New Orleans 'kind of fits the pirate persona, having a good time, partying and wenching and drinking'.[54] So although the first Pirates of the Caribbean amusement ride might have been *physically* located in a theme park in California, the fantasy begins and ends in New Orleans.[55]

Strangely, when the amusement ride was duplicated in Florida, there were initial concerns that it would not be exotic enough, because of Florida's proximity to the Caribbean. There is a difference between New Orleans fantasy and Florida reality. Disney did consider building a ride in Florida

---

[53] Of course, the 'Pirates of the Caribbean' series is by no means the only filmic placing of the island. There is the 1961 low-budget film, *Pirates of Tortuga*, directed by Robert Webb, best known for his many westerns—although he also directed *The Caribbean Mystery* in 1945. There is also the more recent, and more interesting children's film, *The Pirates of Tortuga: Under The Black Flag*. It begins in a museum, where the three boy heroes discover a golden bowl, not the Henry James variety, rather the remnant of an ancient Aztec treasure. Examining the bowl, they accidentally set off the secret time-travelling device and find themselves transported to a pirate ship in the eighteenth century, and so to the pirates' paradise island of Tortuga, governed in this case by a beautiful pirate queen. The boys must rescue the queen from Blackbeard and the Spanish Armada, and then find their way back to their own place and time.

[54] 'New Orleans Spirit Upbeat as Recovery From Hurricane Continues', *The Voice of America*, 24 April 2008 <http://www.51voa.com/voa_standard_english/VOA_Standard_English_21075.html> [20.5.2012].

[55] Where its façade is topped by the thirty-one star US flag, that being the flag that added the Californian star as the 31st in 1850, although it only lasted as the official flag for seven years.

that would be different from the 'Pirates of the Caribbean' in New Orleans, California, but which would have equivalent iconographic status. It would have featured cowboys and Native Americans known as Indians, as well as banditos and coyotes, and it was tentatively called the Western River Expedition. However, the cowboys and Indians were shelved after too many complaints about the lack of pirates.

State-sponsored pirates, or privateers, employed to plunder Spanish ships in the seventeenth century, became known in English as 'buccaneers'.[56] They were extremely diverse: they were French, English, Dutch, and African runaway slaves; religious refugees; escapee prisoners of war transported to the Americas by Cromwell; exiled Huguenots; deported Irish; criminals; runaway apprentices. But they imagined themselves as an entity, and at their base on Tortuga, where they were 1500 strong, they called themselves the Brethren of the Coast. As an emergent micronation, claiming free sovereignty yet un-recognised by even those states that sponsored them, from a European perspective they formed a terrorist dystopia. Yet they had a constitution, and voting rights, and some even had the beginnings of a welfare state, with workers compensation. They were a geopolitical and a political entity, sponsored but never recognised, the focal point of what some commentators have dubbed a 'pirate commonwealth'.[57] Hobbes's defense and justification of the kingly state coincides precisely with the ascendancy of Tortuga, the *dark shadow* of the kingly state, in many ways an anticipation of things to come. Looking back in 1724, in his *General History of the Robberies and Murders of the Most Notorious Pirates*, Captain Charles Johnson—once thought to be Daniel Defoe—has the American buccaneer Samuel Bellamy proclaim himself 'a free Prince... with Authority to make War on the whole World'.[58]

This, according to Bobbitt,[59] makes the pirate not only the nemesis

---

[56] After the French *boucanier*, which derives in turn from the Carib word for the smoking of meat, *bukan* (which is also the origin of the English word 'barbecue').

[57] See, for example, Manuel Schonhorn's Introduction to *A General History of the Pyrates* [attrib. Daniel Defoe] [1972], rev. ed. Mineola: Dover Publications, 1999, p. xix; Doris Garraway, *The Libertine Colony. Creolization in the Early French Caribbean*, Durham: Duke University Press, 2005, pp. 100–101; Angus Konstam, *Blackbeard: America's Most Notorious Pirate*, Hoboken NJ: John Wiley & Sons, 2007, p. 108; Janis E. Thomson, *Mercenaries, Pirates, and Sovereigns: State-Building and Extraterritorial Violence in Early Modern Europe*, Princeton NJ: Princeton University Press, 1996, p. 48, 68, and passim.

[58] Daniel Defoe [Charles Johnson], *A General History of the Pyrates*, Mineola, NY: Dover, 1999, p. 587.

[59] Bobbitt, *Terror and Consent*; p. 32 and n. 26.

of Hobbes and the kingly state, but also looks forward to the sentiments expressed in Rudyard Kipling's short story, 'The Man Who Would be King' (1888): 'We will ... go away to some other place where a man isn't crowded and can come into his own ... in any place where they fight ... Then we will subvert that King and seize his throne and establish a Dynasty'.[60] While the story is set in remote Afghanistan—Kāfiristān (now Nuristān)—and was partly inspired by the exploits of Josiah Harlan, the US traveller who became the Prince of Ghor, it also draws upon the example of James Brooke, the first White Rajah of Sarawak (1842–1861). The diversity of these eighteenth- and nineteenth-century sources is interesting for two reasons: first, it reminds us of Cicero's definition of the pirate, as 'the common enemy of all'—which, as Daniel Heller-Roazen hardly need tell us, is a crucial contemporary trope;[61] second, it links colonialism with both nation-building and piracy. The Brethren of the Coast were transitional figures in the sequence of piratical definitions traced by Heller-Roazen, from the Enlightenment's 'enemy of humanity' to today's 'universal foe' (a legal and political category of exception, inhabiting an extraterritorial region).

The pirate society of Tortuga features prominently in Raphael Sabatini's hugely popular 1922 pirate novel, *Captain Blood*, in the subsequent film starring Errol Flynn, and in a great number of popular pirate films since then, from the swashbuckling to the comedic—from *The Black Swan* (1942, starring Tyrone Power, and again based on a Sabatini novel) and *Abbott and Costello Meet Captain Kidd* (1952) to Disney's *Pirates of the Caribbean* series. It is also the familiar setting of many a popular pirate novel, most of which draw heavily upon the French author Alexandre Olivier Exquemelin's *History of the Buccaneers of America*, first published in Dutch (*De Americaensche Zee-Roovers*) in 1678. Robert Louis Stevenson is said to have borrowed heavily from it for *Treasure Island* (1883).[62] Exquemelin wrote from first-hand experience, having lived on Tortuga and sailed with the legendary Captain Henry Morgan; he is thought to have settled eventually in Holland to avoid persecution as a Huguenot in France. (In fact, Jean Le Vasseur, the first French buccaneer governor of the island, had sought to establish a Huguenot republic there, but was assassinated in 1653.) But the meaning of 'America'

---

[60] Rudyard Kipling, *The Man Who Would Be King and Other Stories*, Oxford: Oxford University Press, 2008, p.64.

[61] Daniel Heller-Roazen, *The Enemy of All. Piracy and the Law of All Nations*, New York: Zone Books, 2009, p.11.

[62] A. James Arnold, 'From Piracy to Policy: Exquemelin's Buccaneers and Imperial Competition in "America"', *Review: Literature and Arts of the Americas*, 40, no. 1 (2007), pp.9–20, at 11.

that the various French and Dutch editions of Exquemelin's influential text bestowed to the future was, as A. James Arnold has shown, far from stable.[63]

Between the late 1670s and the mid-1680s no fewer than five editions of the book known today as *The Buccaneers of America* were published in Dutch (1678), German (1679), Spanish (1681), English (1684), and French (1686). Considerable mystery continues to surround these early editions, the interpretation of which has taken place within national histories of colonisation. Each national tradition has positioned Exquemelin's book within its own socio-historical perspective. Confusion concerning the nationality of the author and the original purpose of the texts has led to parallel paths of transmission, with the result that quite divergent social and political meanings have coalesced around them.

While the Spanish were the first to settle the island, the French and English arrived soon after. At times they coexisted on various parts of the island, only to be expelled by the Spanish, but they soon returned. The Dutch came too, naming the island 'Ter Tholen', after an island off the west coast of Holland. But it is the French and the English who have added most to the literary geography of Tortuga, by a voluminous and multi-faceted literature featuring their most famous historical anti-heroes.

These are François L'Ollonais (Jean-David Nau), 'Le Fléau des Espagnols' [The Flail of the Spaniards], whom Exquemelin claims was torn to pieces by the Indians of Panama, and thrown limb by limb into a fire. He features, for example, in *The Island* (1979) by novelist Peter Benchley, best known for *Jaws* and *The Deep*. Benchley's pirates, based on the Brethren of the Coast and descending from the seventeenth to the twentieth century, are now terrorising the Caribbean yachts of the Bermuda Triangle—at the heart of which, of course, lies the Sargasso Sea. Bertand D'Orgeron is another, the *filibustier* governor who arranged the import of prostitutes from France in a vain effort to end the system of *matelotage*—a kind of marriage among men, with a declared line of inheritance. And of course the Welsh privateer, Captain Henry Morgan, who replaced the Dutch corsair Edward Mansvelt following his death in 1666, and went on to govern Jamaica and was eventually knighted for his services to the English crown. His literary appearances are far too many to list, onwards from William F. Wu's *Marauder* (the second volume of the 'Robots In Time' series) based on the fictional universe of Isaac Asimov. Most importantly, though, Morgan provided John Steinbeck not only with the subject of his first novel, *Cup of Gold* (1929), but also with the vehicle for its allegory of 'the Faustian bargain implicit in the American dream', as Susan F. Beegal argues: 'whether the

---

[63] Arnold, 'From Piracy to Policy'.

dream of an aggressive young nation, Steinbeck's "Republic of Buccaneers"— or the dream of an aggressive young individual ambitious for fortune, fame, and love'.[64] Tortuga, in Steinbeck's novel, is the home of the 'Free Brotherhood', and the Dutchman, Mansveldt, who preceded Morgan as the leader of this 'mob of ragamuffin heroes', has 'the power of dream in him': the dream of 'a strong durable nation, a new, aggressive nation in America'.[65]

But Tortuga is also a sargasso island. In Brad Strickland's and Thomas E Fuller's historical fiction for children, *The Guns of Tortuga* (2003), the child-hero sneaks ashore on a secret mission, but soon finds himself 'darting like a minnow through seaweed'.[66] He is caught up in the carnivalesque cornucopia of the pirates' market—French waistcoats, barrows of mangoes, dried fish, bright knives, 'deadly little pistols': a kind of 'trash island', where the currents meet and all the flotsam and jetsam of the empires converge, *like and unlike*, as they do at the centre of the Sargasso Sea. Amidst this trash—revalued in the pirate market economy—the spy feels safe, outside the gaze, untraceable.

Peace between England and Spain was proclaimed in the Caribbean in 1671, and Tortuga came to an end as a micronation of pirates and buccaneers in 1673. Morgan's physical assault on Panama (the pirate's 'cup of gold'), according to Susan Beegal, allowed Steinbeck an imaginative channeling of his own intended literary assault on New York (the writer's 'Cup of Gold').[67] Fifty years after Steinbeck's *Cup of Gold*, another US novelist, Herbert Gold, published a novel about 'the intersection of Haiti and San Francisco in the specialised commerce of homosexual concubinage' titled *Slave Trade*.[68] But it is Gold's 1991 Haitian travel memoir, *The Best Nightmare on Earth*, that best exemplifies the historical idea of Tortuga as a proto-capitalist society. Gold narrates how a Texan company called Dupont Caribbean, Inc., acquired a 'contract' to take over the pristine Île de la Tortue, at a cost of two dollars an acre, in order to build 'a combination freeport, resort, retirement community, convention park, harbor town and industrial center' and so to create 'a kind of sovereign nation'.[69] The CEO of Dupont Caribbean, Don

---

[64] Susan F. Beegal, *Introduction* to John Steinbeck's *Cup of Gold. A Life of Sir Henry Morgan, Buccaneer, with Occasional Reference to History*, London: Penguin, 2008, p. xxv.

[65] Steinbeck, *Cup of Gold*, p. 82.

[66] Brad Strickland and Thomas E. Fuller, *The Guns of Tortuga*, New York: Aladdin Paperbacks, 2003, p. 85

[67] Beegel, *Introduction*, p. xxiv.

[68] Herbert Gold, *Slave Trade* [1991], Piscataway, NJ: Transaction Publishers, 2001, p. 210.

[69] Gold, *Slave Trade*, p. 164.

Piersen, apparently also owned a bank, and he took his banker with him to Haiti to negotiate 'a 100-year contract' with the President of the Bank of Development in one of the poorest nations on earth to make Île de La Tortue a satellite 'utopia for the world's wealthy'.[70] The brutal military dictator, Papa Doc Duvalier, granted the contract in 1971. The banker, Michael Collins, who became vice-president of Dupont Caribbean, also wrote a memoir, entitled *Cornucopia of Evil* (2005). In it he implicitly links the island's days of piracy in the seventeenth century to an alleged Mafia involvement in the twentieth century. He dubs Piersen 'the man who would be king',[71] and blames him for the death of the contemporary pirate dream of a tax haven for the rich on Tortuga. Piersen and Collins fell out, the president suing the vice-president for 5.6 million US dollars, though at the close of the trial this was reduced to one cent—and even then, Collins was acquitted of all charges. All that remains of the twentieth-century pirate utopia the pair had sought to build on an island with neither roads nor vehicles, and a below-subsistence economy, is the abandoned airfield.

Hakim Bey thinks that the seventeenth-century pirate utopias of Tortuga, Madagascar, and Nassau are wrongly identified as proto-capitalist. For him they are proto-anarchist. And the ideal that survives the fall of Tortuga ('the Buccaneer ideal') is that of the TAZ, which he specifically relates to the founding of 'Libertatia' on Madagascar noted in *The General History of the Pyrates* (1724).[72] Tortuga, as part of the same literary geography, lies at the root of the Libertarian and Free Nation movements of America, but also suggests the shadow of their greatest desire and their greatest fear: their terrorist dystopia. That is why Somalia, from the US perspective, often appears as the New Tortuga.

Tortuga obviously invites *both* nostalgia and speculation. The question is: why is it necessary to reinvent Tortuga? Would democracy, for that matter terrorism, have been possible without it? The fate of Tortuga, reinvented over and over, appears to be the fate of America remembered. The nostalgia is for a time when America mattered, the dream and the nightmare, what Linda Hutcheon calls the 'structural doubling-up of two different times, an inadequate present, and an idealized past'—the 'imperialist nostalgia' that Renato Rosaldo defines as the paradoxical phenomenon of 'people mourn[ing] the passing of what they themselves have transformed'.[73] The

---

[70] Michael Collins, *Cornucopia of Evil*, Austin: Armstrong Printing, 2005, p. 81.

[71] Collins, *Cornucopia of Evil*, p. 81

[72] Bey, *The Temporary Autonomous Zone*, p. 418. The pirate utopia, Libertatia, is the micronation setting of William Burroughs's novella, *Ghost of Chance* (1991).

[73] Linda Hutcheon, 'Irony, Nostalgia, and the Postmodern', University of Toronto

pirate in this sense stands in for the primitive. The proto-micronation of Tortuga is America itself in future retrospect. Thus, in Jessica D. Russell's 2007 novel, *Monday's Child*, in 'the spaceport city of New Tortuga all things are possible'. This Tortuga, the busiest port in three galaxies, is more than a legendary den of smugglers; it is also a 'crossroads [where] new lives begin and old ones are lost'.[74] If Somalia now is the Tortuga of the twenty-first century,[75] it is partly because of nostalgia for a speculative otherworld.

The Somali pirates argue that they are in a fight for survival and that it is the USA and Europe that 'have been pirating humanity' for centuries. Tortuga, for them, offers an inspired model of resistance. They may identify more broadly with Haiti too, the poorest nation of the Americas, home of the revolution that led to the first African Republic in the Americas, invaded and occupied by the USA, starved and impoverished by vindictive and coercive imperialist economic policies, for the Somalis have been moulded by similar forces. But Tortuga inspires the US discourse of vilification, and paradoxically drives the Somali counter-discourse as well. In the wake of the 2010 earthquake, the Somali pirates offered to donate a significant share of what they had pillaged from US and European shipping to the Haitian earthquake victims. Intent on sidestepping the usual aid agencies and distribution networks, they claimed to have their own connections all over the world, and promised to deliver the money undetected by Western 'enemy' governments. As they dispute the 'moral authority' of the West and its First World states, and set about dismantling Somalia as a nation, they build from the wreckage a new Island in the Net, a New Tortuga. Tortuga has gone global. It is the catch-cry of the twenty-first century phenomenon, 'pirate internationalism'.[76]

English Library, Criticism and Theory Resources (1998) <http://www.library.utoronto.ca/utel/criticism/hutchinp.html> [13 May 2012]. Renato Rosaldo, 'Imperialist Nostalgia', *Representations*, 6 (Spring 1989), pp. 107–122, at 107. See also Jennifer Wenzel, 'Remembering the Past's Future: Anti-Imperialist Nostalgia and Some Versions of the Third World', *Cultural Critique*, 62 (Winter 2006), pp. 1–32.

[74] Jessica D. Russell, *Monday's Child*, Aurora, CO: Aspen Mountain Press, 2007, p. 6.

[75] See Marina Angeloni, 'Somalia: The Tortuga of the 21st Century', *Transition Studies Review*, 16, no. 3 (2009), pp. 755–767.

[76] Veronique de Rugy refers to the port of Eyl as 'the Tortuga of Somalia', *Reason* (1 July 2009) <http://reason.com/archives/2009/06/15/paying-the-pirates-price> [15.8.2010].

The Kingdom of Redonda

However, the oldest existing Caribbean micronation of modern times is the Kingdom of Redonda, established in 1865, on a small island between Nevis and Montserrat within the inner arc of the Leeward Islands. Although it is legally today a dependency of Antigua and Barbuda, there are at least four, and possibly as many as nine, competing claimants to the throne of this rocky remnant of an extinct volcanic cone, which has no source of fresh water and no human inhabitants. It also has only poor anchorage and is almost completely unprotected against the prevailing wind and swell.

Columbus named the island 'Santa María la Redonda', but the invention of the kingdom is thought to originate with M. P. Shiel, a British/West Indian fantasy and science-fiction writer. Shiel is credited with possibly the first future history series in science fiction,[77] his lasting literary reputation being secured by the first in the series, *The Purple Cloud*, in 1901. This was recently republished by the University of Nebraska Press, whereupon it was hailed in the *Times Literary Supplement* as 'one of the most impressive treatments' of the theme of the last man journeying through a dead world.[78] The purple cloud consists of poisonous gas that seemingly kills all the planet's inhabitants except one. Adam (a nostalgic/speculative trope of both the first and here the last man) is the lone survivor, who travels the world like a tourist destroying every locale he visits—until of course he finds that he is *not* the only person left after all. *The Purple Cloud* is thought to have inspired the 1959 science-fiction doomsday film, *The World, the Flesh and the Devil*, starring musician, actor, and social activist Harry Belafonte, a film which ends with a new beginning, and which Stephen King cites as an influence in turn on his novel *The Stand* (1978).

The second volume in Shiel's series, titled *Lord of the Sea* (1901), has a more direct bearing on its author's claim to the Kingdom of Redonda.[79] It contains a critique of the private ownership of land, based on the theories of the political economist Henry George (1839–1897), who invented Georgism, proposing that everyone has an equal right to the use of all that nature so impartially offers, especially land. ('There is in nature no such thing as a fee

---

[77] David G. Hartwell, Introduction to M. P. Shiel, *The Purple Cloud*, Upper Saddle River, NJ: Gregg Press, 1977, p. 8.

[78] Edward James, 'Fiction in Brief,' *Times Literary Supplement*, 29 December 2000, p. 20.

[79] The Kingdom of Redonda was not mentioned in print until 1929, in a booklet advertising the reissue of four of Shiel's novels. See Harold Billings, *M. P. Shiel: A Biography of His Early Years*, Austin: Roger Beacham, 2005, pp. 83–85.

simple in land'.)[80] Dashiell Hammett, in *The Gutting of Couffignal* (1925), has his own detective hero on a slow night reading *Lord of the Sea*, which he describes as the story of 'a strong, tough and violent fellow ... whose modest plan was to hold the world in one hand'. Hammett's island lies at the northern end of San Francisco Bay, and is occupied by 'well-fed old gentlemen' who have colonised it 'so they may spend what is left of their lives nursing their livers and improving their golf, while admitting only as many working people and similar riffraff as are needed to keep them comfortably served'.[81]

Shiel proclaimed himself King Felipe, the second king of Redonda, in 1929. Allegedly, his father was the first king, a prosperous sea-trader from Montserrat, who claimed descent from the ancient Irish Kings of Tara, and who was so overjoyed at the birth of his son (after a succession of eight daughters) that he celebrated the event by establishing his birthright. When Guy Fletcher, the keyboard player with Dire Straits, visited the island in 1984, he was told by locals on Montserrat that in the early days of European colonisation the only requirement for ruling your own island was that there had to be a post office there.[82] So the first king built one, even though mostly sheep then inhabited the island, and the ruins of that post office can still be found there today.

The son's coronation at age fifteen took place on the island on 21 July 1880. Despite strong protests from the Shiel family, however, the British Government shortly afterwards annexed the island in order to exploit its phosphate deposits, which explains how Redonda eventually came to be administered by Antigua. The young king moved to England, and the Redondan monarchy has been technically in exile ever since. The British abandoned the phosphate trade with the outbreak of the First World War, and the island now is home for sea-birds, reptiles, a herd of goats, and more recently a colony of burrowing owls displaced from Antigua. Since the physical jurisdiction of the island is no longer in the control of the title owner, the kingship is regarded in law as Incorporeal Property (that is, similar to the Lordship of an English Manor).

The third king, Terence Ian Fytton Armstrong (better known by his *nom de plume* 'John Gawsworth') took the title in 1947 as King Juan I. After that

---

[80] Henry George, *Progress and Poverty* [1879], Cambridge: Cambridge University Press, 2009, p. 304.

[81] Dashiell Hammett, 'The Gutting of Couffignal', in *The Big Knockover: Selected Stories and Short Novels*, New York: Vintage, 1989, p. 6, 4.

[82] Guy Fletcher, 'A Day Trip to Redonda' (2011) <http://www.guyfletcher.co.uk/index.php/gallery/A_Day_Trip_to_Redonda> [10.5.2012].

it gets messy. As mentioned earlier, the title is contested by at least four claimants, and I do not propose here to try to decide that storm in a teacup. It seems clear, however, that this state of affairs in part derives from the fact that the third king's talents as a poet and man of letters failed to sustain him, so that he gradually fell upon evil days and spent most of his time in a tavern in West London, where in return for a drink he is known to have at times bestowed a dukedom—so why not a kingdom?—emblazoned on the back of a beer-coaster.[83] The literary duchy of the realm include the Welsh horror novelist, Arthur Machen, publisher Victor Gollancz, J. B. Priestley, Dorothy Sayers, Arthur Ransome, George Barker, Henry Miller, Dylan Thomas, Lawrence Durrell and many others.

Jon Wynne-Tyson, British activist and founder of Centaur Press, author and publisher of the Redondan novel, *So Say Banana Bird* (1984), whose signature in my copy has in parenthesis 'Juan II, fourth King of Redonda', says that the kingdom is 'a pleasing and eccentric fairy tale; a piece of literary mythology to be taken with salt, romantic sighs, appropriate perplexity, some amusement, but without great seriousness'.[84] It was real enough at one stage, however, for his ambassador in California to entertain plans for a floating extension to the island to be suspended from its peak by heavy cables.[85] And the Kingdom of Redonda does appear after all in *Fodor's Caribbean Guide to the Bahamas and Bermudas* (1974), in *The Caribbean & the Bahamas* (Cadogan Guide, 1994), and in the *Caribbean Islands Handbook (with the Bahamas)*—in the Footprint series, USA Passport Books (1996). But King Juan II dedicates *So Say Banana Bird* to 'those who love islands and want them left alone', as well as for 'those with doubts about today's priorities'.[86]

Another claimant, the eminent Spanish author Javier Marías (King Javier I), says he inherited the title to the kingdom 'through irony and writing, never through solemnity or blood', even though at heart he is a republican and islands make him nervous.[87] He tells the story of his own coronation in *Dark Back of Time* (originally in Spanish as *Negra espalda del tiempo*

---

[83] 'A Brief History of the Island Kingdom Redonda: in the West Indies' (2000) <http://www.redonda.org/redonda.html> [20.8.2010].

[84] Jon Wynne-Tyson, 'Two Kings of Redonda: M. P. Shiel and John Gawsworth', *Books at Iowa*, 36 (April 1982) <http://www.lib.uiowa.edu/spec-coll/bai/wynne.htm> [20.8.2010].

[85] King Robert the Bald, 'The Isle of Redonda: "The Only Island Kingdom in the Caribbean"' <http://jalypso.com/redonda/> [10.8.2010].

[86] Jon Wynne-Tyson, *So Say Banana Bird*, Brighton: Pythian Books, 1984, Author's Note.

[87] Esther Allen, the English translator of *Dark Back of Time*, London: Chatto & Windus, 2003, gives this as 'by irony and writing' (p. 317).

[1998]). His earlier Oxford novel, *All Souls* (1989) begins with a prefatory note stating that any resemblance of any character to any other person living or dead is purely coincidental, except for the characters John Gawsworth and Terence Ian Fytton Armstrong'.[88] But since the author had spent two years in the same academic Oxford post that he gave to his nameless narrator, many readers collapsed all distinction between the two. Marías found that the fiction invaded his life in unexpected and unsettling ways. He says in *Dark Back of Time* that it is a doomed attempt to tell the truth about that invasion. But there was another side to it too. Readers of *All Souls* had also *refused* to believe the *true* story of Terence Ian Fytton Armstrong ('John Gawsworth')—'The Man Who Could Be King'—believing the Kingdom of Redonda to be Marías' own 'Kiplingesque invention, pure make-believe'.[89] Testimony in the end proved futile, itself partaking of fiction. In *Dark Back of Time* he describes Redonda as 'both real and fantastical … with and without territory', a 'literary island'—but one 'that can be located and does figure on certain maps … but not on others'.[90] The reality of this micronation exists in a relation of seeming co-dependency to a whole series of literary other-worlds. Redonda is like Frankenstein, a character in a novel that became a myth, where the identity of the creator and his creation often overlap in confusion. It exists in a geography where, as I said in my discussion of the old/new cyberspace, nature seems no longer to precede ontologically its technical elaboration. The narrator of *Dark Back of Time* even claims that, since his invasion by the fiction of *All Souls*, the former King of Redonda has come to live with(in) him. Not Armstrong the man, but Gawsworth the poet-king (for Armstrong wrote under various pseudonyms). This king—King Javier—has turned the kingdom, or at least his version of it, into a literary foundation. The Redonda Publishing House publishes the works of former Redondan kings and nobles, but also offers a Redondan literary prize worth a considerable sum.

Marías playfully suggests that Redonda may bear a relation of some kinship to George Eliot's final novel, *Daniel Deronda*, itself a mixture of satire and serious moral purpose. Edward Said has argued that Eliot's novel is a Restorationist text, a justification of what later became known as Zionism,

---

[88] Javier Marías, *All Souls*, trans. Margaret Jull Costa, London: The Harvill Press, 1999, Author's note.

[89] Javier Marías's alleged first reference in writing to Gawsworth was in a non-fiction piece entitled 'El Hombre Que Pudo Ser Rey', *El Pais*, 23 May 1985; republished in *Pasiones Pasadas*, Barcelona: Editorial Anagrama, 1991—see *Dark Back of Time*, p. 139 (also p. 18).

[90] Marías, *Dark Back of Time*, p. 92.

allowing Britain to re-invent Palestine as a Jewish homeland.[91] In *Dark Back of Time*, Marías adopts the trope of 'a wanderer in nothingness' to describe the fate of one member of the 'intellectual aristocracy' of Redonda, Hugh Olaff de Wet, the man who made Gawsworth's death mask, a writer himself and a pilot (whom Marías imagines as a pirate, with 'a piratical pony-tail … [and] a black patch or smoked monocle over one eye'—' a seventeenth-century corsair or noble or both things together').[92] De Wet was in fact a French spy, imprisoned by the Gestapo in 1941, and author of various memoirs about his experiences in the Spanish Civil War (*Cardboard Crucifix: The Story of a Pilot in Spain* [1938]) and in prison in Germany (*The Valley of the Shadow* [1949]). The German newspaper report of the trial in Berlin that led to his imprisonment, translated into English by De Wet himself and included in his prison memoir—and quoted in full ('more or less') in *Dark Back of Time*—describes the pirate-pilot De Wet in 1941 as belonging to a society 'without a country'. The ideal of this society, it says, is Colonel T. E. Lawrence, the legendary 'Lawrence of Arabia'. Gawsworth too was a member of that society, though falling short of the unattainable ideal: a society consisting of those 'scattered members of a race whose way of life has become infamous', for which De Wet (and Marías) gives the image of the 'uprooted limbs of a tree that once flourished fruitfully'.[93] De Wet disputes the newspaper account generally, which prefaces his own version of events, beginning 'on the shores of Avernus',[94] where Virgil locates the entrance to the underworld in *The Aeneid*.

In ancient Roman times Port Julius was located on that crater-lake, home to the western fleet of Rome's Imperial Navy—the Fleet of Misenum. Port Julius was built to honour Julius Caesar, and to secure Italy's grain supply from Egypt by putting an end to the piracy that plagued the shipping lanes from Africa. The Mediterranean of that time has four things in common with the seventeenth-century Caribbean: an expansive empire, swarms of pirates, a systematic slave trade, and a plantation economy. Port Julius, like the fabled Atlantis, eventually sank. But according to myth, the Sibylline Books (*Libri Sibyllini*) survived. The Cumaean Sibyl, who also made her home by the lake, burnt six but sold three to the last King of Rome. There

---

[91] Edward Said, 'Zionism from the Standpoint of Its Victims', in *Anatomy of Racism*, ed., David Theo Goldberg Minneapolis: University of Minnesota Press, 1980, pp. 210–246.

[92] Marías, *Dark Back of Time*, pp. 254, 256 and 276.

[93] Marías, *Dark Back of Time*, p. 285.

[94] Marías, *Dark Back of Time*, p. 285.

is reference to them in George Eliot's *Daniel Deronda* notebooks,[95] and the novel's own prose style is sometimes observed as '"sibylline".[96] Did the first King of Redonda, Matthew Shiel, consult Eliot's novel in the way that the ancients consulted the Sibylline Books, as a means of expiation or to stave off some apocalyptic disaster? Is this the source of the invention of Redonda?

In *Lord of the Sea* we witness the rise of anti-Semitism and the expulsion of the Jews from mainland Europe to England. Shiel's protagonist, Richard Hogarth, is falsely imprisoned for murder by his Jewish landlord. But he escapes, builds an empire, institutes Georgist land reforms in England, buys Palestine back from Turkey for the occupation of the Jews and—to ensure their repatriation—evicts all Jews from England. Later, he loses his empire and discovers his own Jewish identity. As John D. Squires summarises the narrative's final phase: he then joins the new exodus to Palestine, and there is 'recognized as the Messiah returned to lead Israel, by example, in the redemption of the world'.[97]

This then is the legacy of Redonda, an uninhabited Caribbean micronation, the smallest of the three islands that constitute the nation of Antigua and Barbuda. While it has failed to establish itself as a recognised nation, it has survived into the present day as a unique literary foundation with its own literary aristocracy, but it continues to be the focus of a battle for title between Spanish and English authors—not to mention King Robert the Bald, who lives on Antigua (and claims to have written eight books, though mostly self-confessed nonsense). The Trojan War is said to have spawned the civilisation of Europe and seeded the story of Europe;[98] the Redondan War gives us a repeat history of the squabbles for sovereignty in the Americas, but with the most likely home for the exiled Kingdom of Redonda within a *literary* economy. Redonda is the imaginative home of artists and intellectuals who, as Theodor Herzl put it when outlining his Zionist vision of *Der Judenstaat*, aspire to 'high pride and the joy of an inner liberation of their existence'. The Jewish Question, for Herzl, was 'neither a social nor a religious one, even though it sometimes takes these and other forms'. It was 'a national question'.[99] The same might be said of Redonda, especially when we consider

---

[95] *George Eliot's Daniel Deronda Notebooks*, ed., Jane Irwin, Cambridge: Cambridge University Press, 1996, p. 149.
[96] See, for example, John P. Kearney, 'Time and Beauty in *Daniel Deronda*: "Was She Beautiful or not ..."', *Nineteenth-Century Fiction*, 26, no. 3 (1971), pp. 286–306, at 292.
[97] John D. Squires, 'Rediscovering M. P. Shiel (1865–1947)', *The New York Review of Science Fiction*, 13, no. 9 (May 2001), pp. 12–15.
[98] Paul Beekman Taylor, 'The Chicano Translation of Troy: Epic Topoi in the Novels of Rudolfo A. Anaya', *MELUS*, 19, no. 3 (1994), pp. 19–35.
[99] Theodor Herzl, *Der Judenstaat* (*The Jewish State*) [1896], trans. Sylvie D'Avigdor,

Marías's archetype, the 'wanderer in nothingness', as an un-housed—rather than unhinged—intellectual community, with T. E. Lawrence as its ideal. Lawrence's map of the Middle East, presented to the British War Cabinet in November 1918 and now displayed in the Imperial War Museum in London, might have made a different world from the one we know, if only because it included a separate state of Palestine. Its view of the Middle East was not unlike a pirates' view of the Caribbean, based on tribal affinities and trade routes, and it drew the borders accordingly. In fact, Lawrence thought of his publisher 'always as part pirate, like Kidd, part buccaneer like Morgan, with moments of legitimacy like Farragut'.[100] Marías notes that many writers—at least three of the Redondan nobility, himself included—have had difficulties with one eye, even James Joyce, who appears in many photographs 'with a bulky black patch over his left eye, though there are those who say he wore it less out of necessity than out of affectation, to make himself more original'.[101]

In *The Dragon of Redonda*, an illustrated children's tale by Frané Lessac and Jan Jackson (with an introduction by Marías rival, King Juan II), three young friends are shipwrecked on the island. All of its people have fled in fear of the volcano, for Redonda, 'just a little rock in the middle of the big Caribbean Sea',[102] is little more than an eruption in space. But inside the volcano lives a great green dragon, caught like a fish in a bowl, though he is ambiguously both the island's custodian and prisoner. Desperately lonely and wanting to escape and see the world, he must first learn to fly. According to the myth of the crater-lake 'Avernus' (meaning: 'without birds'), any bird flying above it would fall down dead. Birds now are almost the only inhabitants of Redonda, boobies mostly. But a wise old pelican teaches the dragon to fly so that he can make his escape, rescue the children, and travel, in the hope of one day meeting the king. It is hard not to think of Quetzalcoatl, the Mesoamerican feathered serpent-god of the winds—often identified with the Aztec Huracan, and the Mayan Kukulan—returning from the land of the dead to make the world human.

American Zionist Emergency Council, 1946 <http://www.jewishvirtuallibrary.org/jsource/Zionism/herzlex.html> [20.8.2010].

[100] David Glasgow Farragut (1801–1870) is remembered particularly for the Battle of Mobile Bay, and his command: 'Damn the torpedoes!' He was the first vice-admiral with the US Navy during the American Civil War.

[101] Marías, *Dark Back of Time*, p. 299.

[102] Frané Lessac and Jan Jackson, *The Dragon of Redonda*, London: Macmillan Caribbean, 1986, p. 12.

The Republic of New Atlantis

The Republic of New Atlantis was founded by its elected first president, Leicester Hemingway, brother of Ernest, on a raft thirty feet by eight feet anchored off the south coast of Jamaica in 1964. Leicester had written a celebrated biography of Ernest to finance this construction of iron pipes, stones, bamboo, and stainless steel cables. Named after Bacon's New Atlantis, this is the micronation that elected the former US president, Harry Truman, as its presidential advisor, and which placed Lyndon Johnson—'protector of the entire free world'—on its first postage stamp.[103] A 40 cent stamp was soon issued also honouring the US 4th infantry division for their role in helping to liberate Europe—combat correspondent Ernest Hemingway had been an 'Ivyman' of that division—and there were plans for a stamp to honour the establishment of the provisional government of the Dominican Republic in 1965.

To fulfil United Nations requirements, a nation must have its own constitution, flag, currency, and postal system: the Republic of New Atlantis developed all of these. Its currency was the scruple: two cents or one hundredth of a scruple was a carob bean with a hole drilled through it; a half a scruple was a small shark's tooth. Having no scruples was literally equivalent to having no money. The purpose of New Atlantis is given in the Preamble to its Constitution: 'to form a more perfect government, establish justice, insure domestic tranquility, promote the general welfare, and secure the blessings of liberty to ourselves and our posterity'.[104] While this is clearly based on the Preamble to the US Constitution, the minor changes in wording are revealing. The New Atlantis constitution omits completely the US reference to defence, and it replaces the abstract ambition of 'perfect union' with 'perfect government'. This signals a particular change in purpose and emphasis, since the US phrase is interpreted in US law as disallowing any state nullification of federal law or dissolution of the Union.

The New Atlantis Constitution was signed by Lady Pamela Bird, a Montego Bay socialite and Vice-President of the alleged twenty-second republic in the Western Hemisphere; it was duly reported in the *Kingston*

---

[103] The postage stamps—and all other items discussed below, including the Constitution from which I quote—are held in the New Atlantis Collection, 1964–1966, Harry Ransom Center, University of Texas at Austin. See: 'Leicester Hemingway: An Inventory of His New Atlantis Collection in the Manuscript Collection at the Harry Ransom Humanities Research Center' <http://research.hrc.utexas.edu:8080/hrcxtf/view?docId=ead/00327.xml> [8.5.2012].

[104] See n.103.

Daily Gleaner, along with the fact that the raft was strategically anchored in international waters beyond the three-mile limit and the hundred-fathom curve of Jamaica's claim. President Hemingway gave his assurances that the New Atlantis would be 'a peaceful power and would pose no threat to Jamaica'.[105] One of the more important functions of the republic, he said, would be to negotiate fishing treaties with the Jamaican and US governments to put an end to the interference of coastal steamers in the fishing grounds adjacent to the raft. This is not unlike the stated purpose of present-day Somali pirates, whose fishing grounds, since the collapse of the Somali government in 1991, have been so ravaged by Europe and polluted by its dumping of nuclear waste that the Somali fishermen have (according to their own testimony) been forced into piracy in order to survive.

In the case of New Atlantis, however, the *Gleaner* reported that the US government almost immediately claimed the northern portion of the raft under the provisions of the Guano Act, passed by Congress a century ago, Chapter 8 of which states:

Whenever any citizen of the United States discovers a deposit of guano on any island, rock, or key, not within the lawful jurisdiction of any other government, and not occupied by the citizens of any other government, and takes peaceable possession thereof, and occupies the same, such island, rock, or key may, at the discretion of the President, be considered as appertaining to the United States.[106]

In reality, Leicester Hemingway had taken advantage of the Act to assist his claim to sovereignty. President Hemingway is reported as saying that shortly after the inhabitable part of the island—that is, the raft—had risen from the sea, he had discovered a small deposit of guano there. He planned in time, he said, to expand the island to some three miles or more; in any case, having formed a sovereign government they were entitled to buy land, and the sovereign rights to that land.

Guano is basically seabird excrement, though it is also sometimes harvested from bat colonies. The Incas in Peru were the first to harvest it, and it was there, in the early nineteenth century, that Alexander von Humboldt 'discovered' its usefulness as an agricultural fertiliser. By the 1840s guano was in great demand, not only for agriculture but also as an ingredient for the making of gunpowder. It is worth noting here that in the 1860s, a US firm—the Redonda Phosphate Company—paid the British government

---

[105] 'New Atlantis Holds First Election', *The Daily Gleaner*, 4 February 1965, p. 1.
[106] The Guano Islands Act, Title 48 of the United States Code, 1411–1419.

as represented in Antigua (for Redonda was then a British dependency) 'a royalty of twelve cents a ton' to mine the island of Redonda.[107] Some maps of the island show the remains of a mining shaft now named the Centaur's Cave, suggestive of a previous 'lost race' of island hybrids, half-human and half-animal.

The utopian aim of Leicester Hemingway's republic was to provide 'a test tube for democracy'[108] in the Caribbean less than a hundred miles from Cuba (where in 1951 his brother had written his epic fishing tale, *The Old Man and the Sea*), but also to establish New Atlantis as headquarters of the International Marine Research Society and promote research into Caribbean marine life. Bacon's New Atlantis proposes something similar: a society of 'generosity and enlightenment, dignity and splendour, piety and public spirit',[109] the 'eye' and the foundation of which is Salomon's House, named after the King of Israel. Most commentators regard Salomon's House as the ideal of the modern research university in both applied and pure sciences; in fact, Bacon's New Atlantis did inspire the founding of the Royal Society in England in 1660. Leicester Hemingway's New Atlantis, however, was more like the fabled old Atlantis: it was destroyed in the first hurricane season.

This New Atlantis now is a long forgotten relic, archived in the Harry Ransom Research Centre at the University of Texas in Austin: a torn flag, a few stamps, and the odd scruple or two.

Conclusion

Micronations are inventions of nations in places where none exist. The continuing proliferation of micronations in the Caribbean over so many years says a number of things: primarily, as we might expect for a place so profoundly affected by migrations, that we cannot think of place without a sense of movement, movement within place, place thickened by migrations of imagination as well as the massive forced movements of people there.[110]

---

[107] Frederick A. Ober, *A Guide to the West Indies*, New York: Dodd, Mead & Company, 1908, p. 343.

[108] 'New Atlantis – The World's Newest Country', p. 30, unidentified newspaper clipping.

[109] Introductory Note to Francis Bacon, *The New Atlantis*, Scott's Valley, CA: IAP, 2009, p. 1.

[110] Editors Murat Aydemir and Alex Rotas, in their Introduction to *Migratory Settings*, Amsterdam: Rodopi, 2008, p. 7, propose a shift in the way we view migration: as 'installing movement *within* place' rather than simply moving 'from place to place'. Place, they argue, is 'neither reified nor transcended' by this view of migration, but 'thickened' as it becomes 'the setting of the variegated memories, imaginations,

After all, those forced movements first to the Americas and then, after the War of Independence, to Australia, were, as Alan Atkinson says, themselves a result of 'increasing aptitude with pen and paper'. They not only amplified the skills of administrating the empire but also the sense of geography, apparent within England for example by renewed attention to parish settlement laws.[111] But in the wider realm this greater literacy and administrative capacity inadvertently threw many English-speaking individuals beyond the reach of authority, so that 'enlightenment increased disorder at the edge of empire'.[112] Tortuga is one good example. The pirate, more than any other figure, represents that 'spirit of free movement and resistance which was the underside of the new order',[113] intent as it was through writing to fix people in their place. The Kingdom of Redonda, the Republic of New Atlantis, and others that are beyond the scope of this essay—like the Principality of New Utopia proposed 120 miles west of Grand Cayman, or the many Tortuga game-worlds that have extended the Caribbean into so-called 'cyber-space'—are in reality dream worlds. Like the utopian and dystopian fictions that literary scholars generally take more seriously, however, they do real work. If anything, it should be even more obvious that these 'texts' help to shape the world they re-represent. Literary and non-literary geographies are inseparable categories in this sense. In *The Guns of Tortuga*, as the ship limps toward the pirates' den, the boy-hero asks what the islands are like. The captain, who has been writing up the ship's log from his hastily scribbled notes, crumples a piece of paper into a wad and tosses it onto the table: 'Like that', he says.[114]

Micronations by definition lack formal recognition, and they are festive in their quality, so they invite laughter. We should at least take them seriously enough, however, in the ways they are variously *invented* and *situated*, to ask what sense of the extended Caribbean—the American Tropics—they might provide. The indications from my own case studies in this essay are both complex and contradictory: libertarian and pirate haven, social experiment and social disorder, in-between-ness, sargasso, floating or flying islands. New Atlantis speaks particularly of the Caribbean as a laboratory. The exiled kingdom of Redonda reminds us how literature circulates, and how the literary economy of Europe in part still depends on the topos of the

---

dreams, fantasies, nightmares, anticipations, and idealizations of both migrants and native inhabitants that experiences of migration bring into contact with each other'.

[111] Atkinson, *The Europeans in Australia*, vol. 1, p. 29.

[112] Atkinson, *The Europeans in Australia*, vol. 1, p. 29.

[113] Atkinson, *The Europeans in Australia*, vol. 1, p. 32.

[114] Strickland and Fuller, *The Guns of Tortuga*, p. 32.

uninhabited Caribbean island. It speaks of the importance of islands to the development of European literature. Tortuga is a key part of the 'Project of Disney', as Karen Klugman calls it, the reduction of the world to simulacra, where representations take the place of the place represented.[115] It combines do-it-yourself democracy and terrorism in one word, a word that speaks of a lost world on the one hand, and a dystopian future on the other. The precise experience depends on the theme park.

---

[115] The Project on Disney, *Inside the Mouse: Work and Play at Disney World*, Durham: Duke University Press, 1995, p. 103.

Golden Kings, Cocaine Lords, and the Madness of El Dorado: Guayana as Native and Colonial Imaginary

Neil L. Whitehead

This essay explores the idea of Guayana as a space of cultural imagination for the American Tropics. The notion of 'exploration' is perhaps particularly apposite here as 'Guayana' defies any stable physical delimitation. The national societies of the Guayana region—Brazil, the Guianas, and Venezuela—quite overtly construct themselves through a contrast between the historically settled coasts and a still-unexplored or unconquered interior.[1] The fluvial border created by the connection of the Amazon, Orinoco, and Rio Negro rivers thereby constitutes the frontier between the imagined space of Guayana and the historically constituted space of national and post-colonial identity. In the contemporary era all kinds of development projects, national parks and forest preserves, police or military actions in this space can partly be understood as a sign of the emplacement of national societies in the as yet wild and alien landscapes of the 'interior'. Historically, for both the colonial and national imaginaries of this region of north-eastern South America, the notion of 'Guayana' signals both numerous dangers and obstacles, but also wonders and marvels, to those who travel within its conceptual and physical spaces. As the Venezuelan proverb puts it: *Quien se va al Orinoco, si no muere, se vuelve loco.*[2]

---

[1] The term 'Guyana' refers to the independent country formerly known as 'British Guiana', while the term 'Guianas' is used to refer collectively to the colonial enclaves of British Guiana, Surinam, and Guyane (or French Guiana). Some writers also use the term 'Guianas' to refer to the territories of those colonial enclaves, plus the regions of Brazil and Venezuela that lie south of the Orinoco and north of the Amazon.

[2] Whoever goes to Orinoco, if they do not die, they come back loco.

Nor can this imaginative reputation be simply reduced to a case of European or non-native credulity and confusion in a strange land, since the marvellous and dangerous are present for Amerindian explorers and adventurers no less than European ones. Both ritually and cosmologically, the space of Guayana represents for native peoples a zone of distinct ritual and cultural practice, the site of ancient routes by which sacred knowledge was spread by the first people and the site where the great earth tree, from which all plants and animals sprouted, once stood.[3] In the highlands at the core of Guayana can still be seen the stump of this first tree, petrified into one of the *tepuis*[4] that rise from the forest, the site of Conan Doyle's 'Lost World'. As the Ye'cuana tell us in their creation myth, the *Watunna*, in Weyana, under one of those *tepuis*, all the good people of the world are still waiting to be born, and will wait until they are shamanically discovered and ritually released.[5] So too, in the reading of Sir Walter Ralegh's *Discoverie of the Large Rich and Bewtiful Empyre of Guiana* (1596), the first European publication to explore this space, we are magically transported to realms of wonder, in quest of visions of exotic possibility. But in this text the prospect of virgin penetration, gratefully invited, also vies with the lure of gold and reputation, as a promised political redemption for colonial desires of complete and sated possession. Both ethnological and literary materials are thus relevant to understanding how 'Guayana' has emerged through time, in indigenous, colonial, and national discourses, as an epitome of threatening alterity, simultaneously alluring for its promise of hidden wealth and knowledge. Fantastic marvels, an abundance of wealth, unnatural sexuality, cannibal violence, as well as the ever-present threat of moral and mental dissolution, are deeply inscribed as the defining features of this land of Amazon women, gilded men, and vengeful shamanic jaguars. In the following pages both the utopian and dystopian, native and non-native visions of Guayana and how they are interconnected will be examined.

---

[3] In the summer of 2009 an archaeological survey sponsored by the US National Science Foundation, for which I was Principal Investigator, uncovered the site of an urban-scale settlement along the Berbice River that was radio-carbon dated to 5,000 BP, and so contemporary with the ancient Egyptian, Sumerian, and Harappan civilisations of the Old World.

[4] The Amerindian term for the flat-topped mountains that have eroded out over millions of years, the upland region of Guayana emerging from the most ancient rock formations on the planet, hence its mineral wealth.

[5] Marc de Civrieux and David Guss, *Watunna: An Orinoco Creation Cycle*, Austin: University of Texas Press, 1977.

Imaginaries of gold, jade, and gender

El Dorado literally means the 'gilded' or 'golden' man, the myth actually referring to a person, even though El Dorado is usually taken to be a place, a city literally made of gold or built from vast wealth.[6] Accounts of El Dorado as reported during the initial conquests of the sixteenth century allude to a diversity of native cultural practices with regard to golden metals, although there is no reason to think that such practices were uniform for native people themselves. But an ancient tradition of gold working certainly did exist in South America outside of the Inca world, as is evident from the archaeological record. So it is important to note that El Dorado tales described gold working outside of the major empires of the Inca and Aztec and were thought to refer to as yet unknown cultures that had gold working traditions. Specifically, the archaeological record tells of both the production of native gold work as well as the diverse symbolic and ritual uses to which such golden metals were put. Given the vast metallic wealth extracted by the Europeans from both Central and South America, it is not surprising that the notion of El Dorado should have seemed most credible. Add to this that in the sixteenth century there was a general expectation, partly deriving from previous encounters in Africa, that gold was especially engendered as a geo-physical property of the torrid zone, or equatorial latitudes. In the case of some explorers, like Christopher Columbus or Walter Ralegh, a personal interest in alchemy and mysticism gave them additional reasons to want to seek out a 'golden king' who might also be a source of arcane knowledge.

Historians have tended to focus on the absurdities and failures of the Spanish quest for the 'Golden One' but, by considering native ritual and symbolic uses for golden metals, and not just the 'rationality' of the colonial mystic quest, El Dorado emerges as a mutually meaningful myth, rooted in native ritual practice. The idea of a 'Golden One' was elaborated by the notion that a king or paramount chief was annually anointed by the sprinkling of gold dust onto his body. This El Dorado was then paddled to the centre of a vast lake where he would deposit votive offerings of gold work. The names of this lake are variously given as Paytiti, Parime, or Rupununi and the great and golden city which stood on its edge is called Manoa. Certainly there is much in this narrative which matches ethnohistorical and archaeological

---

[6] Further details and citations to sources for the following analysis can be found in Walter Ralegh, *The Discoverie of the Large, Rich and Bewtiful Empire of Guiana by Sir Walter Ralegh*, edited, annotated and transcribed by Neil L. Whitehead, Exploring Travel Series Vol. 1, Manchester: Manchester University Press and American Exploration & Travel Series Vol. 71, Norman: Oklahoma University Press, 1977.

reconstructions of the ritual practices of the native cultures of what are now the territories of Colombia, Venezuela, and Guyana. The city of Manoa was thought to lie in an upland area, perhaps recalling locations such as Tenochtitlan and Cuzco, and so El Dorado was sought in the highlands of the upper Amazon, as well as in what are now Colombia, Venezuela, Guyana, and Surinam. It is therefore important to remember that variations in the colonial reports relate as much to the expansion of cultural and geographical knowledge in the sixteenth century as they do to inconsistency and credulity in colonial reports of a native El Dorado.

In fact there were plausible reasons for seeking El Dorado in these three regions, and these reasons remain valid, whatever may have been the cultural and geographical ignorance of the early colonial expeditionaries who acted on them.[7] This unwillingness to abandon the idea of an El Dorado shows the role of the myth in the service of the ideology of colonial expansion. Early encounter with the Muisca, and the other Colombian gold-working cultures, could not completely satisfy all the elements or promise of the El Dorado myth, and so only encouraged the search for another location.

The name Paytiti is associated with fabled locations of this kind in the Bolivian Andes, while Manoa is the name which attaches to the El Dorado idea in the eastern Amazon and Orinoco region. Initially Manoa, the supposed 'golden city' on the shores of a great lake, was transposed to the upper Amazon/Rio Negro region during the 1530–1540s and then during the 1580–1590s to the Guayana highlands of the Sierra Parima and Sierra Pakaraima, these transpositions closely matching the chronology of the expansion of European geographical understanding and colonial ambition.

The lake on which El Dorado resided in his city of Manoa was called Parime or Rupununi, and various locations in the Branco and Essequibo watersheds, subject to annual flooding, were investigated. Native gold work was often encountered but the identification of a single source repeatedly frustrated. This was due partly to the transposition of key elements of the El Dorado myth by Europeans from the Colombian context, and partly to the fact that gold-sources in north-eastern Amazonia are rarely to be found in concentrated volcanic geological contexts like those in Colombia, but rather are alluvial or river-based and therefore dispersed in character. However, the annual formation of vast seasonal lakes due to the annual flooding of rivers, as well as the cultural pattern of the working and wearing of gold as elite activities, meant that any one of the complex polities of the Amazon

---

[7] In particular Lake Guatavita in Colombia has repeatedly been the source of archaeological finds of gold work depicting a king and retinue aboard a raft, in a striking confirmation of the mythic account.

or Orinoco basins could have provided an empirical context for European readings of the El Dorado legend.

The final and still controversial location for El Dorado was in the uplands of Guayana where recent archaeological work has uncovered ancient and large-scale settlements, while the region's significance as a major intra-continental trading crossroads underlines the past ritual and political significance of upland peoples.[8] Walter Ralegh's name is most often associated with this location and his published work was the occasion for a number of depictions of El Dorado. Moreover, the connection of the Guayana region with the production of gold work can now also be better understood in archaeological terms since, in 1990, a sample of such gold work was recovered from precisely the area that Ralegh records as the site of the border of the domain of El Dorado, which he called—like most other writers—Manoa. In the last century anthropologists thought this region to be generally poor or marginal to human settlement in South America, with a corresponding scepticism as to its potential for producing complex societies. This has now to be re-evaluated in the light of emerging archaeological evidence (see note 2) while the persistent ideological desire for an El Dorado reveals the functions the idea served for Europeans, acting as a constant stimulus to further colonial conquest and occupation of the continent in a way that abstract appeals for 'exploration' or 'discovery' never could have.

The first extensive accounts of the existence of native gold work come from the Caribbean region during the early Spanish occupation. From these descriptions we learn that gold objects from the islands were distinguished from the gold alloy or *guanin* pieces that originated in Guayana. Naturally occurring gold-copper alloys are not present in the Caribbean islands, nor did the indigenous population use metallurgical techniques to produce such alloys. In the Antilles the technique was to beat out relatively pure nuggets of gold (called *caona* or *tuob*) into thin sheets, or to form nuggets into rings which were worn in the ear and nose. But the source of the gold-copper alloy *guanin* was, according to native testimony, to the southeast, in Guayana. In turn *guanin*, in the form of crescent shaped chest pendants called *caracoli*, was exchanged for *takua*, carved-jade often rendered in the form of frog-like pendants, which originated in the Amazon basin, especially the Trombetas River.

Gold and jade therefore had key roles to play in the long distance exchanges of elite groups between the Antilles and the Amazon, and the

[8] See Neil L. Whitehead, Michael J. Heckenberger, and George Simon, 'Materializing the Past among the Lokono (Arawak) of the Berbice River, Guyana', *Antrópologica*, 53, no. 114 (2011), pp. 23–59.

myth-cycles of both the Amazons and El Dorado are key to the interpretation of archaeological and historical evidence—particularly that concerning the production and exchange of *takua*, *guanin*, and *caracoli* as an elite activity in the Guayana region. It has been suggested that the *takua* are representative of the water, nature, and woman, and the *caracoli* are representative of the sun, culture, and man. This symbolic gender opposition is also strongly evinced in the gender polarity of the Arawak languages, and the myth of the Amazons or women from Matinino. In native interactions the Amazons are glossed as 'the women-without-men' and *Matinino* (often identified with the island of Martinique), along with the Amazon River, were thought to be places where they resided. The *takua* were also thought to mainly originate from the Amazon region and the archaeology and history of these objects certainly confirm this. By contrast, according to Ralegh, the *caracoli* pectorals and nose-plates were evidently at one time symbols of chiefly authority or elite lineage in a way that the curative greenstones were not. Ralegh also tells us that the *takua* were owned by 'every king or *Casique*' but that they were usually worn by their wives.[9] However, over time, and given the clear dangers of displaying gold, the *takua* became more generally worn as tokens of spiritual power or understanding. So too, native leadership itself became less dynastically based as the old elite genealogical structures were swept away by colonial conquest, and the *takua*, rather than *caracoli*, became associated with chiefly authority. This association was probably always present in the use of *takua* south of the Amazon, among the Tupian peoples, who called them *murayataka*.

Our understanding of this ritual and symbolic context of the exchange of gold work is deepened by analysis of the native use of gold on the Caribbean islands, especially through the writings of Father Ramón Pané.[10] His fifteenth-century account of native conceptions on *Aitij* (Hispaniola) tells us that in the origin myth of Antillean society *Guahayona*, culture-hero and source of ancestral authority for the native elite, took all the women from the islands to *Matinino* and then travelled on to the island of *Guanin*, 'origin' of metals, that is *caona* (pure gold) and *guanin* (gold alloy). In this way a close connection between the ancestors and golden metals is immediately established and was the reason for the noted link between the honorific titles of the elite and the names of metals. There was a similar association of chiefly authority and golden metals seen in the decorative

---

[9] Ralegh, *The Discoverie of the Large, Rich and Bewtiful Empire of Guiana*, chapter 24.

[10] See Neil L. Whitehead, *Of Cannibals and Kings: Primal Anthropology in the Americas*, University Park: Pennsylvania State University Press, 2011.

treatment of the skeletons of Warao chiefs from the Orinoco delta. Among the chieftains of Hispaniola we can recognise Caona-bo, meaning 'he who is like gold', and his wife *Ana-caona*; also *Turei-ga Hobin*, the honorific of the cacique Bohechio, meaning 'king as dazzling and heavenly as guanin'. On Puerto Rico among the names of the native provinces, often treated as equivalent to the personal names of caciques by the Spanish, we find *Guaynia, Guaynabo, Guayama*, and *Guayaney*, all containing the radical for *guanin* and the ancestor *Guahayona*. The 'name' (title) of the *acarewana* of the Yao, *Anacajoury*, reflects both the name of the ancestor who accompanied *Guayahona* to the isle of *guanin*, *Anacacuya*, and the meaning of that name as 'brilliance that guides'. Given the inter-changeability of the personal titles and names of leaders with the names of places, there is also a link to toponyms. The Arawakan word for gold, *caona*, and the Cariban word in the orthographic version *carocori*, also form linguistic radicals for the place names associated with gold working on Trinidad and in Orinoco recorded by Ralegh; for example, *Carowa, Paracow, Caroni, Caura*, and *Carricurina*.

So Ralegh's identification of these places, implying the occurrence of gold, was not suggestive for the reason that we might assume (that there was a connection between naming of place and its geological features), but rather because the toponyms were derived from the native association of political authority with the use of *guanin*. Despite the scepticism which has generally gone along with the evaluations of the written records, it has to be emphasised that in fact, as well as in mythology, the Europeans were directed by the *caciques* of Cuba, Hispaniola, and Puerto Rico towards the lesser Antilles (*Matinino*) and Guayana (isle of *Guanin*) as the source of gold, also indicating that in this direction lived the *canibales*. In the political ideologies of these island chieftains the first ancestor, *Guayahona*, when he left Hispaniola for *Matinino* and persuaded the women to accompany him, also forced them to abandon their husbands but bring with them their children, as well as a cargo of the narcotic snuff *digo*. They travelled to *Matinino* where they were entranced by the sight of beautiful sea-shells (*cobo*) which, following the example of *Guayahona*'s brother-in-law, they descended into the sea to admire. Here the women were left by *Guayahona*, who returned to Hispaniola with the first *guanin* and *cibas* (magic stones, that is *takua*). In other versions of this myth-cycle the fate of the children differs—either they are simply abandoned in a ditch at *Matinino* or they become frogs.[11] In this latter version there are strong thematic connections to both the *takua* and to the Amazons of the continent.

---

[11] Similar themes are present in Aztec mythology. For the Aztec Chalchiuhtlicue ('She of the Jade Skirt') was a goddess of all the waters and of storms as well as being

For the islanders the important feature of the myth was that it provided the ideological grounds for taking *Guayahona* to be not only the originator of political authority, but also the first to partly base this authority in exchanges with outsiders, the *caribe canibales*. In this light the myth-cycle as a whole may be said to represent the ideological underpinning of an elite trade in which drugs (*digo*), shell money (*cobo/quiriquiripa*), and persons (women and children) were exchanged for *guanin* and *takua*, the latter significantly being carved mostly in the form of frogs. In this context *Matinino* (Martinique), the 'island of women-without-men', represents the site of these exchanges, just as the land of the Amazons is the source for the 'greenstones' of Ralegh's account, and the *caribe canibales* emerge as economic or marital, but not gastronomic, consumers of persons. One might also note the further connection of *Matinino* with the Amazon myth cycle in the manner of origin of the *ciba*, that is from female water spirits. The continental *takua* were also said to be made by the 'water-mama', who to this day supplies the stones for smoothing pottery among native potters.

It is therefore significant that the initial establishment of many of the Spanish colonial enclaves mimicked this native political process through the exchanges made between Spanish and native leaders, matching these gold objects against steel tools and 'European *guanin*' in the form of hawk bells, rattles, and buckles made of brass. Indeed, along the Atlantic coast, even into the seventeenth century, golden artifacts were an important medium of exchange in both the surviving native economy and the burgeoning colonial one. The apparent willingness of native people to exchange gold work at rates the Europeans perceived as laughably favourable to themselves was actually not evidence of native commercial naiveté, but an indication of alternative economic values. These derived from cultural attitudes to metals where gold alloys were particularly valued for their brilliance and smell—*guanin* objects being sometimes referred to as *taguagua* after the odoriferous Caribbean plant of the same name—rather than their absolute gold content. For the same reasons—brilliance and smell—European alloys, especially brass, were valued as much, or more, than their native equivalents. Because of its otherworldly brilliance, the people of Cuba called it *turey*, a word for the most luminous part of the sky. The smell of brass, its reddish hue, its exotic origins, and iridescence, were all qualities that made brass a ritually important substance and therefore considered as sacred *guanin*. Local chieftains wore it in pendants and medallions to show their wealth,

---

associated with children and childbirth. She was also the wife/sister of the rain god, Tlaloc (himself associated with frogs), and she was the mother of Tecciztecatl, an Aztec moon spirit who was associated with sea shells, like the *cobo*.

influence, and connection to the supernatural realm. Elite women and children were buried with it.

Ralegh notes that, as a medium of exchange within the surviving native economy, the natives exchanged their carpentry for tobacco out of Trinidad and gold work out of Guayana, where it was also reported by Lawrence Keymis that gold images were 'everywhere current money'.[12] Whatever the ritual significance of gold objects, some native leaders were perfectly content to exchange them for the powerful political potentialities inherent in the control of the distribution of European manufactures. Moreover, the native store of gold in the sixteenth century was considerable enough to be used to finance the Spanish conquests in Orinoco, and overall the early descriptions of the region make it clear that gold work, in the form of pectorals and other bodily adornments, were common in Guayana.

Gold sources were also magical for the natives, just as they were mystical for the Europeans, and were usually guarded by spirit forces in the form of lizards or other ground reptiles. European minds imagined these native spirits as dragons since dragons were guardians of gold in Europe. So the issue of 'secrecy' affects our interpretations of reported native knowledge of gold sources, with the European conquerors inevitably becoming very aware of the difficulties of uncovering such 'secret' knowledge. This secrecy then becomes a main plank of the El Dorado legend as it has come down to us as a hidden city, a lost city, and so on, that is then miraculously discovered by adventurers. Once colonies had been established, the Europeans themselves, in a political imitation of native symbols of power, became suppliers of their versions of gold objects and generally used metal as a way of influencing native populations, for whom metals of all kinds, not just gold, had magical and symbolic properties.

Metalworking traditions persisted in Guayana into the eighteenth century, but mostly the production of silver items, rather than gold ones, given the dangers of displaying the latter in front of Europeans. Today silver is preferred to gold, owing to its association with 'spiritual light' and the association of gold with the yellow jaundice of disease stemming from the identification of historical epidemics with the European search for gold. In fact this association between the search for gold and the impact of strange diseases continues into the present as the whole of the highlands has become a mining area for gold and diamonds. The legend of El Dorado has proved to be true, but not as envisioned in that great and golden city of Manoa. Gold is strongly symbolic of all of the pre-Hispanic world and, as Michael

---

[12] Lawrence Keymis, *A Relation of the Second Voyage to Guiana*, London: Thomas Dawson, 1596, p. 44.

Taussig has noted, in the current moment the sign 'coca' is equated with that of 'gold' and has now become another facet of the unending conquest of South America based on the search for fabulous wealth and marvellous experience.[13]

But the Golden King has been changed by this unceasing violence and exploitation. In the poetry of Al Creighton, this transformation is a madness, with El Dorado now becoming:

> This madman,
> bound by the cult of vengeance to seek redress,
> knew a saner state once,
> before this rot and I was poisoned vicious,
>
> I am no longer what I seem,
> I don't suffer fools,
> I kill them like rats
> and envy other men their grief,
>
> But beware,
> this rage is real,
> do not believe it is a play
> because I sit with you in the audience
> like a spectator,
>
> And wait for proof,
> while men steal governments,
> make widows and reduce men to ghosts wondering,
> who shall revenge?
>
> The furious faculties of my guilty mind revolt,
> and I am mad, mad, mad ...[14]

If El Dorado was the very paradigm of limitless wealth and power, then the drug-lord, epitomised by Al Pacino in the cinematic character of 'Scarface',

---

[13] Michael Taussig, *My Cocaine Museum*, Chicago: Chicago University Press, 2004.
[14] 'The Mad Prince of Denmark' read by Al Creighton at the XVI International Poetry Festival of Medellín (24 June–2 July 2006); Creighton is a Guyanese poet and currently Dean of the School of Education and Humanities at the University of Guyana.

is his mad, modernist guise.[15] Anointed no longer with golden dust but smothered, choking, with the white powder of cocaine, such reflections, echoes, transmutations, revivals, revisions, and appropriations show the continuing force of the native cultural imaginary in the construction of the American Tropics. In this way the fabulous wealth and sacral ornamentation of the vanished native kings is supplanted by an imagination of Guayana as a zone of crazed violence and dissolution of self, illicit wealth, and relentless vengeance, marked now by the sign of kanaimà.

The sign of kanaimà

'My father was so Amerindian … he could kill and resurrect you in a day' (Patamuna Roger Edwin, 1995)

The shamanic complex of kanaimà has become a representation of the savage in both colonial and national cultures of Guayana.[16] Together with the more diffuse cannibal sign, kanaimà is used to construct a vision of the Satanic Majesty of sorcerers and dark shamans. This vision of a Satanic Majesty holding sway over indigenous cultures is used in turn to produce a Demonology of Development. This Demonology pictures tradition and ritual as nothing but superstition and primitiveness, serving the ghoulish and violent desires emanating from the Satanic Majesty of Kanaimà, the hidden and vengeful enemy of Development and Progress. This idea of Development, in western discourse, alludes to forms of both material and spiritual redemption and advancement, and is understood here as part of the colonial and national conquest and incorporation of autonomous communities under the power of the state and government.

Kanaimà is a form of mystical assault that ritually requires the extensive physical maiming of its victims in order that they may be produced as a divine food. This carnal violence, primarily a mutilation of mouth and anus, renders the victim near dead but the process of slow death that occurs allows the formation of the magic substance *maba* within the body of the victim. Kanaimà is currently a key cultural practice of the Patamuna, Akawaio and Makushi of the Guayana highlands, but it is important to notice that it is not just a form of internal dialogue amongst 'natives', but also enters

---

[15] *Scarface*, screenplay by Oliver Stone, directed by Brian da Palma, Universal Pictures, 1983.

[16] Neil L. Whitehead, *Dark Shamans: Kanaimà and the Poetics of Violent Death*, Durham: Duke University Press, 2002.

into the self-fashioning of the national societies of the Guianas, Venezuela, and Brazil. As a profoundly 'authentic' icon of Amerindian survival, it has been appropriated by the national societies of the region as a sign of their emplacement in the wild and alien landscapes of the 'interior' or 'deep bush'.

This idea of the 'interior' posits Guayana as the endpoint of exploration, the counterpoint of modernity and the obstacle to development. Accordingly, the language of conquest and occupation still suffuses the national imagining of this region and kanaimà comes to stand for that alterity. In turn, the encounter with kanaimà becomes a token of the traveller's—or anthropologist's or missionary's or miner's—penetration to that inner mystery. The Demon Landscape that comprises the zone of kanaimà is thus an intellectual construct, a physical space, and an aesthetic inspiration.

Contemporary Amerindian cultural practices have to be recognised as engaging with a wider cultural imaginary, no less than with the imaginary cartographies of the demonic that orientate national governments in their actions towards, and creation of, the indigenous. Thus, as in the case of the work of George Simon, a Lokono Arawak painter, or the Makushi sculptor Sydney Facundes, the invocation of kanaimà may also be a re-appropriation of the cannibal sign, as was the case for the Brazilian modernists, Mário de Andrade, and the *antrofagistas*.[17] Such cannibal constructions of the 'native' or 'indigenous', in public political discourse, the representations of the media, and in anthropological and ethnographic writing, have all served to enable and encourage violence against indigenous communities. From the initial charges of cannibalism made against Amazonian peoples in the sixteenth century to the supposed fierceness of the contemporary Yanomamö in Venezuela,[18] there has been a continuous external discourse on Guayanese savagery and wildness, most usually demonstrated through their supposed Satanic proclivities (shamanism) and demonic customs (cannibalism). No less relevant to the fate of native peoples today than it was five hundred years ago, this discursive production of 'native Guayana' continues to create a broad cultural framework in which violence against indigenous and marginalised persons can be more easily obscured or justified. As successive waves of spiritual and material development have pounded native and other

---

[17] Luís Madureira, 'Lapses in Taste: "Cannibal-tropicalist" Cinema and the Brazilian Aesthetic of Underdevelopment', in *Cannibalism and the Colonial World*, eds., Francis Barker, Peter Hulme, and Margaret Iversen, Cambridge: Cambridge University Press, 1998, pp. 110–125.

[18] The journalist Patrick Tierney's book *Darkness in El Dorado: How Scientists and Journalists Devastated the Amazon*, New York: W. W. Norton & Company, 2002, provides a controversial critique of this violent production of native peoples.

interior communities[19] but not yet destroyed their autonomy, this has led to the continuous ideological construction of indigenous peoples as obstacles to 'progress'. This is signalled by iconic cultural practices, such as kanaimà, that have allowed the governmental regimes to separate out the 'good' and the 'bad' Amerindian, as was the case with the ethnological categories of 'Arawak' and 'Carib'.[20]

In a more diffuse sense, as a result of the presence of Carib-speaking peoples throughout Guayana, the literary and ethnological production of 'the cannibal' has gone hand in hand with the military and political domination of the native population. The violence of conquest in the region mimetically referenced cannibalism as its justification, and representations of the native population suppressed description of Arawak torture and cannibalism, emphasising always the barbarity of the Carib. However, in response to this repeated failure of modernity to establish itself, a 'hyper-traditionality' (or perhaps a native fundamentalism) has emerged that is inimical to both external and indigenous notions of modernity and for which kanaimà is the signal. The external projection of kanaimà as a cultural tradition has therefore become increasingly entwined with its meaning for practitioners and their victims. So the kanaimà killer takes his place alongside the 'thug', 'bogeyman', 'cannibal', 'head-hunter', 'zombie' , 'vampire', and now 'terrorist' or 'pirate', as another ghoul in the colonial and modern nightmare of irrational, cultic violence that springs from enigmatic and atavistic cultural proclivities. Like vampires and these other ghouls, kanaimàs emerge at the intersection of rapidly changing cultural and economic regimes; like vampires, kanaimàs mediate the confrontation of local lives with invasive regional and global systems of political authority and economic exploitation; like vampires, kanaimàs speak with profound force to the cultural fears and anxieties of Euro-American mentalities. Refusing all tokens of modernity and scientific rationalism, the kanaimàs, like vampires, also appear to us as heroic and attractive figures both despite, and because of, their exotic violence.

As a result there has been a notable literary mediation of the idea of kanaimà, which is evident from its earliest poetical treatment by the missionary William Brett in his *Legends and Myths of the Aboriginal Indians of British Guiana* (1880). This work versifies various indigenous 'myths'

---

[19] Such as the descendants of maroons (rebel slaves) that can be found throughout Guayana as well as in Surinam, where they have received extensive scholarly attention.

[20] See Peter Hulme and Neil L. Whitehead, eds., *Wild Majesty. Encounters with Caribs from Columbus to the Present Day*, Oxford: Oxford University Press, 1992.

including Kanaimà, and Brett writes over eighty lines of verse (see Appendix I) in the following vein—

> From the base of high Roráima
> To the widespread Eastern sea,
> Votaries of dread Kanáima
> Track their victims secretly.
> Deadly vow must each fulfill,
> Real or fancied foe to kill ...
>
> One who passed us on the water,
> Had his victim lately slain;
> There triumphant, fresh from slaughter,
> He was hast'ning home again.
> Feathered crown adorned his head,
> Bright red spots his skin o'erspread—
>
> *Spots*, to show that, nightly ranging
> (So do their sorcerers declare),
> He, into a jaguar changing,
> Could his victims seize and tear.
> As the 'were-wolf' of the East
> Prowls, on human flesh to feast.

However, in current treatments kanaimà is inspiring in virtue of its very cultural opacity, as in the case of the poetry of Pascale Petit (1998) or Leah Fraser, a Guyanese poet who sent me the following poem about my own experiences in the Pakaraima highlands:

> *Kanaimà Man*
> Today I met a man who swore he'd seen an older truth.
> Deep in the Pakaraima where the haraballi touch the sky
> Sightless arrows fly - linking life to death,
> And back again.
> Shifting shapes and shadows
> The piya stalk the night,
> Stilling tongues that cry to know their fate.
> Armadillo fire burns bitter to the core,
> And beneath the baramalli's feet [21]

---

[21] *Baramalli* is a large tropical hardwood tree.

Honey flows from lifeless veins.

Today I met a man who swore he'd seen an older truth,
Dark and deadly as the forest's night.
Cosmic circles linked to form a chain,
We feed, are fed,
Then, eaten by the Gods
Who suck the honey from our veins
And crush our hearts and skulls to dust.
So too in turn the hunters track their prey
And from the forest's floor
The spirits eat their fill.

Kanaimà was also used as a literary trope by Rómulo Gallegos, the one-time President of Venezuela, in *Canaima* (1935), a novel set in the Caroni and Yuruari region during the 1930s. In Gallegos's writing 'Canaima' is the very spirit of the deep forest itself, not the elfin spirit of Petit's eco-fantasy, but a malignant 'goblin' whose realm we enter only with 'temerity' towards the forest. The result is to risk a loss of humanity, in the 'demon landscape' of the dark forest, which becomes an 'inhuman jungle'. Those who ever penetrate it begin to be 'something more or something less than men', until the intruder utters 'the words that set madness free—"We're lost"'.[22]

Gallegos defines 'Canaima' as: 'The devil ... of the Waikas, the frantic god, principle of evil and cause of all evils, [who] disputes the world with Cajuña, the good'.[23] 'Canaima' is the demon without a definite shape, who sets free in the heart of man the tempest of infrahuman elements. In this way, 'Canaima' for Gallegos acts as the trigger that unleashes an already formed human nature which contains the capacity for violence, whereas native theory sees kanaimà as a means to produce such violence. Gallegos also speaks of 'The obsession of penetrating it [the forest], errant as a goblin ...'[24] and so identifies 'Canaima' with both a spirit in the forest and the spirit which draws men to it. In this sense he sees Marcos Vargas, the protagonist of the novel, as mimetically assuming its forms, and so acquiring 'the barbaric experience of feeding himself with a piece of the prey ... unsalted and half roasted ... and later raw and bleeding', just like a jaguar.[25] For those who

---

[22] Rómulo Gallegos, *Canaima* [1935], trans. Jaime Tello, Norman: University of Oklahoma Press, 1984, pp. 177–179.
[23] Gallegos, *Canaima*, p. 181.
[24] Gallegos, *Canaima*, p. 204.
[25] Gallegos, *Canaima*, p. 207.

do not choose to initiate themselves in this way the pernicious influence of the kanaimà is expressed in more petty ways:

> the dehumanizing influence of the savage loneliness was producing in those men a somber tendency characteristic of the jungle ... a certain frenzy of cruelty, not ardent and impetuous as the one produced by open spaces, but, on the contrary, frightfully calm, of bestial abysses. Crimes and monstrosities of all kinds, narrated and commented with sadistic details, were almost the exclusive subjects of conversation ... Several of them, applying these crazy experiences to themselves, had self-inflicted wounds to become unable to work ... it was also the tempest of subhuman elements stirred by Canaima in the hearts of men.[26]

Thus, with an invocation of *The Tempest,* Gallegos conjures up that vivid Carib cannibal of the European imagination, Caliban, thus closing the poetical circle of savagery where it began.

As a literary device for suggesting the upwelling of atavistic and ancestral forces into the 'modern' world, kanaimà appears in Wilson Harris's 1964 short story 'Kanaima', first published in 1964, and in his novel *Palace of the Peacock* (1988).[27] This novel in turn inspired the mural which is at the entrance to the School of Education and Humanities at the University of Guyana, painted by the Amerindian artists George Simon, Philbert Gajadhar, and Anil Roberts in 2009. In an article for the *Stabroek News* Al Creighton has extensively discussed the relation between the painting and Harris's novel, with a particular focus on the shape-shifting figure of the kanaimà.[28] The persistent presence of the idea of kanaimà is therefore an important feature of Guyanese cultural life and, indeed, Wilson Harris's work in particular reflects this in many more ways than can be discussed here.[29] In the novels *Carnival* and *The Four Banks of the River of Space,* for example, the kanaimà plays a substantive role in the ordering of the narrative. Harris himself, in an essay significantly titled, 'Living Absences and Presences', explicitly discusses the role of kanaimà in his writing of

---

[26] Gallegos, *Canaima*, p. 220.

[27] Wilson Harris, 'Kanaima', in V. J. Ramraj, ed., *Concert of Voices,* Peterborough: Broadview, 1995, pp. 145–151; *Palace of the Peacock*, London: Faber and Faber, 1988.

[28] <http://www.stabroeknews.com/2009/features/06/28/artists%E2%80%99-homage-to-a-writer/> [22.4.2011].

[29] I am very grateful to Lori Shelbourn, who is currently preparing a doctoral thesis on the work of Wilson Harris, for her guidance and insight into this aspect of Harris's writing.

The Four Banks of the River of Space. In essence kanaimà is a sign of the activity rather than passivity of landscape, that contains a 'living deposit of the action of unconscious memory', which is mysterious and beyond language.[30] Kanaimà is a means through which such 'deposits' are made, and in concluding his essay Harris explicitly considers his vicarious encounter with kanaimà through his alter-ego in *The Four Banks*, the character Anselm. In ethnological terms Harris's understanding of kanaimà is limited and strikingly reflects that given by Gallegos. Harris writes: 'Kanaimà is the god of vengeance of Amerindian peoples, an evil god, it is said. I gathered he had had a long-standing feud with the Arekuna Indians who had wronged him, he claimed, and he had come to settle his account with them. He spirited away some of their able young men and women ... He speaks the language of the unconscious, eruptive elements...'. [31] Harris also alludes to the shape-shifting capabilities of kanaimà, in particular their appearance as familiar or closely related persons, a spirit force that animates such appearances as well as the physical landscape through flood or wind.

There are also more sensationalist presentations, such as in *The Skull of Kanaima*, a pulp fiction piece by the English author Victor Norwood. *The Skull of Kanaimà* actually makes no use at all of the imagery of kanaimà killing but uses the exoticism of the word to refer to a shrunken skull 'the size of a small orange' which is decorated with thousand-year-old inscriptions, made by a 'powerful witch-doctor'.[32] This talismanic object, having been stolen from a tribe who happens to occupy the site of a rich uranium deposit, then becomes the key to enabling Norwood's American and British heroes—Rocks O'Neill and Jim Trent—to outwit their Russian competitors in the South American jungle. In fact the figure of Jacare, Norwood's bid to create an American Tarzan, is the key protagonist and it seems clear that this work was written with possible film-rights in mind. Norwood also wrote his own account of British Guiana, *Jungle Life in Guiana* (1964), as well as *A Hand Full of Diamonds* (1960), *Man Alone! Adventures in the Jungles of British Guiana and Brazil* (1956) and *Drums Along the Amazon* (1974), recycling much of the same material for different audiences. However, Norwood's hypermasculinity,[33] as evidenced in the jaguar-killing prowess of

---

[30] Wilson Harris, 'Living Absences and Presences', in Vera Mihailovich Dickman, ed., *'Return' in Post Colonial Writing: A Cultural Labyrinth*, Amsterdam: Rodopi, 1994, p. 2.

[31] Harris, 'Living Absences and Presences', pp. 3–4.

[32] Victor Norwood, *The Skull of Kanaima*, London: Scion, 1951, p. 6.

[33] However, Norwood's hypermasculinity as evidenced in these works is curiously complemented by an interest in gender ambiguity shown in another work of his

Jacare, invokes the persistent presence of the shamanic were-jaguar in the visual and literary iconography of Guyana—a presence which has reached beyond the American Tropics, as in the case of the Ukrainian death-metal band Tesseract who had a hit with the track *Black Kanaimà* (see Appendix II) and which also uses the motif of kanaimà to reference the 'Obliteration of the Indians! Tropical death irruption!'

The American Tropic of Guayana: a *triste tropique* indeed, no longer the realm of golden kings, those warrior women and cannibals adorned with jade, but rather a space of death and exploitation in which kanaimà mimetically engages the violence of logging, mining, and drug-trafficking. So indeed darkness falls on El Dorado and, as the Ye'cuana say, the good people of the world, those still beneath the *tepuis* of Weyana, are still waiting to be born, but perhaps they never will ….

Appendix I

From W. H. Brett, *Legends and Myths of the Aboriginal Indians of British Guiana*. London: William Wells Gardner, 1880, pp. 152–154. This work versifies various indigenous 'myths' and in the section devoted to the 'Legends of the Acawoios' appears the following:

Kanáima

From the base of high Roráima
To the widespread Eastern sea,
Votaries of dread Kanáima
Track their victims secretly.
Deadly vow must each fulfill,
Real or fancied foe to kill.

He who that dread vow is taking,
Family and friends must leave;
Wife and children all forsaking,
No discharge can he receive.
Still around his victim's way,
Hovering night and day to slay.

If the victim warned of danger,

written under the pseudonym Mark Shane, *Sex Gauntlet to Murder*, London: Fabian, 1957, also released under the title *The Lady Was a Man*.

To some other place should fly,
Soon th'assassin, though a stranger,
Will to that retreat draw nigh,
Patiently he bides his time,
Waiting to commit the crime.

Stealthily each step he traces,
Hiding till he strikes the blow.
Poison in the mouth he places
Of his victim, lying low.
Then if found with swollen tongue,
None will know who did him wrong.

When the grave has closed upon him,
The destroyer hovers round:
Dread Kanáima's spell is on him;
By it he must still be bound,
Till he pierce, with pointed wood,
Through the grave, and *taste the blood.*

Stern Kanáima thus appeasing,
Who withdraws his direful aid,
All his horrid influence ceasing
When that off'ring has been made.
Uncontrolled, the votary then,
Goes, and lives with other men.

One who passed us on the water,[1]
Had his victim lately slain;
There triumphant, fresh from slaughter,
He was hast'ning home again.
Feathered crown adorned his head—
Bright red spots his skin o'erspread—

Spots, to show that, nightly ranging
(So do their sorcerers declare),
He, into a jaguar changing,
Could his victims seize and tear.[2]
As the 'were-wolf' of the East
Prowls, on human flesh to feast.

* * * * *

Should the victim 'scape him living,
Or, if dead, be borne away;
He, no horrid off'ring giving,
Finds Kanáima on him stay.
Still the spell upon him lies;
Mad, he wanders till he dies.

One, who sank with forests round him,
To our Mission hill was borne;
First, an ocelot, which found him,
Horribly his head had torn.
Head and hands he raised in pain,
Scared the beast, then sank again.

Sank--for life no longer striving,
Christian Indians found him then.
Arawâks, his strength reviving,
Bore him to his countrymen.
Healed and fed, Kanáima still,
Christians all he vowed to kill!

[1] Archdeacon Jones and myself, on the Upper Demerara, in 1865. That 'Kanáima' murderer, we found, had followed his victim and friends from the vicinity of Roráima to Georgetown and back, killing him on his return.

[2] A set of jaguar's claws, hung up in the sorcerers hut, have the same threatening signification.

Appendix II

Lyrics from TESSERACT 'Groundless Translethargical Groaning' demo 1992
(MC 2000—Bloodhead Productions)

Black Kanaima
Ritual dance accursed voice
Millions moans of Indians
Iron rumble with hawking of dog's
Feeling the death. Ceaseless

Jaguar's skull on long pole
Symbol of death and psychotic ghoul
Black Kanaima murder in him
Send to Indians emaciating dread

Wild jungle unnerving Indians
Owing to Kanaima incursion
Black vice born the fear
That live in the brain dungeons

Spacious virgin nature in night
Glimmer by death in ritual fight
Tribe wizard gabbing in dance
Blows of drum, calling to death!

Jaguar's skull on long pole
Symbol of death and psychotic ghoul
Black Kanaima murder in him
Send to Indians emaciating dread

Jaguar's skull on long pole
Throwing the power from eyehole
Dark energy from infernal skull
Burn flowing blood at human fall

Fume of burning blood
Above Amazonian forest
Throbbing according drum
Ritual drum of possessed wizard!

Earthquake
Rage of Kanaima
Flame from ground
Nowhere asylum

Sacrifice
Kanaima vengeance
Blood of child
Sacrilege vice

Obliteration of the Indians!
Tropical death irruption!

Jaguar's skull on long pole
Glimmer by empty of eyeholes
Show the fangs in frightful smile
Gnash under wind and wait for you die!

Suriname Literary Geography: The Changing Same

Richard Price and Sally Price

In a recent call for papers for a conference on Léon-Gontran Damas (hosted by the Postcolonial Research Group of the University of Antwerp in December 2008), the organisers asked: 'Why has Guyanese literature (in Dutch, French, and English) remained thus far overlooked, particularly within Caribbean scholarship and more generally speaking in postcolonial literary studies?'[1] If indeed literature from and about the Guianas has been overlooked, it is not because of its scarceness. Restricting ourselves for a moment to Suriname, the geographic centre of the Guianas, we would note that in 2002 the indefatigable Michiel van Kempen defended a nearly 1,500-page dissertation on Surinamese literature up to 1975, and a year later published an updated 1,400-page version, in two volumes, covering the whole history.[2] Including more than 100 pages of bibliography, it is both a monumental accomplishment and an engaging read, ranging from oral literature, including dance, theatre, and song (Carib, Arawak, Trio, Ndyuka, Saamaka, Creole, Hindustani, and Javanese), to all forms of written literature since the end of the sixteenth century.[3] The whole of the thick second volume is devoted to literature written since 1957 and, like the earlier volume, includes numerous word portraits of authors. Getting this book out in English would, in one fell swoop, bring Surinamese literature into critical

---

[1] <http://www.gensdelacaraibe.org/index.php?option=com_content&view=article& id=3283:pour-saluer-leon-damas-his-heirs-and-legacy-revisited-thirty-years-after-his-death&catid=355&Itemid=193> [22.5.2011].

[2] Michiel van Kempen, *Een geschiedenis van de Surinaamse literatuur*, band I: 1596–1957, band II: 1957–2000, Breda: Uitgeverij De Geus, 2003.

[3] Beginning in mid-2010, the people formerly known as 'Saramaka' began calling themselves, in their official documents in English, 'Saamaka', to conform to their own pronunciation.

285

dialogue with other Caribbean (and world) literatures and go a long way toward responding to the challenge posed by the Antwerp postcolonialists. It's not, then, the scarcity of literature, but rather mainstream scholars' non-mastery of the relevant languages as well as scholarly fashions, that has left 'Guyanese literature ... overlooked'.

Before beginning, a few words about how we situate ourselves in these geographic/literary spaces. Our own nostalgia for Suriname is always contrasted to our home base in seaside Martinique, where, as Derek Walcott writes, one has that 'sense of elation you get in the morning in the Caribbean ... the width of the ocean'.[4] The clarity of the green-blue water, through which you can see the rocks on the bottom of the sea, the warm, sensual trade winds, the luscious air, the hills behind hills behind hills on three sides, the black snow drifting down and depositing a fine layer of ash from cane fields burning on the other side of the island over the mountains—all this is where we start from, where we think from, where we write from. This contrasts, for us, with the firmly continental world of the Guianas, whether the spectacular rivers and forests of Suriname or the urban squalor of Paramaribo: equatorial, damp, hot, and largely still—no hurricane ever touches there, not to mention trade winds. And the sea, as one encounters it at the mouth of the Suriname or the Marowijne, washes an always muddy coast, stretching all the way to the mouth of the Amazon— mangroves, mud flats, the detritus from the great rivers that flow northeast from the Orinoco to the Amazon, leaving the seaside brown and ugly, a place of murk and miasma, what early travellers called 'The Wild Coast'.[5]

The relationship between Suriname and the other two Guianas has changed through time. When J. J. Hartsinck published his massive historical, geographical, and ethnological *Beschrijving van Guiana* in 1770, he included in his subtitle 'Essequebo, Demerary, Berbice, and Suriname' and there is an additional chapter on French Guiana—indeed his frontispiece map covers the region from just north of the mouth of the Orinoco to just south of the mouth of the Amazon.[6] But by the end of the eighteenth century, most

---

[4] Derek Walcott, 'Reflections on *Omeros*', *The South Atlantic Quarterly*, 96 (1997), pp. 229–246, at 235.

[5] This paragraph is adapted from Richard Price, *Travels with Tooy: History, Memory, and the African American Imagination*, Chicago: University of Chicago Press, 2008, p. 13.

[6] J. J. Hartsinck, *Beschrijving van Guiana, of De wilde kust in Zuid-Amerika, betreffende ... de bezittingen der Spanjaarden, Franschen en Portugeezen en voornaamelyk de volksplantingen der Nederlanderen, als Essequebo, Demerary, Berbice, Suriname ... Waarby komt, eene verhandeling over den aart en de gewoontes der neger-slaven....*, Amsterdam: Gerrit Tielenburg, 1770.

writers clearly separated out from one another Suriname, French Guiana, and those Dutch colonies that had effectively become by that time British Guiana. In the early years, there was a certain amount of cross-language plagiary and bowdlerisation—George Warren's 1667 *Impartial Description of Suriname* was plagiarised by Adriaan van Berkel in his 1695 *Amerikaansche voijagien*,[7] large portions of Hartsinck were simply set in French (without acknowledgement or citation) in Accarias de Sérionne's 1778 *La richesse de la Hollande*,[8] and even J. G. Stedman, in his famous *Narrative*, lifted a good deal of Hartsinck for his lengthy description of Maroon history.[9] But subsequently, with a few notable exceptions,[10] the literature on the three Guianas has tended to restrict itself by political and linguistic boundaries: English for British Guiana/Guyana, French for Guyane (French Guiana), and Dutch for Suriname.

*

Two major tensions have marked the literature on Suriname since Europeans and their descendants first began describing the place. The natural environment appears alternatively as a menacing jungle (home to barbaric primitives) and an edenic paradise (inhabited by Noble Savages). The master/slave relationship is depicted either in terms of brutality/rebellion or of paternalism/docility. These tensions, and their linked tropes, constitute the changing same of our title.[11] A related tension, which emerges from these earlier oppositions, concerns contemporary realities. Present-day Suriname is at times depicted as an idyllic land of ethnic harmony and ecological riches

---

[7] Adrian van Berkel, *Amerikaansche voijagien, behelzende een reis na Rio-de-Berbice, enz., en na de colonie van Suriname*, Amsterdam: Johan ten Hoorn, 1695.

[8] J. Accarias de Sérionne, *La richesse de la Hollande*, London, aux Depens de la Compagnie, 1778.

[9] John Gabriel Stedman, *Narrative of a Five Years Expedition Against the Revolted Negroes of Surinam*, Newly Transcribed from the Original 1790 Manuscript, Edited, and with an Introduction and Notes, by Richard Price and Sally Price, Baltimore: Johns Hopkins University Press, 1988.

[10] The most prominent are Nassy's late eighteenth-century history of Suriname, in French, which was a preferred language of the local intelligentsia of the day: David de Ishak Cohen Nassy et al., *Essai historique sur la colonie de Surinam*, Paramaribo, 1788, and the Belgian P. J. Benoit's nineteenth-century book on Suriname, also in French: P. J. Benoit. *Voyage à Surinam: description des possessions néerlandaises dans la Guyane*, Bruxelles: Société des Beaux-Arts, 1839.

[11] This felicitous expression was first used by Amiri Baraka to refer to the development of African American music: LeRoi Jones, *Black Music*, New York: William Morrow, 1967.

and at others as a lawless cesspool of crime, corruption, and despoilation of the environment. Following a thumbnail introduction to these tensions, this essay focuses on some eighteenth-century texts where they come into play, and ends by evoking a different, non-Western representational perspective on this same geographical space.

The menacing jungle vs. the bountiful rainforest

Stedman's *Narrative* overflows with both of these tropes. First the menacing jungle: his description of the forest rarely goes for more than a few paragraphs without evoking one or more of the menaces that he met at every turn—ringworm, running sores and ulcers, blood-sucking vampire bats, frenzy fevers, scurvy, yaws, leprosy, parasitic worms, dropsy, and bloody boils, together with quagmires, both torrential rains and life-threatening dry spells, and even 'hurricanes'. Larger-than-life insects are a frequent contributor to this litany: 'So very thick were the Musquitoes now that by Clapping my two hands against each other I have kill'd in one Stroke to the number of 38 upon my honour'.[12] There are moments when the tempestuous natural environment is further darkened by the human element. During one night on the Cassipora Creek, for example, he

> past such a Night as no Pen can discribe being crowded with all Sorts of People, the Seek groand, the Jew prayd, the Soldiers Swore, the Negroes beg'd, the Women Sung the Child Skweek'd the fire Smoaked, the Rains poured down and the whole Stunk to such a Degree that I vow to God I began to think myself little better off than in the black Hole of Calcutta.[13]

Or, to skip right up to the late twentieth century, here is Alex Haley (author of *Roots*) describing his friends' expedition to the Saamakas in the 1970s:

> As extremely nervous passengers in dugout canoes, they went skimming through treacherous rapids, watching the thick boulders against which obviously any collision would immerse all hands into waters abounding with man-eating piranha—not to mention their near panic each time the dugouts passed under overhanging jungle vines and foliage from which large snakes could fall into the dugouts.[14]

---

[12] Stedman, *Narrative*, p. 127.
[13] Stedman, *Narrative*, p. 134.
[14] Alex Haley, in S. Allen Counter and David L. Evans, *I Sought My Brother: An*

On the other side of the coin, the trope of the magnificent forest shows
similar persistence through time, from Stedman's romantic descriptions

> Most Enchanting Were some Parts of the Forrest which we Past during
> this March to Which the dry Season much Contributed And Where
> Simple Nature greatly out Shone and Overpast the most Strenuous
> Endeavours of Art, Such as Open green Savannah's interspear[s]ed
> with Meandring brooks of Limpid Watter, the Borders Adorn'd with
> Rural flowers, While here and there Small Clumps of Elegant Shrubs,
> or a Single Beautiful Tree Scorn'd to be left Growing Designedly to
> Enrich the Scene. The Whole Surrounded by a Vast Wood of Lofty
> Palmetos, Waving their Sea-Green Foliage above the Variegated Copses
> of Never-fading Verdure, blossom, & Fruit, as if to invite the Panting
> Wanderer Under its Cooling Shades … One Universal Silence Reigning
> All Around[15]

to those of the twentieth century, where the discourse often takes on an
ecological edge:

> Chuck [Hutchinson, senior director of conservation and tourism
> planning with Conservation International] tells us that the tourism
> centre [in the rainforest, upriver] … epitomizes the new conservation
> economy and gives hope for a sustainable future in South America.
> The Amazon forest might be a dying animal—in Brazil, a few hundred
> kilometers to the south, it is already far gone—but here, on the Guiana
> Shield, there is still hope. As the conservationist, the ecotourist, and
> humanity itself stumbles after Eden, Suriname serves as a quiet example
> of all we've got left to save.[16]

During the Jazz Age of the 1920s and 1930s, fascination with the 'jungle'
and the 'negro' helped to shape images of Suriname. John Vandercook's
Tom-Tom, a 1926 travelogue about Saamakas that anthropologists Melville
and Frances Herskovits carried with them to Suriname in 1928, preached
that 'The civilized negro must lose his contempt for his "heathen" brethren
in Africa and in the jungles of … Suriname. He must learn that the fathers
of the race had and still possess blessed secrets, wonderful lores, and great

---

Afro-American Reunion, Cambridge: MIT Press, 1981, p. x.

[15] Stedman, *Narrative*, pp. 447–448.

[16] Andrew Westoll, *The Riverbones: Stumbling After Eden in the Jungles of Suriname*,
Toronto: Emblem Editions, 2008, p. 8.

philosophies, that rank the jungle negro's civilisation as the equal, and in many respects the superior, of any way of life that is to be found anywhere in the world'.[17] The more ethnographic accounts of the Herskovitses, *Rebel Destiny* and *Surinam Folk-lore*,[18] and their friend the physician Morton Kahn, *Djuka*,[19] veer between science, romance, and sensationalism but are strongly influenced by this 1920s sensibility. The 1930s also saw sensationalised images of Maroons in Hollywood films. *Too Hot to Handle* (1938), starring Clark Gable and Myrna Loy, featured Matawai Maroons who were turned into veritable Hollywood savages, speaking a made-up primitive language, dancing in what appears to be North American Indian choreography, and dressed in what look like costumes for *King Solomon's Mines* (ostrich feathers and the like). *Land of the Djuka*, a related ten-minute clip presented as 'news', reeks of Vandercookean discourse.[20] A decade later, the Brazilian press offered similarly sensational commentary on Pierre Verger's photos taken during his brief stay among the Ndyuka and which were published under the headline: 'The most primitive of all the black tribes in the world'.[21]

The space of death, torture and heroic resistance vs. the idyllic plantation

Aphra Behn provides the earliest of iconic Suriname images of torture and resistance in her fictional 1688 *Oroonoko*:

> He [Oroonoko-Caesar] had learned to take Tobacco; and when he was
> assur'd he should die, he desir'd they would give him a Pipe in his
> Mouth, ready lighted; which they did: And the Executioner came, and

---

[17] John W. Vandercook, '*Tom-Tom*', New York: Harper & Brothers, 1926, p.xv. The book is filled with Maroon-as-Noble-Savage howlers such as: 'So vain are the [Saamakas] of their magnificent physiques that all young men who do not attain a stature of at least six feet are driven out to die' (pp. 227–228).

[18] Melville J. Herskovits and Frances S. Herskovits, *Rebel Destiny: Among the Bush Negroes of Dutch Guiana*, New York: McGraw-Hill, 1934, and *Suriname Folklore*, Columbia: University Contributions to Anthropology, 27, New York: Columbia University Press, 1936. See also Richard Price and Sally Price, *The Root of Roots: Or, How Afro-American Anthropology Got Its Start*, Chicago: Prickly Paradigm Press/ University of Chicago Press, 2003.

[19] Morton C. Kahn, *Djuka: The Bush Negroes of Dutch Guiana*, New York, Viking, 1931.

[20] James A. Fitzpatrick, *Dutch Guiana—'Land of the Djuka'*, MGM, 1933. Watch it at: <http://www.youtube.com/watch?v=B3AfV__zcjo&eurl=http://sranan-news.blogspot>.

[21] *Diario da Noite*, 1 December 1948. See R. Price et al., *Pierre Verger, un pont au dessus de l'Atlantique*, Cayenne: DRAC Guyane, 2009.

first cut off his Members, and threw them into the Fire; after that, with an ill-favour'd Knife, they cut off his Ears and his Nose, and burned them; he still smoak'd on, as if nothing had touched him; then they hack'd off one of his Arms, and still he bore up, and held his Pipe; but at the cutting off the other Arm, his head sunk, and his Pipe dropt, and he gave up the Ghost, without a Groan, or a Reproach ... They cut Caesar [Oroonoko] into Quarters, and sent them to several of the chief Plantations.[22]

These are quickly followed by descriptions, including eyewitnessing, of similar scenes by J. D. Herlein (1718) and Stedman (1790),[23] the latter accompanied by William Blake's oft-reproduced engravings,[24] as well as Voltaire's well-known 'Suriname' passage from *Candide* (1759):

As they drew near the town they came upon a Negro lying on the ground wearing only half his clothes, that is to say, a pair of blue cotton drawers; this poor man had no left leg and no right hand. 'Good heavens!' said Candide to him in Dutch, "what are you doing there, my friend, in that horrible state?"

'I am waiting for my master, the famous merchant Monsieur Vanderdendur'.

'Was it Monsieur Vanderdendur', said Candide, 'who treated you in that way?'

'Yes, sir', said the Negro, 'it is the custom. We are given a pair of cotton drawers twice a year as clothing. When we work in the sugar mills and the grindstone catches our fingers, they cut off the hand; when we try to run away, they cut off a leg. Both these things happened to me. This is the price paid for the sugar you eat in Europe'.[25]

---

[22] Aphra Behn, 'The History of Oroonoko; or, the Royal Slave' (1688), in *All the Histories and Novels Written by the Late Ingenious Mrs. Behn, Intire in Two Volumes*, London: 1722, pp. 199–200.

[23] J. D. Herlein, *Beschryvinge van de Volk-plantinge Zuriname*, Leeuwarden: Meindert Injema, 1718, p. 117. Stedman, *Narrative*, pp. 546–549; see also p. 103.

[24] Stedman, *Narrative*, p. 548; see also p. 105.

[25] Voltaire, *Candide*, trans. Richard Aldington, in *The Portable Voltaire*, ed., Ben Ray Redman, New York: Penguin, 1977, pp. 229–328, at 281–282. The historical truth of the Behn-Voltaire-Stedman vision of Suriname slavery as having been unusually brutal has been questioned (as being politically motivated) by Gert Oostindie in *Het paradijs overzee: De 'Nederlandse' Caraïben en Nederland*, Amsterdam: Bert Bakker, 1997, pp. 68–107, but after this critique was itself called into question it was not included

Visions of the idyllic plantation appear quite early in Suriname, as elsewhere in the Caribbean ('delicate engravings of sugar mills and harbors, of native women in costume ...'[26]) but the iconic figure remains Stedman's happy slave family, immortalised in William Blake's engraving that accompanies Stedman's description:

> a Negro Family in that State of Tranquil Happiness to Which they are all entitled When they are Well treated by their Owners ... he Carrys a Basket with Small Fish on his Head & a net, While a large Fish is in his Hand, All Caught by Himself; & While his Wife /who is Pregnant/ is employ'd in Carrying Different kinds of Fruit, Spinning a Thread of Cotton and Comfortably Smoking her pipe of Tobacco—Still besides All Which She has a boy on her back And another Playing by her Side—
>
> Under Such a mild Government no Negroes work is more than a Healthy Exercise, which ends with the Setting sun, Viz at 6. O'Clock & When the Rest of the time is his Own, Which he employs in Hunting, And Fishing, Cultivating his Little Garden, or making Baskets, Fishnets &c for Sale; With Which Money he buys a Hog, Sometimes a Couple, or a Quantity of Fowls or Ducks, All Which he Fattens with the Spontaneous Growth of the Soyl, Without they Cost him eyther Cash, or much Trouble & which in the End Afford him Considerable Profit Thus Pleasantly Situated he is Exempt from every Anxiety, And looks up to his Master as the Common Protector of him and his Family, Whom he Adores not from Fear or Flattery but from a Conviction of his being the Object of his Care and Attention—He Breathes in a Luxorious Warm Climate like his Own, thus Wants no Cloaths besides Which incumberance & Expence, he Saves the Time of dressing, Undressing, Washing &c, & enjoys much more Health and Pleasure by Going naked[27]

Stedman drew on both of these tropes liberally, and subsequent authors returned to them again and again, adopting his engravings to illustrate slavery elsewhere in the Americas and making them the most widely reproduced images in the literature.[28]

---

in the English-language version of the book: *Paradise Overseas*, Oxford: Macmillan Caribbean, 2005.

[26] Derek Walcott, *The Antilles: Fragments of Epic Memory. The Nobel Lecture*, New York: Farrar, Straus and Giroux, 1992 [unpaginated].

[27] Stedman, *Narrative*, pp. 534–536.

[28] Recently, a major exhibition in Amsterdam, 'Black is Beautiful: Rubens to Dumas', was criticised for sanitising Dutch depictions of blacks through history, with the set-piece example being the choice to show the Stedman/Blake image depicting the

The multi-ethnic paradise vs. the contemporary narcocracy

Depictions abound of contemporary Suriname as a peaceful, multiethnic democracy with immense natural beauty, one of the world's only untouched tropical forests, indigenous and Maroon populations eager to be visited, and an exciting, historic capital city. But equally common are descriptions of the same society as a narcocracy run by thuggish politicos involved in the international arms and drug trade, who traffic in under-the-table deals granting mining and timber concessions to shady multinational companies from China, Malaysia, Indonesia, Canada, and elsewhere, with the city (and parts of the interior) now overrun by Brazilian goldminers, Dominican and other prostitutes, with wild-west levels of violence, and with casino gambling playing a major role in international money laundering.

In November 2008, as we were drafting this paper, we saw the contrast in two examples. Suriname's leading newspaper reported that

> World leaders and business representatives congratulated President Ronald Venetiaan on the way that his government managed the peaceful coexistence of different peoples in Suriname. These compliments came after Venetiaan had presented Suriname as a multiethnic land to the world leaders conference [attended by, among others, former president Bill Clinton] sponsored by the Club of Madrid.[29]

And Andrew Westoll published an account of five months travelling through what the book's cover describes as 'the most surreal country in South America' that details the full range of modern horrors.[30] His take on the kind of ecotourism proposed by Conservation International:

> Ecotourism here looks like a new form of imperialism. The new visitor's centre [at Raleigh Falls, Suriname], financed by money from Wal-Mart and Intel, will dwarf the very forest it was built to promote. Soon, it will host an internet café, crowds of Dutch tourists drinking Coca-Cola, hordes of European teenagers performing cannonballs into the water

---

Loango slave family but none of the tortures or executions (see 'The Schwartzlist 291. Image of the Beautiful Black', <http://www.gsah.nl/schwartzlist/?id=127> [24.6.2012].

[29] Eric Mahabier, 'Club de Madrid lovend over Surinames multi-etniciteit', *De Ware Tijd*, 15 November 2008.

[30] Westoll, *The Riverbones*.

and getting high on the rocks, gaggles of young women on vacation looking to bed a wild, primitive Maroon.[31]

*

Suriname's eighteenth century began with a famous publication by a female pioneer, Maria Sibylla Merian's *Metamorphosis Insectorum Surinamensium*.[32] Recent attention to this work has been inflected with late twentieth-century concerns that turn it in curious directions. A decade ago, distinguished historian Natalie Zemon Davis devoted a third of her *Women on the Margins* to Merian, depicting her, as well as the African slave women and Amerindian women who served as her guides and mentors, as feminists avant-la-lettre.[33] But as anthropologists, what strikes us reading Merian's book is how surprisingly little ethnographic description it contains about women or men, how very few mentions there are about Africans and Amerindians or, for that matter, any aspects of life in the colony.

Consider the much-cited passage about the way Amerindian and African women used the seeds of the *flos pavonis* plant to induce abortions, allowing them to prevent their offspring from being born into slavery or even to allow adult suicide.[34] It is this single three-sentence-long passage that carries almost all the weight of Merian's recently-forged reputation as an ethnographer and proto-feminist. Given that she spent two years in Suriname, this seems to us a pretty thin reed. A recent book-length assessment by naturalist Kim Todd sticks more closely to Merian's entomological and literary efforts, portraying her as a naturalist's naturalist, a person who insisted on the ecological contextualisation of her discoveries (well before it was the fashion), taking care, for example, to place a particular butterfly on a particular plant in particular surroundings.[35] Writing about Merian's *flos pavonis* passage, Todd observes that it is 'a rare glance up from her pigments and magnifying glass', adding that 'it's the only time ... that Merian describes any conditions of human society in Surinam'.[36] So, while we can salute Merian as a pioneer in natural history observation, we would caution against

---

[31] Westoll, *The Riverbones*, pp. 12–13.

[32] Maria Sibylla Merian, *Metamorphosis Insectorum Surinamensium ofte Verandering der Surinaamsche Insecten*, Amsterdam: 1705.

[33] Natalie Zemon Davis, *Women on the Margins: Three Seventeenth-Century Lives*, Cambridge: Harvard University Press, 1997.

[34] Merian, *Metamorphosis*, commentary on Plate XLV.

[35] Kim Todd, *Chrysalis: Maria Sibylla Merian and the Secrets of Metamorphosis*, New York: Harcourt, 2007.

[36] Todd, *Chrysalis*, p. 180.

ideological impositions from the present in interpreting her scant remarks on the society and on the individuals who surrounded her.

Shortly after Merian's return from Suriname, one of her sponsors and friends from Amsterdam, Jonas Witsen, sent the artist Dirk Valkenburg out to the colony in part to make paintings of his several plantations there. In 1983, *First-Time* was published with Valkenburg's *Slave Dance* (1707) on the cover,[37] launching a set of commentaries that attempted to read the painting as ethnographic text.[38] As Elmer Kolfin claims, 'This is probably the very first time that a black community in the New World is represented in such a detailed way in its social context'.[39] Valkenburg's depiction, then, is in some way the human equivalent of the ecological representations that Merian made of insects. What it offers us are human beings in an ethnographically contextualised setting, not isolated portraits or caricatures, even if certain features of seventeenth-century Dutch genre painting, such as the man vomiting or the couple kissing, are also present.

We are at a 'play' organised by enslaved African Americans—a dance/drumming/singing performance in honour of the gods—dominated by the massive snake-god drum, the *agidá*. People are depicted wearing the clothes that, as we know from written sources, slaves wore—and that their Maroon descendants still wear today: loincloths, wrap skirts, fanciful hats, necklaces, and metal earrings. They drink from calabash bowls and use gourds for carrying water. Some of the women have *kammbá* on belly and arms, decorative cicatrisations that Maroons associate with eroticism and beauty. The postures of the people who are standing and dancing are true to life—for example, the two men dancing at one another in the *susa* style of modern Maroons. A woman wipes the sweat from a drummer's face with a handkerchief, and two women carry babies tied to their backs, exactly as is done today. There are several tobacco pipes, which were used by enslaved men and women as one of their few permitted pleasures. From our Saamaka Maroon friends, we know that the ancestors of the large Dombi clan of Saamakas escaped from this exact plantation (Palmeneribo-Surimombo) five years after the painting was made, suggesting that many of the individuals it depicts were among those who rebelled and chose freedom in the forests

---

[37] Richard Price, *First-Time: The Historical Vision of an Afro-American People*, Baltimore: Johns Hopkins University Press, 1983. The painting hangs in the Royal Museum of Fine Arts, Copenhagen. The best reproduction known to us is in Sally Price and Richard Price, *Les arts des Marrons*, La Roque d'Anthéron: Vents d'ailleurs, 2005, p. 168.

[38] Davis, *Women on the Margins*, pp. 190–191. Elmer Kolfin, *Van de slavenszweep & de Muze*, Leiden: KITLV Uitgeverij, 1997, pp. 23–29.

[39] Kolfin, *Van de slavenszweep*, p. 25.

over a life in slavery. (As a Saamaka Dombi, descended from these people on this plantation, told a Dutch government official in 1917: 'The silk-cotton tree with the large iron ring where our forefathers were attached for punishment is still standing there'.)[40] This extraordinary painting manages to encompass both the trope of the idyllic plantation (its ostensible intent) and (unknowingly to the painter) the only contemporary representation ever made of enslaved men and women, some of whom were already planning their rebellion and escape into the forest to become Saamaka Maroons.

Here, as with Merian's paintings, there's a temptation to read present ideologies into the past. In commenting on this painting, Natalie Davis asks us to look at the woman sitting in the foreground. 'She is pensive and sober', she writes, 'as she looks beyond our viewer's eye ... perhaps she is waiting for the god to come ... [She is] the kind of woman who might have told Maria Sibylla Merian about the hardships of slavery'.[41] Personally, we doubt the woman would have told Maria Sibylla much of anything, as that venerable lady would hardly have consorted with field slaves, such as those depicted here. So we would prefer to leave Merian to her beloved caterpillars and butterflies and the enslaved dancers to their dreams of freedom.

*

John Gabriel Stedman's *Narrative* towers over the literature on Suriname in the late-eighteenth century. During his four-year stay, Stedman's ongoing and intimate dealings with members of all social classes, from the governor and the wealthiest planters to the most oppressed slaves, gave him special opportunities to observe and describe the full panorama of life in the colony. The *Narrative* consists of a half-dozen interwoven strands: Stedman's romance with the slave Joanna and his efforts to gain her freedom; the military campaigns against the rebel slaves; his relations with other soldiers, particularly his commanding officer; the description and investigation of exotic flora and fauna; the description of Amerindian and African slave life; most important, the description and analysis of relations between planters and slaves—all structured by a chronological framework taken from his Suriname diaries. It stands as one of the richest, most vivid accounts ever written of a flourishing slave society.

Since the publication of our critical edition twenty years ago, a number

---

[40] See Price, *First-Time*, pp. 108–111, where other Valkenburg plantation depictions are also reproduced and discussed.
[41] Davis, *Women on the Margins*, p. 191.

of scholars have engaged the *Narrative*.[42] Here, we take up two of the more recent challenges, the first dealing with torture and resistance, the second with the relationship between Stedman and Joanna.

For twenty-first-century historians, any attempt to interpret the systematic use of torture and terror in eighteenth-century plantation societies begs two theoretical/methodological questions. Can we understand, much less re-present, such phenomena given that, as Michael Taussig puts it, 'terror makes mockery of sense making?'[43] Can we, in the current epistemological and moral climate of postcolonialism, legitimately explore and re-present the African American past at all?

Jamaican anthropologist David Scott has been raising the latter question with insistence.[44] Singling out the work of Melville Herskovits and Richard Price, he argues that 'both turn on a distinctive attempt to place the "cultures" of the ex-African/ex-slave in relation to what we might call an authentic past, that is, an anthropologically identifiable, ethnologically recoverable, and textually re-presentable past'.[45] He recommends against such futile and perhaps even morally suspect efforts to represent or verify or corroborate 'authentic Afro-American pasts' ('what really happened'), instead suggesting that scholars focus on 'discourse'—how African Americans in various parts of the hemisphere envision and talk about and act in terms of their pasts.[46] In a similar postcolonial spirit, Marcus Wood reads representations by Stedman and Blake of slaves under torture as if what really matters (or what interests him, or all that perhaps is legitimately recoverable) is, once again, discourse—deconstructing the eighteenth-century author's or artist's intent, intellectual influences, audience reactions, and so forth.[47]

Wood's reading of Stedman claims that his depiction of tortures portrays

---

[42] One of the more interesting discussions, focusing on Blake's illustrations, is Debbie Lee, *Slavery & the Romantic Imagination*, Philadelphia: University of Pennsylvania Press, 2002, pp. 89–119.

[43] Michael Taussig, *Shamanism, Colonialism, and the Wild Man: A Study in Terror and Healing*, Chicago: University of Chicago Press, 1987, p. 132.

[44] David Scott, 'That Event, This Memory: Notes on the Anthropology of African Diasporas in the New World', *Diaspora*, 1 (1991), pp. 261–284, and David Scott, *Refashioning Futures: Criticism After Postcoloniality*, Princeton: Princeton University Press, 1999.

[45] Scott, 'That Event', 263.

[46] For a discussion of Scott's criticisms, see Richard Price, 'On the Miracle of Creolization', in Kevin A. Yelvington, ed., *Afro-Atlantic Dialogues: Anthropology in the Diaspora*, Santa Fe: SAR Press, 2006, pp. 113–145.

[47] Marcus Wood, *Blind Memory: Visual Representations of Slavery in England and America, 1780–1865*, New York, Routledge, 2000.

'a fantasy of complete insensitivity [on the part of the victims] ... an inability to suffer which is inhuman' and even that 'Stedman's set piece descriptions of the torture of black men present the victims as dropping into a nihilistic buffoonery'. He goes so far as to write of 'the disempowering aspects of Stedman's accounts'.[48] We would opt to take Stedman's descriptions of resistance under torture rather more literally, noting that with all Wood's concern about discourse (and Foucault), he never tries to understand what the victims (except, perhaps, as generalised, unhistoricised human beings) might have been thinking and feeling and acting in terms of. When he writes, 'The black male victim in Stedman's writing is an involved parody of the controlled violence of European torture', he is denying the possibility that parodic agency (and the ability to enact an ultimate act of resistance) could be the prerogative of the victim and not just a device of the clever writer's imagination. We have elsewhere tried to show that black stoicism in the face of whitefolks' tortures is neither 'buffoonery' nor 'gallows humor' but can be read, when compared to depictions of black pain in the face of torture mandated by the black community, as an extreme case of resistance.[49] Our own claim is that the Stedman/Blake depictions of the deaths of Neptune (on the rack) and the anonymous black man (on the gallows) involve more than a trope, and that we can legitimately read in these representations (combining them with other types of contemporary evidence, and fully accepting the problematic nature [the inevitable constructedness and perspectivality and incompleteness] of available historical and ethnological 'sources') something of value about the actors' mind-sets, and not just those of the observers.[50] What is at stake here is not just the interpretations of modern literary critics, who might be considered consummate outsiders to the eighteenth-century world of Suriname slavery. It is also the interpretations of the black actors and their descendants who participated in that world. The fact that Maroons continue to recount folktales with the explicit moral that survival (and triumph!) depends on refusing to accept the whiteman's definition of the situation, even (or especially) when he brandishes the power of execution

---

[48] Wood, *Blind Memory*, pp. 231–234.

[49] Richard Price, 'Dialogical Encounters in a Space of Death', in John Smolenski and Thomas J. Humphrey, eds., *New World Orders: Violence, Sanction, and Authority in the Colonial Americas*, Philadelphia: University of Pennsylvania Press, 2005, pp. 47–65.

[50] Michel-Rolph Trouillot's warning about African American historiography may be worth repeating: 'As social theory becomes more discourse-oriented, the distance between data and claims in debates about creolization ... increases. Historical circumstances fall further into a hazy background of ideological preferences': see 'Creolization on the Edges: Creolization in the Plantation Context', *Plantation Society in the America*, 5 (1998), pp. 8–28, at 15.

and torture, stands as persuasive evidence that there is more involved here than modern critics have allowed.[51]

We would also suggest that Mary Louise Pratt, who says almost nothing about Stedman's depiction of slavery and instead focuses on the story of his romance with Joanna, uses the *Narrative* for rhetorical purposes that add little to our understanding of its broader significance.[52] She treats the story as an exemplar of a common late eighteenth-century 'transracial love plot' (involving interracial sex and romantic love [often with a 'mulatta'] and ending with the white man's return to Europe) and argues that such plots serve to mask or mystify colonial relations of brutal domination. Our own view is that historical specificities are always crucial—in this case, Joanna's mother having offered Stedman 'the use of her daugter, while here, for a sertain soom', Stedman having first slept with her as part of a threesome, and so forth.[53] For us, the historical realities of this relationship (and of Stedman's relationships with other women in Suriname) combine with his depictions of planter brutality and slave resistance to make his *Narrative* a searing eyewitness *testimony to*, rather than a *mystification of*, the brutality of late eighteenth-century colonial relations. In a similar way, Pratt's assimilation of *First-Time* into a body of slave and freedman autobiographical literature begun in Stedman's time, and her treatment of it as an almost agentless or passive 'collection' of stories, erases the complex acts of contestatory ethnography that are crucial to understanding that work.[54] Once again in this particular cultural studies mode, historical and ethnographic specificities have been elided in the interests of a theoretical argument, with an understanding of the texts themselves very much the loser.[55]

---

[51] See Richard Price and Sally Price, *Two Evenings in Saamaka*, Chicago: University of Chicago Press, 1991, pp. 126–138, and Price 'Dialogical Encounters'.

[52] Mary Louise Pratt, *Imperial Eyes: Travel Writing and Transculturation*, London: Routledge, 1992, pp. 90–102.

[53] Price and Price, 'Introduction' to Stedman's *Narrative*, pp. xxx–xxxvi.

[54] Pratt, *Imperial Eyes*, p. 102; Price, *First-Time*, pp. 5–30.

[55] Pratt's claim (p. 102) that 'many [of the 'oral tales and histories provided' by Price] hark back to the dramatic events of the 1770s and 1780s' described by Stedman, further reflects her insouciance about historical detail. *First-Time* explicitly ends with the Peace of 1762 (and the great Saamaka celebration of that Peace in 1763). There is not a single story relating to the 1770s Maroon wars that involved Stedman, which in any case were fought with the ancestors of the Aluku (Boni) Maroons, not the Saamakas. History matters.

*

As anthropologists, we would stress the importance of listening to other voices, to ways of conceptualising the universe that are far from our own, whether expressed through writing or through other means of communication. Toward this end, we devote the next section of this essay to a strategy that the Saamaka Maroons recently developed to represent their conceptual geography to outsiders.[56]

Suriname's Maroons, descendants of runaway (rebel) slaves who today number some 120,000 people, are the largest Maroon population in the Americas.[57] The Saamakas, one of the two largest Maroon peoples, number about 55,000. Although the territory in which they have lived for over three hundred years began to be threatened by State and other outside interests in the middle of the twentieth century, their organised struggle to protect their lands began only in the late 1990s.[58]

In 1996, Saamaka women on their way to their gardens began to find their paths blocked by Chinese labourers. They heard heavy earth-moving machinery in the distance. When village headmen went to have a look, they were told that the land now belonged to the Chinese and that if they interfered with logging operations, they would be arrested and imprisoned. Soon, soldiers from the Suriname army were standing guard at the logging sites, refusing entry to Saamakas. The Saamakas began to organise against this invasion of their lands, but the depredations continued. Large swaths of the territory their ancestors had fought for, and which had been granted to Saamakas by the Dutch in the treaty of 1762, were now occupied by Chinese loggers, who had by the mid-1990s received official concessions to much of Saamaka territory.

Over the course of several years, as the logging continued, Saamaka leaders went from village to village—there are nearly seventy—to explain what was happening and conduct consultations. Despite the fact that most of them were not literate, they learned GPS techniques from NGO advisors and painstakingly created a richly detailed map of Saamaka territory—some

---

[56] For a fuller discussion of the case, see Richard Price, *Rainforest Warriors: Human Rights on Trial*, Philadelphia: University of Pennsylvania Press, 2011.

[57] Numerous references to Suriname Maroon (and Saamaka) history and ethnography may be found at www.richandsally.net.

[58] In the 1960s, the colonial government and Alcoa (which had mined bauxite in coastal Suriname since 1916) constructed a massive hydroelectric dam to provide electricity for Alcoa's smelter, with the excess going to light up nearby Paramaribo. Some forty-three Saamaka villages, home to some 6,000 inhabitants, disappeared under the new artificial lake that covered nearly half of traditional Saamaka territory.

9,500 square kilometres of forest. Then in 2000, with the assistance of human rights lawyers, they filed a petition with the Inter-American Commission on Human Rights. Based on this petition, the Commission requested in 2002, and again in 2004, that Suriname suspend all logging concessions and mining exploration in Saamaka territory until the substantive claims raised in the case had been investigated. These 'precautionary measures', in effect injunctions, did slow logging activities, but after the government of Suriname failed to comply with the substantive remedial measures adopted by the Commission in its report of March 2006, the Commission passed the case along to the Inter-American Court for Human Rights.

In choosing what features to mark on their map and which to silence, the Saamakas combined their pride in their environmental knowledge with their reticence to reveal culturally private information. Their cartographic legend, and their actual markings on the map show both natural features such as sandbanks, rapids, waterfalls, and boulders and social features, such as villages, cemeteries, and the sites of former villages. But they also show places of everyday Saamaka engagement with their environment: places where certain fish can be caught, where particular animals can be hunted, where there are trees suitable for making canoes or reeds for making baskets, where various species of palm nuts can be harvested, where wild mangos grow, where white clay is mined for rituals, and much else. What they chose not to show are sites of ritual importance (including the abodes of various gods and spirits) and the sites that played a role in their ancestors' century-long war against the colonists. The presentation of that map to the Court during the hearings in May 2007 was a highpoint in the testimony that won Saamakas the legal right to control their own territory, over the vehement protests of the Republic of Suriname.

In the Court's landmark decision of November 2007, which establishes a precedent for all Maroon and indigenous peoples in the Americas, the Saamaka were granted collective rights to the lands on which their ancestors had lived since the early eighteenth century, including rights to decide about the exploitation of natural resources within that territory.[59] The decision was explicitly based in part on Saamaka ideas about their historical relationship to the land, on the stories and events narrated in *First-Time* and in *Alabi's World*. In April 2009, two of the Saamaka leaders of this effort, Captain Wazen Eduards and law student Hugo Jabini, acting on behalf of the

---

[59] The full text of the judgment is available at: <www.forestpeoples.org/documents/s_c_america/suriname_iachr_Saramaka_judgment_nov07_eng.pdf> [22 April 2011].

Saamaka people, accepted the Goldman Environmental Prize, often called the Nobel Prize for the Environment, in recognition of their efforts.[60]

Our more general point here is that, without disparaging what cultural studies practitioners call 'discourse', we need to pay careful attention as well to 'event' (to 'what [we believe on the basis of careful historical and ethnographic research] really happened'). Indeed, these two aspects of literary geography are complexly intertwined, for Saamakas as well as Western critics. We would argue that on both ethical and epistemological grounds discourse and event must always be considered together, whether in thinking about torture in the eighteenth century or analysing land rights in the twenty-first.

Saamakas Discover America

We end this essay with a perspective on the literary geography of Suriname that would be unlikely to appear in an essay written by most card-carrying literary scholars. It comes to us courtesy of the Saamaka Maroons, whose ancestors arrived from Africa in chains. For Saamakas, their lived environment includes not only the forests and rivers of the interior where they have villages, gardens, and hunting grounds, but also the sea, which became an important part of their everyday world once Saamaka canoemen began work on the Oyapock River in French Guiana more than a century ago. The ways they conceptualise this environment might be divided into what they consider on the one hand the domain of the 'real', (both the 'historical' and the 'everyday') and, on the other hand, what they consider to be 'fictional'—the imaginary world they create and delight in through their folktale (and related) performances. This distinction crosscuts and challenges standard Western ways of thinking, in that the Saamaka 'real' includes normally invisible beings of many sorts. But it is a distinction that may throw light on the degree to which European historical visions of this same stretch of literary geography also reflect particular, culturally constructed perspectives.

We begin with Saamakas's vision of the real. Oral accounts of their history,[61] told in small doses in particular settings, stress that the earliest generation of enslaved Africans who escaped to freedom found themselves in a markedly inhospitable forest and struggled to develop means of survival appropriate to this new and unfamiliar environment. They recount in detail

---

[60] For a five-minute video about the case, prepared by the Goldman Foundation and narrated by Robert Redford, see <http://goldmanprize.org/2009/southcentralamerica> [22.4.2011]

[61] See Price, *First-Time*, *Alabi's World*, and *Travels with Tooy*.

the creation of rituals of an enormous variety, based largely and loosely on models from West and Central Africa, to assist them in coping. They follow the early runaways as they moved into the forest, periodically discovering kinds of gods previously unknown to them who inhabited the trees and boulders and streams of their new surroundings. Each new kind of god, as well as each individual deity, taught these pioneers how to worship them, how to lay out their gardens safely and successfully, how to hunt in their territory, and much else. From the perspective of today's Saamakas, their ancestors literally discovered America, finding in the forest a panoply of usually-invisible powers that continue to make their world what it is today.[62]

Saamakas recount, for example, the experiences of their earliest remembered ancestors, soon after their successful rebellion and escape from the Suriname plantation of Imanuël Machado in 1690. These stories invoke individual names and personalities in describing how, during the group's stay at Matjáu Creek (while fomenting new rebellions among slaves they had known in whitefolks' captivity, and conducting periodic raids on vulnerable plantations), the Matjáu-clan people were engaged in building new lives in the unfamiliar forests—forging anew everything from horticultural techniques to religious practices, drawing on their diverse African memories as well as their New World experiences with both transplanted Europeans and local Amerindians. The stories tell how, as these early Maroons prepared their fields for planting, they encountered for the first time local forest spirits and snake spirits and had to learn, by trial and error, to befriend and pacify each of them and integrate them into their understanding of the landscape of their new home. They tell how a mother of twins from the Watambíi clan inadvertently discovered, through the intervention of a monkey, the complex rituals that would forever thereafter be a necessary accompaniment to the birth of Saamaka twins. And they tell how newly-found gods of war joined those remembered from across the waters in protecting and spurring on Saamaka raiders when they attacked plantations to obtain guns, pots, and axes, and to liberate their brothers and, particularly, sisters still in bondage.

Their stories describe how the early bands of Saamakas engaged in communal divination, with people from a diversity of African origins asking questions together (through a spirit medium or other divinatory agent) of a god or ancestor in order to grasp the nature of the kinds of gods who now

---

[62] For a more detailed exposition of Saamaka discoveries of their new environment, see Richard Price, 'Africans Discover America: The Ritualization of Gardens, Landscapes, and Seascapes by Suriname Maroons', in Michel Conan, ed., *Sacred Gardens and Landscapes: Ritual and Agency*, Washington, DC: Dumbarton Oaks Research Library and Collection, 2007, pp. 221–236.

surrounded them. The detailed pictures that emerged of the personality, family connections, habitat, whims, and foibles of each local deity permitted the codification by the nascent community of new religious institutions— classes of gods such as *vodús* (boa constrictor deities) and their close cousins *watawenús* (anaconda deities) or *apúkus* (forest spirits), each with a complex and distinctive cult, including shrines, drum/dance/song plays, languages, and priests and priestesses.[63]

The process of discovery did not end with the pioneer generations. Gods (speaking in possession or through other means of divination) have continued to instruct Saamakas about landscapes, riverscapes, and seascapes ever since. Elsewhere we have described nineteenth-century discoveries of powerful new forest spirits as well as the discovery at the dawn of the twentieth century, by Saamaka men working in French Guiana on the Oyapock River, of some of the most important sets of normally invisible actors in modern Saamaka life, including *wéntis* (seagods) and Dúnguláli-*óbia* (a major protective and curing cult). Each of these discoveries is chronicled in the stories, rituals, and songs recounted by Saamakas today.[64]

It would take far more space than we have here to introduce the extraordinary variety of sometimes invisible beings that people the historical and everyday world of Saamakas.[65] In recounting their stories about the past and in their everyday activities in the present, Saamakas engage numerous individually-named gods and spirits who inhabit particular parts of the natural environment, from the forests to the rivers and streams and the sea. And many of these gods manifest themselves in possession, making them very real indeed.

But alongside the 'real' world of Saamaka daily life—including the gods and spirits that men and women deal with as they make their gardens, go hunting, or cure an illness—there is an alternative universe that Saamakas have created: a literary/fictional (oral) world, that carries great meaning for them. This parallel world manifests itself in *kóntu*, the folktales told as part of Saamaka funeral celebrations.[66]

---

[63] While twentieth-century Saamakas recounting their ancestors' early years in the forest envision a repeated process of discovery—an unfolding series of divine revelations that occurred in the course of solving the practical problems of daily life—anthropologists or historians might describe the process, rather, as one in which these particular spirits were being created or invented to fit into a generalised religious model that was familiar to most members of the various African ethnic groups present.

[64] Price, *Alabi's World*; *Travels with Tooy*.

[65] See Price, *Travels with Tooy* for an overview.

[66] For detailed discussion and examples of Saamaka folktales, see Richard Price and Sally Price, *Two Evenings*, from which much of the following discussion is borrowed.

Amidst the hectic weeks of drumming, dancing, singing, feasting, and complex rituals that contribute to these festivities, the telling of folktales constitutes a special moment for people of all ages. The setting is more intimate than other funeral-related gatherings, typically involving some thirty to forty kinsfolk and neighbours, sitting on stools before the deceased's doorstep. Together, they in effect agree to transport themselves into a separate reality that they collectively create and maintain—'folktale-land', an earlier time as well as a distant place, where animals speak, where the social order is often inverted, where Saamaka customs have been only partially worked out, and where the weak and clever tend to triumph over the strong and arrogant.

Saamaka folktales are seen as entertainment, as fictions with deep moral lessons for the present—not as history or cosmological myths. Sitting by torchlight or the light of the moon, the participants at a tale-telling wake come face-to-face with age-old metaphysical problems and conundrums; by turns, frightened by the antics of a villainous monster, doubled over with laughter at a lascivious song, or touched by a character's sentimental farewell, they experience an intellectually and emotionally rich evening of multimedia entertainment. To participate in an evening of Saamaka tale-telling is to join speakers and listeners in the collective creation and maintenance of a fictional but richly significant separate reality, a reality that has its own geography, peopled with both familiar and exotic creatures.

The stock characters of these folktales number in the scores and have diverse historical proveniences. Some, like the 'scrawny little kid' (usually the youngest sibling who saves his sister from disaster), appear, albeit in different guise, throughout Afro-America. This 'scrawny little kid' (*makisá miíi*) is the Saamaka version of the Chiggerfoot (or Jiggerfoot) Boy of Anglophone West Indian tales, described by Roger Abrahams as

> an almost invisible character ... a 'dark' figure: an 'Old Witch Boy', a dirty and diseased misfit, a mysterious member of the [white] king's family ... He lives at the margins between the family and the wilds, and can be seen as something of a contaminating anomaly, and ... the upsetter of order. Described variously as 'dirty', 'smelly', 'covered with ashes' (like Cinderella), he is best known for his ugly foot, which is described alternatively as diseased, constantly surrounded by fleas and nits ... or as a clubfoot ... [He is] contrasted with the king's beautiful daughter, ostensibly his sister.[67]

---

[67] Roger D. Abrahams, *Afro-American Folktales: Stories from Black Traditions in the New World*, New York: Pantheon, 1985, pp. 22–23.

In certain ways the Saamaka kid resembles his West Indian counterpart. In Saramaccan, *makisá* means crushed, mashed up, messed up, weak, frail, and generally in a dilapidated state; *miíi* is the word for child, kid, or boy. So, physically, the two are much alike. But there is also a crucial difference between them. In Saamaka, this ubiquitous character is not the younger brother of a white princess in the family of a king but a member of a 'normal' Saamaka family living in a rainforest village—in Saamaka terms, he is one of 'us', not one of 'them'. The difference is cardinal and points to an ideological contrast that helps us understand how Saamaka tales—while in general very much a part of the Afro-American tale-telling world—also stand alone in that comparative context.

As Abrahams glosses a common West Indian plot involving the Chiggerfoot Boy,

> the daughter [the white princess] is courted by many of the best men in the land, but she rejects them all until one man comes riding by with whom she falls madly in love. Their courtship and marriage is therefore quickly achieved, and her new bridegroom carries her off with him to his home in the bush. The boy, through snooping or using one of his witching powers, is able to follow the couple and discover that his sister has married an animal or bush spirit that has been able to transform itself into human form.[68]

Here, the West Indian audience is meant to empathise and identify, at least to a point, with this rather bizarre royal family; it is the princess whose life is in danger, and her brother who is the hero. But in Saamaka, though white kings and princesses occasionally appear in tales, they are consistently portrayed as part of an alien, foreign world. (Indeed, in the most fully-developed depiction of a princess in Saamaka tales, she appears as a prototypical bitch—self-centred, fickle, spoiled, condescending, and nasty.[69]) In Saamaka, the scrawny little kid who, like his counterpart elsewhere in Afro-America, saves his sister(s) from disaster, always saves *black*, 'normal' sister(s), not—as in the West Indian cases—a strange white one.

Other stock characters, such as the fearsome, giant, oafish, but amusing 'devils' (*didíbi*) have at least partial Christian/European roots. Employed as blacksmiths for Great God, they reside beyond the boundary of Saamaka habitation (sometimes just down a forest path from a Saamaka village,

[68]   Abrahams, *Afro-American Folktales*, p. 22.
[69]   See for example the tale of the 'one-sided boy' in Price and Price, *Two Evenings*, pp. 314–346.

sometimes across whole seas that can be forded only with the help of a friendly cayman, who offers his back for transport). In some ways, devils are inversions of normal Saamakas. They eat through their assholes (swallowing pots and plates along with the food), cannot tolerate contact with water (which turns them into stones), catch fire and turn to ashes when they die, and speak Sranan (the language of coastal Surinamers). They are supremely territorial, aggressively defending their land against human intruders—most commonly, the scrawny little kid who arrives in search of something for the betterment of Saamaka society (e.g. one or another kind of drum) or simply to liberate a stretch of forest or a particular path for Saamaka use. When threatened, devils become frantic, throwing things around, burning houses, running wildly in circles, and yelling out in characteristic excitable, repetitive speech. Their lechery knows no bounds; their gluttony is equally impressive; and they are the original owners of drums, horns, and other musical instruments. Their ritual powers allow them to dry up rivers or seas by throwing in a tooth or cast up mountains to block their enemy's escape with a magical charm. Their sensitivity to the smell of humans alerts them to the presence of intruders but their susceptibility to the charms of music and dance generally brings their demise. Often, a scrawny little kid succeeds in distracting a devil by playing a drum, finger-piano, or horn; a beautiful nubile girl achieves the same end by singing or dancing or exposing herself; either one of them (often with the help of monkeys) may inspire a devil to sing or dance until he drops from exhaustion.

Still other folktale characters, such as Anasi the Spider (and his numerous progeny) or—more remarkably—Elephant (an animal whose memory is preserved by Saamakas at a remove of three centuries), are African to the core. Anasi, at once man and spider, participates in the social world of Saamakas, wearing a breechcloth, courting human women, hunting large animals with a gun, building canoes, and dancing at community funerals; at the same time, his spider attributes figure importantly in the stories about him, as he spins a web that other animals must walk on in a special ordeal, hides in the rafters when chased by Death, or escapes from an enemy due to his light weight.

Like his counterpart elsewhere in Afro-America, the Saamakas's Anasi displays 'tremendous ingenuity in stirring things up and keeping them boiling; how he gets into a stew of his own making on many occasions, and how, as often as not, he uses his wits to get out of this trouble .... [His] unbridled egotism runs as high as his clever wit'.[70] He is admired for his creativity in meeting the boundless demands of his own ego and is

---

[70] Abrahams, *Afro-American Folktales*, p. 180.

much appreciated for the entertainment that his incorrigible naughtiness contributes to an evening of tale-telling. Win or lose, Anasi epitomises the valued Saamaka (and Afro-American) strategy of trying things out, keeping multiple options open, and relying largely on one's wits to stay a step ahead of the competition.

But the bulk of the denizens of Saamaka folktale-land are either humans, more or less like Saamakas themselves, or familiar animals of their own South American rainforest—Bushfowl, Jaguar, Howler Monkey, Deer, Hummingbird, Cayman, and Anaconda, as well as a host of others. If Lion is king in much of Africa, it is Jaguar who reigns over the other animals in the rainforest of Suriname. Saamakas underscore his absolute authority in folktale-land by repeating the formulaic 'all the animals called him *tío*' ('mother's brother', the ultimate authority in this matrilineal society). But though Chief of all the animals and physically powerful, Jaguar—like his less-exotic counterparts elsewhere in Afro-America—often comes up short in the end, being tricked by smaller but smarter creatures such as Shrimp, Turtle, or Hummingbird. In addition, Saamaka folktales feature frequent cameo appearances by special figures such as Death and the Great God. One memorable character is the mysterious stranger whose impressive dancing inspires Anasi to run up to him and offer a congratulatory embrace; only after the damage has been done does he, and the other spectators who smell his soiled body, realise that the stranger was Shit himself.

What partially differentiates Saamaka (and other Suriname Maroon) folktale characters from those elsewhere in Afro-America (including coastal Suriname or French Guiana) is less their bare identities than the roles and significance they take on for tellers and listeners. This has to do with the way geographic and social boundaries are drawn. Saamaka folktales contrast with those of other Afro-Americans in portraying the white world (with its kings and princesses, palaces and cannons, horses and coaches, ships and their crews, as well as slavemasters and wage-labour bosses) as completely 'other', fully beyond the boundaries of Saamaka society. When Bajans or Nevisians or Alabamians or coastal Surinamers depict those same characteristics, they are talking about a much more integral—if still in many ways distant—part of their own social universe. In this sense, then, the contrast in folktale conventions reflects social realities: those of the descendants of Maroons vs. those of the descendants of plantation slaves. In this broader Afro-American context, the special ideological stance of Saamakas toward whitefolks renders unique the specific transformations that they have effected on African, other Afro-American, and European tales.

Another example of the distinctiveness of Saamaka tales can be seen in what Abrahams calls 'Afro-American "In the beginning" stories [which] underscore the value of accommodating yourself to the way things are (and always will be) ... [and] underscore the fact that [one must accept that] life isn't usually very fair'.[71] But while the West Indian Chiggerfoot Boy, through his cleverness or witching powers, saves his sister or solves some other *domestic* problem, his Saamaka counterpart solves *community-wide* problems. Many Saamaka tales describe the way a particular individual— often the scrawny little kid—refuses to accept a difficult, 'unfair' status quo and sets out to alter it, changing some aspect of the world into the (better) way it now is. In various tales (often unlikely) heroes render a particular stretch of forest (or a path into the forest), which had been inhabited by devils or monsters, safe for humans; in others, through their courage and initiative, they introduce central aspects of life—drums, fire, polygyny, all-night dancing—into the Saamaka world. No accommodation here! The contrasts seem clear: slaves vs. maroons and tales of playful antagonism within a world of social inequities vs. genuine 'hero tales'.

One ideologically central Saamaka tale may serve as a final illustration of these contrasts.

There was a great hunter called Bási Kodjó. He had hunting dogs that were killing off all the Bush Cows in the forest. [The Bush Cow is a mythical animal, resembling—but fiercer than—a tapir.] Finally, the Bush Cows held a council meeting. They said, 'What can we do to kill this man? Soon there will be none of us left'. One of them, a female, spoke. 'I'll go to him. I have a plan to lure him back here so we can kill him'. And she changed herself into a beautiful woman in order to trick Bási Kodjó.

She arrived in his village with a basket on her head, saying that the man who could knock it to the ground would become her husband. She was really beautiful! No one could do it. Finally Bási Kodjó tried, and the basket fell. So this beautiful woman became his wife. Every night, when they were in their hammock, making love, she would ask Bási Kodjó what his secret was, how it was that he was able to kill so many Bush Cows without their ever hurting him. Each night she asked, and each night he told her a little more. She was so beautiful!

Often, during the night, the woman would go out behind the house to stare at the row of Bush Cow skulls that her husband had nailed against the rear wall as trophies. She would weep and weep, silently, for her dead relatives. When she had finished crying, she would return to the house, and Bási Kodjó would ask, 'Where have you been?' 'I went

---

[71] Abrahams, *Afro-American Folktales*, p. 39.

to urinate', she would say. But every few minutes she would go back out and just stare at those skulls and weep.

Every night, she asked Bási Kodjó over and over, 'Those animal skulls at the back of your house. How in the world did you kill those animals? They're fiercer than any animal alive!'

One night, Bási Kodjó finally told her, 'Woman, those animals live in savannahs. I go all the way to the middle of the savannah and fire my gun. When they come charging, I toss my gun aside and climb an awara [palm] tree. The animals circle round and furiously chew at the trunk to fell it. Meanwhile, my mother is back in the village, stirring the boiling pap that she feeds to my hunting dogs at the proper moment, to excite them. When I see that the palm tree is about to fall, I turn myself into a chameleon, sitting on the trunk, and I call out, *'fiiii'*, and this makes the trunk grow even thicker than it was at first. I do this until I know that the dogs have had time to gobble up all the boiling pap, and really feel it. Then I let the tree fall. By then, the Bush Cows have realized that I am the chameleon, so I turn into a spot of sand. When they try to eat that up, I use my final disguise and turn myself into a ....' Just then, Bási Kodjó's mother shrieked from her house, 'Bási Kodjó. Bási Kodjó. Hurry. Snake. Snake!' [It was really the god in her head that was calling out.] Bási Kodjó jumped out of his hammock and ran to kill the snake. When he got to his mother's house, she pulled him close and whispered, 'There's no snake. But I must warn you. That beautiful woman is not really a woman! Don't tell her the last thing you know how to turn yourself into. Instead, tell her that you become a *nóuna*'. Bási Kodjó returned to his wife. She said, 'That thing you were about to tell me, the very last thing you turn yourself into, when the Bush Cows come charging at you, what is it?' He said, 'I become a *nóuna* [a nonsense word, a word with no meaning]'. At last, she was satisfied. They slept.

In the middle of the night, the woman arose very quietly and went to her basket and took out a razor. She prepared to cut Bási Kodjó's throat. Bási Kodjó's gun said, 'I will shoot her *kpóó*!!' His machete said, 'I will cut her *vélevélevélevéle!*' His magical belt [*óbiatatái*] said, 'I will tie her *kilikilikilikili*'. All the posts of the house groaned loudly, '*hiiiiii*'. Bási Kodjó awoke with a start, saying, 'What's going on?' She answered, 'I have no idea. I was asleep'. Not a single thing in the house slept during the rest of the night.

At dawn, the beautiful wife asked Bási Kodjó to go off to the forest with her to collect awara palm seeds. He told his mother to prepare the pap for the dogs. And they set off. The woman led them deeper and deeper into the forest until they finally reached the savannah. Bási Kodjó climbed the awara tree and began picking fruit. Suddenly, the woman turned back into her natural form, a Bush Cow, and called out to her relatives. In a moment, the savannah was black with Bush Cows, all coming to eat Bási Kodjó. Quickly, he turned himself into a chameleon. She told them he was now the chameleon. So they began felling the tree. When it finally fell, they couldn't find the chameleon. She said, 'Eat that spot of sand. *It* is Bási Kodjó'. After a while, they could not find the sand. Bási Kodjó had turned himself into a tiny awara palm thorn, and hidden himself by sticking himself into a leaf. She said, 'Destroy the *nóuna*. He's turned himself into a *nóuna*'. The Bush Cows milled around in confusion. None of them knew what a *nóuna* was!

Meanwhile, Bási Kodjó's hunting dogs, who by then had finished eating their boiling pap and had been untied, arrived on the scene and they ripped every last Bush Cow to shreds. Except for one. Bási Kodjó saw that this last Bush Cow was pregnant, and he called off the dogs. This Bush Cow was hiding in a cave near a stream. She called out, 'Bási Kodjó, have mercy. You're about to kill your own offspring!' He grabbed her by one side, ripping off the whole leg, and then shoved her back into the cave.

Now you know the importance of *nóuna*.[72]

In the common West Indian plot (glossed by Abrahams, above), a white princess is seduced by an evil animal-in-disguise; the action unfolds on a purely domestic plane, involving personal dangers and triumphs, and the central characters are empathetic (if a bit strange) whitefolks. But in the *nóuna* tale (and others of the genre in Saamaka), two worlds are pitted in mortal battle—'our' world (that of Maroons) and another (rhetorically that of 'bush cows', historically and structurally that of 'whitefolks' and the plantation); the seduction is carried out in the service of the 'bush cow' state, and the renunciation of the beautiful 'woman' and her eventual destruction are carried out by the Saamaka hero on behalf of his people.

---

[72] This version of *nóuna* is considerably condensed from two tellings recorded in 1978 from the late Kandámma, then ailing and in her hammock. As has been pointed out elsewhere (Price, *First-Time*, p. 159), the rhetorical structure of *nóuna* almost exactly parallels that of a central First-Time historical account—that of the faithful slave/spy, Kwasimukámba, who arrived in Saamaka feigning friendship, who *almost* learned the secret of Saamaka invulnerability, 'escaped' back to the whites to lead a giant whitefolks' army against the Saamakas, and in the final battle was maimed by the Saamaka chief in an ultimate act of vengeance.

While the West Indian tale is largely entertainment, the Saamakas's story (in addition to its entertainment value) encodes perhaps their strongest ideological concern—community betrayal, treason vis-à-vis whitefolks, and the fear that 'those times [the days of whitefolks' slavery] shall come again'.

In short, we have been arguing that Saamakas view their history and everyday environment through a cultural lens that is quite different from the ones used by European (or coastal Suriname) writers, and that Saamakas also have a rich fictional universe that creates a world that is equally unique.

Our quick and highly selective tour through aspects of the literary geography of Suriname has come to an end. We hope that it will stimulate further attention to this sometimes neglected corner of the postcolonial world.

The Art of Observation: Race and Landscape in *A Journey in Brazil*

Nina Gerassi-Navarro

Tropical nature evokes a distinctive kind of geographical setting with its own characteristic flora and fauna.[1] Its representation, however, has been varied, shaped by distinct perceptual frames and ideologies that in turn have produced an array of visual images and verbal accounts. During the early nineteenth century the study of nature was closely intertwined with science and religion. Alexander von Humboldt, the renowned Prussian naturalist and explorer who travelled extensively throughout Latin America, argued that the key to understanding the divinely-ordered natural world was through careful observation. He encouraged scientists and artists to travel and observe nature, especially in the tropics—the American tropics—where the exuberance of the natural world exceeded what the European eye knew. Humboldt offered a comforting mixture of rational science and firm belief in the existence of a world structure created by a supreme being that famed Harvard naturalist Louis Rodolphe Agassiz, in turn, advanced in the USA. However, in 1859, Charles Darwin's evolutionary theory produced a major change in the apprehension of the natural world, generating new lenses for observation. This essay contrasts three contemporary perspectives of a scientific expedition to Brazil that illustrate the ways in which this important shift reshaped the scientific and artistic representations of the tropics. Focusing on the travel narrative *A Journey in Brazil* (1868), co-authored by Agassiz and his wife Elizabeth Cary Agassiz, and the journal and letters of William James, psychologist and philosopher—at the time Agassiz's

---

[1] The research for this essay was made possible by a National Endowment for the Humanities Fellowship. Any views, findings, conclusions, or recommendations expressed in this publication do not necessarily reflect those of the National Endowment for the Humanities.

student—I argue that new evolutionary paradigms altered the concept of observation, complicating the ways in which nature and cultures were perceived. As Cary Agassiz and James negotiate the role of the viewer in observation, their descriptions of the tropics challenge Agassiz's 'godlike' explanations geared at providing certainty, signalling the epistemological shift introduced with the theory of evolution.

Considered the 'founding father' of the American scientific tradition, Swiss-born naturalist Agassiz revolutionised the study of natural science in the USA, both promoting and advancing its professionalisation.[2] He was instrumental in the establishment of the American Association for the Advancement of Science, Harvard's Museum of Comparative Zoology, and the Lawrence School of Science. An inspiring teacher, researcher, and a successful fundraiser, Agassiz trained a whole generation of scientists. He made science vibrant, exciting, and accessible.[3] His approach, similar to that of his mentor and benefactor, Alexander von Humboldt, was based on observation; when asked what his greatest achievement had been, Agassiz replied, 'I have taught men to observe'.[4] Continuing Humboldt's teaching methods, Agassiz believed students should be outside, in the field, experiencing the confusing complexity of nature. Science, he argued, did not proceed in a linear fashion as it was portrayed in books. Books offered coherent explanations in which all the steps had been put in a logical order, but they were not in the sequence in which they had necessarily occurred. The only way students could truly understand nature was by rigorous and meticulous observation in the field. His mandate was clear: 'Study nature, not books'.[5] He was known for handing students a single fish or a whole drawer of oyster or turtle shells and telling them to simply 'look'. A week later, when the student would present his assessment, it would not be uncommon to have Agassiz respond, 'Look again, look again!' and perhaps even add, 'a

---

[2] The most complete biography of Agassiz is Edward Lurie, *Louis Agassiz: A Life in Science*, Chicago: University of Chicago Press, 1960. See also Louis Menand, *The Metaphysical Club*, New York: Farrar, Straus and Giroux, 2001, chapter five; Elizabeth Cary Agassiz, ed., *Louis Agassiz: His Life and Correspondence* [1885], Boston: Houghton, Mifflin and Co., 1997; and most recently Christoph Irmscher, *Louis Agassiz: Creator of American Science*, Boston: Houghton Mifflin Harcourt, 2013.

[3] Cary Agassiz, ed., *Louis Agassiz*, p.406; Lurie, *Louis Agassiz*, p.126.

[4] Lane Cooper, *Louis Agassiz as a Teacher: Illustrative Extracts on his Method of Instruction*, Ithaca: Comstock Publishing Co., 1917, p.1.

[5] Elizabeth Higgins Gladfelter, *Agassiz's Legacy. Scientists' Reflections on the Value of Field Experience*, Oxford: Oxford University Press, 2002, p.7; Edward Lurie makes a similar reference in *Nature and the American Mind: Louis Agassiz and the Culture of Science*, New York: Science History Publications, 1974, p.23.

pencil is one of the best of eyes', and then walk away.[6] For Agassiz, drawing was a form of documentation that forced the eyes to focus on details that in turn helped unveil the object in its complexity and specificity.

Observation had been a decisive factor for Humboldt in his travels and discoveries of the New World. In his multivolume work *Cosmos* (1845), a compendium on a wide variety of disciplines from astronomy to biology, geology, and meteorology, which he analyses in great detail, he synthesises the existing scientific knowledge about the world into a grand theoretical system to explain the underlying principles of the universe—an understanding that could only be achieved through direct observation. Humboldt's vision was based on the union and positive interaction between feeling and analysis, sentiment and observation.[7]

Agassiz was a key figure in extending Humboldt's scientific thought across the Atlantic. He came to the USA in 1846, invited by John Amory Lowell to give a series of public lectures at the Lowell Institute. Although Agassiz was well known in Europe for his studies on ichthyology and his theory of glaciation, he had not yet achieved the prestige of his mentors, Humboldt and Georges Cuvier. His visit to the USA granted him that opportunity. On this side of the Atlantic, Agassiz was received with awe and admiration. The USA, fulfilling what it saw as its Manifest Destiny, was engaged in its nationalist expansion to the west and south of the continent. In its desire for economic progress and intellectual advancement, scientific knowledge was perceived as a fundamental tool for growth. Furthermore, as new disciplines began to emerge within the sciences, the demand for new colleges, teachers, scientific societies, and journals became pressing. Agassiz seemed to embody the US ideal of advancement. His European credentials, his impressive scientific knowledge and curiosity, his charm and capacity to engage the general public and distinguished scientists alike made him a sort of 'cultural hero'. He, in turn, was also impressed with the USA, struck by the determination to educate the population at large, and the fervour with which scientists undertook their studies and the building of their collections. Echoing Emerson's idealism, Agassiz was seduced by the idea of instructing

---

[6] The episode in question is referred to by Samuel Scudder, founder of insect paleontology in the USA, included in Cooper, *Louis Agassiz*, pp. 40–48. For additional first-hand accounts of Agassiz's pedagogical methodology see Joseph Le Conte, *The Autobiography of Joseph Le Conte*, New York: Appleton, 1903, and James David Teller, *Louis Agassiz: Scientist and Teacher*, Columbus: Ohio State University Press, 1947.

[7] Stephen Jay Gould, 'Church, Humboldt and Darwin: The Tension and Harmony of Art and Science', in Franklin Kelly with Stephen Jay Gould, James Anthony Ryan, and Debora Ringe, *Frederic Edwin Church*, Washington: Smithsonian Institution Press, 1989, pp. 94–107, at 98.

scholars and citizens through his work and lectures on the importance of science and especially on the spiritual imprint of nature's creative powers. In a letter to his colleague, French zoologist Henri Milne-Edwards, he stated:

> What a people! ... Their look is wholly turned toward the future ... nothing holds them back, unless, perhaps, a consideration for the opinion in which they may be held in Europe. This deference toward England (unhappily, to them, Europe means almost exclusively England) is a curious fact in the life of the American people.[8]

Thus, in 1847 when Harvard created a position for him at the newly founded Lawrence School, he did not hesitate to accept. In his view, he would free the USA from foreign 'tutelage' and, in so doing, he would become a legitimating (European) authority in the advancement of science in the country.[9]

A few years later, in 1850, Agassiz married Elizabeth Cabot Cary, a Boston Brahmin with strong family ties to Harvard.[10] Intelligent and resourceful, Cary Agassiz helped him secure his position within the Boston and Cambridge cultural elite. George Ticknor, Henry Wadsworth Longfellow, Oliver Wendell Holmes, and, of course, Cary's brother-in-law Cornelius Felton, president of Harvard in 1862, socialised regularly with Agassiz and attended the Saturday Club, a literary and dining society of which he was a founding member.[11] Cary Agassiz did not just anchor her husband within a privileged social network; she was also a devoted stepmother to his three children, as well as his travelling companion, administrator, promoter, collaborator, and biographer.[12] She was also in her own right an educational pioneer. She ran a school for women in her home on Quincy

---

[8] Cary Agassiz ed., *Louis Agassiz*, p.435.

[9] The offer from Harvard coincided with political changes in Europe, most significantly for Agassiz that the canton of Neuchâtel, where he had been teaching, had ceased to be a dependence of the Prussian Monarchy. Agassiz was, as a result, discharged from the service of the King along with the corresponding funds, which had been secured by Humboldt for him to do research in the USA.

[10] Lucy Allen Paton, *Elizabeth Cary Agassiz: A Biography*, Boston: Houghton Mifflin Company, 1919; in relation to her scientific work, Nina Baym, *American Women of Letters and the Nineteenth-Century Sciences: Styles of Affiliation*, New Brunswick: Rutgers University Press, 2002, pp.91–112.

[11] Established in 1855, the Saturday Club was a monthly gathering of writers, historians, scientists, and philosophers, who embodied Massachusetts' intellectual elite. Given Agassiz's prominent role, the club was popularly known as 'Agassiz's Club'. Other well-known members included Charles Sumner, Ralph Waldo Emerson, Nathaniel Hawthorne, Charles Peirce, Henry David Thoreau, and Asa Gray.

[12] Agassiz's first wife, Cécile Braun, estranged from her husband by 1845, had stayed

Street, published a science manual entitled *A First Lesson in Natural History* (1859) under the pseudonym of Actaea, participated in and helped organise Agassiz's two major scientific expeditions, and helped set up and run his science school on Penikese Island, off Buzzard's Bay. In 1869 she was elected to the American Philosophical Society. She continued to work in education after her husband's death, becoming the first president of Radcliffe College (1894–1903). Cary Agassiz was her husband's intellectual partner. From the moment of their marriage, Agassiz's triumph in the USA was complete and he never regretted his decision to stay there.[13]

At Harvard, Agassiz advanced not only the study of science but also his ideas about nature and creation. In his original lectures at the Lowell Institute, he articulated his belief in the spiritual essence underlying all material creation. Drawing on current research in comparative embryology, paleontology, and anatomy, he demonstrated how coherent relations of similarity not explained by material necessity permeated nature. These patterns of similarity were to him evidence of a higher Being. Agassiz believed the world had been created according to a divine plan, and that it was the scientist's task to uncover that order through direct experience. Change and development were everywhere in nature and could be observed in the life history of the embryo, but this process was fixed and determined by the Divine Creator. In his quest for the origin of life he focused on fish fossils because they were present through nearly all the geological ages.

Following Cuvier's theory of catastrophism, Agassiz maintained that the Earth had been periodically hit by global catastrophes, after which new species of animals and plants had appeared. For Cuvier, the biblical flood had been the last catastrophe, for Agassiz it was ice. His glacial theory, which was a fundamental contribution to the understanding of natural history and won him international recognition, was a clear example of the power of the Creator.[14] His reasoning was that ice masses had moved

---

in Neuchâtel because of ill health and died in July 1848. Their children continued to be cared for by her family until their eventual relocation to the USA.

[13] Agassiz would have at least two important opportunities to confirm his decision to remain in the USA. The first was in 1854, when the new University of Zurich called upon his patriotism to consider an endowed professorship. Although not official, Agassiz turned the invitation down (see Cary Agassiz ed., *Louis Agassiz*, p. 513). The second and most important offer came in August 1857, when the French government extended him the Chair of Paleontology at the Museum of Natural History in Paris. Agassiz had coveted heading the Jardins des Plantes for many years, yet he declined without hesitation. In 1863, Agassiz confirmed his decision to stay by becoming a US citizen.

[14] Lurie, *Louis Agassiz*, p. 97.

forward and retreated, grinding the earth into different contours, depositing
drift, boulders, and primitive rocks, thus accounting for the appearance
and distribution of mysterious land configurations. This explained patterns
of extinction of flora and fauna, known only through fossil remains,
as well as their particular geographical distribution. Agassiz considered
glaciers 'God's great plough', a destructive and chaotic natural force which
was part of the divine plan.[15] Agassiz's glacial theory offered scientists
empirical corroboration of change, yet for him it anchored his belief in
the fixity of species because it enabled him to dismiss any disturbing
resemblance between past and present.[16] Charles Darwin and Charles Lyell
were impressed with Agassiz's glacial theory as it solved the geological puzzle
of the parallel roads of Glen Roy in the Scottish highlands, even though
their interpretation regarding the fixity of species differed. Although Agassiz
provided basic insights and discoveries that were instrumental in changing
the study of nature, he 'fought against the implications of these insights
for the new framework of natural history'.[17] This would eventually isolate
him from the scientific community by the time of his death in 1873, once
evolutionary theory had taken centre stage.

Agassiz was caught up in the transition to new paradigms for understanding
nature and the origin of life. Until mid-century there did not seem to be
a conflict between scientists and their religious beliefs; on the contrary, it
was a mutually reinforcing relationship. The elaborate and intricate design
of nature, and the multi-specied array of life was taken as evidence of
God's design—that he had created all living things and maintained them in
majestic permanence. However, as questions of truth and certainty became
foundational elements in the study of science, some scientists began to accept
that religious beliefs did not necessarily have a place in scientific research.
The process was slow. Even as schools, lyceums, and observatories sought
to cope with the growth of scientific knowledge and its dissemination, they
also made a concerted effort to maintain harmonious relations with religious
belief. The Lawrence School stipulated that students should 'attend religious

---

[15] Louis Agassiz, *Geological Sketches*, Boston: James R. Osgood & Co., 1876, p. 99.
The first series of *Geological Sketches* appeared in 1866, and contained ten sketches,
three descriptive of glaciers; the second series published in 1876 (three years after
Agassiz's death) contained five sketches on glaciers, the last one based on Agassiz's
trip to Brazil, all of which had been previously published in the *Atlantic Monthly*. Also
see Lurie, *Louis Agassiz*, pp. 94–105. For Agassiz's investigations regarding the ice-age
in the USA see: Louis Agassiz, 'Ice-Period in America', *Atlantic Monthly* (July 1864),
pp. 86–93.

[16] Agassiz, *Geological Sketches*, p. 42.

[17] Lurie, *Louis Agassiz*, p. 98.

worship' and John Lowell Jr. of the Lowell Institute left precise instructions in his will that students were to take a course once a year on 'the historical and internal evidences of Christianity'.[18]

By 1850, scientists had begun to accumulate evidence of geological changes and species variation that unsettled the reigning harmony. In 1856 Lyell noted, 'belief in species as permanent, fixed and invariable … is growing fainter'.[19] But the absence of a plausible theory to understand these facts left them as exceptions to the divinely ordained rule. This belief would begin to crumble as of 1859, when Charles Darwin published his groundbreaking work, *On the Origin of Species,* stirring both scientific and religious communities.[20]

Agassiz dismissed evolutionary theory because it did not offer proof; it was only a theory of plausibility. In his view 'Theories that presupposed change as the result of physical agents were as false as they were fanciful; they were the curse of science'.[21] Darwin's account of the origin of species was shocking to the religious and scientific communities because it implied a world without morality and questioned religious truths.[22] Although he did not give proof, Darwin offered highly probable explanations regarding the development of new species: they were created by and evolved according to processes that were entirely natural, chance-generated, and blind. It was a new way of thinking.[23]

Agassiz was appalled. In the copy of *On the Origin of Species* that Darwin sent him, he highlighted numerous passages he found disturbing; on the margins of a section in which Darwin speculates on the aquatic transformation that could affect the black bear in North America through natural selection Agassiz wrote: 'This is truly monstrous!'[24] As one of the

---

[18] Paul Jerome Croce, 'Probabilistic Darwinism: Louis Agassiz vs. Asa Gray on Science, Religion, and Certainty', *The Journal of Religious History*, 22, no. 1 (1998), pp. 35–58, at 40.

[19] Charles Lyell, cited in Michael Ruse, *The Darwinian Revolution: Science Read in Tooth and Claw*, Chicago: University of Chicago Press, 1999, p. 202.

[20] Prior to Darwin's *On the Origin of Species,* Robert Chambers argued for the evolution of species in his anonymously published *The Vestiges of Creation* [1844]. The book's hostile reception most likely contributed to Darwin's delay in publishing his own theory.

[21] Cited in Lurie, *Louis Agassiz*, p. 254.

[22] Croce, 'Probabilistic Darwinism', p. 41; Ruse, *Darwinian Revolution*, p. 229.

[23] Menand, *The Metaphysical Club*, p. 121.

[24] Agassiz's copy of Charles Darwin's *On the Origin of Species*, London: John Murray, 1859, p. 184, housed in the Mayr Library, Museum of Comparative Zoology, Harvard University.

foremost scientists of his times, Agassiz would take on Darwin's theory to prove its fallacy. In 1859, he debated fellow Harvard colleague, botanist Asa Gray, at the American Academy of Arts and Science. The debate demonstrated that Agassiz was familiar with the factual evidence advanced by Darwin, but not with the logic that bolstered his argument. This new science operated according to probabilities; in other words, it was a science that found plausible, persuasive explanations as patterns in the midst of indeterminate events.[25] Agassiz found this unacceptable: species were determined by God and did not change. Darwin could not explain why some characteristics remained the same and others did not in conditions that Agassiz argued should effect changes. Thus, in Agassiz's view, Darwin's argument did not stand up to special creationism:

> Until they can tell us why certain features of animals and plants are permanent under conditions which, according to their view, have power to change certain other features no more perishable or transient themselves, the supporters of the development theory will have failed to substantiate their peculiar scientific doctrine.[26]

Eventually the scientific community would be swayed by Darwin's argument, but Agassiz, convinced of his own authoritative position, remained firmly undeterred. Yet he could not avoid the impact. By the time he died, he was essentially alone in his opposition, and had lost a good deal of his prestige, despite the efforts of friends, family, and colleagues. As his biographer Edward Lurie states, 'He was the victim of both his European education and his authoritative role in American science'.[27] Rather than argue against evolution, Agassiz preferred to focus on the building of the Museum of Comparative Zoology, which was also founded in 1859. He had been collecting both live and fossil specimens for years, keeping them in his house or stored in deposits. It was to be an educational institution with

---

[25] Croce, 'Probabilistic Darwinism', p. 35.

[26] Agassiz, *Geological Sketches* [1866], p. 43. During the debates at the American Academy of Arts and Science, Gray stated that Agassiz's theory 'offers no scientific explanation of the present distribution of species over the globe, but simply supersedes explanation, by affirming, that as things now are, so they were at the beginning; whereas facts of the case ... appear to demand from science something more than a direct reference of the phenomena as they are to the Divine will' (in Lurie, *Louis Agassiz*, p. 277). For an excellent analysis of the debate see Croce, 'Probabilistic Darwinism'.

[27] Lurie, *Louis Agassiz*, p. 384.

its own faculty.[28] As soon as construction began, Agassiz demonstrated his capacity to mobilise people. Circulars were sent out to citizens interested in collaborating with his project instructing them in the proper way of mailing fish and other specimens to Cambridge.[29]

The museum was the first of its kind. Popularly known as the Agassiz Museum, it was unique because it demonstrated how comparative zoology could explain taxonomic categories. It was composed of an admirable zoological library, well-equipped laboratories, public exhibition rooms, and a large collection of dried and preserved specimens for the use of students. In 1901, when Alfred Russel Wallace, the naturalist who shared with Darwin the theory of natural selection (though with less publicity), visited the museum, he declared it embodied the ideal of what a museum should be because it covered the whole range of the animal kingdom necessary to illustrate the order of nature. The museum 'is far in advance of ours as an education institution, either as regards the general public, the private student, or the specialist'.[30] Wallace was impressed with the originality and breadth of mind of its founder.

The Thayer expedition

By 1865 Agassiz was suffering from ill health, worn out by the work on his museum. A trip to Brazil was planned as a rest, but when the wealthy businessman Nathaniel Thayer offered to cover the cost of an expedition, Agassiz embraced the opportunity. Agassiz had never been to Brazil and had yet to make an important scientific voyage as Humboldt or Darwin had done.[31] The Thayer expedition, as it was known, set sail on 1 April 1865 from New York to Rio de Janeiro on *The Colorado*, a Pacific Mail Steamship, returning sixteen months later in early August 1866. The expedition comprised a small group of Harvard scientists and students in addition to Agassiz and his wife. Among the six professionals were Charles Frederick Hartt, a geologist, who would return to Brazil to continue his

---

[28] For details on the process of the building of the museum see Lurie, *Louis Agassiz*, pp. 212–251.

[29] Christoph Irmscher, *The Poetics of Natural History. From John Bartram to William James*, New Brunswick: Rutgers University Press, 1999, p. 237.

[30] 'The "Agassiz Museum"; Harvard Museum of Comparative Zoology Regarded as an Ideal Institution by Dr. A. R. Wallace', *The New York Times*, 9 February 1901.

[31] His first book, *Brazilian Fishes* (1829), was based on research carried out by Johann Baptist von Spix and Carl Friedrich Philipp von Martius, who had travelled to Brazil between 1818 and 1820.

own explorations,[32] and Jacques Burkhardt, a draftsman who had worked with Agassiz for many years in Europe and who would produce more than two thousand watercolours of Brazilian fish.[33] The Brazilian engineer and naturalist, João Coutinho, would join the expedition upon the group's departure for the Amazon from Rio de Janeiro, courtesy of Brazil's Emperor Dom Pedro II. The students included Stephan van Rensselaer Thayer (Ren), Newton Dexter, Walter Hunnewell, who would become the expedition's photographer, and William James, future psychologist and philosopher. The expedition spent the first three months in Rio de Janeiro, then travelled to Belém, Manaus, and followed the Amazon River practically to the Peruvian border, exploring many of its tributaries and visiting numerous river towns along the way to collect fish specimens.

At the time of the trip, William James was twenty-three years old and was in his second year of Medical School, still undecided about his profession. The expedition would help him realise that he was not interested in collecting and classifying. Instead, he would eventually take Agassiz's teachings on observation and shift them to the psychological process that integrated knowledge into the subjective world of the individual. His reflections on the trip are scattered in his letters, drawings, brief personal journal, and an incomplete narrative of his collecting expedition on the Solimões River, all of which offer insights regarding the expedition and his own personal development.[34] James did not share Agassiz's rejection of evolutionary theory, but he was fascinated by his passion and work ethic, and considered him one of his favourite professors. Henry James Sr. knew Agassiz well through his participation in the Saturday Club, and shared the professor's scientific and creationist beliefs. In guiding his son's professional choices, James Sr. resisted the emerging view of scientific materialism and exerted a strong influence on his son's education to avoid this tendency.[35]

---

[32] In 1876, Hartt became director of a section of the *Museo Nacional*, Brazil, a teaching museum dedicated to educating the public in the natural sciences. Magali Romero Sá and Heloisa Maria Bertol Domínguez, 'O Museu Nacional e o Ensino das Ciências Naturais no Brasil no Século XIX', *Revista da Sociedade Brasileira de História da Ciência*, 15 (1996), pp. 79–88, at 82.

[33] The other scientific members of the expedition included Orestes St. John, geologist; George Sceva, preparator; John G. Anthony, conchologist; John Allen, ornithologist. The latter two returned to the USA because of ill health shortly after their arrival.

[34] María Helena Machado has put together most of James's texts related to the Thayer Expedition in a bilingual edition entitled *Brazil Through the Eyes of William James. Letters, Diaries, and Drawings, 1865–1866*, trans. John M. Monteiro, Cambridge, MA: David Rockefeller Center for Latin American Studies, Harvard University, 2006.

[35] James's disagreements with his father regarding his profession were a source of

James spent only eight months in Brazil. He was seasick for much of the trip and shortly after his arrival in Rio he contracted small pox and briefly lost his eyesight. These events prompted his decision to leave early, defining his trip as an 'expensive mistake'.[36] But once recovered, as he began to explore the 'earthly paradise', he changed his mind, arguing he would get a valuable training from Agassiz.[37] In his narrative, James implicitly confronts Agassiz's scientific as well as racial theories as he negotiates his own thoughts on race and cultural difference.

The goal of the expedition was twofold: to investigate the distribution of Brazil's freshwater fish species and collect specimens for the Museum of Comparative Zoology, and to disprove evolutionary theory: 'The origin of life is the great question of the day. How did the organic world come to be as it is?' announced Agassiz during his second lecture aboard the ship.[38] Agassiz hoped to find traces of the continental ice sheet to negate the continuity of species and thus refute Darwin. Although finding traces of ice in the tropics seemed unlikely, Agassiz believed the ice age was cosmic:

Indeed, when the ice-period is fully understood it will be seen that the absurdity lies in supposing that climatic conditions so intense could be limited to a small portion of the world's surface. If the geological winter existed at all, it must have been cosmic; and it is quite as rational to look for its traces in the Western as in the Eastern hemisphere, to the south of the equator as to the north of it.[39]

Agassiz spent considerable time studying the Amazon's 'stupendous' geological structure, reflected in his extensive discussion that encompasses most of Chapter XIII of *A Journey in Brazil* (a total of 44 pages). Agassiz

---

tension: Paul Jerome Croce, *Science and Religion in the Era of William James*, Chapel Hill: The University of North Carolina Press, 1995, pp. 49–81.

[36] James was constantly worried about the expenses incurred in his trip and kept a detailed list of what he owed and was owed to him in his diary. He repeats that the trip is a mistake several times in his letter to his father on 3 June 1865, Machado, *Brazil*, p. 62.

[37] James had criticised Agassiz in his letter to his brother Henry James for being 'so self-seeking & illiberal to others', 10 May 1865; Machado, *Brazil*, p. 59.

[38] Louis and Elizabeth Agassiz, *A Journey in Brazil* [1868], Boston: Fields, Osgood, & Co., 1871, pp. 7–8. The authors appear as Professor and Mrs. Louis Agassiz. Subsequent references to the text will be noted parenthetically as *Journey*. Unless otherwise noted, quotes belong to Cary Agassiz; when corresponding to Louis Agassiz, the initials LA precede the title.

[39] Agassiz, *Geological Sketches*, p. 154.

argued that the drift he found was proof of Brazil's glacial past (LA, *Journey*, 425)—though what he interpreted as such were layers of laterite soil, extremely common in the tropics.[40] Upon his return he announced he had found 'Traces of Glaciers under the Tropics'.[41] This shocked the scientific community and prompted the influential geologist and one-time admirer of Agassiz, Lyell, to state 'Agassiz ... has gone wild about glaciers', evidence of the growing distance between Agassiz and his colleagues.[42]

Narrating science

A Journey in Brazil (1868), the travel narrative of the expedition, is a hybrid text that illustrates two forms of knowledge based on direct 'observation'. It is authored by both Agassizs, but was primarily written by Cary Agassiz, who was the expedition's 'self-appointed clerk' and historian.[43] She recorded the daily activities, her husband's lectures on board and on land, as well as her own observations that make up the bulk of the text. Following Agassiz's methodology of observation, she describes their experience in the Amazon in great detail. We see her trekking through the jungle, sleeping in hammocks, fighting off insects, and hear her thoughts on women, slavery, and Brazil's racial diversity. Agassiz is present in the narrative through his 'lectures', the inclusion of some of his letters and his scientific assessments, in addition to numerous signed footnotes that expand or correct information presented and several appendices. A number of woodcut illustrations of Brazilian scenery and local inhabitants accompany the text. Cary Agassiz's goal was to show her husband 'the comprehensiveness of his aims and the way in which he carried them out'.[44] Her gaze oscillates between her impressions of what she sees—the landscape, the people she meets—and Agassiz's 'geologizing and botanizing' (*Journey*, 328) and inexhaustible collecting of fish, butterflies, turtles, palms, etcetera. Yet, while maintaining Agassiz's scientific rigour for observation, her rich and nuanced portrait of Brazil opens up fissures, and leads her to confront many of her own prejudices. Thus her view gives way to a narrative that pushes scientific knowledge to the margins.

---

[40] Marcus Vinicius de Freitas, *Hartt: expedições pelo Brasil Imperial (1865–1878)*, São Paulo: Metalivros, 2001, p. 38.

[41] This was the title of the paper Agassiz delivered at the National Academy of Sciences in Washington on 12 August 1866. See Lurie, *Louis Agassiz*, p. 353.

[42] Cited in Lurie, *Louis Agassiz*, p. 354.

[43] Paton, *Elizabeth*, p. 69.

[44] Paton, *Elizabeth*, pp. 106–07.

Aware of this discursive hybridity, Agassiz states in his preface how the book came about:

> Partly for the entertainment of her friends, partly with the idea that I might make some use of it in knitting together the scientific reports of my journey by a thread of narrative, Mrs. Agassiz began this diary... In this volume I have attempted only to give such an account of my scientific work and its results as would explain to the public what were the aims of the expedition, and how far they have been accomplished. (LA, *Journey*, ix)

The scientific discourse, serious and empirical, merges with the fictional or minor "thread" that turns text into "entertainment". Each discourse reflects two forms of knowledge: the scientific one, through Agassiz's lectures, his research, and opinions, all geared at disproving evolutionary theory, and the subjective and personal travel narrative. The travel narrative tells us about Brazil, its geography, flora, and fauna, including its inhabitants. In fact, it is because of this 'other' discourse that the text presents a valuable portrayal of the country's landscape. When read together with James's narrative of the trip, the paradigm shift in how to observe and represent the tropics becomes apparent as direct experience, subjectivity, and science are negotiated.

James's account is less structured and more personal than *A Journey in Brazil*. James was more interested in his own development and deciding what he wanted to do professionally: 'I said to myself before I came away, "W.J. in this excursion you'll learn to know yourself and your resources somewhat more intimately than you do now, & will come back with your character considerably evolved & established".[45] Hence, his perception of Brazil and the expedition reveals an awareness of the interrelation between the subject and the world outside the individual. His interest fluctuates from the Brazilian landscape and its people (as well as other members of the expedition) to his own personal views, as he struggles to discern his emotions and goals. He seems fond of Mrs Agassiz for her good temper and curiosity, though at times he is irritated by her way of seeing things 'in such an unnatural romantic light'.[46] James constantly reassesses his observations as he moves along the Amazon, signalling his awareness of how experience shapes perception.

---

[45] James to James Sr., 3 June 1865; Machado, *Brazil*, p. 61.

[46] James praises her in his letter to his mother, 23 August 1864; Machado, *Brazil*, p, 67. His more negative comments are from his diary, 10 November 1865, Machado, *Brazil*, p. 88.

Until recently, both texts have received relatively little attention. James's account is not well known to Latin Americanists, and critics in the USA tend to read his experience in Brazil as an early but minor stepping stone in the development of his professional career.[47] Likewise, *A Journey in Brazil* received little attention from professional scientists compared to other travel narratives such as Henry Walter Bates's account of his trip to the Amazon, *The Naturalist on the River Amazons* (1863), Darwin's *Expedition of the Beagle* (1839), or Humboldt's *Personal Narrative* (1810; translated into English 1814). Perhaps because of its amalgamation of discourses, it was not as seriously considered, but friends such as Longfellow and Emerson praised it, and Holmes remarked: 'So exquisitely are your labors blended, that as with the Mermaidens of ancient poets, it is hard to say where the woman leaves off and the fish begins. The delicate observations from the picturesque side relieve the grave scientific observations'.[48] For Holmes, science through careful and direct observation of the outside world appears opposed to the subjective world, in which the observations are 'delicate' and pleasing to the senses. The opposition of the fish (serious and concrete) to the mermaid (imaginary and intangible) encompasses two forms of knowledge, two modes of perception: male versus female.

James also observed the amalgamation of discourses in his letter to the Agassizs thanking them for their book. He wrote in 1868 'it was even more interesting than I thought it would be … you have so skillfully picked out the more picturesque incidents + sandwiched the narrative with science so artfully that one is led on from chapter to chapter and finishes the book without knowing it'.[49] Agassiz's 'scientific observations' are not the meat of the text, but rather the frame for the more substantive part, the narrative in which Cary Agassiz observes Brazilian life and nature.

Agassiz was impressed with what Brazil offered in terms of science. Yet his determination to discredit evolution led him to undermine his 'scientific observations' as he pushed his conclusions without evidence. His reading exemplifies the changes science underwent during the nineteenth century. In their historical study of 'objectivity', Lorraine Daston and Peter Galison note that as notions of objectivity and subjectivity were revamped by Kantian philosophy and became defining in the quest for scientific knowledge,

---

[47] See Croce, *Science and Religion*, pp. 123–124. A few biographers recognise the importance of the trip: Daniel Bjork, *William James: The Center of His Vision*, New York: Columbia University Press, 1988, pp. 53–67; Howard M. Feinstein, *Becoming William James*, Ithaca: Cornell University Press, 1984, pp. 169–181.

[48] Cited in Lurie, *Louis Agassiz*, p. 357.

[49] James to Agassiz, MS Am 1419 (435), Houghton Library, Harvard University.

there was a concern that the subjective self might idealise or regularise observations to fit theoretical expectations; in Daston and Galison's words, the fear was that the self would 'see what it hoped to see'.[50] Agassiz's obsessive quest to find ice exemplifies the process of 'making science fit'.

In constructing his argument regarding the geological structure of the Amazon, Agassiz states that all the different deposits belonged to the ice period and, as if already anticipating his critics, adds, 'I am aware that this suggestion will appear extravagant. But is it, after all, so improbable that ... in this epoch of universal cold, the valley of the Amazon also had its glacier poured down into it from the accumulations of snow in the Cordilleras?' His answer overrides facts and even probability as he affirms: 'The movement of this immense glacier *must have* been eastward ... It *must have* ploughed the valley-bottom over and over again' (LA, *Journey*, 425; my emphasis). He admits lacking evidence, nevertheless he asserts the glacial origin of the Amazon: 'there cannot, in my opinion, be any doubt' (LA, *Journey*, 427). Categorical and determined, Agassiz affirms over and over his claims with emphatic pronouncements such as 'I reject', 'I have found', 'I can truly say', 'it seems certain', and 'it must be', as if his own remarks could plough through the scientific debates and stand as proof.

Cary Agassiz had no particular theory to prove. Furthermore, she did not hide her own views; instead, she exposed them, recognising the possibility of misreading her surroundings. In her first outing in Rio de Janeiro, while Agassiz has gone to pay his respects to Dom Pedro II, her party wanders the streets and encounters a group of slaves, singing and dancing a 'fandango'. Her description is preceded by a brief statement that qualifies her place as observer, which she will often repeat: 'So far as we could understand, there was a leader who opened the game with a sort of chant ... he broke into a dance which rose in wildness and excitement, accompanied by cries and ejaculations' (*Journey*, 48). Perhaps because she recognises her own limitations and has no prior knowledge of these dances, she cannot assign them a specific meaning and, therefore, relates them incorrectly to an Andalusian dance that has little in common with any dances of African origin that might have been popular in Brazil at the time. Travellers visiting Brazil were often struck by the spectacle black people offered, and wrote

---

[50] Lorraine Daston and Peter Galison, *Objectivity*, New York: Zone Books, 2007, p. 34. As Daston and Galison explain, the line between objective and subjective for Kant is generally between universal and particular, not between word and mind. Notions of objectivity and subjectivity are redefined throughout the history of science, but as the authors stress in their introduction, the history of objectivity is almost by definition 'part of the history of the self' (p. 37).

about their 'strange' dances and religious ceremonies.[51] The impossibility of interpreting the dance (as well as numerous encounters with local inhabitants) compels her to describe it as strange, thus exposing her own class and racial prejudices.

Depicting tropical nature

Perhaps because of the origin of species question and the fact that Brazil was such a racially diverse country, tropical nature seems to be secondary in this expedition—at least in the terms that Humboldt had portrayed. More than anyone else Humboldt defined tropical nature for the nineteenth century. His travel writings comprise 34 volumes with illustrations that address botany, zoology, and barometric measurements, as well as geography and geopolitical descriptions. *Views of Nature* (1808) and his unfinished *Personal Narrative* (1814) are his best known works regarding South America. Humboldt not only collected and illustrated the tropics, he measured it, quantified it, and mapped it to determine the laws that governed the physical world to apprehend what he called 'terrestrial physics'.[52] Throughout his travels, he created an image of the tropics as exuberant and lush, inspiring the sublime:

> When a traveller newly arrived from Europe penetrates for the first time into the forests of South America, he beholds nature under an unexpected aspect. He feels at every step, that he is not on the confines but in the centre of the torrid zone; not in one of the West India Islands, but on a vast continent where everything is gigantic,— mountains, rivers, and the mass of vegetation ... It might be said that the earth, overloaded with plants, does not allow them space enough to unfold themselves.[53]

---

[51] George Ermakoff, *O Negro na Fotografia Brasileira do Século XIX*, Rio de Janeiro: G. Ermakoff, Casa Editorial, 2004, especially pp. 283–286; Lilia Moritz Schwarcz, *The Emperor's Beard: Dom Pedro II and the Tropical Monarchy of Brazil*, trans. John Gledson, New York: Hill and Wang, 2004, pp. 184–231.

[52] Michael Dettelbach 'Humboldtian Science', in N. Jardine, J. A. Secord, and E. C. Spary, eds., *Cultures of Natural History*, Cambridge: Cambridge University Press, 1996, pp. 287–304, at 288–289.

[53] Alexander von Humboldt, *Personal Narrative of Travels to the Equinoctial Regions of America, During the Years 1799–1804*, trans. Thomasina Ross, 3 vols., London: Henry G. Bohn, 1852, I, pp. 215–216.

In his writings, America is scrupulously and carefully 'observed'.[54] To explain nature and uncover her laws, landscape and its representation played a fundamental role. He was so clear on this that he dedicated a chapter to landscape:

> Descriptions of nature, I would again observe, may be defined with sufficient sharpness and scientific accuracy, without on that account being deprived of the vivifying breath of imagination.[55]

Humboldt advocated on-site sketching, recording detailed facts with scientific accuracy based on observation. He did not, however, expect the painter to offer a photographic transcription of the landscape, but rather to capture the 'essence' of a particular region. The result would be a 'heroic landscape painting' that used creative imagination and maintained a connection with the great traditions of painting but was modern in its scientific accuracy.[56] This mixture of science and aesthetics inspired numerous followers to the tropics, from naturalists like Darwin, Bates, and Wallace, to artists such as Johann Rugendas, Frederic Edwin Church, and Martin Heade.[57] But as the authority of science to depict empirical reality grew (enhanced by new technologies such as photography), and the origin of species question took centre stage, Humboldt's vision of heroic landscape began to recede.

Both James and Cary Agassiz were struck by the beauty of their surroundings. However, Humboldt's abundant and luxurious images of the sublime in their eyes became picturesque, rough but contained. James is initially unimpressed with the scenery:

---

[54] Mary Louise Pratt analyses Humboldt's portrayal of tropical nature as part of the process of the reinvention of America, in which he attenuates the human imprint: *Imperial Eyes: Travel Writing and Transculturation*, London: Routledge, 1992, pp. 111–143.

[55] Alexander von Humboldt, *Cosmos: A Sketch of the Physical Description of the Universe*, trans. by E. C. Otté, 2 vols., Baltimore: Johns Hopkins University Press, 1997, II, p. 81.

[56] Franklin Kelly, 'A Passion for Landscape: The Paintings of Frederic Edwin Church' in Kelly et al., *Frederic Edwin Church*, pp. 32–93, at 47.

[57] Ann Shelby Blum, *Picturing Nature. American Nineteenth-Century Zoological Illustration*, Princeton: Princeton University Press, 1993; Barbara Novak, *Nature and Culture. American Landscape and Painting, 1825–1875*, New York: Oxford University Press, 1980; Katherine Emma Manthorne, *Tropical Renaissance. North American Artists Exploring Latin America, 1839–1879*, Washington: Smithsonian Institution Press, 1989; Nancy Leys Stepan, *Picturing Tropical Nature*, Ithaca: Cornell University Press, 2001.

[T]he tropic Atlantic certainly is just like the northern sea. I thought the sky would be of a deep prussian blue over a sea of the same color, with spice laden winds, and birds of paradise; nautili & flying fish; porpoises & bonitas phosp[h]orescence at night rivalling the moonlight, & all that kind of stuff. Neither skies nor sunsets nor sea are of any livelier hues than with us. We have seen a few little flying fish skip, but they are not near as interesting as toads at home.[58]

But a month later his perspective has changed:

The affluence of nature here is wonderful. The ease with which the vegetation invades every thing, with which moss grows on every wall a few years old for instance, and weds what is artificial to what is natural, makes every thing very beautiful & very different from the colorless state of things at home.[59]

James's impressions vacillate as he scrutinises his feelings and his role in the expedition. He goes from being bored and unimpressed, complaining about not even encountering a monkey, to describing the discovery of 'picturesque' scenes and the warmth of Brazilians. In a letter to his father, he presents the following description of Rio: 'On my left up the hill there rises the wonderful, inextricable, impenetrable forest, on my right the hill plunges down into a carpet of vegetation which reaches to the hills beyond, which rise further back into mountains'. As he continues, his gaze falls upon the human landscape: 'Down in the valley I see 3 or four of the thatched mud hovels of negroes, embosomed in their vivid patches of banana trees'.[60] Unlike Humboldt's unpeopled landscapes, in James's and Cary Agassiz's narratives Brazil's human landscape is enmeshed in the tropical exuberance, reframing the representation of the tropics.

As Cary Agassiz tours Rio de Janeiro, she too displaces Humboldt's sublime with the picturesque. The old narrow streets with balconied windows and peeling stucco walls are crowded with people of all types. Moving from one group to another she forms a collage of snapshots from 'half-naked black carriers' and 'mules laden with fruits and vegetables', to a striking black woman dressed in white muslin and turban, to another fruit vendor resting against a wall. In spite of the 'dirt and discomfort' they create a 'motley scene entertaining enough to the new-comer' (*Journey*, 50). The

---

[58] James to James Sr., 21 April 1865; Machado, *Brazil*, p. 53.
[59] James to James Sr., 10 May 1865; Machado, *Brazil*, p. 59.
[60] James to James Sr., 15 July 1865; Machado, *Brazil*, p. 65.

human landscape for Cary Agassiz was just as impressive as the natural landscape. Even when confronted with the exuberance and exoticness of nature, the human imprint is always present, although at times barely discernable, shaping her perspective. Her first drive outside Rio leaves her with 'an impression of picturesque decay' (*Journey*, 53), in William Gilpin's terms: beautiful but varied with a certain roughness:[61]

> The first view of high mountains, the first glimpse of the broad ocean, the first sight of tropical vegetation in all its fullness, are epochs in one's life. This wonderful South American forest is so matted together and intertwined with gigantic parasites that it seems more like a solid, compact mass of green than like the leafy screen ... Many of the trees in the region we passed through to-day seemed in the embrace of *immense serpents*, so large were the stems of the *parasites winding about them*; orchids of various kinds and large size grew upon their trunks and the vines climbed to their summits and threw themselves down in garlands to the ground. (*Journey*, 54; my emphasis)

An illustration from a photograph by George Leuzinger entitled 'Tree entwined by Sipos's accompanies the text presenting a distinctly large tree struggling to overcome its unwieldy parasites: vines and orchids encroach, practically stifling it (Figure 6). The woodcut also shows a man sitting at the base of the tree, almost imperceptible, which may be why there is no description of him in the text. With scrutiny, his hut emerges from the landscape on the side with a small fire, implying perhaps some activity. His plough, on the other side of the picture, is resting, like the man himself. Given the persistent portrayal of the native population as 'lazy', the man's absence from the description might be read as casting him as one more indolent parasite. The densely overgrown background of trees encloses the human presence. Nature is active, as the vines 'embrace', 'climb', and thrust themselves down, while men linger idly.

The portrait of unruly nature stands out against the drawing of the botanical garden that boasts of its unique and beautiful long avenue of palm trees, some eighty feet high (Figure 7). This illustration is from a photograph by Auguste Stahl and Germano Wahnschaffe, the imperial photographers

---

[61] Based on the characteristics Gilpin assigns to the picturesque (roughness, variety, contrast), the object presented in picturesque beauty is rich and complex, which in this sense is more 'real' than the static beauty. William Gilpin, *Three Essays: on Picturesque Beauty; on Picturesque Travel; and on Sketching Landscape To Which is Added a Poem on Landscape Painting*, London: Blamire, 1794.

Figure 6   Tree Entwined by Sipos Vine.

of Dom Pedro II: 'I wish it were possible to give in words the faintest idea of the architectural beauty of this colonnade of palms, with their green crowns meeting to form a roof. Straight, firm, and smooth as stone columns, a dim vision of colonnades in some ancient Egyptian temple rises to the imagination as one looks down the long vista' (*Journey*, 61). The matted derelict forest has given way to sculpture; the elegance and architecturally structured image of the trees whose tips unite harmoniously as crowns emblemises Edmund Burke's notion of beauty: neat, controlled, firm, and

Figure 7   Vista down the Alley of Palms in the Botanical Gardens.

smooth.[62] The gardens are beautiful, but the tropical forest is rough, diverse, and picturesque.

Unlike landscape artists such as Church and Heade who painted the tropics without any human imprint to capture nature at its purest (the Edenic paradise), in Cary Agassiz's and James's narratives the human aspect is integrated into the tropical scenery, in part because, as Lilia Moritz

[62]   Edmund Burke, *A Philosophical Enquiry into the Origin of Our Ideas of the Sublime and Beautiful* [1757], Oxford: Oxford University Press, 1990.

Schwarcz states, Brazil offered the greatest 'spectacle of humans'.[63] But more significantly the human presence, in particular evidence of miscegenation in the tropics, was so disturbing to Agassiz that it could not be overlooked.

Classifying race

Agassiz corresponded with Samuel Morton, whose work *Crania Americana* (1839) impressed him. Morton was the 'great data-gatherer' who ranked races 'objectively' by physical characteristics of the brain, particularly their size.[64] Upon Morton's death, Josiah Nott and George Gliddon carried his ideas further, arguing in their monumental tribute to his work, *Types of Mankind* (1854), that Morton's findings supported polygeny. Agassiz contributed an essay to that volume supporting this view, contending that the distinction between races coincided with their geographical distribution.[65]

Shocked by the human spectacle of Brazil, and determined to offer proof of the dangers of racial mixing, Agassiz established a photographic lab in the city of Manaus to document, as Morton did, the physiognomy of hybrid Amazonians with the lens of his student, Walter Hunnewell. Agassiz was well aware of the power of visual images, evident in his scientific illustrations and his interest in photography.[66] In 1850 he commissioned fifteen daguerreotypes of African slaves working on plantations outside Columbia, South Carolina, from the photographer J. T. Zealy. These powerful images of naked slaves are among the very few antebellum photographs of slaves presently known.[67]

---

[63] Lilia Moritz Schwarcz, *The Spectacle of Races. Scientists, Institutions, and the Race Question in Brazil, 1870–1930*, trans. Leland Guyer, New York: Hill and Wang, 1999, p. 4.

[64] For a succinct explanation of his work see Stephen Jay Gould, *The Mismeasure of Man*, rev. edn., New York: W. W. Norton & Company, 1996, pp. 82–101.

[65] Louis Agassiz, 'Sketch of the Natural Provinces of the Animal World and their Relation to the Different Types of Man', in J. C. Nott and George R. Gliddon, eds., *Types of Mankind*, Philadelphia: Lippincott, Grambo & Co, 1855, pp. lviii–lxxviii.

[66] For Agassiz's influence on zoological illustrations see Blum, *Picturing Nature*, pp. 169–237.

[67] These are extremely striking images of both men and women, meant to illustrate Agassiz's theory of 'separate creation'. The daguerreotypes are housed in the Archives of the Peabody Museum at Harvard University. On these photographs see: Melissa Banta, Curtis M. Hinsley; with the assistance of Joan Kathryn O'Donnell, *From Site to Sight: Anthropology, Photography and the Power of Imagery*, Cambridge, MA: Peabody Museum Press, 1993, pp. 54–61; Alan Trachtenburg, *Reading American Photographs: Images as History, Mathew Brady to Walker Evans*, New York: Hill and Wang, 1989, pp. 52–60, offers an excellent analysis of the photos, highlighting the ways in which the subjects defy the scrutinising gaze of the viewer. For a recent analysis of the photos

Figure 8   'Mina Negress'.

For Agassiz they were a form of visual documentation of racial differences, much like Morton's measurements. Brazil, with its multifarious 'hybrid' population, was the ideal place to illustrate his views and demonstrate what he so clearly believed.

Photography was extremely popular in Brazil; it was a symbol of modernity as well as a mark of civilisation. Dom Pedro II played an important role in stimulating its development. In 1840 when he took over the throne at the age of fourteen, and only a few months after the official announcement of the daguerreotype, he had already acquired a camera.[68] Dom Pedro had the royal family photographed for his private collection, as well as his public outings and official activities to help publicise the rapid

see Molly Rogers, *Delia's Tears. Race, Science, and Photography in Nineteenth-Century America*, New Haven: Yale University Press, 2010.

[68] Pedro Vasquez, *Dom Pedro II e a Fotografia no Brazil*, Rio de Janeiro: Fundação Roberto Marinho: Internacional de Seguros, 1985, p. 14.

process of modernisation his country had embarked on.[69] Between 1840 and
1855, itinerant daguerreotypists visited Brazilian cities. They photographed
the elite, documented the construction of buildings, roads, and railroads,
and accompanied scientific expeditions. Most of these photographers were
foreigners who would return to their countries of origin after a few months
or years. But as technology improved and interest in photography grew, a
number of photographers set up shop in Rio de Janeiro's Ouvidor Street.[70]

One of these foreigners was Leuzinger, who established a firm specialising
in landscapes and panoramas, where Hunnewell trained to 'become quite
expert in taking likenesses' (*Journey*, 276).[71] Agassiz commissioned Stahl and
Wahnschaffe to take a series of photographs of 'pure' races. The result was two
sets of photographs of men and women: a series of portraits—two of which
were reproduced as woodcut illustrations in *A Journey in Brazil* (Figure 8),
and a number of physiognomic photographs of 'pure racial types', mainly
Africans and a few Chinese.[72] These physiognomy photographs present the
subjects nude and in fixed positions: back, profile, front (Figure 9).[73] Their
origin is stated in French or Portuguese, in pencil, on the bottom left hand
corner (Island of Mozambique, Chinese, etcetera). The imperial seal is stamped
on the top left hand corner. They are carefully crafted artists' photographs,
taken inside a studio, that contrast with Hunnewell's unrefined images taken
outdoors. But in Hunnewell's rudimentary setting in Manaus, his subjects
seem less distant to the viewer than in the staged studio poses, and at times
the subject's gaze at the viewer evokes an eerie resemblance to the powerful
Zealy photographs of slaves that Agassiz had commissioned in South Carolina.

Cary Agassiz only mentions the photographic studio in passing to
highlight the backwardness of the locals who feared photography might

---

[69] E. Bradford Burns, *A History of Brazil*, 3rd edn., New York: Columbia University
Press, 1993, pp. 140–80.

[70] For a history of photography in Brazil see Vasquez, *Fotografia no Brasil*; Ermakoff,
O Negro na Fotografia; Gilberto Ferrez, *Photography in Brazil 1840–1900*, trans. Stella
de Sá Rego, Albuquerque: University of New Mexico Press, 1990; also Schwarcz, *The
Emperor's Beard*, pp. 260–266.

[71] Many of the scenic woodcut illustrations in *A Journey in Brazil* produced by
Burkhardt were based on photographs by Leuzinger and Marc Ferrez. Ferrez also
apprenticed at Leuzinger's studio and became one of the most successful photographers
in Brazil in his own right.

[72] The other portrait is 'Mina Negress and Child' found in *Journey*, p. 84.

[73] The complete collection of photographs of the Thayer expedition was originally in
three albums. For conservation purposes, the photographs have been placed in boxes,
housed in the Archives of the Peabody Museum at Harvard University. I would like
especially to thank India Spartz, Patricia Kervick, and Jessica Desany-Ganong for
their assistance in viewing and information regarding the photographs.

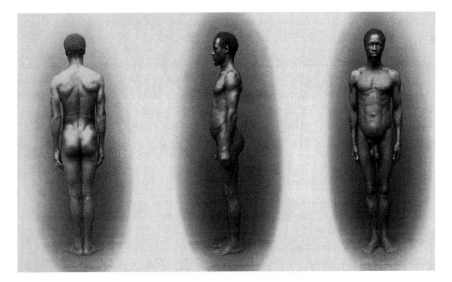

Figure 9 'Physiognomic Photograph'.

rob their vital energy or even kill them (*Journey*, 276–277). She implies that a good deal of time was spent helping the subjects overcome their fear. In James's account, Agassiz's effort to dissipate his subjects' fear is portrayed in a completely different light:

> I then went to the photographic establishment and was cautiously admitted by Hunnewell with his black hands. On entering the room found Prof. engaged in cajoling 3 moças whom he called pure Indians, but who, I thought as afterwards appeared, had white blood. They were very nicely dressed in white muslin + jewelry with flowers in their hair + an excellent smell of pripioca. Apparently refined, at all events not sluttish, they consented to the utmost liberties being taken with them and two without much trouble were induced to strip and pose naked. While we were there Sr. Tavares Bastos came in and asked me mockingly if I was attached to the Bureau of Anthropology.[74]

James is evidently embarrassed and bothered at being identified as a participant in the disturbing scene. Machado suggests that he was able to recognise the nuances of tropical society by underscoring the women's

---

[74] William James, *Brazilian Diary*, MS Am 1092.9 (4498), p. 8, Houghton Library, Harvard University.

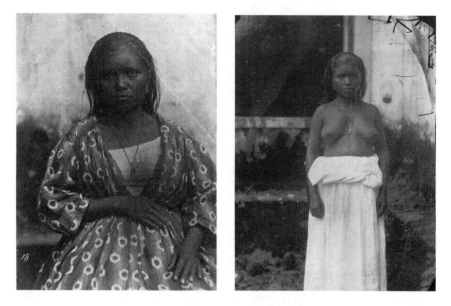

Figure 10   'Frontal Portrait of a Girl'.   Figure 11   'Frontal Portrait of a Girl'.

Figure 12   'Profile Portrait of a Girl'.

pleasant scent and elegant dress. His observation that the women looked white despite Agassiz's categorisation of them as pure Indians points to the lack of negative connotations hybridism might have had for James.[75] The irony embedded in Tavares Bastos's question unmasks Agassiz's seduction of the young women, stripping the bureau of its false pretense.[76]

Unlike the photographs taken by Stahl and Wahnschaffe, most of Hunnewell's 40 to 50 photos were taken outside, in natural sunlight, in front of the 'picturesque barrack of a room ... [that] serves as a photographic saloon' (*Journey*, 276). The photographs were inspired by the series presented by Stahl and Wahnschaffe, the imperial photographers, but they are amateurish and crude (Figures 10, 11, & 12). Hunnewell's collection, as well as that of the professional photographers, include several postcards of classical statues: a bust of Juno Ludovisi, Apollo Belvedere, or a semi-draped Venus de Milo, that loosely correspond with the pose of the images that follow (Figure 13). These postcards highlight the Western model of beauty against which the racial types are compared. The women in the photographs are well-dressed and many of them wear jewellery. Their colourful long dresses or crisp white petticoats contrast with the dingy outside of the deteriorated barrack. They either stand or sit. A rickety old chair is often seen as the only prop where their dress lies when posing naked. The subjects are tense and restrained and, for the most part, young. Although the majority are women there are a few men photographed, as well as older women and a couple of dressed children. In Agassiz's view, Hunnewell's photographs are geared not just at documenting the different racial types he encountered; but at demonstrating the dangerous consequences of miscegenation. While this is not the main focus of Agassiz's expedition and he claims not to be able to offer a thorough study, it is a topic of great concern to him.

In a section in which his wife discusses the 'amalgamation' of races in the USA and Brazil, saying that in Brazil 'the free negro has full access to all the privileges of any free citizen', Agassiz adds a footnote:

Let any one who doubts the evil of this mixture of races, and is inclined, from a mistaken philanthropy, to break down all barriers between them, come to Brazil. He cannot deny the deterioration consequent upon an amalgamation of races, more widespread here than in any other country in the world, and which is rapidly effacing

---

[75] Machado, *Brazil*, p. 23.

[76] Aureliano Cândido Tavares Bastos was a well-known politician who, in the name of progress, advocated opening up the Amazon to international trade and maintaining a close relationship with the USA. See, Burns, *A History*, pp. 180–181.

the best qualities of the white man, the negro, and the Indian, leaving a mongrel nondescript type, deficient in physical and mental energy. (LA, *Journey*, 293)

As a proponent of polygenism, Agassiz argued that racial types showing clear physical distinctness might also reasonably be viewed as different species.[77] This was what he had affirmed when, in the midst of the Civil War, S. G. Howe, a member of Lincoln's Inquiry Commission, had asked him to give his opinion about the role of blacks in a reunited nation. While Agassiz opposed slavery, he did not believe in social equality with blacks or Indians, and argued that races should remain separate so as not to degenerate.[78] As his wife introduces a slight ambivalence toward the racial structure in Brazil, Agassiz disciplines her narrative with a footnote, trying to determine the way we should understand her comments.

Despite his efforts, Agassiz's science remains at the margins of the narrative. While his views are clear, the images he provides through the photographs, like the data he cites regarding drift, do not reflect any obvious form of 'degeneration' nor the presence of glaciers. Unable to rely completely on facts, Agassiz imposes his theory on the narrative and tries to guide our gaze. As Gwyniera Isaac states in her analysis of these photographs, 'History, like the photographic image, may have numerous readings and involves the negotiation of the past in the present'. In addition, she notes, 'A shift in meaning can also occur when an image or a visual perception of

---

[77] Lurie, *Louis Agassiz*, pp. 264–265. Monogenism mantained that all races originated from a single source. However, neither monogenism nor polygenism ratified racial equality. For an excellent analysis see John Haller, 'The Species Problem: Nineteenth-Century Concepts of Racial Inferiority in the Origin of Man Controversy', *American Anthropologist*, 27 (1972), pp. 1319–1329; Gould, *Mismeasure*, pp. 76–77, argues that when confronted with the sight of black people for the first time upon his arrival in the USA, Agassiz felt a pronounced revulsion, which he relayed in a letter to his mother in 1846. This would lead him to develop his arguments supporting polygenism. However, it should also be noted that having lived in Boston for several years, where there were numerous legal cases regarding school segregation, including one argued in part by Agassiz's friend, US senator Charles Sumner who was a member of the Saturday Club and a champion of blacks' rights, Agassiz never changed his view of blacks. On racial struggles in Boston see Stephen Kendrick and Paul Kendrick, *Sarah's Long Walk. The Free Blacks of Boston and How Their Struggle for Equality Changed America*, Boston: Beacon Press, 2004.
[78] Gould, *Mismeasure*, pp. 79–82; Menand, *Metaphysical Club*, pp. 114–116. See Agassiz's correspondence with Samuel Gridley Howe in Elizabeth Cary Agassiz ed., *Louis Agassiz*, pp. 591–617.

Figure 13   Postcard of *Venus de Milo*.

an event is transformed into language'.[79] The images might have been clear for Agassiz, but the scientific theories that motivated their creation do not speak through the images for a contemporary viewer. Perhaps Agassiz was implicitly aware of this, despite his intentions to publish the photographs (LA, *Journey*, 529), which he never did. It is unclear as to how he might have conceived the photographic project, but given the shift in the scientific community by the 1870s, it would have been extremely problematic for him to continue making the same arguments about race.

Cary Agassiz shared her husband's views on racial mixing and did not hesitate to articulate how specific racial traits are transformed through 'amalgamation'. Her description of the population of Breves, a municipality in the state of Pará, follows:

---

[79]   Gwyniera Isaac, 'Louis Agassiz's Photographs in Brazil. Separate Creations', *History of Photography*, 21, no. 1 (1997), pp. 3–11, at 3.

Its population, like that of all these small settlements on the lower Amazon, is made up of an amalgamation of races. You see the regular features and fair skin of the white man combined with the black, coarse, straight hair of the Indian, or the mulatto with partly negro, partly Indian features, but the crisps taken out of the hair; and with these combinations comes in the pure Indian type, with its low brow, square build of face and straight line of shoulders. (*Journey*, 154)

Despite endorsing her husband's theories, Cary Agassiz is able to question them, and thus recognise advancement in Brazil:

It seems to me that we may have something to learn here in our own perplexities respecting the position of the black race among us ... The absence of all restraint upon free blacks, the fact that they are eligible to office ... without prejudice on the ground of color, enables one to form some opinion as to their ability and capacity for development. (*Journey*, 129)

James's perspective regarding race is much less troubled. His mode of observation is neither pessimistic nor optimistic. In fact, he seems intrigued by a different way of living and thinking. His diary and several notebooks are full of lists of words or sentences in Portuguese and Tupí, one of the many languages spoken in the Amazon, prefaced by 'How do you say?', revealing his effort to establish more direct contact with the locals. He is frustrated when a young woman with whom he dances understands absolutely nothing of his talk: 'Ah Jesuina, Jesuina, my forest queen, my tropic flower, why could I not make myself intelligible to thee?'[80] In his view, the Indians are not only nice but 'of a beautiful brown color with fine black hair. Their skin is dry and clean looking'.[81]

In different ways, Cary Agassiz and James's form of observation is interactive. She is constantly assessing and comparing what she observes with what she knows, which often brings her gaze upon herself as a woman or a US citizen. Unlike her husband who uses analogies to confirm his views, her comparisons often lead her to suspend categorical affirmations to introduce fluctuation; fixity confronted with uncertainty. Both Baym and Irmscher contend that Cary Agassiz performed a 'disappearing act', effacing her own contributions or simply positioning them as a weaker feminine perspective.[82]

---

[80] James to Alice James, 31 August 1865; Machado, *Brazil*, p. 74.
[81] James to Alice James, 31 August 1865; Machado, *Brazil*, p. 72.
[82] Baym, *American Women*, p. 92; Irmscher, *Poetics of Natural History*, pp. 249–251.

Linda Bergmann, however, argues that Cary Agassiz offers a clearer view of Brazil 'precisely because she does not efface herself or her experiences'.[83] Fabiane Vinente dos Santos's analysis of Cary Agassiz's portrayal of women offers substantial evidence supporting Bergmann's opinion.[84] Her personal letters make it clear that Cary Agassiz does not want to upstage her husband and consciously avoids asserting her own achievements in the narrative. Yet she confesses to her family that this does not mean she does not want recognition; she simply does not want to detract attention from her husband, which in her view would reflect poorly on her duties as a devoted spouse.[85]

Cary Agassiz's subjective views are evident when portraying Amazonian women 'whose life is perfectly free and a thousand times pleasanter than the ladies' life'.[86] She is struck by their moral and physical autonomy, their physical strength and freedom to move about without men's supervision, travelling alone in canoes, pipe smoking, as well as their sexual habits (they have no shame in their illegitimate children). These observations take her beyond the stereotyped portrayal of indigenous women and allow her to develop a variety of views of Amazonian women as she sifts through her own notions of nature and culture, progress and backwardness. Although she finds indigenous women, with their hair hanging uncombed, generally ugly and dirty, she notes that 'the primitive life of the better class of Indians on the Amazon is much more attractive then the so-called civilised life in the white settlements' (*Journey*, 175). In her view, they are superior to Native Americans from the USA as they show an aptitude for the arts of civilisation 'so uncongenial to our North American Indians' (*Journey*, 192). In observing them she realises that she is perceived as a 'very extraordinary specimen', as they touch her clothes and refer to her as the white woman ("branca"). [87] Western institutions, clothing, and values such as marriage did not hold the same meaning in Amazonian society, which forces Cary Agassiz briefly to shift her gaze onto herself. While she certainly does not question her cultural values, they are momentarily suspended so that she

---

[83] Linda S. Bergmann, 'A Troubled Marriage of Discourses: Science Writing and Travel Narrative in Louis and Elizabeth Agassiz's *A Journey in Brazil*', *Journal of American Culture*, 18 (1995), pp. 83–88, at 83.

[84] Fabianne Vinente dos Santos, '"Gold Earrings, Calico Skirts": Images of Women and their Role in the Project to Civilize the Amazon, as Observed by Elizabeth Agassiz in *A Journey in Brazil*: 1865–1866', *História, Ciências, Saúde-Manguinhos*, 12, no. 1 (2005), pp. 1–21.

[85] Cary Agassiz in Paton, *Elizabeth*, p. 84, 91.

[86] Cary Agassiz in Paton, *Elizabeth*, p. 90.

[87] Cary Agassiz in Paton, *Elizabeth*, p. 90.

can recognise her privileged position ('everything is forgiven to a stranger') and acknowledge differences.[88]

Both Cary Agassiz and James are less disturbed than Agassiz by the racial mingling in Brazil, mostly because both had more personal relationships with the inhabitants: Cary Agassiz with the women and servants; James with the boatmen and guides that escorted him on his individual outings, as well as the few women that he may have been attracted to. These situations clearly enabled them to move and look beyond Agassiz's scientific theories. In his diary James ponders, 'Is it race or is it circumstance that makes these people so refined and well bred? No gentleman of Europe has better manners and yet these are peasants'.[89] James's and Cary Agassiz's place as tourists, or scientific dilettantes, limits them from making categorical judgments, as they mingle with Indians, blacks, and *mestizos*, spending evenings with them, admiring their hospitality without fear or revulsion. Where Agassiz sees degeneration, his wife sees 'a *curious* illustration of the amalgamation of races' (my emphasis), as in the portrait of her 'little house-maid' Alexandrina, whose hair of wiry elasticity has lost 'its compact negro crinkle' (*Journey*, 246). After his month-long collecting trip along the Solimões River with Signor Urbano, James writes in his journal:

> I now feel perfectly domesticated in this place and with these people. Never were there a more decent worthy set of gentry. Old Urbanno especially, by his native refinement, intelligence and a sort of cleanliness and purity is fit to be the friend of any man who ever lived, how elevated his birth and gifts. There is not a <u>bit</u> of our damned anglo saxon brutality and vulgarity either in masters or servants.[90]

Yet, neither Elizabeth Cary Agassiz nor William James erases differences between cultures. In their comparisons, the notion of 'civilized' culture belongs to the north. Cary Agassiz notes that Brazilians have been brought in contact 'with a less energetic and powerful race than the Anglo-Saxon' (*Journey*, 129), and James complains that 'I am beginning to get impatient with the brazilian sleepiness & ignorance. These Indians are particularly exasperating by their laziness & stolidity ... I had no idea before of real greatness of American energy'.[91]

---

[88]   Cary Agassiz in Paton, *Elizabeth*, p. 90.
[89]   James, *Brazilian Diary*, pp. 12–13.
[90]   James, *Brazilian Diary*, pp. 19–20.
[91]   James to Henry James Sr. 12 September 1865; Machado, *Brazil*, pp. 76–77.

A Journey in Brazil is a hybrid text in which science and personal experience are interlaced, but the more complete portrayal is offered through the personal and not the scientific observation. The value of Cary Agassiz's portrait rests on recognising her own subjectivity. Her narrative subverts her husband's because she makes science relative not absolute. Juxtaposed with James's narrative, it becomes clear that at this crossroads, in which evolutionary theory began to unravel scientific racial theories, Louis Rodolphe Agassiz's resistance would, in the end, reveal his inability to observe nature in its complexity, as he could not include in her parameters the human component other than to conform to his racial categories. Cary Agassiz and James were not as rigid and allowed for uncertainty. By focusing not on categories but on discrete individuals they offered a much more complex human landscape than Agassiz ever could. Their narratives unstitch preconceptions and hypotheses about the tropics (though they certainly had them) by taking into account variety and details of the human phenomena. In that sense, their gaze, both personal and un-scientific, opens a third space that signals an expansion and shift of scientific observation. Evoking once again the image of Holmes's mermaid, Cary Agassiz's narrative submerges the fish in the water as she displaces science to the margins of *A Journey in Brazil* to reaffirm those 'delicate observations in the picturesque'. In the end, her observations, as well as James', held much more empirical weight in exploring and uncovering the American tropics and its inhabitants than Agassiz's long lost glaciers.

Notes on Contributors and Editors

María del Pilar Blanco is University Lecturer in Spanish American Literature and Fellow in Spanish at Trinity College, University of Oxford. She is the author of *Ghost-Watching American Modernity: Haunting, Landscape, and the Hemispheric Imagination* (2012) and co-editor, with Esther Peeren, of *Popular Ghosts: The Haunted Spaces of Everyday Culture* (2010).

Maria Cristina Fumagalli is Professor in the Department of Literature, Film, and Theatre Studies at the University of Essex. Her publications include the monographs *The Flight of the Vernacular: Seamus Heaney, Derek Walcott and the Impress of Dante* (2001) and *Caribbean Perspectives on Modernity: Returning Medusa's Gaze* (2009). She is also editor of *Agenda: Special Issue on Derek Walcott* (2002–2003), and joint editor of *The Cross-Dressed Caribbean: Writing, Politics, Sexualities* (2013). She is currently working a monograph entitled *On the Edge: A Literary Geography of the Border between Haiti and the Dominican Republic*, which is part of the *American Tropics* series..

Nina Gerassi-Navarro is Associate Professor of Latin American Literature at Tufts University. Her research focuses primarily on nineteenth-century Latin American literature and visual culture. She has worked on outlaws, travel narratives and popular culture. She is the author of *Pirate Novels: Metaphors of Nation Building* (1999) and co-editor of a special issue of *Revista Iberoamericana* entitled *Otros estudios transatlánticos: Lecturas desde lo latinoamericano* (2009). She is currently working on a book centred on the cultural and scientific debates between the USA and Latin America during the nineteenth century.

Susan Gillman is Professor of Literature and American Studies at the University of California, Santa Cruz. Her publications include *Dark Twins: Imposture and Identity in Mark Twain's America* (1989), *Blood Talk: American Race Melodrama and the Culture of the Occult* (2003), and most recently, co-edited with Russ Castronovo, *States of Emergency: The Object of American*

Studies (2009). Her book *Our Mediterranean: American Adaptations, 1820–1975* is forthcoming.

Hsinya Huang is Dean of the College of Arts and Humanities and Professor of American and Comparative Literature at National Sun Yat-Sen University, Taiwan. Her book publications include *(De)Colonizing the Body: Disease, Empire, and (Alter)Native Medicine in Contemporary Native American Women's Writings* (2004) and *Lesbigay Literature in Modern English Tradition* (2008). She is Editor-in-Chief of *Review of English and American Literature* and *Sun Yat-sen Journal of Humanities*. She edited the English translation of *The History of Taiwanese Indigenous Literatures* and is editing two essay volumes, *Aspects of Transnational and Indigenous Cultures* and *Ocean and Ecology in the Trans-Pacific Context*. Her current research project focuses on Trans-Pacific indigenous literatures.

Peter Hulme is Professor of Literature in the Department of Literature, Film, and Theatre Studies at the University of Essex. His research interests centre on the relationships between literature, travel writing, anthropology, and colonialism, especially in the Caribbean, and on postcolonial studies in its widest sense. He is the author of *Colonial Encounters: Europe and the Native Caribbean, 1492–1797* (1986, paperback 1992) and *Remnants of Conquest: The Island Caribs and Their Visitors, 1877–1998* (2000), and joint editor of *Wild Majesty: Encounters with Caribs from Columbus to the Present Day* (1992), *Colonial Discourse/Postcolonial Theory* (1994), *Cannibalism and the Colonial World* (1998), and *The Cambridge Companion to Travel Writing* (2002). His book, *Cuba's Wild East: A Literary Geography of Oriente*, was published in 2011 as the first volume in the *American Tropics* series.

Gesa Mackenthun teaches American Studies at Rostock University, Germany. Her research centres on the analysis of colonial discourse in the Americas and postcolonial theory. Her publications include *Metaphors of Dispossession. American Beginnings and the Translation of Empire, 1492–1637* (1997) and *Fictions of the Black Atlantic in American Foundational Literature* (2004). Her current research deals with nineteenth-century travel writing in the Americas and the concurrent scientific discourses about antiquity.

Russell McDougall is Professor in the School of Arts at the University of New England. His research interests include postcolonial subjectivities, the relationship between anthropology and travel writing, and literary studies of Sudan. His publications include the edited collection (with Peter Hulme) *Writing, Travel, and Empire: Colonial Narratives of Other Cultures* (2007).

Martha Jane Nadell is Associate Professor of English at Brooklyn College of CUNY. She is the author of *Enter the New Negroes: Images of Race in American Culture* (2004), as well as essays about race and modernism, the Harlem Renaissance, and African American history. She is currently at work on a literary and cultural history of Brooklyn.

Jak Peake is Lecturer in American Literature in the Department of Literature, Film, and Theatre Studies at the University of Essex. His current research examines Caribbean, and specifically Trinidadian, literature. His recent publications include an article in the journal *Sargasso*, a book chapter in *The Caribbean Short Story* (2011) and a forthcoming article in the journal *Moving Worlds*. He is also working on a monograph entitled *Between the Bocas: A Literary Geography of Western Trinidad*.

Alasdair Pettinger is an independent scholar based in Glasgow. He is the editor of *Always Elsewhere: Travels of the Black Atlantic* (1998), and has published a number of essays reflecting his (overlapping) interests in travel literature, the cultures of slavery and abolitionism, and representations of Haiti. His current projects include a study of Frederick Douglass's visit to Scotland in the 1840s and a history of the word 'voodoo' in English.

Richard Price retired in 2011 as Duane A. and Virginia S. Dittman Professor of Anthropology, American Studies, and History at the College of William and Mary. His research focuses on Afro-America, particularly the Maroons of Suriname and French Guiana, and ethnographic history. He is the author and co-author of many books, including *Maroon Societies: Rebel Slave Communities in the Americas* (1973), *The Convict and The Colonel* (1998), *Maroon Arts: Cultural Vitality in the African Diaspora* (with Sally Price, 1999), *Travels with Tooy: History, Memory, and the African American Imagination* (2008), and *Rainforest Warriors: Human Rights on Trial* (2011).

Sally Price retired in 2011 as Duane A. and Virginia S. Dittman Professor of American Studies and Anthropology at the College of William and Mary. Her research interests are on Afro-America, particularly in the area of aesthetics and museums. Her many publications include *Co-Wives and Calabashes* (1984), *Primitive Art in Civilized Places* (1989), *Romare Bearden: The Caribbean Dimension* (with Richard Price, 2006), and *Paris Primitive: Jacques Chirac's Museum on the Quai Branly* (2007).

Owen Robinson is Senior Lecturer in US Literature in the Department of Literature, Film, and Theatre Studies at the University of Essex. Specialising in writing of the US South, he is the author of *Creating Yoknapatawpha: Readers and Writers in Faulkner's Fiction* (2006), and several journal articles and book chapters on William Faulkner, George Washington Cable, and New Orleans. With Richard Gray, he has co-edited *A Companion to the Literature and Culture of the American South* (2004).

Mimi Sheller is Professor of Sociology and Director of the Center for Mobilities Research and Policy at Drexel University. She is former co-Director of the Centre for Mobilities Research at Lancaster University and founding co-editor of the journal *Mobilities*. She has held recent Visiting Fellowships in the Davis Center for Historical Studies at Princeton University (2008–2009); Media@McGill in Montreal (2009); the Center for Mobility and Urban Studies at Aalborg University, Denmark (2009); the Penn Humanities Forum at the University of Pennsylvania (2010–11). She is the author of the books *Democracy After Slavery* (2000), *Consuming the Caribbean* (2003), *Citizenship from Below: Erotic Agency and Caribbean Freedom* (2012), and the forthcoming *Aluminum Dreams: Lightness, Speed and Modernity* (2013). She is co-editor with John Urry of *Mobile Technologies of the City* (2006), *Tourism Mobilities: Places to Play, Places in Play* (2004), and a special issue of Environment and Planning A on 'Materialities and Mobilities', as well as co-editing *Uprootings/Regroundings: Questions of Home and Migration* (2003).

Neil L. Whitehead was Professor of Anthropology at the University of Wisconsin, Madison until his death in 2012. He worked mainly on South America and the Caribbean, particularly Amazonia. His publications include *Dark Shamans. Kanaimà and the Poetics of Violent Death* (2002), and the editions of (with Michael Harbsmeier) *Hans Staden's True History: An Account of Cannibal Captivity in Brazil* (2008) and *Of Cannibals and Kings: Primal Anthropology in the Americas* (2011).

Lesley Wylie is Lecturer in Latin American Studies at the University of Leicester. Previously she was Senior Research Officer on the 'American Tropics' Project. Her book, *Colonial Tropes and Postcolonial Tricks: Rewriting the Tropics in the 'novela de la selva'* was published in 2009. She is currently editing a collection of critical essays on Amazonian literature.

Index